Zebulon Montgomery Pike, U. S. Army

Exploratory Travels Through the Western Territories of North America

Comprising a voyage from St. Louis, on the Mississippi, to the source of that river, and a journey through the interior of Louisiana, and the north-eastern provinces of New Spain

Zebulon Montgomery Pike, U. S. Army

Exploratory Travels Through the Western Territories of North America
Comprising a voyage from St. Louis, on the Mississippi, to the source of that river, and a journey through the interior of Louisiana, and the north-eastern provinces of New Spain

ISBN/EAN: 9783337127794

Printed in Europe, USA, Canada, Australia, Japan

Cover: Foto ©ninafisch / pixelio.de

More available books at **www.hansebooks.com**

EXPLORATORY TRAVELS

THROUGH THE

WESTERN TERRITORIES

OF

NORTH AMERICA:

COMPRISING A

VOYAGE FROM ST. LOUIS, ON THE MISSISSIPPI,

TO THE

SOURCE OF THAT RIVER,

AND A

JOURNEY THROUGH THE INTERIOR OF LOUISIANA,

AND THE

NORTH-EASTERN PROVINCES OF NEW SPAIN.

Performed in the years 1805, 1806, 1807, by Order of the Government of the United States.

BY ZEBULON MONTGOMERY PIKE,

MAJOR 6TH REGT. UNITED STATES INFANTRY.

LONDON:

PATERNOSTER-ROW.

1811.

DENVER:
W. H. LAWRENCE & CO.
1889.

Copyright 1889
By W. H. LAWRENCE & CO.

DONOHUE & HENNEBERRY
Printers, Engravers and Binders
CHICAGO.

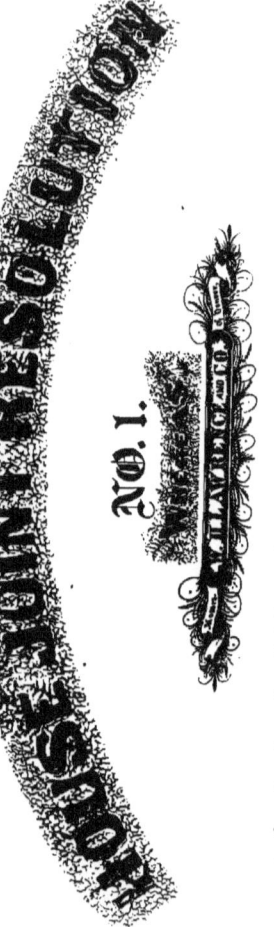

INTRODUCTION.

IN June, 1808, in conformity with law, Zebulon M. Pike secured a copyright for a book, the title of which was as follows: "An account of expeditions to the sources of the Mississippi, and through the western parts of Louisiana, to the sources of the Arkansaw, Kans, La Platte and Pierre Jaun rivers. Performed by order of the Government of the United States, during the years 1805, 1806, and 1807. And a tour through the interior parts of New Spain, when conducted through these provinces by order of the captain-general in the year 1807. By Major Z. M. Pike." It was printed by John Binns, of Philadelphia, who is said to have had the honor of being the first to print the Constitution of the United States, and was published by C. & A. Conrad & Co., of Philadelphia, who appear to have had associated with them in the enterprise other publishing houses in Petersburgh, Norfolk and Baltimore. The date of publication is 1810. The work contained a portrait of Major Pike, and maps and charts of the country traversed in his explorations; though in the case of some of the copies extant the maps were bound separately from the volume. The text is marred by errors, and the book, a cramped octavo, indifferently printed and bound, is quite unworthy of the story it carried to the world. The edition was probably limited to a comparatively small number of copies, and those now existing are to be found only in old libraries, or in the hands of lovers of or dealers in rare books.

Early in 1811 the work was republished in London by Longman, Hurst, Rees, Orme & Brown, in quarto form, on hand-made paper, with type double leaded throughout the body of the text, and with generously margined pages. From the fact that in the "Advertisement," by Thomas Rees, mention is made of manuscript having been transmitted to England, it is to be inferred that this was an authorized edition and that Pike had a share in the proceeds arising from its sale. The publishers ventured upon some liberties with the arrangement of the materials, taking much of the details that had gone to make up Pike's report to the Government—geographical, statistical and scientific records—which in the American edition had been gathered in appendixes, and incorporating them, when practicable, in the body of the work. Some inaccuracies of expression were amended, but the corrections were so few as to leave the narrative practically as the author penned it. In all respects the edition is an improvement on the original one, and gives evidence that the value of the recital had been appreciated by the British publishers. It had probably a large sale on this side of the Atlantic, but at this day copies are rare in America.

The material progress that has characterized the career of our country has nowhere been more marked than in those sections of it that were the scenes of Pike's travels and adventures. The great silent river of his day, flowing through a wilderness rarely trodden save by the foot of the savage, is one of the main arteries of a colossal commerce. Mighty cities adorn its banks. The roar of the Falls of St. Anthony, where he secured from the Indians land for a post, is lost in the ever increasing hum of industry. The buffalo has passed forever from the plains; the idle desert waves in wheat fields, and rustles in seas of corn. Potosi's wealth seems beggarly by the side of the stores of precious metal taken from the Rocky Mountains within thirty years.

Among those inhabiting the portions of our country first explored and described by Pike, there exists a very widespread ignorance of the man. To the majority his name has been kept alive solely because of its connection with the great peak, by which, in what we call early days, a large part of Colorado was known. There is some general knowledge that he crossed the plains and penetrated the mountains, but, at the best, it is extremely vague. That in the century that witnessed the exploits of the pioneer of pioneers, who first raised the flag of the United States within the limits of what is now Colorado, his identity should be virtually lost, and his deeds forgotten by those who, afterward, under very different conditions—stern though they may have been—followed in his footsteps, seems strange enough. But the ingratitude said to be peculiar to republics in all ages has not been the prevailing factor in bringing about this condition; as has been shown, the record made by Pike himself is almost unattainable. This consideration has induced the present publishers to give this volume to the world. In pursuit of the undertaking it has been deemed best to republish the British edition of Pike's book. That edition was much the worthier vehicle of the history. Beside, it had, in all probability, the benefit of a revisal by the author. It has been considered that it would add to the interest of the volume to have it, so far as the text is concerned, as nearly as practicable, a reproduction of the copy. This has been here attempted. A fac-simile of the portrait of Pike, printed in the original edition, has been added, as well as a modern map illustrating, as nearly as may be, the course of his party on the western expedition.

The journal of the voyage to the head of the Mississippi will be read with interest and pleasure. Pike's indomitable perseverance, surmounting all obstacles, is well illustrated in the narration. But his most important work is the record of the expedition to the Rocky Mountains. It will be found of absorbing interest. In point of daring adventure and enduring fortitude it is not surpassed in American history, replete with examples. Poorly provisioned and appointed, Pike led a handful of men, in the dead of winter, into the heart of unknown mountains eight hundred miles from his country's frontier. The simple, unaffected recital of the dangers met and the hardships endured compels our utmost sympathy and admiration. While all the details are not set down—the author seeming rather to abstain from rousing the reader's pity—enough is given to enable us to form some conception of the appalling misery of the march across the mountains from hunger, fatigue and freezing. The picture of that broken file of emaciated, half-clothed heroes, strung out over the January snowfields on the steeps of the Sangre de Cristo Range, will never fade from the memory. In the military annals of the Republic there is nothing more pathetic.

The reader, in perusing the story of suffering, will find himself casting about for an answer to the question,—Why did Pike sacrifice so much in order to cross the mountains from the Arkansas? Why the feverish pressing forward, when that course involved inevitable distress on the part of the entire command as well as the abandonment of several of his men? Good reason for an onward movement nowhere appears, necessitating, as it did, leaving behind the horses, and dropping here and there, singly or in couples, men made cripples by frost, to be exposed to the gravest dangers from disease, starvation, wild beasts and savages, and to certain death should the main body be unable to send back relief. There was every probability of more privation in the mountains than had been experienced upon the plains, where stray buffalo yet lingered. It was a season of intense cold, the snow lay deep upon the hills, where game was known to be scarce, and even to so sanguine a man as Pike the consideration that he knew absolutely nothing of the country ahead of him might well have given pause. The more the matter is studied from every point of view the more irresistible becomes the conclusion that some design or motive not disclosed was a powerful factor in deciding the step that was taken.

His conduct upon reaching the San Luis Valley deepens the seeming mystery. Whether or not he knew he was on the Rio Grande when captured is doubtful, but probably he did not. There are early Spanish maps showing with comparative accuracy the relative courses and positions of the Arkansas, the Rio Grande and the Red River; but Pike may never have had access to one of these, and beside, the direction pursued by Robinson in going west from the fort, on his journey to Santa Fé, indicates ignorance of the country. It is difficult, too, to understand Robinson's actions even on the explanation that Pike has given us. He had no interest in Morrison's claims, ostensibly for the collection of which he went to Santa Fé. Why, when he arrived there, he should represent himself as a Frenchman who had accompanied a hunting party, and tell the fantastic tale that Salcedo writes to Wilkinson in his letter of May 20, 1807; whether he expected to return, and, if so, how; and why Pike denied his being of the force—all this is not easy to comprehend.

The relations between the United States and Spain were under great strain at this time. The Louisiana purchase had been consummated, but the limits of the grant, especially toward the southwest, were disputed, and much jealousy was manifested on both sides. Each power claimed Red River, while the Spaniards asserted dominion far to the northeast of that stream, upon the great plains. War was confidently expected as the outcome of the dispute. In May, 1806, the United States dispatched "the exploring expedition of Red River," a small force under the command of Captain Sparks, instructed to ascend the river "to the country of the

Pawnee Indians." Here he was to buy horses from the Pawnees, to be used in transporting his men and their effects "to the top of the mountains," considered to be distant about three hundred miles. The command was met, while on the river, by a force of Spaniards greatly outnumbering it, and compelled to turn back. In addition to the tension in the far West, the country was agitated by the intrigues of Aaron Burr. He was suspected of cherishing a design of forcing secession of the country west of the Alleghanies, while it was notorious that an invasion and conquest of the northern Spanish provinces was in contemplation. The commander-in-chief of the United States army was James Wilkinson. He was also governor of the Territory of Louisiana. It was generally suspected that between him and Burr some bond of union existed; it subsequently developed that he had been the recipient from Burr of cipher letters bearing upon the conspiracy, and it was charged by Burr, under solemn circumstances, that these letters had been answered. It is true that Wilkinson was the chief witness in, if he was not the instigator of, Burr's prosecution, and that Wilkinson was duly acquitted of complicity in the plot; but the country, almost rocked by revolution, was in a high state of alarm, and Wilkinson labored under the greatest suspicions in some quarters. Pike was a protégé of Wilkinson, and it was from the latter and not from the secretary of war, that the orders for the expedition proceeded. It is not, then, to be wondered at that it was widely charged that Pike was an emissary of the supposed conspirators, and that the expedition bore a very direct relation to Burr's enterprises. Pike, upon his return, promptly and vigorously denounced the calumnies against him, and no one who reads his journal and discerns the lofty, patriotic soul that inspired the writer, can for a moment suspect his fidelity to his country and its laws. Whatever may be thought of Wilkinson, no cloud will rest upon Pike's memory.

But that he had instructions other and further than appear, may well be presumed, and thus may an explanation be found for conduct that seems to need it. There was every probability of war with Spain, in which case a strategic demonstration upon the headwaters of the Red River, or upon those of the Rio Grande, even with the small force at Pike's command—for the Spaniards were not held in high estimation—might be of importance. This will account for his haste to leave the Arkansas after a month's delay in the mountains. Then, too, in anticipation of an invading force follow-

INTRODUCTION.

ing his line of march, it was imperatively demanded that a practicable route to Santa Fé should be known as early as possible. Upon either of these hypotheses we can reconcile his rigorous exposure of his men with his evident love for them. Looking at the party as the pioneers of a possible invading force, Robinson's journey to Santa Fé may be understood, and its value, as well as the supreme danger attending it, appreciated; though we would prefer to have had him in the rear with the crippled soldiers, who were sending forward bones taken from their frozen feet — mute memorials of their distress.

It will be learned from the journal that certain more or less widely accepted notions concerning Pike are erroneous. One is the general belief that he scaled the peak now bearing his name. His diary shows that he failed in the undertaking—a fact not at all to his discredit when his condition, ignorance of the country, and the season of the year are considered. The height he climbed was probably Cheyenne Mountain. Major Long, who did gain the summit of the peak in 1819, is the first who succeeded of whom there is a record. He had a well equipped party, and made the ascent in the summer. He named the eminence James' Peak after the surgeon of his command, but later comers re-christened the mountain as it should be known. The germ of the now threadbare anecdote concerning the tourist starting to climb the peak before breakfast is found in Pike's attempt. It is also supposed that Pike had many encounters with Indians while on the plains and in the mountains. He not only fought none, but saw remarkably few after leaving the neighborhood of the Pawnee villages. There is also a belief that mining was, to some extent, prosecuted by the Spaniards within the limits of the present State of Colorado at the time. As a matter of fact, there was not a white man in the country. Strangely enough, to a citizen of the United States, James Pursley, a Kentuckian, must be accorded the distinction of being the discoverer of gold in what is now Colorado. The story of this man, found at page 314, reads like a romance, but it can hardly be doubted that he did, in the year 1802, find the precious metal in the sands of the Platte, presumably near where Fairplay now stands. Not till fifty-seven years had rolled by was his story shown to be capable of verification. The exact line of march of the party from the time it reached the foot of the Grand Cañon of the Arkansas is not easy to trace. It is likely that it reached the Platte in the South Park, and quite possible that it penetrated to the headwaters of the Gunnison. It is extremely difficult to identify the streams spoken of, owing to the hasty manner in which the country is sketched, the loss of Pike's original notes, and his subsequent borrowing from Spanish maps. Striking southwest, in the last desperate effort to cross the mountains, the Wet Mountain Valley was probably traversed and one of the higher branches either of Grape Creek or of the Huerfano followed to reach the pass. Whether this pass was the Mosca or the Medano (known also as "Sandhill"), or whether it was one still farther to the north as thought by some, cannot be definitely established. In the early days of the settlement of the country the Mosca was well traveled by the Southern Utes on their journeys to the plains, and their "hieroglyphics," of which Pike speaks, were to be seen cut in the bark of the aspen trees; but from the fact that after reaching the San Luis Valley on January 28th, 1807, the party marched some considerable distance on a course lying between the sand dunes and the mountains, the evidence would seem to warrant the belief that the pass used was north of the Mosca, and was probably the "Sandhill." Thence the march led to the western skirt of Sierra Blanca, and thence to the Rio Grande near where Alamosa now stands. The river was descended to the Conejos and upon the north bank of that stream, at a point five or six miles above its mouth, the fort was built. The exact locality of the site (a notable spot in western history) is in dispute, owing to the discovery many years ago of the remains of an ancient log structure farther west on the Conejos which some suppose to have been Pike's fortress; but everything in the narrative, as well as in the Spanish records, indicates the prairie opposite the mineral springs and high hill on the south bank of the Conejos as the spot where the flag of the United States is first recorded as floating above the soil of Colorado.

Pike was essentially a soldier. His intrepidity under disheartening misfortunes, the stern discipline he maintained in his little band, and his dignified bearing in the hands of his captors, stamp him as a leader among men. He did not shield himself behind his rank when danger and hardship were to be met. He was the scout of his force, he was the hunter, he carried the "pack." The West, with few historic associations beyond our own times, and no other remote hero, may look back upon this one fondly and with pride. It is a picturesque and bold figure, that of this young officer, "dressed in a pair of blue trousers, mockinsons, and blanket, coat and cap made of scarlet cloth lined with fox skins," before the Spanish Governor at Santa Fé, in March, 1807. We may be certain that the uncouth attire detracted no particle from the natural dignity of its owner, who was well aware what was due from, as well as to, an American soldier representing his country in a strange land. He was born near Trenton, New Jersey, on the 5th day of January, 1779. His father was an officer in the War of the Revolution. Even as a boy, of slight build and gentle disposition, there showed in him the resolute spirit that was to carry his country's flag over vast tracts of unknown land destined thereafter to constitute an important part of the United States. His conduct on the two expeditions of which he has left accounts was such as to earn him his appointment as Brigadier-General as he entered his thirty-fourth year. While it was awaiting confirmation by the Senate, on April 27th, 1813, his brief but active career was crowned with a soldier's death when he was leading the assault upon the British works at York, Canada. In his last moments he maintained the utmost fortitude. Upon his person after death there was found a pocket volume in which he had written two rules by which he wished his young son to be guided. They were that the boy should always preserve his honor free from blemish, and that he should be ready at all times to die for his country. There can be no doubt that these were the cardinal principles directing Zebulon Montgomery Pike throughout life.

His monument, than which no man has a prouder, looks down upon the scene of his daring western march. To us who know his story, the great "White Mountain" seems to gather a new dignity by the addition of his name, and for all yet to come shall the mighty peak yet preserve his memory even as it holds its everlasting snow. A soldier of the Republic when it and the century were young, earnestly devoted to his duty, he deserved well of his country. For it he lived, and for it he died.

DENVER, 1889. WILLIAM M. MAGUIRE.

REPORT OF THE COMMITTEE,

APPOINTED

ON THE FIFTEENTH OF NOVEMBER, 1808,

TO INQUIRE

WHAT COMPENSATION OUGHT TO BE MADE

TO

CAPTAIN ZEBULON M. PIKE,

AND HIS COMPANIONS.

DECEMBER 16th, 1808.

THE committee of the House of Representatives of the Congress of the United States, to whom was referred the resolution to inquire, Whether any, and if any, what compensation ought to be made to Captain Zebulon M. Pike and his companions, for their services in exploring the Mississippi river, in their late expedition to the sources of the Osage, Arkansaw, and La Plate rivers, and in their tour through New Spain:
REPORT,

That it appears by the documents accompanying this Report, that the objects of each of the exploring expeditions, together with the instructions for executing them, were communicated to and approved by the President of the United States; that the conduct of Captain Pike in each of the expeditions also met with the approbation of the President, and that the information obtained and communicated to the executive on the subjects of his instructions, and particularly in relation to the source of the Mississippi, and the natives in that quarter, and the country generally, as well on the Upper Mississippi as that between the Arkansaw and the Missouri, and on the borders of the latter extensive river to its source, and the country adjacent, is highly interesting in a political, geographical, and historical view; and that although no special encouragement was given to the individuals who performed these laborious and dangerous expeditions, yet it was but reasonable for them, should they fortunately succeed in their objects, to expect some reward from goverment. That the zeal, perseverance,

REPORT OF

and intelligence of Captain Pike as commander, have been meritorious, and the conduct of the individuals generally, who composed the parties respectively, has been faithful, and their exertions arduous. The Committee therefore are of opinion that compensation ought to be made by law to Captain Pike and his companions.

DOCUMENTS.

WAR DEPARTMENT.

To the Hon. J. Montgomery,
Chairman, &c.

December 7th, 1808.

SIR,

I HEREWITH inclose copies of the instructions to Lieutenant Pike, for the government of his conduct on the two exploring expeditions alluded to in your letter; and likewise lists of the names of the men composing those parties. You will perceive that the instructions were given by General Wilkinson, the object however of each party, together with the instructions, were communicated to, and approved by the President of the United States. Although no special encouragement was given to the individuals who performed these laborious and dangerous expeditions, yet it was but reasonable for them, should they fortunately succeed in their objects, to expect a liberal reward from the government; and as there can be no reasonable doubt of the zeal, perseverance, and intelligence of the commander, or of the faithful conduct and arduous exertions of the individuals generally, composing the respective parties, it may, I trust, be presumed that no objection will be opposed to a reasonable compensation for such meritorious services.

I am very respectfully, sir,
Your obedient servant,
H. DEARBORN.

(COPY.)

To Z. M. PIKE, 1st Regiment Infantry.

Head Quarters, St. Louis, July 30th, 1805.

SIR,

HAVING completed your equipments, you are to proceed up the Mississippi with all possible diligence, taking the following instructions for your general government, which are to yield to your discretion in all cases of exigency. You will please to take

THE COMMITTEE OF CONGRESS. xvii

the course of the river, and calculate distances by time, noting rivers, creeks, highlands, prairies, islands, rapids, shoals, mines, quarries, timber, water, soil, Indian villages, and settlements, in a diary to comprehend reflections on the winds and weather. It is interesting to government to be informed of the population and residence of the several Indian nations, of the quantity and species of skins and furs they barter per annum, and their relative price to goods; of the tracts of country on which they generally make their hunts, and the people with whom they trade. You will be pleased to examine strictly, for an intermediate point between this place and the Prairie des Chiens, suitable for a military post, and also on the Ouisconsin, near its mouth, for a similar establishment, and will obtain the consent of the Indians for their erection, informing them that they are intended to increase their trade, and ameliorate their condition. You will please to proceed to ascend the main branch of the river until you reach the source of it, or the season may forbid your further progress without endangering your return before the waters are frozen up. You will endeavour to ascertain the latitude of the most remarkable places in your route, with the extent of the navigation, and the direction of the different rivers which fall into the Mississippi; and you will not fail to procure specimens of whatever you may find curious, in the mineral, vegetable, or animal kingdoms, to be rendered at this place. In your course you are to spare no pains to conciliate the Indians, and to attach them to the United States; and you may invite the great chiefs of such distant nations as have not been at this place to pay me a visit. Your own good sense will regulate the consumption of your provisions, and direct the distribution of the trifling presents which you may carry with you, particularly your flags. I wish you a speedy, pleasant, and safe tour, and am, sir, with sentiments of respect and esteem,

Your obedient servant,
(Signed) JAMES WILKINSON.

P. S. In addition to the preceding orders, you will be pleased to obtain permission from the Indians, who claim the ground, for the erection of military posts and trading houses at the mouth of the river St. Pierre, the Falls of St. Anthony, and every other critical point which may fall under your observation; these permissions to be granted in formal conferences, regularly recorded, and the ground marked off.

(COPY.)

To Lieutenant Z. M. Pike.

St. Louis, June 24th, 1806.

SIR,

YOU are to proceed without delay to the cantonment on the Missouri, where you are to embark the late Osage captives, and the deputation recently returned from Washington, with their presents and baggage, and are to transport the whole up the Missouri and Osage rivers to the town of the Grand Osage. The safe delivery of this charge at the point of destination constitutes the primary object of your expedition, and therefore you are to move with such caution as may prevent surprise from any hostile band, and are to repel with your utmost force any outrage which may be attempted. Having safely deposited your passengers and their property, you are to turn your attention to the accomplishment of a permanent peace between the Kanses and Osage nations, for which purpose you must effect a meeting between the head chiefs of those nations, and are to employ such arguments, deduced from their own obvious interests, as well as the inclinations, desires, and commands of the President of the United States, as may facilitate your purpose and accomplish the end. A third object of considerable magnitude will then claim your attention: it is to effect an interview, and establish a good understanding with the Ietans or Camanches. For this purpose you must interest White Hair of the Grand Osage, with whom and a suitable deputation, you will visit the Pawnee Republic, where you may find interpreters and inform yourself of the most feasible plan by which to bring the Camanches to a conference. Should you succeed in this attempt, and no pains must be spared to effect it, you will endeavour to make peace between that distant powerful nation and the nations which inhabit the country between us and them, particularly the Osage; and finally, you will endeavour to induce eight or ten of their distinguished chiefs to make a visit to the seat of government next September, and you may attach to this deputation four or five Pawnees, and the same number of Kanses chiefs. As your interview with the Camanches will probably lead you to the head branches of the Arkansaw and Red rivers, you may find yourself approximated to the settlements of New Mexico, and therefore it will be necessary you should move with great circumspection, to keep clear of any hunting or reconnoitring parties from that province, and to prevent alarm or offence, because the affairs of Spain and the United States appear to be on the point of amicable adjustment; and, moreover, it is the desire of the President to cultivate the friendship and harmonious intercourse of all the nations of the earth, and particularly our nearest neighbours, the Spaniards.

In the course of your tour, you are to remark particularly upon the geographical structure, the natural history, and population of the country through which you may pass, taking particular care to collect and preserve specimens of everything curious in the mineral and botanical worlds which can be preserved and are portable. Let your courses be regulated by your compass, and your distances by your watch, to be noted in a field book; and I would advise you, when circumstances permit, to protract and lay down in a separate book the march of the day at every evening's halt.

The instruments which I have furnished will enable you to ascertain the variation of the magnetic needle, and the latitude, with exactness; and at every remarkable point I wish you to employ your telescope in observing the eclipses of Jupiter's satellites, having previously regulated and adjusted your watch by your quadrant, taking care to note with great nicety the periods of immersion and emersion of the eclipsed satellite. These observations may enable us after your return, by application to the appropriate tables, which I cannot now furnish you, to ascertain the longitude. It is an object of much interest with the executive to ascertain the direction, extent, and navigation of the Arkansaw and Red rivers; as far therefore as may be compatible

THE COMMITTEE OF CONGRESS.

with these instructions, and practicable to the means you may command, I wish you to carry your views to those subjects, and should circumstances conspire to favour the enterprise, you may detach a party with a few Osages to descend the Arkansaw, under the orders of Lieutenant Wilkinson or Sergeant Ballinger, properly instructed and equipped to take the courses and distances, to remark on the soil, timber, &c. and to note the tributary streams. This party will, after reaching our post on the Arkansaw, descend to Fort Adams, and there wait further orders. And you yourself may descend the Red river, accompanied by a party of the most respectable Camanches to the post of Natchitoches, and there receive further orders. To disburse your necessary expenses, and to aid your negotiations, you are herewith furnished six hundred dollars worth of goods, for the appropriation of which you are to render a strict account, vouched by documents to be attested by one of your party. Wishing you a safe and successful expedition,

I am, Sir, with much respect and esteem,
Your very obedient servant,
(Signed)   JAMES WILKINSON.

(COPY.)

To Lieutenant Z. M. Pike.

Cantonment, Missouri, July 12, 1806.

SIR,

THE health of the Osages being now generally restored, and all hopes of the speedy recovery of their prisoners from the hands of the Potowatomies being at an end, they have become desirous to commence their journey for their villages; you are therefore to proceed to-morrow. In addition to the instructions given to you on the 24th ultimo, I must require you to have the talks under cover, delivered to White Hair and the Grand Peste, the chief of the Osage band which is settled on the waters of the Arkansaw, together with the belts which accompany them; you will also receive herewith a small belt for the Pawnees, and a large one for the Ietans or Camanches. Should you find it necessary, you are to give orders to Maugraine, the resident interpreter at the Grand Osage, to attend you. I beg you to take measures for the security and safe return of your boats from the Grand Osage to this place. Doctor Robinson will accompany you as a volunteer; he will be furnished with medicines, and for the accommodation which you give him, he is bound to attend your sick.

Should you discover any unlicensed traders in your route, or any person from this territory, or from the United States, without a proper license or passport, you are to arrest such person or persons, and dispose of their property as the law directs.

My confidence in your caution and discretion has prevented my urging you to be vigilant in guarding against the stratagems and treachery of the Indians; holding yourself above alarm or surprise, the composition of your party, though it be small, will secure to you the respect of a host of untutored savages.

You are to communicate from the Grand Osage, and from every other practicable point, directly to the secretary of war, transmitting your letters to this place, under cover to the commanding officer, or by any more convenient route. I wish you health, and a successful and honorable expedition, and am yours, with friendship,
(Signed) J. WILKINSON.

To Captain Zebulon M. Pike.

War Department, February 24, 1808. .

SIR,

IN answer to your letter of the 22d instant, I can with pleasure observe, that although the two exploring expeditions you have performed were not previously ordered by the President of the United States, there were frequent communications on the subject of each, between General Wilkinson and this department, of which the President of the United States was, from time to time, acquainted; and it will be no more than what justice requires to say, that your conduct in each of those expeditions met the approbation of the President, and that the information you obtained and communicated to the executive, in relation to the source of the Mississippi, and the natives in that quarter, and the country generally, as well on the Upper Mississippi as that between the Arkansaw and the Missouri, and on the borders of the latter extensive river to its source, and the country adjacent, has been considered highly interesting in a political, geographical, and historical view. And you may rest assured that your services are held in high estimation by the President of the United States, and if any opinion of my own can afford you any satisfaction, I very frankly declare that I consider the public much indebted to you for the enterprising, persevering, and judicious manner in which you have performed them.

I am, very respectfully, Sir,
Your obedient servant,
H. DEARBORN.

THE COMMITTEE OF CONGRESS. xxi

RETURN

Of Persons employed on a Tour of Discovery and Exploration to the Source of the Mississippi, in the years 1805 and 1806.

Lieutenant, Z. M. Pike.
Interpreter, Pierre Rosseau.
Sergeant, Henry Kennerman.
Corporals { William E. Meek.
{ Samuel Bradley.

PRIVATES.

Jeremiah Jackson	John Brown
John Boley	Jacob Carter
Thomas Dougherty	William Gordon
Solomon Huddleston	John Mountjoy
Theodore Miller	Hugh Menaugh
Alexander Roy	John Sparks
Patrick Smith	Freegift Stout
Peter Branden	David Owings.
David Whelply	

This party left St. Louis the 9th of August, 1805, but had been detached for that duty from the 1st of July. They returned the 30th of April, 1806; from which time until the 15th of July, I was preparing for the second expedition to the westward, which consisted of the following persons, to wit:

Captain Z. M. Pike.
Lieutenant James B. Wilkinson.*
Doctor John H. Robinson.
Sergeants { Joseph Ballenger.*
{ William E. Meek.†
Corporal Jeremiah Jackson.†

21

xxii   REPORT OF THE COMMITTEE, &c.

PRIVATES.

John Boley*	Theodore Miller†
Henry Kennerman	Hugh Menaugh
Samuel Bradley*	John Mountjoy†
John Brown	Alexander Roy
Jacob Carter†	John Sparks†
Thomas Dougherty†	Patrick Smith†
William Gordon	Freegift Stout
Solomon Huddleston*	John Wilson.*

Interpreter, Baroney Vasquez.*

* Those thus marked descended the Arkansaw river, and arrived at New Orleans sometime about the   of February, 1807.

† Those thus marked are still detained in New Spain.

The remainder arrived at Natchitoches on or about the 1st of July, 1807; but it may probably be better to leave the whole time undefined, to be regulated by the honourable secretary of war.

Z. M. PIKE, Major.

CONTENTS.

	PAGE.
JOURNAL OF A VOYAGE FROM ST. LOUIS TO THE SOURCE OF THE MISSISSIPPI	25
INDIAN NATIONS BORDERING THE UPPER MISSISSIPPI	124
THE SACS	ib.
THE REYNARDS	125
THE IOWAS	ib.
WINEBAGOES OR PUANTS	126
MENOMENE OR FOLS AVOIN	127
SIOUX	ib.
MINOWA KANTONG	128
WASHPETONGS	ib.
SUSSITONGS	ib.
YANCTONGS	129
TETONS	ib.
WASHPECONTE	ib.
OBSERVATIONS ON THE TRADE OF THE NORTH-WEST COMPANY	138
JOURNAL OF AN EXPEDITION THROUGH THE INTERIOR OF LOUISIANA	149
OSAGE INDIANS	168
PAWNEE INDIANS	184
KANSES INDIANS	187
IETAN OR CAMANCHE INDIANS	202
JOURNAL OF A TOUR THROUGH THE INTERIOR PROVINCES OF NEW SPAIN	241
GEOGRAPHICAL AND STATISTICAL OBSERVATIONS ON THE INTERIOR PROVINCES OF NEW SPAIN	297
GAUDALAXARA	ib.
VALLADOLID	298

CONTENTS.

	PAGE
MEXICO	298
OAXACA	299
VERA CRUZ	ib.
PUEBLA	ib.
GUANAXUATO	300
ZACATECAS	ib.
ST. LUIS POTOSI	ib.
NEUVO SAN ANDER	ib.
NEW LEON	301
NEW MEXICO	302
BISCAY	316
SENORA	323
SINALOA	326
COGQUILLA	ib.
TEXAS	329
APPENDIX	353

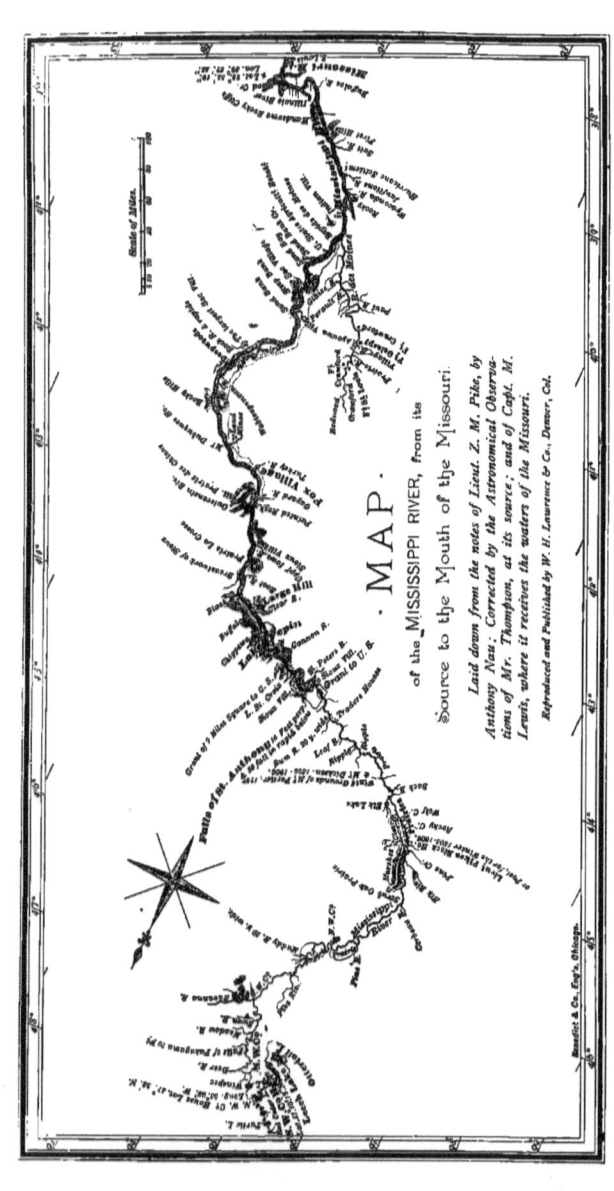

EXPLORATORY TRAVELS,

&c., &c.

JOURNAL OF A VOYAGE FROM ST. LOUIS TO THE SOURCE OF THE MISSISSIPPI, PERFORMED IN THE YEARS 1805 AND 1806.

ON the afternoon of *Friday*, the 9th of *August*, 1805, I sailed, agreeably to my instructions, from my encampment near St. Louis, with one sergeant, two corporals, and seventeen privates, in a keel boat about seventy feet long, provisioned for four months, in order to make a survey of the river Mississippi to its source. Encamped at night on the eastern side of the river, at the head of an island.

We embarked again early on the following morning, and breakfasted opposite to the mouth of the Missouri, near Wood Creek; about 5 o'clock P. M. a storm came on from the westward. Having gone out with two men, to march behind a cluster of islands, one of my soldiers swam a channel in the night, to inform me that the boat had stopped during the storm. I remained on the beach all night. We had this day proceeded by computation twenty-eight miles.

From St. Louis to the mouth of the Missouri, the eastern shore consists of a rich sandy soil, timbered with button wood, ash, cotton wood, hacberry, etc. The western is composed of high land, for a short distance above the town, bordered by a small prairie or natural meadow; after which bottom land occurs, with the same timber as on the eastern side. The current is rapid, and the navigation, at low water, obstructed by sand bars. Immediately on the peninsula, formed by the confluence of the rivers Mississippi and Missouri, is a small Kikapoo settlement, occupied in summer only. On the western shore there is a rich prairie, with small skirts of wood, and the eastern generally consists of hills from eighty to one hundred feet in height, extending to the mouth of the Illinois. The current of the Mississippi, above the entrance of the Missouri, is quite gentle, until you arrive at the mouth of the Illinois, where, owing to the large sand bars, and many islands, it is rendered extremely rapid.

On the 11th of *August*, the boat came up in the morning, and stopped opposite to the Portage de Sioux. We here spread out our baggage to dry, discharged our guns at a target, and scaled out our blunderbusses; dined at the cave below the Illinois; at the mouth of which river we remained some time. From the course of the Mississippi, the Illinois might be mistaken at its junction with it for a part of the principal stream. The Illinois river is about four hundred and fifty yards wide at its mouth, and bears from the Mississippi N. 75° W.: the current appears not to exceed two and a half miles an hour. The navigation and the tributary streams of this river are too well known to require a description. We encamped at night on the lower point of an island, about six miles above the Illinois. We were much detained in passing some islands, and obliged to get into the water, and haul the boat through.

On the 12th of *August*, we made several miles to breakfast, and about three o'clock P. M. passed Buffalo or Bœuf river, above which, about five miles, commences a beautiful cedar cliff. Having passed this, the river expands to nearly two miles in width, and contains four islands, whose lowest points are nearly parallel; these we called the Four Brothers. We encamped on the point of the easternmost. It rained very hard all night; caught one catfish. We advanced this day thirty miles.

From the Illinois to the Buffalo river, the eastern shore exhibits hills, but of easy ascent; on the west the land is a continued prairie, but not always bordering on the river. Timber is found on both sides, generally hacberry, cotton wood, and ash; the Buffalo river enters on the west, and appears to be about one hundred yards wide at its mouth. It bears from the Mississippi S. 30° W. From the Illinois to this river, the navigation is by no means difficult, and the current is mild.

On the 13th of *August*, it was late before we sailed. In our course we passed a great number of islands, on one of which we left one of our dogs.

We were much impeded by sand bars, and obliged to haul our boat over several of them. We observed, on our way, several encampments which had been lately occupied: rained all day; distance sailed, twenty-seven miles.

On the following morning, 14th of *August*, we had rain, but a fine wind springing up, we put off at half past six o'clock: passed a camp of Sacs, consisting of three men, with their families ; they were employed in spearing and scaffolding a fish, about three feet in length, with a long flat snout: they pointed out the channel, and prevented us from taking the wrong one. I gave them a small quantity of whiskey and biscuit, and they, in return, presented me with some fish. Sailed through a continuation of islands, for nearly twenty miles : met a young gentleman (Mr. Robedoux) by whom I sent a letter to St. Louis. At night encamped on an island; caught a considerable number of small fish. The rain continued the whole day. Distance sailed, twenty-eight miles.

On the 15th of *August*, it continued still to rain ; from the uninterrupted series of wet weather, the men were quite galled and sore. I met this day a Mr. Kittletas, of New York, who gave me a line to Mr. Fisher, of the Prairie des Chiens. Passed a small river, to the west, with a sand bar at its entrance: we also passed Salt river, which I do not recollect to have seen laid down on any chart: it is a considerable stream, and at high water is navigable for at least two hundred miles. We left here another dog; distance sailed, twenty-six miles.

From the Illinois to Salt river, or Oahahah, the eastern shore is either immediately bordered by beautiful cedar-cliffs, or the ridges may be seen at a distance. On the west there is a rich low soil, through which two small rivers flow into the Mississippi. The first I called Bar river, which is about twenty yards in width; the second is about fifteen yards. Salt river bears from the Mississippi, N. 75° W. and is about one hundred or one hundred and twenty yards wide at its junction, and when I passed the current appeared to be perfectly gentle. At high water it is navigable for boats at least two hundred miles above its mouth. About one day's sail up the river, there are salt springs, which have been worked for four years ; but I am not informed as to their qualities or produce.

In this distance the navigation of the Mississippi is very much obstructed by bars and islands, indeed, to such a degree, as to render it difficult in many places to fix the proper channel. The shores generally consist of a sandy soil, timbered with sugar maple, ash, pecan, locust, and black walnut. The eastern side has generally the preference as to situations for building.

We embarked early on the morning of the 16th of *August*, but were so unfortunate as to get fast on a log, and did not extricate ourselves until past eleven o'clock, having to saw off a part of it under the water. At three o'clock P. M. arrived at the house of a Frenchman, situate on the western side of the river, opposite to Hurricane Island. His cattle appeared to be in fine order; but his corn in a bad state of cultivation. He is married to a woman of the Sac nation, and lives by a little cultivation and the Indian trade. About one mile above his house, there is a very handsome hill, which he informed me was level on the top, with a gradual descent on either side, and a fountain of fine water. He likewise told me that two men had been killed on the Big Bay or Three Brothers, and desired to be informed what measures had been taken in consequence. Caught three catfish and one perch. Encamped four miles above the house, having proceeded in all this day eighteen miles.

Embarked the following morning, and came on remarkably well; at ten o'clock stopped for breakfast, and in order to arrange our sail, when the wind serving we put off, and continued under easy sail all day; passed three batteaux. In the evening we had, by computation, proceeded thirty-nine miles.

On the 18th of *August*, about eleven o'clock, passed an Indian camp, on the eastern side; they fired several guns, but we passed without stopping. We had very hard head winds part of the day; caught six fish; advanced twenty-three miles.

19th *August.*— Embarked early, and made fine way; but at nine o'clock, in turning the point of a sand bar, our boat struck a sawyer: at the moment we did not know it had injured her, but in a short time after we discovered her to be sinking; however, by thrusting oakum into the leak, and bailing, we got her to shore on a bar, where, after entirely unloading, we with great difficulty keeled her sufficiently to cut out the plank, and put in a new one. This I conceived at the time to be a great misfortune; but we afterwards discovered that the injury resulting from the accident was greater than we were at first induced to believe; for, upon inspection, we found our provision and clothing considerably damaged. The day was usefully and necessarily employed in assorting, sunning, and airing those articles. One of my hunters (Sparks) having gone on shore to hunt, swam the river about seven miles above, and killed a deer; but finding we did not come on, he returned and joined us by swimming. Whilst we were at work at our boat on the sand beach, three canoes, with Indians, passed on the opposite shore. They cried "How do you do?" wishing us to give them an invitation to come over; but receiving no answer they passed on. We then carried our baggage on board, and put off, designing to go where our hunter had killed the deer, but after dark we became entangled among the sand bars, and were obliged to stop and encamp on the point of a beach. Caught two fish; distance advanced, fourteen miles.

From the Salt river to the River Jauflione, which is five miles above Hurricane settlement, and forms the boundary between the Sac nation and the United States, on that side of the Mississippi, the western shore is hilly, but the eastern consists of low lands, timbered with hickory, oak, ash, maple, pecan, &c.; the western exhibits also the same wood, with a greater proportion of oak: the eastern is a rich sandy soil, and has many very eligible situations for cultivation. The Jauflione is about thirty yards wide at its mouth, and bears from the Mississippi about S. W. In this part of the river the navigation is good.

From hence to the Wyaconda river the navigation is easy, with very few impediments, and the soil on both sides pretty good. This river pays its tribute to the Mississippi, about twenty miles above the Jauflione, by a mouth one hundred yards wide, and bears from the former nearly due west. Just below its entrance is a small stream of fifteen yards wide, which discharges itself into the Mississippi. Between this and the river Des Moines, there is one small stream emptying itself into the Mississippi, on the west, of about fifty-five yards in width, and bearing S. by W. The first part of the distance is obstructed by islands, and the river expands itself to a great width, so as to render the navigation extremely difficult; but the latter part affords more water, and consequently an easier passage. The timber is principally oak and pecan. The soil is the same as that on the river below. Seventy-five miles above the Frenchman's settlement, and two hundred and thirty-two from the Missouri, the Rivière des Moines comes in from the north-west. The width of the Mississippi is here three-fourths of a mile.

On *Tuesday*, the 20th of *August*, we arrived at the foot of the Rapids des Moines, which are immediately above the confluence of the river of that name with the Mississippi. Although no soul on board had passed them before, we commenced ascending without delay. Our boat being large, and moderately loaded, we found great difficulty. The rapids are eleven miles long, with successive ledges and shoals extending from shore to shore across the bed of the river; the first fall is the most difficult to ascend. The channel (which is a bad one) is on the eastern side at the first two falls. It then passes under the edge of the third, crosses to the west, and ascends on that side all the way to the Sac village. We had passed the first and most difficult shoal, when we were met by Mr. Wm. Ewing (who, I understand, is an agent appointed by the United States to reside with the Sacs, to teach them agriculture), with a French interpreter, four chiefs and fifteen men of the Sac nation, in their canoes, bearing a flag of the United States. They came down to assist me up the rapids, and took out thirteen of my heaviest barrels, and put two of their men in the barge as pilots. We arrived at the house of Mr. Ewing, opposite the village, at dusk. This establishment is in latitude 30° 32′ N. The land on both sides of the rapids is hilly, but the soil rich; distance sailed, sixteen miles.

The next morning after our arrival, all the chief men in the village came over to my encampment, where I spoke to them to the following purpose:

"That their great father (the President of the United States) wishing to be more intimately acquainted with the situation, wants, &c., of the different nations of the Red People on our newly acquired territory of Louisiana, had ordered the General (Wilkinson, the commander on that station) to send a number of his young warriors in different directions, to take them by the hand, and make such inquiries as might afford the satisfaction required; also, that I was authorized to choose situations for their trading establishments, and wished them to inform me, if that place would be considered by them as central."

"That I was sorry to hear of the murder that had been committed on the river below; but, in consideration of their assurances that it was done by none of their nation, and of the concern exhibited by them on the occasion, I had written to the General and informed him of what they had said on the subject."

"That in their treaty they had engaged to apprehend all traders who came amongst them without license; for that time, I would not examine their traders on this point, but that on my return I would make a particular examination. That, if they thought proper, they might send a young man in my boat, to inform the other villages of my mission."

I then presented them with some tobacco, knives and whiskey. They replied to the following purport:

"That they thanked me for the good opinion I had of their nation, and for what I had written to the General. That themselves, their young warriors, and the whole nation, were glad to see me amongst them."

"That as for the situation of the trading houses, they could not determine, being but a part of the nation. With respect to sending a young man along with me, if I would wait until the following day, they would choose and appoint one. And finally, thanked me for my presents."

I wrote to my friends, and to the General; and not wishing to lose any time, I then embarked, and made six miles above the village. Encamped on a sand bar. One canoe of savages passed.

Embarked *Thursday*, 22d *August*, at five o'clock, A. M., with head winds; passed a great number of islands. The river was here very wide, and full of sand bars; proceeded in all, twenty-three miles.

Having sailed about five miles on the following morning, we came on the western shore to a very handsome situation for a garrison. The channel of the river passes under the hill, which is about sixty feet perpendicular height; the top is level for about four hundred yards. In the rear, there is a small prairie of eight or ten acres, which would be a convenient spot for gardens; and, on the eastern side of the river, there is a beautiful prospect over a large prairie, as far as the eye can extend, occasionally interrupted by groves of trees. Directly under the rock is a limestone spring, which, after an hour's work, will afford water amply sufficient for the consumption of a regiment of men. The landing is bold and safe, and at the lower part of the hill a road may easily be made for a team. Black and white oak timber are found here in abundance. The hill continues about two miles; and gives rise to five springs in that distance. We here met four Indians and two squaws; having landed with them, we gave them one quart of *made*, or diluted whiskey, a few biscuits, and some salt. I requested some venison of them; they pretended they could not understand me; but after we had left them, they held up two hams, and hallooed and laughed at us in derision. We remained nine hours on the shore, and observed some traces of Indians. We afterwards passed a handsome prairie on the eastern side, and encamped at its head; three batteaux from Michillimackinac stopped at our camp; we were told they were the property of Mr. Myers Michaels: we were here informed that the largest Sac village was about two and a half miles out on the prairie; and that this spot was called half way to the Prairie des Chiens, from St. Louis.

Saturday, 24th *August*.—Passed in the morning a number of islands; before dinner Corporal Bradley and myself took our guns, and went on shore. We got behind a savannah, by following a stream which we conceived to be a branch of the river, but which led us at least two leagues from it. My two favourite dogs having gone with us gave out in the prairie, owing to the heat, high grass, and want of water; but thinking they would follow, we continued our march. We heard the report of a gun, and supposing it to be from our boat, answered it; but shortly after we passed an Indian trail, which appeared as if the persons had been hurried, I presume at the report of our guns, for with this people all strangers are enemies. We soon struck the river, and the boat appeared in view. We stayed some time for my dogs, when two of my men volunteered to go in search of them. Encamped on the western shore, nearly opposite a chalk bank. My two men had not yet returned, which I thought extraordinary, as they knew my boat never waited for any person on shore: they endeavoured, it afterwards appeared, to strike the Mississippi ahead of us. We fired a blunderbuss at three different times, to let them know where we lay. Advanced this day, twenty-three and a half miles.

Sunday, August 25.—Stopped on the sand bank prairie on the east, from which there is a beautiful prospect of at least forty miles down the river, bearing SE. and E. We discovered that our boat leaked very fast, but secured her inside so completely with oakum and tallow, as nearly to prevent the leak. Fired a blunderbuss every hour, as signals for our men. We this day passed the river Iowa, and encamped at night on the prairie, marked Grant's Prairie. The men had not yet arrived. Proceeded in all, twenty-eight miles.

The Iowa river* bears from the Mississippi SW., and is one hundred and fifty yards wide at its mouth. The shore of the Mississippi consists here of high prairie, with yellow clay banks, and in some places red sand; the western shore is prairie also, but bounded by skirts of wood. About ten miles up the Iowa river, on its right bank, is a village of the Iowas.

Monday, 26th *August.*—Rained, with a very hard head wind: towed our boat about nine miles, to where the river Hills joins the Mississippi: here I expected to find the two men I had lost, but was disappointed. The mercury in Reaumur was at 13°, whereas, yesterday, it was 26°. Met two perroques full of Indians, who commenced hallooing, "How do you do," &c.: they then put to shore, and beckoned us to do so likewise, but we continued our course. This day was very severe on the men: distance sailed, twenty-eight miles.

Tuesday, 27th *August.*—Embarked early, with a cold north wind; mercury 10°, the wind so hard ahead that we were obliged to tow the boat all day. Met one perroque of Indians, and late in the day, passed the Rock river. Some Indians, who were encamped there, embarked in their canoes, and ascended the river before us. The wind was so very strong, that although down the stream, they were near sinking. Encamped about four miles above Rock river, on the western shore. This day passed a pole on a prairie, on which five dogs were hanging: distance advanced, twenty-two miles.

From the Iowa to Rock river, we generally had beautiful prairies on the west, and in some places very rich land, with black walnut and hickory timber.

Rock river† is a large stream, emptying itself into the Mississippi on the east, and is about three hundred yards wide at its mouth. It bears

---

* In ascending Iowa river thirty-six miles, you come to a fork, the right branch of which is called Red Cedar river, from the great quantity of that wood found on its banks. It is navigable for batteaux, nearly 300 miles. It then branches out into three forks, called the Turkey's Foot: these shortly after lose themselves in Rice lake.

† Rock river takes its source near Green Bay, on Lake Michigan, upwards of 450 miles from its mouth, and is navigable for more than 300 miles.

from the Mississippi almost due east. About three miles up this river, on the south bank, is situated the third town of the Sac nation, which, I was informed, was burnt in the year 1781 or 1782, by about three hundred Americans, although the Indians had assembled seven hundred warriors to give them battle.

Wednesday, August 28.—About an hour after we had embarked, we arrived at the camp of Mr. James Aird, a Scotch gentleman, of Michillimackinac. He had encamped with some goods on the beach, and was repairing his boat, which had been injured in crossing the rapids of Rock river, at the foot of which we now were. He had sent three boats back for the goods he had left behind. We breakfasted with him, and obtained considerable information. We afterwards commenced ascending the rapids; in the first we carried away our rudder, but after getting it repaired, the wind rising, we hoisted sail, and although entire strangers passed through them with a perfect gale blowing all the time: had we struck a rock, in all probability we must have bilged and sunk. On our way we met with Mr. Aird's boats (which had pilots) fast on the rocks. These shoals are a continued chain of rocks, extending about eighteen miles in length, and reaching in some places from shore to shore. They afford more water than those of La Rivière des Moines, but are much more rapid and difficult to pass.

Thursday, 29th *August.*—Breakfasted at the Reynard or Fox village, which is above the rapids: this is the first village of the Reynards. It consists of about eighteen lodges. I expected to have met my two men here, but was again disappointed. Finding they had not passed, I lay by until four o'clock, P. M.; the wind fair all the time. The chief informed me, by signs, that in four days they could march to Prairie des Chiens; and promised to furnish them with mockinsons, and put them on their route; upon this we set sail, and made at least four knots an hour. I was disposed to sail all night, but the wind lulling, we encamped on the point of an island on the western shore, having advanced twenty miles.

Friday, August 30th.—Embarked at five o'clock, with the wind fair, but not very high; sailed all day. Passed four perroques of Indians; distance made, forty-three miles.

Saturday, 31st *August.*—Embarked early. Passed one perroque of Indians; also two encampments, one on a beautiful eminence on the western side of the river. This place had the appearance of an old town. Sailed almost all day, and made thirty-one miles.

Sunday, 1st *Sept.*—Embarked early, with the wind fair; arrived at the lead mines at twelve o'clock. A dysentery, with which I had been afflicted several days, was suddenly checked this morning, which I believe to have been the occasion of a very violent attack of fever about eleven o'clock. Notwithstanding it was very severe, I dressed myself, with an intention to execute the orders of the General relative to this place. We were saluted with a field piece, and received with every mark of attention by Monsieur Dubuque, the proprietor. There were no horses at the house, and as it was six miles to the mines, it was impossible to make a report from actual inspection. I proposed, in consequence, ten queries, on the answers to which my report was formed.* Dined with Mr. D., who informed me that the Sioux and Sauteurs were as warmly engaged in opposition as ever; that not long since the former had killed fifteen of the latter, who, in return, killed ten Sioux, at the entrance of the St. Peter's; and that a war party, composed of the Sacs, Reynards, Puants, to the number of two hundred warriors, had embarked on an expedition against the Sauteurs, but that they had heard that, the chief having had an unfavourable dream, persuaded the party to return, and that I should meet them on my voyage. At this place I was introduced to a chief, called the Raven of the Reynards. He made a very flowery speech on the occasion, which I answered in a few words, accompanied by a small present. I had now given up all hopes of my two men, and was about to embark, when a perroque arrived, in which they were with a Mr. Blondeau, and two Indians, whom that gentleman had engaged above the rapids of Rock river. The soldiers had been six days without any thing to eat, except muscles, when they met with Mr. James Aird, by whose humanity and attention their strength and spirits had in a measure been restored; and they had been enabled to reach the Reynard village, where they met with Mr. B. The Indian chief furnished them with corn and shoes, and showed his friendship by every possible attention.

* The substance of the answers was, that the mines were supposed to extend about twenty-seven leagues in length, and from one to three leagues in breadth. The ore yielded about 75 per cent. and from 20 to 40,000 lbs. were annually formed into pigs.

I immediately discharged the hire of the Indians, and gave Mr. Blondeau a passage to the Prairie des Chiens. Left the lead mines at four o'clock: distance made this day, twenty-five miles.

From the first Reynard village to the lead mines, the Mississippi evidently becomes narrower, but the navigation is thereby rendered much less difficult. The shores consist, in general, of prairie, which if not immediately bordering on the river, can be seen through the thin skirts of forest that in some places line the banks; the timber is generally maple, birch, and oak, and the soil very excellent. To this place we have seen only a few turkeys and deer, the latter of which are pretty numerous from the River Des Moines.

Monday, 2d *September*.—After making two short reaches, we commenced one which is thirty miles in length; the wind serving we just made it, and encamped on the eastern side, opposite to the mouth of Turkey river.

From the lead mines to Turkey river, the Mississippi continues about the same width, and the banks, soil, and productions are entirely similar. The Turkey* river empties in on the west, bearing from the Mississippi about SW. and is about one hundred yards wide at its mouth: half a league up this river, on the right bank, is the third village of the Reynards, at which place they raise sufficient corn to supply all the permanent and transient inhabitants of the Prairie des Chiens.

In the course of this day we landed to shoot pigeons; the moment a gun was fired, some Indians who were on the shore above us ran down, and put off in their perroques with great precipitation. Upon which Mr. Blondeau informed me that all the women and children were frightened at the very name of an American boat; and that the men held us in great respect, conceiving us to be very quarrelsome, much disposed for war, and at the same time very brave. This information I used as prudence suggested. We stopped at an encampment about three miles below the

---

* Between the Iowa and Turkey rivers, you find on the west the Wabisapenkun river. It runs parallel to the Red Cedar river, and has scarcely any wood on its banks. The next water we met with was the Great Macottite, and a little higher the little river of the same name. These two streams appear to approach each other, and present nothing remarkable, excepting some lead mines which are said to exist on their banks.

town, where they gave us some excellent plums. They despatched a perroque to the village, to give notice, as I supposed, of our arrival. It commenced raining about dusk, and rained all night. Distance advanced, forty miles.

Tuesday, September 3d.—Embarked at a pretty early hour; the weather cloudy. We met two perroques of family Indians; they at first asked Mr. Blondeau, "if we were for war, or going to war?" I now experienced the good effect of having some person on board who could speak their language; for they presented me with three pair of ducks, and a quantity of venison sufficient for all our crew for one day: in return, I made them some trifling presents. We afterwards met two perroques carrying some of the warriors. They kept at a good distance until spoken to by Mr. B., when they informed him that their party had proceeded up as high as Lake Pepin, without effecting anything. It is surprising what a dread the Indians in this quarter have of the Americans: I have often seen them go round islands to avoid meeting my boat. It appears to me evident that the traders have taken great pains to impress the minds of the savages with the idea of our being a very vindictive, ferocious, and warlike people. This impression was made perhaps with no good intention; but when they find that our conduct towards them is guided by magnanimity and justice, instead of operating to our prejudice, it will have the effect of causing them to respect, at the same time that they fear us. Distance advanced this day, twenty-five miles.

Wednesday, September 4.—Breakfasted just below the Ouisconsin; arrived at the Prairie des Chiens about eleven o'clock. Took quarters at Captain Fisher's, and were politely received by him and Mr. Frazer.

Thursday, 5th September.—Embarked about half past ten o'clock in a Schenactady boat, to go to the mouth of the Ouisconsin, in order to take the latitude and look at the adjacent hills for a situation for a fort; was accompanied by Judge Fisher, Mr. Frazer, and Mr. Woods. We ascended the hill on the western side of the Mississippi, and made choice of a spot which I thought most eligible, being level on the top, with a spring in the rear, and commanding a view of the country around. A shower of rain came on, which completely wetted us, and we returned to the village without having ascended the Ouisconsin as we had intended. I marked four

VOYAGE TO THE SOURCE

trees with A.B.C.D. and squared the sides of one in the centre. Wrote to General Wilkinson.*

Friday, 6th *September*.—I held a small council with the Puants, and a chief of the lower band of the Sioux. I afterwards visited and laid out a position for a post, on a hill called the *Petit Gris*, on the Ouisconsin, three miles above its mouth. Mr. Fisher, who accompanied me, was taken very ill, in consequence of drinking some water out of this river. The Puants never have any white interpreters, nor have the Fols Avoin nation. In my council I spoke to a Frenchman, he to a Sioux, who interpreted to some of the Puants.

My men beat all the villagers here in jumping and hopping.

The Ouisconsin enters the Mississippi in latitude $43°\ 44'\ 8''$ and is nearly half a mile wide at its mouth. It bears from the Mississippi nearly NE.† This river is the grand source of communication between

---

*The letters to General Wilkinson, noticed here and elsewhere, are omitted, as containing only the official report of what is given in the journal.—E.

† The voyage from the Michillimackinac to the Prairie des Chiens, by the Ouisconsin and Fox rivers, is as follows, viz.:

"The distance between Michillimackinac and the settlements at the bottom of Green Bay is calculated to be eighty leagues. On leaving Mackinac, there is a traverse of five miles to Point St. Ignace, which is the entrance into Lake Michigan; four leagues from Mackinac, is an island of considerable extent, named St. Helens, and may be seen from that place in a clear day. The shore from Mackinac to the Point au Chene, which is a league distant from the island, is rocky, and from this to the island Epouvette, which is a very small one, and stands near the banks of the lake, is high and covered with pine, the soil very barren. From this island to the river Meno Cockein, the distance is five leagues; two small islands occur on the way, and a river where boats or canoes may take shelter in a storm. The river Meno Cockein is large and deep, and takes its rise near Lake Superior. From this to Shouchoir, the distance is ten leagues; the shore is dangerous from the number of shoals that extend a great way into the lake. This rock, called Shouchoir, forms an excellent harbour for canoes. The entrance, however, when the wind blows from the lake, is difficult, but when once in, canoes and boats may lie during any storms without unlading. A custom prevails here among the voyagers for every one to have his name carved on the rock the first time he passes, and pay something to the canoe-men. From this to the river Manistique the distance is five leagues; this is a large river. The entrance is difficult, from a sand bank at its mouth, and the surf is very high when the wind blows from the lake; at certain seasons sturgeons are found here in great numbers. The banks of this river are high and sandy, covered with pine. It takes its rise from a large lake,

the Lakes and the Mississippi, and is the route by which all the traders of
Michillimackinac convey their goods for the trade of the Mississippi, from

and nearly communicates with Lake Superior. From this to the Detour, the distance
is ten leagues; the shore rocky, flat, and dangerous. Here begins the traverse at the
mouth of Green Bay. The first island is distant from the main land about a league,
and is called the Ile de Detour, and is at least three leagues in circumference. There
are generally a few Sauteaux lodges of Indians on this island during the summer
months. From this to Ile Brulée, the distance is three leagues. There are two small
islands between these and Ile Veste, whence the distance is two leagues to Ile des
Poux; so called from Poutowatomies having once had a village here, which is now
abandoned. In the months of May and June, there is here a fishery of trout; they are
taken in great quantities by trolling: there are also white fish in vast numbers. The
ship channel is between this island and Ile Veste; from thence to Petit Détroit, the
distance is three leagues; some lodges of Otowas and Sauteaux have raised here
small quantities of corn, but their subsistence during the summer months chiefly
depends upon the quantities of sturgeon and other fish with which the lake abounds.
From Petit Détroit to the main land the distance is three leagues, and is called the
Port des Morts, from a number of canoes having been wrecked at this place, where
every one perished; the shore is bold and rocky. Hence the distance is four leagues
to the Ile Racro, which is a safe harbour, inaccessible to all winds. From hence to
Sturgeon bay the distance is eight leagues; the shore is bold and rocky, and several
large islands lie a few miles distant. A few Sauteaux families raise corn here, and
reside during the summer season; trout and sturgeon are found in great numbers.
Sturgeon bay is two miles across, and about four leagues in length, and communicates
by a portage with Lake Michigan, near Michillimackinac; distant from the bay about
two leagues, in the Ile Vermillion. There were here, a few years ago, a number of
Fols Avoin inhabitants, who were accustomed to raise corn; but why they have left
this place I cannot learn. There are thirteen leagues from hence to the entrance of
the Fox river. On leaving Ile Vermillion, the woods and general appearance of the
country begin to change, and have a very different aspect; from the northern parts of
this lake, a small river called Rivière Rouge, falls into the lake about half way between
Ile Vermillion and La Baye. On approaching La Baye, the water of the latter assumes
a whiter appearance, and becomes less deep. A channel which winds a good deal
may be found for vessels of fifty and sixty tons burden, and loaded vessels of these
dimensions have gone up the river Fox to the French settlement, opposite which is
the Fols Avoin village, which consists of ten or twelve bark lodges. A great number
of Sauteaux and some Otowas come here in the spring and fall. Three leagues from
La Baye is a small village of the same nation, and another three leagues higher at the
portage of Kakalin. This portage is a mile long, the ground even and rocky; there
is a fall of about ten feet, which obstructs the navigation for three leagues higher,
and almost continual rapids succeed as far as the fall of Grand Konomee, which is
about five feet high; above this the river opens into a small lake, at the end of which

VOYAGE TO THE SOURCE

St. Louis to the River de Corbeau, and the confluent streams which are in those boundaries.

is a strong rapid, called Puant's Rapid, which issues from a lake of that name. This lake is ten leagues in length, and from two to three wide; at its entrance stands the first Puant village, consisting of ten or twelve lodges. At the upper end of the lake stands another Puant village of about the same number of lodges, and at the end of this is a small river, which, with the intervals of a few portages, communicates with Rock river. About midway between the two Puant villages, there is a Fols Avoin village, on the south side of the lake, containing fifty or sixty men. Five leagues from the entrance of the lake on the north side, the Fox river falls in, and is about two hundred yards wide: ascending two leagues higher there stands a small Fols Avoin village, where there is a lake of more than two leagues in length; and about a league above this lake the river de Loup joins the Fox river near a hill called the Butte des Morts, where the Fox nation were nearly exterminated by the French, and confederated Indians. The river and lakes are at certain seasons full of wild rice. The country on the borders of this is finely diversified with woods and prairies. Any quantity of hay may be made, and it is as fine a country for raising stock as any in the same latitude through all America.

"From the Butte des Morts to the Lac Puckaway, the distance is twenty-eight leagues; there is here another Puant village of seven or eight large lodges. This lake is three leagues in length: four leagues above it, Lac du Bœuf begins, which is also four leagues long, and full of wild rice, and a great many fowls in their season. From Lac du Bœuf the next stage is to the Forks, five leagues from the Portage of the Ouisconsin; ten leagues above the Forks, there is a very small lake called the Lac Vaseux, which is so choked with wild rice as to be almost impassable. The river, although very winding, becomes here more and more serpentine on approaching the Portage, and narrows so much as almost to prevent the use of oars. The length of the Portage to the Ouisconsin is two miles, and when the waters are high, canoes and boats loaded pass over.

"Here the waters at such times separate, the one part going to the Gulf of Mexico, and the other to that of St. Lawrence. In wet seasons the Portage road is very bad, the soil being of a swampy nature; there is for nearly half the way a kind of natural canal, which is sometimes used; and I think a canal between the two rivers might be easily cut. The expense at present attending the transports is one-third of a dollar for one hundred weight; for a canoe, five dollars; and a boat eight dollars; but this is not in cash, but in goods, at the rate of two hundred per cent. advance on the sterling price.

"There are at present two white men who have establishments there, but they are much incommoded by the Puants of Rock river, who are troublesome visitors. The Ouisconsin is a large river, its bottom sandy, full of islands, and sand-bars, during the summer season. The navigation is difficult even for canoes, owing to the lowness of the water; from the Portage to its confluence with the Mississippi is sixty leagues.

OF THE MISSISSIPPI.

The village of the Prairie des Chiens* is situated about one league above the mouth of the Ouisconsin, on the eastern bank; there is a small pond, or marsh, which extends in the direction of the river: the town is in the front of the marsh; it consists of eighteen dwelling houses, arranged in two streets; sixteen in Front street, and two in First street. In the rear of the pond, are eight dwelling houses; some of them are framed; and instead of weather-boarding, there are small logs let in mortises, made in the uprights, joined close, daubed on the outside with clay, and handsomely white-washed within. The interior furniture of their houses is decent, and indeed, in those of the most wealthy, display a degree of elegance and taste.

There are eight houses scattered in the country, at the distance of one, two, three, and five miles; there are also, on the western side of the Mississippi, three houses situated on a small stream, called Giard river, making in the village and vicinity thirty-seven houses, which it will not be too much to calculate at ten persons each, making the population three hundred and seventy souls; but this calculation will not answer for the spring or autumn, as there are at those seasons at least five or six hundred white persons resident here: this is owing to the concourse of traders and their engagers from Michillimackinac, and other parts, who make this their last stage previous to their launching into the savage wilderness: they again meet here in the spring on their return from their wintering grounds, accompanied by three hundred or four hundred Indians; when

---

The Jacques and Reynards formerly lived on its banks, but were driven off by the Sauteaux. They were accustomed to raise a good deal of corn and beans, the soil being excellent. Opposite to the Detour du Pin, half way from the Portage on the south side, are lead mines, said to be the best in any part of the country, and may be wrought with great ease. Boats of more than four tons are improper for the communication between the Mississippi and Michillimackinac."

"DICKSON."

* The present village of the Prairie des Chiens was first settled in the year 1783, and the settlers were Mr. Giard, Mr. Antaya, and Mr. Dubuque. The old village is about a mile below the present, and had existed during the time the French were in possession of the country. It derives its name from a family of the Reynards, who formerly lived there, distinguished by the appellation of dogs. The present village was settled under the English government, and the ground was purchased from the Reynard Indians.

they hold a fair, the one to dispose of the remainder of their goods, and the others their reserved peltries. It is astonishing that there are not more murders and affrays at this place, such a heterogeneous mass assembling here to trade, and the use of spirituous liquors being in no manner restricted; but since the American government has become known, such accidents take place much less frequent than they used to do before.

The prairie on which the village is situated is bounded in the rear by high bald hills, and extends about eight miles from the Mississippi to where it strikes the Ouisconsin, at the Petit Gris, which bears from the village SE. by E. If the marsh were drained (which might be easily done), I am of opinion the situation of the prairie would be rendered healthy; the inhabitants are now subject to intermittent fevers in the spring and autumn.

There are a few gentlemen who reside at the Prairie des Chiens, and many other persons who claim that appellation; but the rivalship of the Indian trade occasioned them to commit acts at their wintering quarters which they would blush to be thought guilty of in the civilized world. They possess, however, the spirit of generosity and hospitality in an eminent degree, but this is the leading feature in the character of the frontier inhabitants; their mode of living had obliged them to have temporary connection with the Indian women; and what was at first policy, is now so confirmed by habit and inclination, that it has become (with a few exceptions) the ruling practice of all the traders; and in fact almost one-half the inhabitants under twenty years of age have the blood of the Aborigines in their veins.

Sunday, 8th *September*.—Having the day before begun to load my two new boats, which I had procured as better adapted for the prosecution of the voyage, I embarked at half past eleven o'clock, the wind fair and fresh. I found myself very much embarrassed and cramped in my new boats, with the provisions and baggage. I embarked two interpreters, one to perform the whole voyage, whose name was Pierre Rosseau; and the other, named Joseph Reinville, paid by Mr. Frazer, to accompany me as high as the falls of St. Anthony. Mr. Frazer is a clerk to Mr. Blackler of Montreal; he was born in Vermont, but has latterly resided in Canada. To the attention of this gentleman I am much indebted; he procured me everything in his power that I stood in need of.

Mr. Frazer despatched his bark canoes, and remained himself to go on with me—his design was to winter with some of the Sioux bands. We sailed well, proceeded eighteen miles, and encamped on the western bank.

I must not omit here to bear my testimony to the politeness of all the principal inhabitants of the village.

Monday, 9th *September*.—Dined at Cape Gartie, or at Gartie river, after which we proceeded to an island on the eastern side, about five miles below the River Iowa, where we encamped. The Iowa river is about one hundred miles wide at its mouth, and bears from the Mississippi, about NW. Distance advanced, twenty-eight miles.

Tuesday, 10th *September*.—The rain still continuing, we remained at our camp—having shot at some pigeons, the report was heard at the Sioux lodges;[*] when Le Feuille, a chief of this nation, sent down six of his young men to inform me, "that he had waited three days with meat, &c., but that last night he had begun to drink, and that on the next day, he would receive me with his people sober." I returned for answer, "that the season was far advanced, that time was passing, and if the rain ceased I must proceed." Mr. Frazer and the interpreter went home with the Indians. We embarked about one o'clock; Mr. Frazer returning, informed me that the chief acquiesced in my reasons for pressing forward; but that he had prepared a pipe (instead of a letter), to present me, to shew to all the other bands of the Sioux above, with a message to inform them that I was a chief of their new father's, and that he wished us to be treated with friendship and respect. On our arrival opposite to the lodges, the men were paraded on the bank with their guns in their hands. They saluted (with ball) with what might be termed three rounds, which I returned with three rounds from each boat with my blunderbusses. This salute, although nothing to soldiers accustomed to fire, would not be so agreeable to many people, as the Indians had all been drinking, and some of them even tried their dexterity to see how near the boat they could strike; they may indeed be said to have struck on every side of us. When I landed, I had my pistols in my belt and sword in hand. I was met on the bank by the chief and invited to his lodge; as soon as my guards were formed and sentinels posted, I accompanied him. Some of my men who were to attend me I caused to leave their arms behind, as a mark of

---

[*] The same I had spoken to, on the 6th, on the Prairie des Chiens.

confidence. At the chief's lodge I found a clean mat and pillow provided for me to sit upon; and the before-mentioned pipe, on a pair of small crutches, was placed before me. The chief sat on my right hand, my interpreter and Mr. Frazer on my left. After smoking, the chief spoke to the following purport:

"That notwithstanding he had seen me at the prairie, he was happy to take me by the hand amongst his own people, and there to shew his young men the respect due to their 'new father:' that when at St. Louis in the spring his father had told him, that if he looked down the river he would see one of his young warriors coming up; he now found it true, and he was happy to see me, who knew the Great Spirit was the father of all, both the white and the red people, and if one died the other could not live long. That he had never been at war with their new father, and hoped always to preserve the same good understanding that now existed. That he now presented me with a pipe to shew to the upper bands, as a token of our good understanding; and that they might see his work and imitate his conduct. That he had gone to St. Louis on a shameful visit, to carry a murderer; but that we had given the fellow his life, and he thanked us for it. That he had provided something to eat, but he supposed I could not eat it myself, and if not, desired I might give it to my young men." I replied, "that although I had told him at the prairie my business up the Mississippi, I would again relate it to him: I mentioned the different objects I had in view with regard to the savages who had fallen under our protection by our late purchase from the Spaniards; the different posts to be established; the objects of these posts as they related to them; supplying them with necessaries, having officers and agents of government near them to attend to their business; and, above all, to endeavour to make peace between the Sioux and Sauteurs. That it was possible on my return I should bring some of the Sauteurs down with me, and take some of the Sioux chiefs to St. Louis, there to settle the long and bloody contest which had existed between the two nations. That I accepted his pipe with pleasure as the gift of a great man * and a brother. That it should be used as he desired."

I then ate of the dinner he had provided. It was very grateful. It consisted of wild rye and venison, of which I sent four bowls to my men.

---

* He is the chief of four bands.

I afterwards went to a dance, the performance of which was attended with many curious manœuvres. Men and women danced indiscriminately. They were all dressed in the gayest manner; each had in their hand a small skin of some description: they frequently ran up, pointed their skin, and gave a puff with their breath, when the person blown at, whether man or woman, would fall and appear to be almost lifeless, or in great agony; but would recover slowly, rise, and join in the dance. This they called their great medicine, or, as I understood the word, the dance of religion, the Indians believing that they actually puffed something into each others bodies, which occasioned the falling, &c. Every person is not admitted to take a part: they who wish to join them must first make valuable presents to the society, to the amount of forty or fifty dollars, and give a feast; they are then admitted with great ceremony. Mr. Frazer informed me that he was once in the lodge with some young men who did not belong to the club, when one of their dancers coming in, they immediately threw their blankets over him and forced him out of the lodge. Mr. F. laughed at them, and the young Indians called him a fool, and said "he did not know what the dancer might blow into his body."

Having returned to my boat, I sent for the chief, and presented him with two carrots of tobacco, four knives, half a pound of vermillion, and one quart of salt. Mr. Frazer asked leave to present them with some rum; we made them up a keg between us of eight gallons.* Frazer informed the chief that he durst not give them any without my permission. The chief thanked me for all my presents, and said, "they must come free as he did not ask for them." I replied, "that to those who did not ask for anything, I gave freely; but to those who asked much, I gave only little or none."

We embarked about half past three, proceeded three miles, and encamped on the western side. Mr. Frazer we left behind, but he came up with his two perroques about dusk. By this time it commenced raining very hard. In the night a perroque arrived from the lodges. During our stay at their camp there were soldiers appointed to keep the crowd from my boats, who executed their duty with vigilance and vigour, driving men, women and children back whenever they approached. At my departure their soldiers said, "as I had shaken hands with their chief,

---

* Two gallons whiskey.

they must shake hands with my soldiers." In which request I willingly indulged them.

Wednesday, 11th *September*.—Embarked at seven o'clock, although raining. Mr. Frazer's canoes also came on until nine o'clock. Stopped for breakfast, and made a fire. Mr. Frazer staid with me, and finding his perroques not quite able to keep up, he despatched them. We resumed our voyage, proceeded until near six o'clock, and encamped on the western side: we saw nothing of his perroques after they left us. I computed that we advanced sixteen miles this day, rain and cold winds the whole time ahead. The river has never been clear of islands since I left Prairie des Chiens. I believe it to be here two miles wide; hills, or rather prairie knobs, on both sides.

Thursday, 12th *September*.—It raining very hard in the morning, we did not embark until ten o'clock, Mr. Frazer's perroques then coming up. It was still raining, and very cold. We passed the Root river, which, at its junction with the Mississippi, is twenty yards wide, bearing from it nearly west, and is navigable for canoes about sixty miles. Opposite to Root river we passed a prairie called La Crosse, from a game of ball played frequently on it by the Sioux Indians. This prairie is very handsome; it has a small square hill, similar to some mentioned by Carver. It is bounded in the rear by hills like the Prairie des Chiens. On this prairie Mr. Frazer shewed me some holes dug by the Sioux when in expectation of an attack, into which they first put their women and children, and then crawl in themselves; they were generally round, about ten feet in diameter, but some were half moons, and formed quite a breastwork. This, I understand, was the chief's work, which was the principal redoubt. Their mode of constructing them is as follows: the moment they apprehend, or discover, an enemy on a prairie, they commence digging with their knives, tomahawks, and a wooden ladle, and in an incredibly short space of time sink a hole sufficiently capacious to secure themselves and their families from the balls or arrows of the enemy. They have no idea of taking these subterranean redoubts by storm, as they would probably lose a great number of men in the attack; and although they might be successful in the event, it would be considered as a very imprudent action.

Mr. Frazer, finding his canoes not able to keep up, staid at this prairie to organize one of them, intending then to overtake us. Advanced three miles farther.

Friday, 13th *September.*—Embarked at six o'clock: came to a sand bar, and stopped to dry my things. At this place Mr. Frazer overtook me. We remained here three hours: we afterwards proceeded together, and passed the mouth of Black river, entering the Mississippi from the east. It is of considerable size, and Indian traders have ventured one hundred and twenty miles up its course. We had rain all day, except about two hours at noon. Distance advanced, twenty-one miles.

Saturday, 14th *September.*—We embarked early; the fog was so thick we could not distinguish objects twenty yards distant. When we breakfasted we saw nothing of Mr. Frazer's canoes; but after breakfast, at the head of an island, we met Frazer's boat. The wind coming on fair we hoisted sail, and found that we were more on an equality with our sails than our oars. The birch canoes sailed very well, but we were able to out-row them. We now met the remainder of the war party (before mentioned) of the Sacs and Reynards, returning from their expedition against the Sauteurs. I directed my interpreter to ask how many scalps they had taken; they replied none: he added, they were all squaws, for which I reprimanded him. We now passed the mountain which stands in the river, called by the French "the mountain which soaks in the river." We proceeded on to the Prairie l'Aile, on the west. Mr. Frazer, Bradley, Sparks, and myself, went out to hunt; we crossed first a dry flat prairie; when we arrived at the hills we ascended them, and had a most sublime and beautiful prospect. On the right we saw the mountains which we had passed in the morning, and the prairie in the rear; and, like distant clouds, the mountains at the Prairie de la Crosse. On our left, and under our feet, the valley between the two barren hills, through which the Mississippi winds in numerous channels, forming many beautiful islands, as far as the eye could embrace the scene. Our four boats under full sail, their flags streaming before the wind, formed altogether a prospect so variegated and romantic as one may scarcely expect to enjoy more than twice or thrice in the course of his life. I proposed keeping the hills until they led to the river, encamping, and waiting the next day for our boats; but Mr. Frazer's anxiety to get to the boats induced me to yield, and after crossing a very thick bottom, fording and swimming three branches of the river, and traversing several morasses, we, at twelve o'clock, arrived opposite our boats, which were moored on the eastern side; we were conveyed over to them. We saw frequent signs of elk, but had not the good fortune to come across any of them: my men saw three on the shore. Distance advanced, twenty-one miles.

Sunday, 15th *September*.—Embarked early; passed the River Embarrass and Clear river, which enter on the west, the former of which is navigable one hundred and thirty-five miles; encamped opposite to Buffaloe river on the western shore. This stream, at the head of which the Chippeways reside, is navigable for perroques forty-five or fifty leagues. On the eastern shore, the river de la Prairie de la Crosse empties itself into the Mississippi, at the head of that prairie. It is about twenty yards wide, and bears N.NW.

Mr. Frazer broke one of his canoes, in consequence of which he did not come on as far as our encampment by three miles. Distance advanced, twenty-five miles.

Monday, 16th *September*.—Embarked late, as I wished Mr. Frazer to overtake me, but came on very well. His canoes overtook us at dinner, at the grand encampment below Lake Pepin. We made the sandy peninsula on the east by dusk, when we passed the Sauteaux or Chippeway river, at the entrance of the lake. This river is at least half a mile wide, and appears a deep and majestic stream; it bears from the Mississippi nearly due north. Some distance up it is scarcely to be distinguished from the Ouisconsin; it has a communication with the Montreal river by a short passage, and by this river with Lake Superior. The agents of the new West India Company supply the Fols Avoins and Sauteaux, who reside at the head of this river, and those of the Michillimackinac, and also the Sioux who hunt on its lower waters.

In the division of the Mississippi which we had passed from La Prairie des Chiens, the shores are more than three-quarters prairie on both sides, or, more properly speaking, bald hills, which, instead of running parallel with the river, form a continual succession of high perpendicular cliffs and low valleys; they appear to head the river and to traverse the country in an angular direction. These hills and valleys exhibit some of the most romantic and sublime views I ever saw; but this irregular scenery is sometimes interrupted by a wide extended plain, which brings to mind the verdant lawn of civilized regions, and would almost induce the traveller to imagine himself in the centre of a highly cultivated plantation. The timber of this division is generally birch, elm, and cotton wood, all the cliffs being bordered by cedars.

The navigation, as far as the Iowa river, is good, but from thence to the Sauteaux river is very much obstructed by islands. In some places the Mississippi is uncommonly wide, and divided into many small channels, which, from the cliffs, appear like so many distinct rivers, winding in a parallel course through the same immense valley. But there are few sand bars in those narrow channels; the soil being rich, the water cuts through it with facility.

"The mountain which soaks in the river" stands in the Mississippi, near the eastern shore, about fifty miles below the Sauteaux river, and is about two miles in circumference, with an elevation of two hundred feet, covered with timber. There is a small river that empties into the Mississippi in the rear of the mountain, which, I conceive, once bounded it on the lower side, while the Mississippi formed its upper boundary, the mountain being then joined to the main by a neck of prairie low grounds, which in time was worn away by the spring freshes of the Mississippi, and thus forming an island of this celebrated spot.

Lake Pepin (so called from the French) appears to be only an expansion of the Mississippi. It commences at the entrance of the Sauteaux river, and bears N. 55. W. twelve miles, to Point de Sable, which is a neck of land projecting about one mile into the lake from the western shore, and is the narrowest part of the lake; from hence to the upper end of the course it stretches nearly due west, about ten miles, making its whole length twenty-two miles, and from four to one and a half miles in width, the broadest part being in the bay below Point de Sable. This is a beautiful place; the contrast of the Mississippi, full of islands, and the lake with not one in its whole extent, gives more force to the grandeur of the scene. The French, under the government of M. Frontenac, drove the Reynards (or Ottiquamies) from the Ouisconsin, and pursuing them up the Mississippi, built as a barrier a stockade on Lake Pepin on the western shore, below Point de Sable, and, as was generally the case with that nation, blended the military and mercantile professions by making their fort a factory for the Sioux. The lake at the upper end is three fathoms deep, but I am informed this is its shallowest part. From the Iowa river to the head of Lake Pepin, the elk is the prevailing species of wild game, with some deer and a few bear. By observation I found the head of Lake Pepin to be in latitude 44° 58' 8".

After supper, the wind being fair, we put off, with the intention to sail across the lake; my interpreter (Rosseau) telling me that he had passed it twenty times, but never once by day, giving as a reason that the wind frequently rose and detained them in the day-time on the water. But I believe the traders' only reason, generally, is their fear of the Sauteurs, as they have made several strokes of war at the mouth of this river, never distinguishing between the Sioux and their traders. However, the wind serving, I was induced to proceed; my boat bringing up the rear, for I had put the sail of my big boat on my batteau, and a mast of twenty-two feet. Mr. Frazer embarked in my boat. At first the breeze was very gentle, and we sailed with our violins and other instruments playing; but the sky afterwards became cloudy, and the wind blew quite a gale. My boat ploughed the swells, sometimes almost bows under. When we came to the traverse, which is opposite to Point de Sable, we thought it most advisable, the lake being very much disturbed and the gale increasing, to take harbour in a bay on the east. One of the canoes and my boat came in very well, and together, but having made a fire on the point, to give notice to the boats in the rear, they both ran on the bar before they doubled it, and were near foundering; by jumping into the lake, however, we brought them to a safe harbour. Distance advanced, forty miles.

Tuesday, 17th *September*.— Although there was every appearance of a very severe storm, we embarked at half past six o'clock, the wind fair; but before we had all hoisted sail, those in front had struck theirs. The wind came on hard ahead, the sky became inflamed, and the lightning seemed to roll down the sides of the hills which bordered the shore. The storm in all its grandeur, majesty and horror burst upon us in the traverse, while making for Point de Sable, and it required no moderate exertion to weather the point and get to the windward side. Here we found Mr. Cameron, who had sailed from the prairie on the fifth; he had three barks and one wooden canoe with him. He had been lying here two days, his canoes unloaded and turned up for the habitation of his men, his tents pitched, and living in all the ease of an Indian trader. He appeared to be a man of tolerable information, but rather indolent in his habits; a Scotchman by birth, but an Englishman by prejudice. He had with him a young man of the name of John Rudsdell, and also his own son, a lad of fifteen.

The storm continuing, we remained here all day.. I was shown a point of rocks from which a Sioux woman cast herself and was dashed into a thousand pieces on the rocks below: she had been informed that her friends intended marrying her to a man she despised; and having refused her the man she had chosen, she ascended the hill singing her death song, and before they could overtake her, and frustrate her purpose, took the lover's leap and ended her troubles with her life—a wonderful display of sentiment in a savage! Distance advanced, three miles.

Wednesday, 18th *September*.— Embarked after breakfast. Mr. Cameron with his boats came on with me; crossed the lake, sounded it, and took an observation at the upper end. I embarked in one of Mr. C.'s canoes, and we came up to Canoe river, where there was a small band of Sioux, under the command of *Red Wing*, the second war chief in the nation. He made me a speech, and presented a pipe, pouch, and buffaloe skin. He appeared to be a man of sense, and promised to accompany me to Saint Peter's. He saluted me, and had his salute returned. I made him a small present. We encamped on the end of the island, and although not more than eleven o'clock, were obliged to stay all night. Distance advanced, eighteen miles.

Thursday, 19th *September*.— Embarked early, and dined at the St. Croix river. Messrs. Frazer and Cameron having some business to transact with the savages, we left them at the encampment; but they promised to overtake me, though they should be obliged to travel till twelve o'clock at night. Fired a blunderbuss for them at Tattoo. The chain of my watch became unhooked, by lending her to my guard: this was a very serious misfortune.

Friday, 20th *September*. — Embarked after sun rise; cloudy with hard wind; a small shower of rain: cleared up in the afternoon, and became pleasant. Encamped on a prairie on the eastern side, on which is a large painted stone, about eight miles below the Sioux village. The traders had not yet overtaken me. Distance advanced, twenty-six miles.

VOYAGE TO THE SOURCE

Saturday, 21st September. — Embarked at a seasonable hour, breakfasted at the Sioux village, on the eastern side. It consists of eleven lodges, and is situated at the head of an island, just below a ledge of rocks. The village was deserted at this time, all the Indians having gone out upon the lands to gather Fols Avoin. About two miles above, saw three bears swimming over the river, but at too great a distance for us to kill one of them; they made the shore before I could come up with them. Passed a camp of Sioux, of four lodges, in which I saw only one man, whose name was *Black Soldier*. The garrulity of the women astonished me, for at the other camps they never opened their lips; but here they flocked around us with all their tongues going at the same time. The cause of this freedom must have been the absence of their lords and masters. We passed the encampment of Mr. Fenebault, who had broken his perroque, and had encamped on the western side of the river, about three miles below St. Peter's. We made our encampment on the north east point of the Big island, opposite to St. Peter's. The Mississippi became so very narrow this day, that I once crossed it in my batteau with forty strokes of my oars.

The water of the Mississippi, since we passed Lake Pepin, has been remarkably red, and where it is deep appears as black as ink. The waters of the St. Croix and St. Peter's appear blue and clear for a considerable distance below their confluence.

From the head of Lake Pepin, for about twelve miles to the Cannon river, the Mississippi branches into many channels, and is speckled with numerous islands. There is a hill on the western shore, about six miles above the lake, called the Grange; from the summit of which, you have one of the most delightful prospects in nature. When turning to the east, you have the river winding in three channels at your feet; on the right, the extensive bosom of the lake, bounded by its chain of hills; in front, over the Mississippi, a wide extended prairie; on the left, the valley of the Mississippi, open to view quite to the St. Croix; and partly in your rear, the valley through which passes the Cannon river. When I viewed it, on one of the islands below appeared the spotted lodges of the Red Wing's band of Sioux, the white tents of the traders and my soldiers, and three flags of the United States, waving on the water; which gave a contrast to the still and lifeless wilderness around, and increased the pleasure of the prospect.

From the Canoe river to the St. Croix, the Mississippi evidently becomes narrower, and the navigation less obstructed by islands; the St. Croix river joins the Mississippi on the east, and bears from it almost due north. It is only eighty yards wide at its mouth, and five hundred yards up, commences Lake St. Croix, which is from one and a half to three miles wide, and thirty-six miles in length; this river communicates with Lake Superior, by the Burnt river, by a portage of half a mile only, and in its whole extent has not one fall or rapid worthy of notice; this, with the mildness of its current, and its other advantages, renders it by far the most preferable communication that can be had with the north-west, from this part of our territories. Its upper waters are inhabited by the Fols Avoin and Sauteaux, who are supplied by the agents of the north-west company, and its lower division by the Sioux, and their traders.

From the Cannon river, the Mississippi is bounded on the east by high ridges, but the left shore consists of low ground; the timber is generally ash and maple, except the cedar of the cliffs, sugar-tree, and ash. About twenty miles below the entrance of the river St. Peter's on the eastern shore, at a place called the Grand Marais, is situated the Petit Corbeau village, of eleven log-houses.

I observed a white flag on shore to day, and, on landing, discovered it to be white silk; it was suspended over a scaffold, on which were laid four dead bodies, two enclosed in boards and two in bark. They were wrapped up in blankets which appeared quite new; I was informed they were the bodies of two Sioux women, (who had lived with two Frenchmen,) one of their children and some other relative; two of whom had died at St. Peter's and two at St. Croix, but were brought here to be deposited upon this scaffold together; this is the manner of a Sioux burial, when persons die a natural death; but when they are killed, they suffer them to lie unburied. This circumstance brought to my recollection the bones of a man I found on the hills below the St. Croix—the jaw-bone I brought on board,—he must have been killed on that spot.— Distance advanced, twenty-four miles.

Sunday, 22nd *September*.—Employed in the morning in measuring the river—about three o'clock Mr. Frazer arrived with his perroques, and in three hours after, the Petit Corbeau, at the head of his band, arrived with one-hundred and fifty warriors; they ascended the hill, in the point between the Mississippi and St. Peter's, and gave me a salute *á-la-mode Sauvage* with balls; after which, we settled the affairs for the council to be held next day. Mr. Frazer and myself took a bark canoe and went up to the village, in order to see Mr. Cameron. We ascended the St. Peter's to the village and found his camp, (no current in the river,) he engaged to be at the council, and promised to let me have his barge. The Sioux had marched on a war excursion, but hearing (by express) of my arrival, had returned by land. .We were treated very hospitably, and hallooed after to go into every lodge to eat. We returned to our station about eleven o'clock, and found the Sioux and my men peaceably encamped.

Monday, 23d *September.*—Prepared for the council, which we commenced about twelve o'clock. I had a bower, or shed, made of my sails on the beach, into which only my gentlemen (the traders) and the chiefs entered. I then addressed them in a speech, which, though long and touching on many points, had for its principal object, the obtaining of a grant of land at this place (the Falls of St. Anthony) and at St. Croix, and the making peace between them and the Chippeways. I was replied to by Fils de Penichon, Le Petit Corbeau, and L' Original Levé. They gave me the land required, about one hundred thousand acres, (equal to two hundred thousand dollars in value,) and promised me a safe passport for myself and the chiefs I might bring down;˙but spoke doubtfully with respect to the peace. I gave them presents to the amount of about two hundred dollars, and as soon as the council was over, I allowed the traders to present them with some liquor, which, with what I gave, was equal to sixty gallons. In half an hour they were all embarked for their respective villages. The chiefs in the council were, Le Petit Corbeau, he signed the grant; Le Fils de Penichon, he also signed ; Le Grand Partisan, L' Original Levé, La Dimi Douzaine, Le Bucasse, and Le Bœuf qui Marche. It was somewhat difficult to get them to sign the grant, as they conceived their word of honour should be taken without any mark ; but I convinced them it was not on their account, but my own, I wished for their signatures.*

---

* The following is the substance of my conversation on this occasion:

"BROTHERS—I am happy to meet you here at this council fire, which your father has sent me to kindle, and to take you by the hand as our children. We having but lately acquired from the Spaniards the extensive territory of Louisiana, our general

Tuesday, 24th *September.*— In the morning I discovered that my flag was missing from my boat. Being in doubt whether it had

has thought proper to send out a number of his young warriors to visit all his red children; to tell them his will, and to hear what request they may have to make of their father. I am happy the choice has fallen on me to come this road, as I find my brothers, the Sioux, ready to listen to my words.

"It is the wish of our government to establish military posts on the upper Mississippi, at such places as might be thought expedient; I have therefore examined the country, and have pitched on the mouth of the River St. Croix, this place, and the Falls of St. Anthony; I therefore wish you to grant to the United States, nine miles square at St. Croix, and this place from a league below the confluence of the St. Peter's and Mississippi, to a league above St. Anthony, extending three leagues on each side of the river; and as we are a people accustomed to have all our acts written down, in order to have them handed to our children, I have drawn up a form of an agreement, which we will both sign in the presence of the traders now present. After we know the terms we will fill it up, and have it read and interpreted to you.

"These posts are intended as a benefit to you; the old chiefs now present must see that their situation improves by a communication with the whites. It is the intention of the United States to establish at these posts factories, in which the Indians may procure all their things at a cheaper and better rate than they do now; or, that your traders can afford to sell them at to you, as they are single individuals who come far in small boats. But your fathers are many and powerful, and will come with a strong arm in larger vessels. There will also be chiefs here, who can attend to the wants of their brothers, without their sending or going all the way to St. Louis; and who will see the traders that go up your rivers, and know that they are good men.

"Another object your father has at heart is, to endeavour to make peace between you and the Chippeways. You have now been a long time at war, and when will you stop? if neither side will lay down the hatchet, your paths will always be red with blood; but if you will consent to make peace, and suffer your father to bury the hatchet between you, I will endeavour to bring down some of the Chippeway chiefs with me to St. Louis, where the good work can be completed under the auspices of our mutual father. I am much pleased to see, that the young warriors have halted here to hear my words this day: and as I know it is hard for a warrior to be struck and not strike again, I will, by the first Chippeway I meet, send words to their chief, that if they have not felt your tomahawk, it is not because you have no legs or the hearts of men, but because you have listened to the voice of your father.

"If the chiefs do not listen to the voice of their father, and continue to commit murders on you and your traders, they will call down the vengeance of the Americans; for they are not like a blind man walking into the fire. They were once at war with us, and together with their allies, all the northern Indians, were defeated at Roche de Butte, and obliged to sue for peace; that peace we granted them. They know we are not children, but like all wise people, are slow to shed blood.

been stolen by the Indians, or had fallen overboard and floated away, I sent for my friend L' Original Levé, and sufficiently evinced to him by the vehemence of my action, by the immediate chastisement of my guard, (having on one of them inflicted severe corporal punishment,) and by sending down the shore three miles in search of it, how much I was displeased that such a thing should have occurred. I sent a flag and two

"Brothers—Your old men know that not many years since, we received Detroit, Michillimackinac, and all the posts on the lakes, from the English, and now, but the other day, Louisiana from the Spaniards; so that we put one foot on the sea at the east, and the other on the sea at the west; and if once children, are now men. Yet, I think the traders who come from Canada are bad birds amongst the Chippeways, and instigate them to make war on their red brethren, the Sioux, in order to prevent our traders going up the Mississippi. This I shall enquire into; and if I find the case to be so, warn those persons of their ill conduct.

"Brothers—Mr. Cheteau was sent by your father to the Osage nation, with one of his young chiefs, he sailed some days before me, and had not time to procure the medals which I am told he promised to send up, but they will be procured.

"I wish you to have some of your head chiefs to be ready to go down with me in the spring. From the head of St. Peter's also, such other chiefs as you may think proper, to the number of four or five. When I pass here on my way I will send you word at what time you will meet me at the Prairie des Chiens.

"I expect you will give orders to all your young warriors to respect my flag, and the protection which I may extend to the Chippeway chiefs, who may come down with me in the spring: for were a dog to run to my lodge for safety, his enemy must walk over me to hurt them.

"Brothers—Here is a flag which I wish to send to the Gens de Feuille, to shew them they are not forgotten by their father. I wish the comrade of their chief to take it on himself to deliver it with my words.

"Brothers—I am told, that hitherto the traders have made a practice of selling rum to you. All of you in your right senses must know that it is injurious, and occasions quarrels and murders amongst yourselves. For this reason your father has thought proper to prohibit the traders from selling you any more. Therefore I hope my brothers the chiefs, when they know a trader to sell an Indian rum, will prevent that Indian from paying his credit. This will break up the pernicious practice, and oblige your father. But I hope you will not encourage your young men to treat our traders ill from this circumstance, or from a hope of the indulgence formerly experienced, but make your complaints to persons in this country, who will be authorized to do you justice.

"I now present you with some of your father's tobacco, and some other trifling things, as a memorandum of my good will, and before my departure I will give you some liquor to clear your throats."

carrots of tobacco by Mr. Cameron, to the Sioux at the head of the St. Peter's. Made a small draft of the position at this place: sent up the boat I got from Mr. Fisher, to the village on the St. Peter's, and exchanged her for a barge with Mr. Duncan; my men returned with the barge about sun-down, she was a fine light vessel, eight men were able to carry her—employed all day in writing.

Wednesday, 25th *September*.—I was awakened by Le Petit Corbeau, (head chief,) who came up from his village to see if we were killed, or if any accident had happened to us; this was in consequence of his having found my flag floating three miles below their village, (fifteen miles hence,) from which they concluded some affray had taken place, and that it had been thrown overboard. Although I conceived this an unfortunate accident for me, I was exceedingly happy at its effect; for it proved the means of preventing much blood-shed among the savages. A chief called the Outarde Blanche had his lip cut off, and had come to the Petit Corbeau, and told him, "that his face was his looking-glass, that it was spoiled, and that he was determined on revenge." The parties were charging their guns and preparing for action, when lo! the flag appeared like a messenger of peace, sent to prevent their bloody purposes; they were all astonished to see it, the staff being broken: when the Petit Corbeau arose and spoke to this effect, "That a thing so sacred had not been taken from my boat without violence, that it was proper for them to hush all private animosities, until they had revenged the cause of their elder brother; that he would immediately go up the St. Peter's, to learn what dogs had done it, in order to take steps to get satisfaction of those who had committed the outrage." They all listened to this reasoning, and he immediately had the flag put out to dry, and embarked himself for my camp.

I was much concerned to hear of the blood likely to have been shed, and gave him five yards of blue stroud, three yards of calico, one handkerchief, one carrot of tobacco, and a knife, in order to make peace among his people. He promised to send my flag by land to the falls, and make peace with the Outarde Blanche. Mr. Frazer went up to the village, and we embarked late and encamped at the foot of the rapids.

Thursday, 26th *September*.—Embarked at the usual hour, and after much labour in passing through the rapids, arrived at the foot of the falls about three or four o'clock; here we unloaded our boat and had the principal part of the cargo carried over the portage: with the other boat however, full loaded, they were not able to get over the last shoot, and encamped about six hundred yards below—I pitched my tent and encamped above the shoot. The rapids mentioned here, might properly be called a continuation of the Falls of St. Anthony, for they are equally entitled to this appellation with the falls of the Delaware and Susquehannah. Killed one deer—distance advanced, nine miles.

Friday, 27th *September*.—Brought over the residue of my loading this morning. Two men arrived from Mr. Frazer on St. Peter's for my despatches. This business of closing and sealing, appeared like a last adieu to the civilized world: I sent, by this opportunity, a large packet to the General, and a letter to Mrs. Pike, with a short note to Mr. Frazer. Two young Indians brought my flag across by land, and arrived yesterday just as we came in sight of the falls; I made them a present for their punctuality and expedition, and the dangers to which their journey exposed them. We next carried our boats out of the river as far as the bottom of the hill.

Saturday, 28th *September*.—Having conveyed my barge over the portage, we put her into the river above the falls. While we were thus occupied three quarters of a mile from the camp, seven Indians painted black appeared on the height—we had left our guns at camp, and were entirely defenceless. It occurred to me that they were the small party of Sioux, who were obstinately bent on going to war, when the other part of the bands came in; these they proved to be: they were better armed than any I had ever seen; having guns, bows and arrows, clubs, spears, and some of them even a case of pistols. I was at that time giving my men a dram; having presented the cup of liquor to the first Indian he drank it off, but I was more cautious with the others. I sent my interpreter to the camp with them to wait my arrival, wishing to purchase one of their war clubs, it being made of elk-horn and decorated with inlaid work. This and a set of bows and arrows, I wished to obtain as curiosities; but the liquor I had given the Indian beginning to operate, he came back for me, but refusing to go till I had brought up my boat, he returned, and (being I suppose offended) borrowed a canoe and crossed the river. In the afternoon we got the other boat near the top of the hill, when the props giving way she

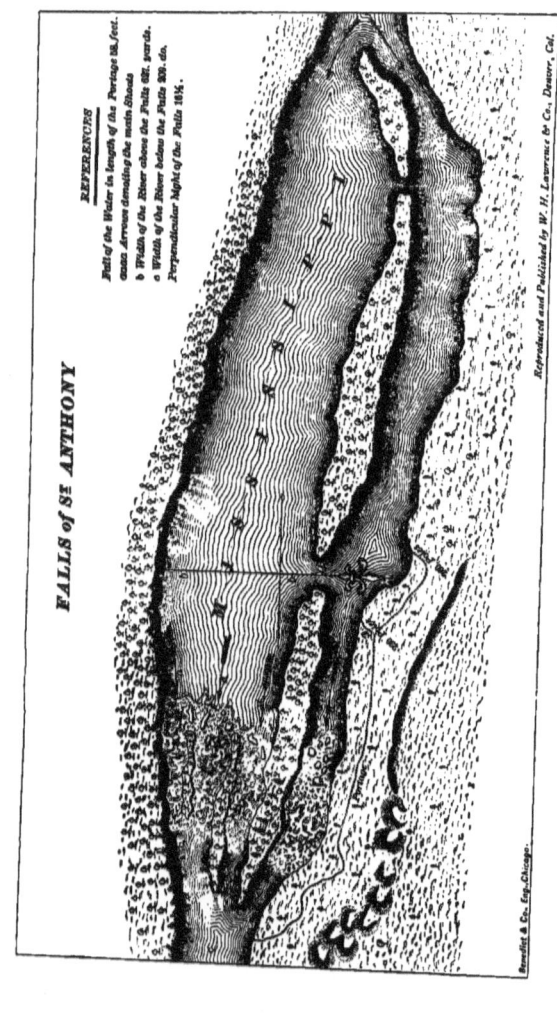

slid down to the bottom, but fortunately without injuring any person —it raining very hard we left her—killed one goose and a rackoon.

Sunday, 29th *September*.—We got our large boat over the portage, and put her in the river, at the upper landing; this night the men gave sufficient proof of their fatigue, by all throwing themselves down to sleep, preferring rest to supper. This day I had but fifteen men out of twenty-two; the others were sick.

Our voyage could have been performed with great convenience, if we had taken our departure in June.

But the most proper time would be to leave the Illinois as soon as the ice would permit, when the river would be of a good height.

Monday, 30th *September*.—Loaded my two boats, moved over and encamped on the island. In the mean time, I took a survey of the falls, portage, &c., to examine whether it be possible to pass the falls at high water, of which I am doubtful*; if practicable, it must be on the eastern side, about thirty yards from shore; as there are three layers of rocks, one below the other, the pitch off of either is not more than five feet.

From the River St. Peter's to the Falls of St. Anthony, the Mississippi is contracted between high hills, and is one continued rapid or fall, the bottom being covered with rocks, which (in low water) are some feet above the surface, leaving narrow channels between them. The rapidity of the current is likewise much augmented by the numerous small rocky islands which obstruct the navigation.

The shores have many large and beautiful springs issuing from them, which form small cascades as they tumble over the cliffs into the Mississippi. The timber is generally maple. This place is not noted for any great number of wild fowls.

The Falls of St. Anthony did not strike me with that majestic appearance which I had been taught to expect from the description of other travellers. On an actual survey I find the portage to be two hundred and sixty poles, but when the river is not very low, boats ascending may put in thirty-one poles below at a large cedar tree, which would reduce it to two hundred and twenty-nine poles. The hill on which the portage is made is sixty-nine feet ascent, with an elevation at the point of debarkation of 45°. The fall of the water between the place of debarkation and of

---
*Never possible, as ascertained in my return.

reloading is fifty-eight feet, the perpendicular fall of the shoot sixteen feet and a half, the width of the river above the shoot six hundred and twenty seven yards, below two hundred and nine. In high water the appearance is much more sublime, as the great quantity of water then forms a spray, which in clear weather reflects from some positions the colours of the rainbow, and when the sky is overcast, covers the falls in gloom and chaotic majesty.

Tuesday, 1st *October*.—We again embarked to proceed on our voyage above the falls. The river at first appeared mild and sufficiently deep for the easy passage of our boats; but after we had advanced about four miles, the shoals commenced, and we had very hard water all day; we passed in all three rapids: killed one goose and three ducks: the sun shone for the first time since we had left the falls; distance advanced seventeen miles.

From the Falls of St. Anthony to the Rum river, the Mississippi is almost one continued chain of rapids, with the eddies formed by winding channels. The land on both sides consists of prairie, with scarcely any timber, excepting small groves of scrub oak. Rum river is about fifty yards wide at its mouth, and takes its source in Le Mille Lac, which is but thirty-five miles south of lower Red Cedar Lake. The small Indian canoes ascend this river quite to the lake, the ground in the neighbourhood of which is considered one of the best hunting stations for some hundred of miles, and has long been a scene of contention between the hunting parties of the Sioux and Sauteaux. The last winter a number of the Fols Avoins, and Sioux, and some Sauteaux, wintered in that quarter.

From Rum river to Leaf river (called by Father Hennipin and Carver the river St. Francis, and formed the extent of their travels) the prairies continue with a few interruptions, the timber scrub oak, with now and then a lonely pine.

Wednesday, 2d *October*.—We embarked at our usual hour, and shortly after passed some large islands, and remarkably hard ripples. Indeed the navigation, to persons not determined to proceed, would have been deemed impracticable. We waded nearly all day to force the boats off shoals, and draw them through rapids: killed three geese and two swans. We observed much appearance of elk and deer; distance advanced, twelve miles.

Thursday, 3d *October*.—The weather was extremely cold in the morning, the mercury being at 0°; we proceeded very well, though some ripples occurred; killed three geese and one rackoon, also a blaireau, an animal I had never before seen; distance advanced, fifteen miles and a half.

Friday, 4th *October*.—Rained in the morning, but the wind serving, we embarked, although extremely raw and cold. Passed Crow river, on the west. The stream is about thirty yards wide, and bears from the Mississippi S. W. Opposite to the mouth of Crow river, we found a bark canoe, cut to pieces with tomahawks, and the paddles broken lying on shore. A short distance higher up we saw five more, and continued to discover similar wrecks until we had found eight. From the form of the canoes my interpreter pronounced them to be Sioux; and some broken arrows he declared to have belonged to the Sauteurs. The paddles were also marked with the Indian sign of men and women killed. From all these circumstances we inferred that the canoes had belonged to a party of Sioux, who had been attacked by the Sauteurs and all killed, or taken prisoners. My interpreter was much alarmed, assuring me that it was probable, that at our first meeting with the Chippeways, we should be mistaken by them for Sioux traders, and be fired at before we could come to an explanation. He stated that they had murdered three Frenchmen, whom they found on the shore about this time last year; but notwithstanding his information, I was on shore all the afternoon in pursuit of elk. During this excursion I caught a curious little animal on the prairie, which my Frenchman termed a prairie mole,. but it is very different from the mole of the states; killed two geese, one pheasant, and a wolf; distance advanced, sixteen miles.

Saturday, 5th *October*.—Had hard water and ripples all day; passed by some old Sioux encampments, all fortified; found five litters in which sick or wounded men had been carried. At this place a hard battle was fought between the Sioux and Sauteurs in the year 1800: killed one goose; distance advanced, eleven miles.

Sunday, 6th *October*.—Early in the morning we discovered four elks, which were the first we saw; they swam the river, I pursued them, and wounded one, but he made his escape into a marsh, saw afterwards two droves of elk, but could not approach them. I killed some small game, and joined the boats at dusk. During my excursion I found a small red capot hung upon a tree, which my interpreter informed me was a sacrifice by some Indians to the Bon Dieu. I determined to lay by and hunt the next day: killed three prairie hens and two pheasants; distance advanced, twelve miles.

Monday, 7th *October*.—Lay by in order to dry my corn, clothing, &c., and to investigate the conduct of my sergeant, against whom charges had been exhibited; sent several of my men out hunting; went myself towards evening and killed four prairie hens; the hunters were unsuccessful, having killed only three prairie hens and six pheasants.

Tuesday, 8th *October*.—Embarked early and made a very good day's progress, but had three rapids to pass on the western side. We passed some woodland, consisting chiefly of oak, but the whole bottom was covered with the prickly ash.

I made it a practice, to oblige every man who complained of indisposition, to march on shore; by which means I had some flankers on both sides of the river, who were excellent guards against surprise; they also served as hunters: distance advanced, twenty miles.

Wednesday, 9th *October*.—Embarked early, the wind a-head. The shores consisted of barrens and prairie; killed one deer and four pheasants; distance advanced, three miles.

Thursday, 10th *October*.—We arrived in the morning at the place where Mr. Reinville and Mons. Portier wintered in 1797; passed a cluster of more than twenty islands in the course of four miles; these I called Beaver Islands, from the great signs of those animals which they exhibited, for they had constructed dams on every island, with roads from them every two or three rods' distance. Encamped in the evening at the foot of the grand rapids: killed two geese, five ducks, and four pheasants; distance advanced, sixteen miles and a half.

Friday, 11th *October*.—Both the boats had passed the worst of the rapids by 11 o'clock, but the men were obliged to wade and lift them over rocks, which had not a foot of water on them, while at times the next step they would be in the water over their heads. In consequence of these circumstances, our boats were frequently in imminent danger of being bilged on the rocks. About five miles above the rapids, our large boat was discovered to leak so fast that it became necessary to unload her. Having done this, and stopped the leaks, we reloaded. Near a war encampment, at this place, I found a painted buckskin, and a piece of scarlet cloth, suspended on a tree; this I supposed to be dedicated to *Matcho Manitou* by the Indians, to ensure the success of their enterprise; but I took the liberty of invading the rights of his diabolical majesty, by appropriating the articles, as the priests of old have often done similar offerings, to my own use: killed only two ducks; distance advanced, eight miles.

From Leaf river to Sac river, a little above the grand rapids, both sides of the Mississippi are generally prairie, with skirts of scrub oak; the navigation still obstructed with ripples, but with some intermissions of a few miles. Sac river is about two hundred yards wide at its mouth, and bears from the Mississippi about south-west.

At the grand rapids the river expands itself to about three-fourths of a mile in width (its general width not being more than three-fifths of a mile), and tumbles over an unequal bed of rocks for about two miles, through which there cannot be said to be any channel, for notwithstanding the rapidity of the current, one of my invalids who was on the western shore waded to the eastern, where we were encamped; the eastern bank at the rapids is a very high prairie, the western scrubby wood land.

Saturday, 12th *October*.—Hard ripples in the morning; but after having passed a narrow rocky place, we had good water: our large boat again sprung a leak, and we were obliged to encamp early and unload: killed one deer, one wolf, two geese, and two ducks; distance advanced, twelve miles and a half.

Sunday, 13th *October*.—Embarked early and came on well with good water, and fair wind; passed a handsome little stream on the east, which we named Clear river; killed one deer, one beaver, two minks, two geese, and one duck. This day we discovered the first buffalo sign, and came to the first timber land above the falls of St. Anthony; distance advanced, twenty-nine miles.

Monday, 14th *October*.—Ripples for a considerable way. My hunters killed three deer, four geese, and two porcupines. While I was out hunting I discovered a trail, which I supposed to have been made by the savages. I followed it with much precaution, and at length started a large bear, feeding on the carcass of a deer; he soon made his escape. This was the first discovery of bear since we left St. Louis, excepting what we saw three miles below St. Peter's: distance advanced, seventeen miles.

Tuesday, 15th *October.*—Ripples all day. In the morning the large boat came up, and I once more got my party together; they had been detained by taking in the game. Yesterday and to-day passed some skirts of good lands, well timbered, swamps of hemlock and white pine. The water continued very hard, and the river became shallow and full of islands. We encamped on a beautiful point on the west, below a fall of the river over a bed of rocks, through which we had two narrow shoots to make our way the next day; killed two deer, five ducks, and two geese. This day made us think seriously of our wintering ground, and of leaving our large boats: distance advanced, five miles.

Wednesday, 16th *October.*—When we arose in the morning, we found that snow had fallen during the night; the ground was covered, and it still continued snowing. This was indeed but poor encouragement for attacking the rapids, in which we were certain to have to wade up to our necks in water. I was determined however, if possible, to make Corbeau or Raven river, the highest point ever reached by traders in the bark canoes. We embarked, and after four hours' work, became so benumbed with cold, that our limbs were perfectly useless; we put to shore on the opposite side of the river, about two-thirds of the way up the rapids, built a large fire, and then discovered that our boats were nearly half full of water; both having sprung large leaks, so as to oblige me to keep three hands bailing. My sergeant, (Kennerman,) one of the stoutest men I ever knew, burst a blood-vessel, and vomited nearly two quarts of blood. One of my corporals (Bradley) also discharged nearly a pint of blood, when he attempted to void his urine.

These unhappy circumstances, in addition to the inability of four other men, whom we were obliged to leave on shore, convinced me, that if I had no regard for my own health and constitution, I ought to have some for those poor fellows, who were killing themselves to obey my orders. After we had breakfasted and refreshed ourselves, we went down to our boats, on the rocks, where I was obliged to leave them. I now informed my men, that we should return to the camp, and leave on this spot some of the party and our large boats. This information proved agreeable to them, and the effort to reach the camp was soon accomplished. My reasons for this step have already been in part stated. The necessity of unloading and refitting my boats, the beauty and convenience of the spot for building huts, the fine pine trees it afforded for perroques, the quantity of game which abounded in the neighbourhood, were additional inducements. By leaving men at this place, I was sure of plenty of provisions for my returning voyage. In the party left behind was one hunter, to be continually employed, who would keep our stock of salt provisions good.

We immediately unloaded our boats and secured their cargoes. In the evening I went out upon a small but beautiful creek, which empties into the falls, for the purpose of selecting pine trees to make canoes; saw five deer, and killed one buck, weighing one hundred and thirty-seven pounds. Distance two hundred and thirty-three miles and a half above the Falls of St. Anthony.

From Sac river to Pine creek, our present station, the quantity of game continued to increase. The borders of the river consist of prairie, with groves of pine on the edge of the banks, but there are some exceptions, where we meet with small bottoms of oak, ash, maple, and lyme. In this distance there is an intermission of rapids for about forty miles, when they commence again, full as difficult as ever. There are three small creeks emptying in on the west, scarcely worthy of notice, and on the east are two small rivers, Lake and Clear rivers, mentioned before; the former, a small stream about fifteen yards wide, bearing N. W. at its mouth. About three miles from its entrance is a beautiful small lake, around which resort immense herds of elk and buffalo. Clear river is a delightful little stream, of about eighty yards in width, and heads in some swamps and small lakes, on which the Sauteaux of lower Red Cedar Lake and Sandy Lake frequently come to hunt. The soil of the prairies from above the falls is sandy, but would raise small grain in abundance; the bottom is rich and fit for corn or hemp.

Pine creek is a small stream which comes in on the western shore, and bears nearly west. It is bounded by large groves of white and red pine.

Thursday, 17th *October*.— It continued to snow; I walked out in the morning and killed four bears, and my hunter three deers. Felled our trees for canoes, and commenced working on them.

Friday, 18th *October*.— Stopped hunting, and put every hand to work; cut sixty logs for huts, and worked at the canoes. This, considering we had only two felling axes and three hatchets, was pretty good work. Weather cloudy with a little snow.

Saturday, 19th October.— Raised one of our houses, and almost completed one canoe. I was employed the principal part of this day in writing letters, and making arrangements which I deemed necessary, in case I should never return.

Sunday, 20th October.— Continued our labour at the houses and canoes, finished my letters, &c. At night discovered the prairie on the opposite side of the river to be on fire, which I supposed to have been occasioned by the Sauteurs. I wished much to have our situation respectable here, or I would have sent the next day to discover them.

Monday, 21st October.— Went out hunting, but killed nothing, not wishing to shoot at small game. Our labour went on.

Tuesday, 22d October.— Went out hunting: about fifteen miles up the creek saw a great quantity of deer, but from the dryness of the woods, and the quantity of brush, only shot one through the body, which made its escape. This day my men neglected their work, which convinced me I must leave off hunting and superintend them. Miller and myself lay out all night in the pine woods.

Wednesday, 23d October.— Raised three block houses, deposited all our property in the one already completed; killed a number of pheasants and ducks, while visiting my canoe makers. Sleets and snow.

Thursday, 24th October.— The snow having fallen one or two inches thick in the night, I sent out one hunter (Sparks) and went out myself: Bradley, my other hunter, being sick. Each of us killed two deer, one goose and one pheasant.

Friday, 25th October.— Sent out men with Sparks to bring in his game; none of them returned, and I supposed them to be lost in the hemlock swamps, with which the country abounds. My interpreter, however, whom I believe to be a coward, insisted that they were killed by the Sauteurs. Made arrangements for my departure.

Saturday, 26th October.— Launched my canoes and found them very small. My hunters killed three deer. Took out Miller and remained out all night, but killed nothing,

Sunday, 27th October. — Employed in preparing our baggage to embark.

Monday, 28th *October.*—My two canoes being finished, launched and brought them to the head of the rapids, where I put my provision, ammunition, &c., on board, intending to embark by daylight. Having left them under the charge of the sentinel, in about an hour one of them, containing the ammunition and my baggage, sunk: the accident was occasioned by what is called a wind shock. This misfortune, and the extreme smallness of my canoes, induced me to build another. I had my cartridges spread out on blankets, and large fires made around them; at that time I was not able to ascertain the full extent of the damage, the magnitude of which none can estimate, excepting those in the same situation with ourselves, fifteen hundred miles from civilized society, and in danger of losing the very means of defence, nay, even of existence.

Tuesday, 29th *October.*—Felled a large pine and commenced another canoe; I was at work at my cartridges all day, but did not save five dozen out of thirty. In attempting to dry the powder in pots, blew it up, and it had nearly blown up a tent and two or three men with it. Made a dozen new cartridges, with the old wrapping paper.

Wednesday, 30th *October.*—My men laboured as usual; nothing extraordinary occurred.

Thursday, 31st *October.*—Enclosed my little work completely with piquets; hauled up my two boats, and turned them over on each side of the gateways, by which means a defence was made to the river; and had it not been for various political reasons, I would have laughed at the attack of eight hundred or a thousand savages, if all my party were within. For, save accidents, it would only have afforded amusement, the Indians having no idea of taking a place by storm.

I found myself this day powerfully attacked with the fantastics of the brain, called ennui, at the mention of which I had hitherto scoffed; but my books being packed up, I was like a person entranced, and could easily conceive why so many persons, who have been confined to remote places, have acquired the habit or drinking to excess, and many other practices which have been adopted merely to pass time.

Friday, 1st *November.*—Finding that my canoe would not be finished under two or three days, I concluded to take six men and go down the river about twelve miles, where we had observed great signs of elk and buffalo. We arrived there early in the afternoon, and all turned out to hunt, but none of us killed anything except Sparks, who shot one doe. A slight snow fell.

Saturday, 2d *November.*—Left the camp with the full determination of killing an elk if possible before my return. I had never yet killed one of these animals. Took with me Miller, whose obliging disposition made him agreeable in the woods. I was determined that if we came on the trail of elk, to follow them a day or two in order to kill one. This to a person acquainted with the nature of those animals, and the extent of the prairies, in this country, would appear, what it really was, a very foolish resolution. We soon struck where a herd of one hundred and fifty had passed, pursued and came in sight about eight o'clock, when they appeared, at a distance, like an army of Indians, moving along in single file; a large buck of at least four feet between the horns leading the van, and one of equal magnitude bringing up the rear. We followed till near night, without being once able to get within point blank shot. I once made Miller fire at them with his musket, at about four hundred yards distance; it had no other effect than to make them leave us about five miles behind on the prairie. We passed several deer in the course of the day, which I think we could have killed, but did not fire for fear of alarming the elk. Finding that it was no easy matter to kill one, I shot a doe through the body, as I perceived by her blood where she lay down in the snow, yet, not knowing how to track, we lost her. Shortly after we saw three elk by themselves, near a copse of wood; approached near them and broke the shoulder of one, but he ran off with his companions. Just as I was about to follow, I observed a buck deer lying in the grass, which I shot behind the eyes, when he fell over. I walked up to him, put my foot on his horns and examined the shot, upon which he snorted, bounced up and fell about five steps from me. This I considered his last effort, but soon after, to our utter astonishment, he jumped up and ran off: he stopped frequently; we pursued him expecting him to fall every minute, by which we were led from the pursuit of the wounded elk. After having wearied ourselves out in this unsuccessful chase, we returned to pursue the wounded elk, and when we came up to the party, found him missing from the flock. Shot another in the body, but my ball being small he likewise escaped; wounded another deer. Being now hungry, cold, and fatigued, after having wounded three deer and two elk, we were obliged to encamp, in a point of hemlock woods, on the head of Clear river. The large herd of elk lay about one mile from us, in the prairie. Our want of success I ascribe to the smallness of our balls, and to our inexperience in following the track, after wounding them, for it is very seldom a deer drops on the spot where he is shot.

Sunday, 3d *November*.—Rose pretty early and went in pursuit of the elk; wounded one buck deer on the way. Made an attempt to drive them into the woods, but their leader broke past us, and it appeared as if the drove would have followed him, though they had been obliged to run over us: we fired at them passing, but without effect. Pursued them through the swamp till about ten o'clock, when I determined to attempt to make the river, and for that purpose took a due south course; passed many droves of elk and buffalo, but being in the middle of an immense prairie, knew it was folly to attempt to shoot them. Wounded several deer, but got none; in fact, I knew I could shoot as many deer as anybody, but neither myself nor companion could find one in ten, where an experienced hunter would have got all he shot. Near night we struck a lake about five miles long, and two miles wide: saw immense droves of elk on both banks. About sundown we saw a herd crossing the prairie towards us, which induced us to sit down; two bucks, more curious than the others, came pretty close. I struck one of them behind the fore shoulder; he did not go more than twenty yards, before he fell and died. This was the cause of much exultation, because it fulfilled my determination, and as we had been two days and nights without victuals, it was a very acceptable prize. We found during our excursion some scrub oak.

After having proceeded about a mile farther, we made a fire, and with much labour and pains got our meat to it; the wolves feasting upon one half, while we were carrying away the other. We were now provisioned, but were still in want of water; the snow being all melted; finding my thirst very excessive in the night, I went in search of water, and was much surprised, after having gone about a mile, to strike the Mississippi: here I filled my hat, and returned to my companion.

Monday, 4th *November*.—Repaired my mockinsons, using a piece of elk's bone as an awl. We both went to the Mississippi, and found we were a great distance from the camp. I left Miller to guard the meat, and marched for camp: having strained my ancles in the swamps, they were extremely painful, and the strings of my mockinsons cut them, and made them swell considerably. Before I had proceeded far, I discovered a herd of ten elk; I approached within fifty yards, and shot one through the body; he fell on the spot, but rose again and ran off. I pursued him at least five miles, expecting every minute to see him drop; I then gave him up. When I arrived at Clear river, a deer was standing on the other bank; I killed him on the spot, and while I was taking out the entrails another came up. I shot him also: this was my last ball, and then only could I kill! I left part of my cloaths at this place to scare the wolves: arrived at my camp at dusk, to the great joy of our men, who had been to our little garrison to inquire for me, and, receiving no intelligence, had concluded we had been killed by the Indians, having heard them fire on the opposite bank. The same night we saw fires on the opposite shore in the prairie; this was likewise seen from the fort, when all the men moved in the works.

Tuesday, 5th *November*.—Sent four of my men with our canoe, loaded with the remains of nine deer that had been killed, with the other two. Went down the river for my meat, stopped for the deer, which I found safe. Miller had just started to march home, but returned to camp. Found all the meat safe and brought it to the river, where we pitched our camp.

Wednesday, 6th *November*.—At the earnest entreaties of my men, and with the hope of killing some more game, I agreed to stay and hunt. We went out and found that all the elk and buffalo had the day before gone down the river from those plains, leaving large roads to point out their course. This did not appear extraordinary to us, as the prairie had unluckily caught fire. After Miller left the camp for home, Sparks killed two deer about six miles off, and it being near the river, I sent the three men down with the canoe, with orders to return early in the morning. It commenced snowing about midnight, and by morning the snow was six inches deep.

Thursday, 7th *November*.—Waited all day with the greatest anxiety for my men. The river became nearly filled with snow, partly congealed into ice; my situation can more easily be imagined than described. I went down the river to where I understood the deer were killed, but discovered nothing of the men. I became very uneasy on their account, for I was well aware of the hostile disposition of the Indians to all persons on this part of the Mississippi, taking them to be traders, and we had not had an opportunity of explaining to them who we were. Snow still continued falling very fast, and was nearly knee deep. Had great difficulty to procure wood sufficient to keep up a fire during the night. Ice in the river thickening.

Friday, 8th *November*—My men not yet arrived, I determined to depart for the garrison, and when the river had frozen, to come down on the ice with a party, or if the weather became mild, by water, with my other perroques to search for them. Put up about ten pounds of meat, two blankets and a bear skin, with my sword and gun; which, together, made for me a very heavy load. I left the meat in as good a situation as possible; wrote on the snow my wishes, and put my handkerchief up as a flag. My anxiety was so great that, notwithstanding my load and the depth of the snow, I entered the bottom above our former hunting camp a little before night. Passed several deer and one elk, which I might probably have killed, but not knowing whether I should be able to secure the meat, and bearing in mind that they were created for the use and not the sport of man, I did not fire at them. Whilst I was endeavouring to strike fire, I heard voices, and looking around, observed my Corporal Meek and three men passing; called them to me, and we embarked together. They were on their march down to see if they could render us any assistance in ascending the river. They were much grieved to hear my report of Corporal Bradley, Sparks, and Miller.

Saturday, 9th *November*.—Snowed a little: the men carried my pack. I was so sore, that it was with difficulty I carried my gun. Fortunately they brought with them a pair of mockinsons, sent me by one of my soldiers (Owings) who had rightly calculated that I was barefoot; also a phial of whiskey, sent by the sergeant, which were both very acceptable to me. They brought also some tobacco for my lost men. We experienced difficulty in crossing the river owing to the ice. Here I set all hands to work making sledges, in order that the moment the river closed, I might descend with a strong party, in search of our missing companions. Issued provision, and was obliged to use six venison hams, being part of a quantity of choice ones I had preserved, to take down if possible to the General and some other friends. Had the two hunters not been found, I must have become a slave to hunting, in order to support my party; the ice still ran very thick.

Sunday, 10th *November.*—Continued making sledges. No news o my hunters; ice in the river very thick and hard. Raised my tent with punchions, and laid a floor in it.

Monday, 11th *November.*—I went out hunting; saw but two deer killed a remarkably large black fox. Bradley and Miller arrived, having understood the writing on the snow, and left Sparks behind at the camp to take care of the meat.

Their detention was owing to their being lost on the prairie the firs night, and not being able to find their deer.

Tuesday, 12th *November.*—Despatched Miller and Huddleston to th lower hunting camp, and Bradley and Brown to hunt in the woods. Mad my arrangements in camp. Thawing weather.

Wednesday, 13th *November.*—Bradley returned with a very large buck which supplied us for the next four days.

Thursday, 14th *November.*—It commenced raining at four o'clock A. M., and continued with lightning and loud thunder. I went down th river in one of my canoes with five men, in order to bring up the mea from the lower camp; but after descending about thirteen miles, foun the river blocked up with ice—returned about two miles, and encampe in the bottom where I had my hunting camp on the first instant Extremely cold towards night.

Friday, 15th *November.*—When we intended to embark in the morn ing, found the river full of ice and hardly moving; returned to camp an went out to hunt, for we had no provision with us: killed nothing but fiv prairie hens, which afforded us this day's subsistence: this bird I took to b the same as grouse. Expecting the ice had become hard we attempted t cross the river, but without success; in the endeavour one man fe through.

Saturday, 16th *November.*—Detached Corporal Meek and one privat to the garrison, to order the sledge down. No success in hunting excep a few fowls: I began to consider the life of a hunter a very slavish on and extremely precarious as to support; for sometimes I have myse (although no hunter) killed six hundred weight of meat in one day; an at others, I have hunted three days successively, without killing any thin but a few small birds, which I was obliged to do to keep my men fro starving. Freezing.

Sunday, 17th *November.*—One of my men arrived, he had attempted to make the camp before, but lost himself in the prairie, lay out all night and froze his toes: he informed us that the corporal and the men I sent with him, had their toes frost-bitten, the former very badly; that three men were on their way down by land, the river above not being frozen over. They arrived a few hours before night. Freezing.

Monday, 18th *November.*—Took our departure down the river on the ice, our baggage on the sledge. Ice very rough; distance twelve miles. Freezing.

Tuesday, 19th *November.*—Arrived opposite our hunting camp about noon, had the meat, &c., moved over; the men had a large quantity. I went out and killed a very large buck. Thawing.

Wednesday, 20th *November.*—Departed to return to the stockade; part of our meat on the sledge, and part in the little perroque, (the river being open in the middle;) killed four deer. Thawing; distance advanced, five miles.

Thursday, 21st *November.*—Marched in the morning—came to a place where the river was very narrow, and the channel blocked up, where we were obliged to unload our perroque and haul her over: the river having swelled a good deal in this place, the ice gave way with myself and two men; we seized the sledge that stood by us, with some little baggage on it, and by jumping over four cracks, the last two feet wide, providentially made our passage good, without losing an individual thing. Encamped opposite Clear river; killed one deer and one otter: freezing.

Friday, 22d *November.*—Were obliged to leave our canoe at Clear river, the Mississippi being closed: made two trips with our sledge. Killed one deer; distance advanced, five miles.

Saturday, 23d *November.*—Having seen a great deal of buffalo signs, I determined to kill one the next day, (forgetting my former chase.) Encamped nearly opposite our camp of the 15th and 16th. Thawing; distance advanced, four miles.

Sunday, 24th *November.*—Took Miller and Boley, and went in pursuit of buffalo. We came up with some about ten o'clock; in the afternoon wounded one, pursued them until night and encamped on the side of a swamp. Thawing.

Monday, 25th *November.*—Commenced again the pursuit of th buffalo, and continued it till eleven o'clock, when I gave up the chase Arrived at the camp about sundown, hungry and weary, having eate nothing since we left it. My rifle carried too small a ball to kill buffalo the balls should not be more than thirty to a pound, an ounce ball woul be still preferable, and the animal should be hunted on horseback: I thin] that in the prairies of this country the bow and arrow could be used t more advantage than the gun; for you might ride immediately alongside and strike them where you pleased, then leave them and proceed afte others.

Tuesday, 26th *November.*—Proceeded up the river; the ice getting very rotten, the men fell through several times. Thawing; distanc advanced, five miles.

Wednesday, 27th *November.*—Took one man with me and marched t the fort, found all well. My hunter, Bradley, had killed eleven deer sinc my departure: sent all the men down to help the party up; they returne accompanied by two Indians, who informed me they belonged to a ban who resided on Lake Superior, called Fols Avoins; but spoke the languag of the Chippeways. They told me that Mr. Dickson's and the othe trading houses were established about sixty miles below—that there wer seventy lodges of Sioux on the Mississippi. All my men arrived at th post. We brought from our camp below the residue of seventeen dee and two elks.

Thursday, 28th *November.*—The Indians departed much pleased wit their reception. I despatched Corporal Meek and one private down t Mr. Dickson with a letter, which would at least have the effect of attachin the most powerful tribes in this quarter to my interest.

Friday, 29th *November.*—A Sioux, (the son of a warrior called th Killeur Rouge, of the Gens des Feuilles,) and a Fols Avoin, came to th post: the young chief said that having struck our trail below, and findin some to be shoe-tracks, he had conceived it to be the establishment c some traders, followed it and came to the post. He informed me, tha Mr. Dickson had told the Sioux, "That they might now hunt where the pleased, as I had gone before and would cause the Chippeways, whereve I met them, to treat them with friendship; that I had barred up th mouth of the St. Peter's, so that no liquor could ascend that river; but they came on the Mississippi, they should have what they wanted: also that I was on the river, and had a great deal of merchandise to give them in presents." This information of Mr. Dickson to the Indians, seemed to have self-interest and envy for its motives; for by giving the Indians the idea of my having prevented liquor from going up the St. Peter's, he led them to understand, that it was a regulation of my own, and not a law of the United States; and by assuring them he would sell to them on the Mississippi, he drew all the Indians from the traders on the St. Peter's, who had adhered to the restriction of not selling liquor; and should any of them be killed, the blame would all be made to rest on me, as he had (without authority) assured them they might hunt in security. I took care to give the young chief a full explanation of my ideas on the above points. He remained all night. Killed two deer.

Saturday, 30th *November.*—I made the two Indians some small presents; they crossed the river and departed. Detached Kennerman with eleven men to bring up two canoes.

Sunday, 1st *December.*—Snowed a little in the middle of the day; went out with my gun, but killed nothing.

Monday, 2d *December.*—Sparks arrived about ten o'clock at night from the party below, and informed me they could not kill any game; but had started up with the little perroque: also that Mr. Dickson and a Frenchman had passed my detachment about three hours before; he left them on their march to the post.

Tuesday, 3d *December.*—Mr. Dickson with one engagee, and a young Indian, arrived at the fort; I received him with every politeness in my power, and after a serious conversation with him on the subject of the information given me on the 29th ult., was induced to believe it in part incorrect. He assured me that no liquor was sold by him, nor by any houses under his direction: he gave me much useful information relative to my future route, which afforded me great encouragement as to the certainty of accomplishing the object of my voyage, to the fullest extent. He seemed to be a gentleman of general commercial knowledge, and possessed of much geographical information respecting the western country, and of open frank manners. He gave me many assurances of his good wishes for the prosperity of my undertaking.

Wednesday, 4th *December.*—My men arrived with one canoe only.

VOYAGE TO THE SOURCE

Thursday, 5th *December*.—Mr. Dickson with his two men departe[,] for their station, after having furnished me with a letter for a young ma of his house, on Lake De Sable, and a carte blanche as to my command on him. Weather mild.

Friday, 6th *December* —I despatched my men to bring up the othe perroque with a strong sledge, on which it was intended to put the cano about one-third, and to let the end drag on the ice. The families of th Fols Avoins arrived and encamped near the fort; also one Sioux, who pre tended to have been sent to me from the Gens des Feuilles, to inform m that the Yanctongs and Sussitongs (two bands of Sioux from the head c the St. Peter's and Missouri, and the most savage of the tribe) had com menced the war dance, and would depart in a few days; in which case h conceived it would be advisable for the Fols Avoins to keep close unde my protection: that making a stroke on the Chippeways would tend t injure the grand object of my voyage, &c., &c. Some reasons induce me to believe he was a self-created envoy; however I offered to pay him or any young Sioux, who would go to those bands, and carry my word; h promised to make known my wishes on his return. My men came back i the evening without my canoe, having been so unfortunate as to split hei in carrying her over the rough hilly ice in the ripples below. So many dis appointments almost wearied my patience; but, notwithstanding, I intende to embark by land and water in a few days.

Saturday, 7th *December*.—An Indian (by the name of the Chie Blanc) of the Fols Avoin tribe, with his family and connections, arrive and encamped near the stockade. He informed me that he had wintere here for ten years past, that the sugar-camp near the stockade was th place where he made sugar: he appeared to be an intelligent man. visited his camp in the afternoon and found him seated amidst his childre and grand-children, amounting in all to ten;· his wife, although of a advanced age, was suckling two infants, who appeared to be about tw years old. I should have taken them to be twins had not one been muc fairer than the other. Upon enquiry, I found that the fairest was th daughter of an Englishman, by one of the Indians lately deceased, sinc whose death the grandmother had taken it to the breast. His lodge wa made of rushes, plaited into mats, after the manner of the Illinois. I wa obliged to give some meat to all the Indians who arrived at the stockad[,]

at the same time explaining our situation: the Chien Blanc assured me it should be repaid with interest in the course of the winter; but that, at this time, he was without any thing to eat. In fact, our hunters having killed nothing for several days, we were ourselves on short allowance.

Sunday, 8th *December.*—An invalid Sioux arrived with information that the bands of the Sussitongs and Yanctongs had actually determined to make war upon the Chippeways, and had formed a party of a hundred and fifty or a hundred and sixty men; but that part of the Sussitongs had refused to join with them, and would be with me on a visit the next day: this occasioned me to delay crossing the river on my voyage to Lake Sang Sue, or Leech lake, as it was possible that by having a conference with them I might still prevent the stroke intended to be made against the Chippeways.

Monday, 9th *December.*—Prepared to embark. Expecting the Sioux, I had two large kettles of soup made for them. As a pastime, had a shooting match with four prizes. The Sioux did not arrive, and we ate the soup ourselves: crossed the river, and encamped above the rapids; wind changed and the weather grew cold.

Tuesday, 10th *December.*—After arranging our sledges* and perroques, we commenced our march, the sledges on the prairie and the perroque towed by three men. We found it extremely difficult to get along, the snow being melted off the prairie in spots. The men who had the canoe were obliged in many places to wade, and drag her over the rocks. I shot the only deer I saw; it fell three times, and afterwards made its escape. This was a great disappointment, for upon the game we took we now depended for our subsistence. This evening disclosed to my men the real danger they had to encounter. Distance advanced, five miles.

Wednesday, 11th *December.*—It having thawed all night, the snow had almost melted from the prairie. I walked on until ten o'clock, and made a fire. I then returned to look for the perroque, and at a remarkable rapid in the river, opposite to a high piney island, made a fire, and waited for them to come up, when we partly unloaded her; I returned and met the sledges. When we arrived at the place pitched on for our camp, I

---

* My sledges were such as are frequently seen about farmers' yards, calculated to hold two barrels or four hundred weight, in which two men were geared abreast.

sent the men down to assist the perroque. In the afternoon, from abou three o'clock, we heard the report of not less than fifty guns a-head and after dusk, much shouting on the prairie. I was at a loss to knov who the party could be, unless they were Sauteurs, and what could be thei object in shooting after dusk: kept a good look out; distance advanced five miles.

Thursday, 12th *December*.—The snow having almost entirely left th(prairie, we were obliged to take on but one sledge at a time, and trebl(man it. In the morning my interpreter came to me with quite a martia air, and requested that he might be allowed to go a-head to discover wha Indians we had heard firing last evening. I gave him permission, anc away he went: shortly after, I went out with Corporal Bradley and ; private; and in about an hour overtook my partisan, on a bottom, close t(the river—he was hunting rackoons, and had caught five. We left him t(his amusement, and after choosing an encampment, and sending th(private back to conduct the party to it, anxious to discover the Indians the corporal and myself marched on. We ascended the river about eigh miles, and saw no Indians, but found that the river was frozen over, whicl pleased me more, for we should now be enabled to walk three times ou usual distance in a day. I was much surprised at discovering no Indians After our return to the camp, I was told that a Fols Avoin Indian had me my party, and informed them, that in the rear of the hills that borderer the prairie there were small lakes, which by portages communicated wit: Lake Superior; that in one day's march along that course, we should fin(English trading houses; that the Chippeways were there hunting; that th Sioux who had visited my camp on the 29th ult. on hearing the firing ha prudently returned, with his companions, to the western side of the Mis sissippi, agreeably to my advice.

How greatly would persons unacquainted with the searching spirit c trade, and the enterprize of the people of the North-west, be surprised t find men who had penetrated from Lake Superior to lakes which were littl better than marshes! It may serve to point out the difficulty of putting barrier to their trade. All my sledges and perroques did not get up unt half past ten o'clock; saw a very beautiful fox, called by my interprete Reynard d'argent, having a red back, white tail and breast; but I had n opportunity of shooting it: killed six rackoons and one porcupine; fin day; distance advanced, seven miles.

Friday, 13th *December*.—Made double trips; embarked at the upper end of the ripples: it commenced snowing at three o'clock. Bradley killed one deer, another man killed one rackoon; storm continued until next morning; distance advanced five miles.

Saturday, 14th *December*.—We departed from our encampment at the usual hour, but had not advanced one mile, when the foremost sledge, which happened unfortunately to carry my baggage and ammunition, fell into the river. We were all in the water up to our middles, recovering the things. Halted and made a fire: came on to where the river was frozen over; stopped and encamped on the western shore, in a pine wood. Upon examining my things, found all my baggage wet, and some of my books materially injured; but a still greater misfortune was, that all my cartridges, and four pounds of double battle super powder, which I had brought for my own use, were destroyed. Fortunately my kegs of powder were preserved dry, and some bottles of common glazed powder, which were so tightly corked as not to admit water. Had this not been the case, my voyage must necessarily have been terminated, for we could not have subsisted without ammunition. During the time of our misfortune, two Fols Avoin Indians came to us, one of whom had been at my stockade on the 29th ult. in company with the Sioux. I signified to them, by signs, the place of our intended encampment, and invited them to come and encamp with us. They left me, and both arrived at my camp in the evening, having each a deer, which they presented to me. I gave them my canoe to keep until spring, and in the morning, at parting, made them a small present. Sat up until three o'clock drying and assorting my ammunition, baggage, &c.: killed two deer; distance advanced four miles.

Sunday, 15th *December*.—Remained at our camp making sledges; killed two deer: crossed and recrossed several Indian trails in the woods.

Monday, 16th *December*.—Remained at the same camp. Employed as yesterday; killed three deer. I wounded a buffalo in the shoulder, and by a fair race overtook him in the prairie, and gave him another shot, but it being near night left him till the morning.

Tuesday, 17th *December*.—Departed from our agreeable encampment at an early hour; found our sledges to be very heavily loaded; broke one sledge runner, and were detained by other circumstances. Bradley, Rosseau (the interpreter) and myself, killed some deer and wounded five others.

Having eleven on hand already, I found it necessary to leave behin
some of my other loading. At night we dug a hole, in which we deposite
one barrel of pork and one barrel of flour, wrapped them up in seven dee
skins, to preserve them from the damps, we then filled up the hole, an
built our fire immediately over it.

Wednesday, 18th *December*.—Did not get off until eight o'clock, fro
the delay in bringing in our meat. The ice was now tolerably good: bega
this day to see the Chippeways' encampments very frequently, but had no
entirely left the Sioux country on the western shore. Beautiful pin
ridges now appeared.

Thursday, 19th *December*.—Were obliged to take to the prairie, fro
the river being open, but the snow was frozen hard, and the sledges di
not sink deep, so that we made a pretty good day's journey: killed on
deer and two otters: river still open; distance advanced, ten miles.

Friday, 20th *December*.—Travelled part of the day on the prairie an
part on the ice; killed one deer; heard three reports of guns just at su
set from the opposite side of the river: deposited one barrel of flou
distance advanced seven miles.

Saturday, 21st *December*.—Bradley and myself went on a-head, an
overtook my interpreter, who had left camp very early in hopes of bein
able to see the Revière de Corbeau or Raven river, where he had twic
wintered. He was immediately opposite a large island, which he suppose
to bear a great resemblance to one at the mouth of the above river; bi
finally he concluded it was not the same, and returned to camp. But th
proved to be actually the river, as we discovered when we got to the hea
of the island, from which we could see its entrance. This fact exposes th
ignorance and inattention of the French and the traders, and, with th
exception of a few intelligent men, shews what little confidence is to b
placed on their information.

We ascended the Mississippi about five miles above the confluenc
found it not frozen, but in many places not more than one hundred yar
over, mild and still; exhibiting indeed all the appearance of a small riv
in a low country. Returned and found my party, having broken sledge
and had only made good three miles, while I had marched thirty-five.

Sunday, 22d *December*.—Killed three deer. Owing to the mar
difficult places we had to pass, made but four miles and a half.

Monday, 23d *December.*—Never did I undergo more fatigue than this day, performing the duties of hunter, spy, guide, commanding officer, &c., sometimes in front, sometimes in the rear, frequently in advance of my party ten or fifteen miles. At night I was scarcely able to write my notes intelligibly: killed two rackoons. From our sledges breaking down, and having to make so many portages on the land, advanced but four miles.

Tuesday, 24th *December.*—Took the latitude of the Raven island, and found it to be in 45° 49′ 50″ N. The Mississippi becomes very narrow above the Raven river, and changes its direction from nearly N. to N. E. generally; distance advanced, ten miles and a half.

From Pine creek to the Ile de Corbeau (or the river of that name) two small streams come in on the western shore. The first is of little consequence, but the second, called Elk river, is entitled to more consideration from its communication with the River St. Peter's. The first ascent to it is a small lake; this being crossed, they ascend a small stream to a large lake, from which they mark a portage of four miles west, and fall into the Sauteaux river, which they descend into the River St. Peter's. On the eastern side is one small stream which heads towards lower Cedar lake, and is bounded by hills. The whole of this distance is remarkably difficult to navigate, being one continued succession of rapids, shoals and falls; but there is one that deserves to be more particularly noted; viz., the place called by the French La Chute de la Roche Peinturée, or the falls of the Painted Rock, which is certainly the third obstacle, in point of important navigation, which I met with in my whole route.

The shore, where it does not consist of prairie, is a continued succession of pine ridges: the entrance of the River de Corbeau is partly hidden by the island of that name, and discharges its waters into the Mississippi, above and below it; the lowest channel bearing from the Mississippi N. 65° W., the upper due west. This place should, in my opinion, be termed the forks of the Mississippi, the other stream being nearly of equal magnitude, and heading not far from the same source, although taking a much more direct course to their junction. It may be observed on the chart, that from St. Louis to this place, the course of the river had generally been north to the west, and that from here it bore north-east.

This river affords the best communication with the Red river, and the navigation is as follows: You may ascend the River de Corbeau one hundred and eighty miles to the entrance of the River des Feuilles, whic falls from the north-west; this you ascend one hundred and eighty mile also, then make a portage of half a mile into the Otter Tail lake, which i a principal source of the Red river. The other branch of the River d Corbeau bears south-west, and approximates with St. Peter's. The whol of the river is rapid, and by no means affording so much water as th Mississippi: their confluence is in latitude 45° 49' 50" N. In this divisio: the elk, deer and buffalo, were probably in greater abundance than in an; other part of my whole voyage.

Wednesday, 25th *December.*—Marched, and encamped at 11 o'clock gave out two pounds extra of meat, two pounds extra of flour, one gill o whiskey, and some tobacco, to each man, in order to distinguish Christma Day: distance advanced, three miles.

Thursday, 26th *December.*—Damaged four sledges, broke into th river four times, and had four carrying places since we left the Ravei river. The timber observed this day was all yellow and pitch pine, o which there was scarcely any below: distance advanced, three miles.

Friday, 27th *December.*—After having to pass two carrying places we arrived where the river was completely closed with ice. After whicl we proceeded with some degree of speed and comparative ease: killed on bear. The country on both sides presented a dreary and barren prospec of high rocks, with dead pine timber: snow; distance advanced, ten mile:

Saturday, 28th *December.*—Two sledges fell through the ice: in th morning passed a very poor country; bare knobs on either side; bu towards evening the bottoms became larger, and the pine ridges well tin bered. Bradley and myself marched ten miles before the sledges: kille one deer: distance advanced, twelve miles.

Sunday, 29th *December.*—Cold windy day; met with no materia interruptions: passed some rapids; the snow blew from the woods on t the river. We found the country full of small lakes, some three miles i: circumference: distance advanced, twenty-one miles.

Monday, 30th *December.*—The snow having drifted on the ice, retarde the sledges: numerous small lakes and pine ridges continued to occui killed one otter; distance advanced, twelve miles.

Tuesday, 31st *December.*—Passed Pine river about eleven o'clock.

From Elk to Pine river the Mississippi continues to become narrower, and has but few islands. In this distance I discovered but one rapid, which the force of the frost had not entirely covered with ice. The shores in general presented a dreary prospect of high barren knobs, covered with dead and fallen pine timber; to this there were some exceptions of ridges of yellow and pitch pine, also some small bottoms of lyme, elm, oak and ash. The adjacent country, at least two-thirds of its surface, is covered with small lakes, some of which are three miles in circumference; this renders the communication impossible in summer, except with small bark canoes. In this distance we first met with a species of pine, called the sap-pine; it was equally unknown to myself and all my party; it scarcely exceeds the height of thirty-five feet, and is very full of projecting branches. The leaves are similar to those of other pines, but project out from the branches on each side in a direct line, thereby rendering them flat, and this form occasions the natives and voyagers to give them the preference on all occasions to the branches of all other trees for their beds, and for covering their temporary camps; but its greatest recommendations consist in its medicinal virtues. The rind is smooth, with the exception of little protuberances of about the size of a hazle nut; the top of which being cut, you squeeze out a glutinous substance of the consistence of honey. This gum or sap gives its name to the tree, and is used by the natives and traders of the country as a balsam for all wounds made by sharp instruments, or for parts frozen, and for almost all other external injuries. My poor fellows experienced its beneficial qualities, by the application made of it to their frozen extremities in various instances.

The Pine river bears from the Mississippi N. 30° E. although it empties in on that which has hitherto been termed the western shore. It is eighty yards wide at its mouth, and has an island immediately at the entrance; it communicates with Lake Sang Sue or Leech lake, by the following courses of navigation. In one day's sail from the confluence you arrive at the first part of White Fish lake, which is about six miles long and two wide; from thence you pursue the river about two miles, and come to the second White Fish lake, which is about three miles long and one wide; then you have the river for three miles to the third lake,* which is seven miles long and two in width.

---

* This I crossed on my return from the head of the Mississippi in February, it is in 46° 32' 32" N. latitude.

From thence you follow the river a quarter of a mile to the fourth lake, which is a circular one of about five miles in circumference. From thence you pursue the river one day's sail to a small lake, thence two days sail to a portage, which conveys you to another lake, from whence, by small portages from lake to lake, you make the voyage to Leech lake The whole of this course lies through ridges of pines or swamps of penenel sap-pine, hemlock, &c.

From the River de Corbeau to this place the deer are very plentiful but we found no more buffalo or elk.

At the mouth of the Pine river there was a Chippeway encampmen of fifteen lodges which had been occupied in the summer, but was now vacant. By the significations of their marks, we understood that they had marched a party of fifty warriors against the Sioux, and killed four men and four women, which were represented by images carved out of pine o cedar. The four men were painted and put in the ground to the middle having above ground those parts which are generally concealed. By their sides were four painted poles, sharpened at the end, to represent the women. Near this were poles with deer skins, plumes, silk handkerchiefs &c.; also a circular hoop of cedar with something attached representing a scalp. Near each lodge they had holes dug in the ground, and bough ready to cover them, as a retreat for their women and children, if attacked by the Sioux or other enemies.

Wednesday, 1st *January*, 1806.—Passed six elegant bark canoes, on the bank of the river, which had been laid up by the Chippeways; also a camp which we conceived to have been evacuated about ten days. My interpreter came after me in a great hurry, conjuring me not to go so fa a-head, and assured me that if the Chippeways encountered me without an interpreter, party, or flag, they would certainly kill me. But, notwithstanding this admonition, I went on several miles farther than usual, in order to make discoveries, conceiving the savages not to be so barbarou or ferocious, as to fire on two men (I had one with me) who were appar ently coming into their country, trusting to their generosity; and knowing that if we met only two or three we were equal to them, I having my gu and pistols and my companion his musket. Made some extra presents fo new year's day.

Thursday, 2d *January*.— Fine warm day; discovered fresh signs c Indians. Just as we were encamping at night, my sentinel informed us that some Indians were coming full speed upon our trail or track. I ordered my men to stand by their guns carelessly. They were immediately at my camp, and saluted the flag by a discharge of three pieces, when four Chippeways, one Englishman, and a Frenchman, of the northwest, presented themselves. They informed us, that some women having discovered our trail gave the alarm; and not knowing but that it might be that of their enemies, they had departed to make a discovery; they had heard of us and respected our flag. Mr. Grant, the Englishman, had only arrived the day before from Lake de Sable; from which he had marched in one day and a half. I presented the Indians with half a deer, which they received thankfully, for they had discovered our fires some days before, and believing us to be Sioux, had not dared to leave their camp. They returned, but Mr. Grant remained all night.

Friday, 3d *January*.— My party marched early, but I returned with Mr. Grant to his establishment on the Red Cedar lake, attended by one corporal. When we came in sight of Mr. Grant's house, I observed the flag of Great Britain flying, and felt indignant, and cannot say what my feelings would have excited me to, had he not informed me that it belonged to the Indians. This was not much more agreeable to me. After explaining to a Chippeway warrior, called Curly Head, the object of my voyage, and receiving his answer, that he would remain tranquil until my return, we ate a good breakfast for the country: departed and overtook my sledges just at dusk: killed one porcupine: distance advanced, sixteen miles.

From Pine river to Red Cedar lake, the pine ridges are interrupted by large bottoms of elm, ash, oak, and maple; the soil would be very proper for cultivation. From the appearance of the ice, which was firm and equal, I conceive there can be but one ripple in this distance. Red Cedar lake lies on the eastern side of the Mississippi, at the distance of six miles from it, and is nearly equally distant from the River de Corbeau, and Lake de Sable. Its form is an oblong, and may be ten miles in circumference.

Saturday, 4th *January*.—We made twenty-eight points on the river. The shores here consisted of broad good bottom, with the usual timber. In the night I was awakened by the cry of the sentinel, calling repeatedly to the men; at length he vociferated, with an oath, " Will you let the lieutenant be burned to death?" This immediately aroused me; at first I seized my arms, but looking around, I saw my tents in flames. The men flew to my assistance, and we tore them down, but not until they were entirely ruined. This, with the loss of my leggings, mockinsons, socks &c., which I had hung up to dry, was no trivial misfortune in such a country and on such a voyage. But I had reason to thank God, that the powder three small casks of which I had in my tent, did not take fire; if it had I must certainly have lost all my baggage, if not my life.

Sunday, 5th *January.*—Mr. Grant promised to overtake me yester day, but has not yet arrived. Distance advanced, twenty-seven miles.

Monday, 6th *January.*— Bradley and myself walked up thirty-one points, in hopes of discovering Sandy lake; but finding a near cut o twenty yards for ten miles, and being fearful the sledges would miss it we returned twenty-three points before we found our camp. They had made only eight points: met two Frenchmen of the North-West company with about one hundred and eighty pounds on each of their backs, with rackets on; they informed me Mr. Grant had gone on with the French man. Snow fell all day, and was three feet deep; spent a miserable night

Tuesday, 7th *January.*—Made but eleven miles, and then were obliged to send a-head and make fires every three miles. Notwithstanding which the cold was so intense that some of the men had their noses, others their fingers, and others their toes frozen, before they felt the cold sensibly: had a very severe day's march.

Wednesday, 8th *January.*—Conceiving I was at no great distance from Sandy lake, I left my sledges, and with Corporal Bradley took my departure for that place, intending to send him back the same evening We walked on very briskly until near night, when we met a young Indian one of those who had visited my camp near Red Cedar lake; I endeavoured to explain to him, that it was my wish to go to Sandy lake that evening. He returned with me until we came to a trail that led across the woods; this he signified was a near course. This I pursued with him and shortly after found myself at a Chippeway encampment, to which believe the friendly savage had enticed me with an expectation that would tarry all night, knowing that it was too late to make the lake in an tolerable time. But upon my refusing to stay, he put us in the right road. We arrived at the place where the track left the Mississippi, a dusk, when we traversed about two leagues of a wilderness without an very great difficulty; and at length struck the shore of Sandy lake, over a branch of which our course lay. The snow having covered the trail made by the Frenchmen, who had passed before with the rackets, I was fearful of losing ourselves on the lake; the consequence of which can only be conceived by those who have been exposed on a lake or naked plain, during a dreary night of January, in latitude 47°, and the thermometer below 0. Thinking that we could observe the bank of the other shore, we kept a straight course, and some time after discovered lights, and on our arrival were not a little surprised to find a large stockade. The gate being open, we entered, and proceeded to the quarters of Mr. Grant, where we were treated with the utmost hospitality.

Thursday, 9th *January.*—Marched the corporal early in order that our men might receive assurances of our safety and success. He carried with him a small keg of spirits, a present from Mr. Grant. The establishment at this place was formed twelve years since, by the North-West Company, and was formerly under the charge of a Mr. Charles Brusky. It has obtained at present such regularity, as to permit the superintendent to live tolerably comfortable. They have horses, which they procured from Red river, of the Indians; raise plenty of Irish potatoes, catch pike, suckers, pickerel, and white fish in abundance. They have also beaver, deer and moose, but the provision they chiefly depend upon is wild oats, of which they purchase great quantities from the savages, giving at the rate of about one dollar and a half per bushel; but flour, pork, and salt, are almost interdicted to persons not principals in the trade. Flour sells at half a dollar, salt a dollar; pork eighty cents, sugar half a dollar; coffee and tea four and a half dollars per pound. The sugar is obtained from the Indians, and is made from the maple tree.

From Red Cedar lake to Lake de Sable, on the eastern shore you meet with Muddy river, which discharges itself into the Mississippi by a mouth of twenty yards wide, and bears nearly NE. We then met with Pike river on the west, about seven miles below Sandy lake, and bears nearly north, up which you ascend with canoes four days' sail, and arrive at a wild rice lake which you pass through, and enter a small stream and ascend it two leagues, then cross a portage of two acres into a lake of seven leagues in circumference, then two leagues of a river into another small lake. From thence you descend the current north-east into Leech lake. The banks of the Mississippi are still bordered by pines of the different species, except a few small bottoms of elm, lyme, and maple The game scarce, and the Aborigines subsist almost entirely on the beaver, with a few moose, and the wild rice or oats.

Sandy lake (or the discharge of the said lake) is large, but is only si: miles in length from the lake to its confluence with the Mississippi The lake is about twenty-five miles in circumference, and has a num ber of small rivers running into it, one of those entitled to particula attention, viz., the River Savannah, which, by a portage of three mile and three-quarters, communicates with the River St. Louis, which emp ties into Lake Superior at the Fond du Lac, and is the channel by which the North-West Company bring all their goods for the trade o the upper Mississippi. Game is very scarce in this country.

Friday, 10th *January*. — Mr. Grant accompanied me to the Mis sissippi, to mark the place for my boats to leave the river. This was th first time I marched on rackets. I took the course of the Lake river from its mouth to the lake. Mr. Grant fell through the ice with his rackets or and could not have got out without assistance.

Saturday, 11th *January*.—Remained all day within quarters.

Sunday, 12th *January*.—Went out and met my men about sixtee miles distant. A tree had fallen on one of them and hurt him very much which induced me to dismiss a sledge, and put the loading on th others.

Monday, 13th *January*. — After encountering much difficulty, w arrived at the establishment of the North-West Company on Sandy lake a little before night. The ice being very bad on the Lake river, owin to the many springs and marshes in the neighbourhood, one sledge fe through. My men had an excellent room furnished them, and wer presented with potatoes and *fille*.* Mr. Grant had gone to an India lodge to receive his credits.

Tuesday, 14th *January*.—Crossed the lake to the north side, that might take an observation; found the latitude 46° 9′ 20″ N. Surveye that part of the lake. Mr. Grant returned from the Indian lodges. The brought a quantity of furs, and eleven beaver carcasses.

---

* A cant term for a dram of spirits.

OF THE MISSISSIPPI.

Wednesday, 15th January.—Mr. Grant and myself made the tour of the lake, with two men whom I had for attendants. I found it to be much larger than could be imagined at a view. My men sawed stocks for the sledges, which I found it necessary to construct after the manner of the country. On our march met an Indian coming into the fort; his countenance expressed no little astonishment when told who I was, and from whence I had come, for the people in the country acknowledge that the savages hold in greater veneration the Americans than any other white people. They say of us, when alluding to warlike achievements, that "we are neither Frenchmen nor Englishmen, but white Indians."

Thursday, 16th January.— Laid down Sandy lake, &c. A young Indian, whom I had engaged to attend me as a guide to Lake Sang Sue, or Leech lake, arrived from the woods.

Friday, 17th January.— Employed in making sledges,* after the manner of the country. Two other Indians arrived from the woods. Engaged in writing.

Saturday, 18th January.— Busy in preparing my baggage, &c., for my departure for Leech lake.

Sunday, 19th January.—Employed as yesterday. Two men of the North-West Company arrived from Lake Superior, with letters; one of which was for their establishment at Athapusco, and had been since last May on their route. While at this place I ate roasted beavers, dressed in every respect as a pig is usually dressed with us; it was excellent; I could not discern the least taste of wood. I also ate boiled Moose's head; when well boiled, I consider it equal to the tail of the beaver; in taste and substance they are much alike.

Monday, 20th January.—The men with their sledges took their departure about two o'clock; shortly after I followed them. We encamped at the portage between the Mississippi and Leech lake river. Snow fell in the night.

Tuesday, 21st January.—Snowed in the morning, but we crossed about nine o'clock. I had gone on a few points, when I was overtaken by Mr. Grant, who informed me that the sledges could not get along in consequence of the water being on the ice; he sent his men forward. We

---

* These sledges are made of a single plank, turned up at one end like a fiddle head, and the baggage is lashed on in bags or sacks.

returned and met the sledges, which had advanced one mile. We unloaded them, sent eight men back to the fort with whatever might be denominated extra articles, but in my hurry sent my salt and ink. Mr. Grant encamped with me, and marched early in the morning.

Wednesday, 22d *January.*—Made a pretty good day's journey. My Indian came up about noon. Distance advanced, twenty miles.

Thursday, 23d *January.*—Marched about eleven miles. Forgot my thermometer, having hung it on a tree; sent Boley back five miles for it. My young Indian and myself killed eight partridges; took him to live with me.

Friday, 24th *January.*—At our encampment this night (Mr. Grant had encamped on the night of the same day he left me) it was three days' march for us. In the evening the father of his girl came to my camp, and staid all night; he appeared very friendly, and was very communicative, but having no interpreter, we made but poor speed in conversation. It was late before the men came up.

Saturday, 25th *January.*—Travelled almost all day through the lands and found them much better than usual. Boley lost the Sioux pipe stem, which I carried along for the purpose of making peace with the Chippeways; I sent him back for it; he did not return until eleven o'clock at night; the weather was very warm; thawing all day. Distance advanced, forty-four points.

Sunday, 26th *January.*—I left my party in order to proceed to a house, or lodge, of Mr. Grant's, on the Mississippi, where he was to tarry until I overtook him. Took with me my Indian, Boley, and some trifling provision. The Indian and myself marched so fast that we left Boley on the route, about eight miles from the lodge. Met Mr. Grant's men on their return to Sandy lake, having evacuated the house this morning, and Mr. Grant having marched to Leech lake. The Indian and myself arrived before sunset. Passed the night very uncomfortably, having nothing to eat, nor much wood, nor any blankets. The Indian slept soundly. I cursed his insensibility, being obliged to content myself over a few coals all night. Boley did not arrive.

Monday, 27th *January.*—My Indian rose early, mended his mockinsons, then expressed by signs something about his son and the Frenchman we had met yesterday; conceiving that he wished to send a message to his family, I suffered him to depart. After he had left me I felt the curse of solitude, although in fact he was no company. Boley arrived about ten o'clock; he said that he had followed us till some time in the night, when believing that he could not overtake us, he had stopped and made a fire, but having no axe to cut wood, he was near freezing. He met the Indian, who made him signs to proceed. I spent the day in putting my gun in order, mending my mockinsons, &c. Provided plenty of wood, but still found it cold with but one blanket. I can only account for the gentlemen of the North-West Company contenting themselves in the wilderness for ten or fifteen years, and some of them for twenty years, by the attachment they contract for the Indian women. It appears to me that the wealth of nations would not induce me to remain secluded from the society of civilized mankind, surrounded by a savage and unproductive wilderness, without books or other sources of intellectual enjoyment, or being blessed with the cultivated and feeling mind of a civilized female companion.

Tuesday, 28th January.—Left our encampment at a good hour; unable to find any trail, I passed through one of the most dismal cypress swamps I ever saw, and struck the Mississippi at a small lake. I observed Mr. Grant's tracks going through it; found his mark of a cut off, agreed on between us: took it and proceeded very well, until we came to a small lake where the trail was entirely hidden, but after some search on the other side, found it again. We then passed through a dismal swamp, on the other side of which I found a large lake, at which I was entirely at a loss as no trail could be seen. I struck for a point about three miles distant, where we found a Chippeway lodge, of one man, his wife, and five children, and one old woman. They received us with every mark that distinguished their barbarity; such as setting their dogs on ours, trying to thrust their hands into our pockets, &c., but we convinced them that we were not afraid, and let them know we were Chewekomen (Americans), when they used us more civilly. After we had arranged a camp as well as we could, I went into the lodge; they presented me with a plate of dried meat. I ordered Miller to bring about two gills of liquor, which made us all good friends. The old Squaw gave me more meat, and offered me tobacco, which, not using, I did not take. I gave her an order upon my corporal, for one knife, and half a carrot of tobacco. Heaven clothes the lilies and feeds the ravens, and the same Almighty Providence protects and preserves these creatures. After I had gone out to my fire, the old man came and proposed to trade beaver skins for whiskey; meeting with a refusal he left me, when presently the old woman came out with a beaver skin; she also being refused, he again returned to the charge, with a quantity of dried meat, (this or any other I should have been glad to have had,) when I gave him a peremptory refusal; then all further application ceased. It really appeared, that with one quart of whiskey I might have bought all they were possessed of. This night proved remarkably cold; I was obliged to sit up nearly the whole of it. Suffered much with cold and want of sleep.

Friday, 31st *January.*—Took my clothes into the Indians' lodge to dress, and was received very cooly; but by giving the man a dram, unasked, and his wife a little salt, I received from them directions for my route. Passed the lake or morass, and opened on meadows, through which the Mississippi winds its course for nearly fifteen miles. Took a straight course through them to the head, when I found we had missed the river; made a turn of about two miles and regained it. Passed a fork, which I supposed to be Lake Winipic, making the course N. W.; the branch we took was on Leech lake branch, course S. W. and W. Passed a very large meadow or prairie; course west; the Mississippi was here only fifteen yards wide. Encamped about one mile below the traverse of the meadow. Saw a very large animal, which, from its leaps, I supposed to have been a panther; but if it was one, it was twice as large as those on the lower Mississippi. He evinced some disposition to approach: I lay down (Miller being in the rear) in order to entice him to come near, but he would not. The night remarkably cold. Some spirits which I had in a small keg congealed to the consistence of honey.

Saturday, 1st *February.*—Left our camp pretty early; passed a continued train of prairie, and arrived at Leech lake at half past two o'clock.

I will not attempt to describe my feelings on the accomplishment of my voyage; for this is the main source of the Mississippi. The Lake Winipic branch is navigable from thence to Red Cedar lake, for the distance of five leagues, which is the extremity of the navigation.

I crossed the lake twelve miles to the establishment of the North-West Company, where we arrived about three o'clock. We found all the gates locked, but upon knocking were admitted, and received with marked attention and hospitality by Mr. Hugh M'Gillis, who provided for us a good dish of coffee, biscuit, butter and cheese, for supper.

In ascending the Mississippi from Sandy lake you first meet with Swan river on the east, which bears nearly due east, and is navigable for bark canoes ninety miles to Swan lake; you then meet with the Meadow river which falls in on the east, and bears nearly east by north, and is navigable for Indian canoes one hundred miles: you next, in ascending, meet with a very strong ripple, and an expansion of the river where it forms a small lake. This is three miles below the falls of Packagama, and from which the noise of the shoot may be heard. The course of the river at the falls was N. 70° W. and just below the river is a quarter of a mile in width, but above the shoot not more than twenty yards. The water thus collected runs down a flat rock which has an elevation of about thirty degrees. Immediately above the fall is a small island of about fifty yards in circumference, covered with sap-pine. The portage, which is on the east (or north) side, is no more than two hundred yards, and by no means difficult. These falls, in point of consideration as an impediment to the navigation, stand next to the Falls of St. Anthony, from the source of the river to the Gulph of Mexico. The banks of the Mississippi to the Meadow river have generally been timbered by the pine, pinênet, hemlock, sap-pine, or the aspen tree. From thence it winds through high grass meadows (or savannas) with the pine swamps at a distance, appearing to cast a deeper gloom on the borders. From the falls, in ascending, you pass the Lake Packagama on the west, celebrated for its great production of wild rice, and next meet with the Deer river on the east. The extent of its navigation is unknown. You next meet with the River la Crosse on the eastern side which bears nearly north and has only a portage of one mile to pass from it into the Lake Winipic branch of the Mississippi. We next came to what the people of that quarter call the forks of the Mississippi: the right branch of which bears northwest, and runs eight leagues to Lake Winipic, which is of an oval form about thirty-six miles in circumference. From Lake Winipic the river continues five leagues to upper Red Cedar lake, which may be termed the upper source of the Mississippi. The Leech lake branch, bears from the forks south-west, and runs through a chain of meadows. You pass Muddy lake which is scarcely any thing more than an extensive marsh of fifteen miles circumference; the river bears through it nearly north, after which it again turns to the west. In many places this branch is not more than ten or fifteen yards in width, although fifteen or twenty feet deep; from this to Leech lake the communication is direct, and without any impediment. This is rather considered as the main source, although the Winipic branch is navigable the greatest distance. To this place the whole face of the country has the appearance of an impenetrable morass, or boundless savannah: but on the borders of the lake are some oak, and large groves of sugar-maple, from which the traders make sufficient sugar for their consumption the whole year. Leech lake communicates with the River de Corbeau by seven portages, and the River des Feuilles also with the Red river by the Otter-tail lake on the one side, and by Red Cedar lake, and other small lakes to Red lake on the other. Out of these small lakes and ridges rise the upper waters of the St. Lawrence, the Mississippi and *Red river, the latter of which discharges itself into the ocean by Lake Winipic and Hudson's bay. All these waters have their upper sources within one hundred miles of each other, which, I think, plainly proves this to be the most elevated part of the north-east continent of America. But we must cross what are commonly termed the Rocky mountains, or a spur of cordeliers, previous to our finding the waters whose currents run westward, and pay tribute to the western ocean.

In this quarter we find moose, a very few deer and bears, but a vast variety of fur animals of all descriptions.

Sunday, 2d *February*.—I remained all day within doors. In the evening sent an invitation to Mr. Anderson, who was an agent of Mr. Dickson; and also for some young Indians, at his house, to come over and breakfast in the morning.

Monday, 3d *February*.—Spent the day in reading, proposing some queries to Mr. Anderson; and preparing my young man to return with a supply of provisions to my party.

Tuesday, 4th *February*.—Miller departed this morning. Mr Anderson returned to his quarters. My legs and ancles were so swelled that I was not able to wear my own clothes, and was obliged to borrow some from Mr. M'Gillis.

---

* Red river discharges itself into Hudson's bay, by Lake Winipic and Nelson's river.

Wednesday, 5th *February.*—One of Mr. M'Gillis's clerks had been sent to some Indian lodges, and was expected to return in four days, but had now been absent nine. Mr. Grant was despatched in order to find out what had become of him.

Thursday, 6th *February.*—My men arrived at the fort about four o'clock. Mr. M'Gillis asked, if I had any objections to his hoisting their flag, in compliment to ours. I made none, as I had not yet explained to him my ideas. In making a traverse of the lake, some of my men had their ears, some their noses, and others their chins frozen.

Friday, 7th *February*—I remained within doors, my limbs being still very much swelled; addressed a letter to Mr. M'Gillis on the subject of the N. W. company's trade in this quarter.*

Saturday, 8th *February.*—Took the latitude, and found it to be 47° 16' 13".

Sunday, 9th *February.*—Mr. M'Gillis and myself paid a visit to Mr. Anderson, who resided at the west end of the lake; found him eligibly situated as to trade, but his houses bad. I rode in a cariole for one person, constructed in the following manner: boards planed smooth, turned up in front about two feet, coming to a point; and about two and a half feet wide behind, on which is fixed a box, covered with dressed skins painted; this box is open at the top, but covered in front about two-thirds of the length; the horse is fastened between the shafts, the rider wraps himself up in a buffalo robe, sits flat down, having a cushion to lean his back against: thus accoutred with a fur cap, &c., he may bid defiance to the wind and weather.

Upon our return, we found that some of the Indians had already returned from the hunting camps; also Monsieur Roussand, the gentleman supposed to have been killed by the Indians; his arrival with Mr. Grant diffused a general satisfaction through the fort.

Monday, 10th *February.*—Hoisted the American flag in the fort: the English Jack still flying at the top of the flag-staff, I directed the Indians and my rifle-men to shoot at it: they soon broke the iron pin to which it was fastened, and brought it to the ground.

Tuesday, 11th *February.*—The Sweet, Buck, Burnt, &c., arrived; all chiefs of note, but the former in particular, a venerable old man; from

---

* See the letter, with Mr. M'Gillis's answer, at the end of this Journal.

him I learnt that the Sioux occupied this ground, when (to use his own phrase,) he was made man, and began to hunt; that they occupied it the year that the French missionaries were killed at the river Packagama. The Indians now flocked in to us.

Wednesday, 12th *February.*—Bradley and myself, with Mr. M'Gillis and two of his men, left Leech lake at ten o'clock, and arrived at the house at Red Cedar lake at sunset, a distance of thirty miles. My ancles were much swelled, and I was very lame.

From the entrance of the Mississippi to the strait is called six miles, along a south-west course; from thence to the south end, south thirty east, four miles; about two and a half from the north side to a large point. This may be called the upper source of the Mississippi, being fifteen miles above little Lake Winipic, and the extent of canoe navigation only two leagues to some of the Hudson's bay waters.

Thursday, 13th *February.*—We were favoured with a beautiful day; took the latitude and found it to be 47° 42' 40" N. It was at this place Mr. Thompson made his observations in 1798, from which he determined that the source of the Mississippi was 47° 38'. I walked about three miles back into the country; one of our men marched to Lake Winipic, and returned by one o'clock for the stem of the Sweet's pipe, a matter of more consequence in his affairs with the Sioux than the diploma of many an ambassador. We feasted on white fish roasted on two iron grates, fixed horizontally in the back of the chimney—the entrails left in the fish.

Friday, 14th *February.*—Left the house at nine o'clock. It becomes me here to do justice to the hospitality of our hosts, one Roy, a Canadian, and his wife a Chippeway squaw; they relinquished for our use the only thing in the house that could be called a bed; and attended us like servants; nor could either of them be persuaded to touch a mouthful until we had finished our repasts.

We made the garrison about sundown, having been drawn at least ten miles in a sledge, by two small dogs, which were loaded with two hundred pounds weight, and went so fast, as to render it difficult for the men with snow-shoes to keep up with them. The chiefs asked permission to dance the calumet dance, which I granted.

Saturday, 15th *February.*—The Flat-mouth, chief of the Leech lake village, and many other Indians arrived. Received a letter from Mr.

M'Gillis, in answer to mine of the 7th. Noted down the heads of my speech, and had it translated into French, in order that the interpreter, might be perfectly master of his subject

Sunday, 16th *February*.—Held a council with the chiefs and warriors at this place, and of Red lake; but it required much patience, coolness, and management to obtain the object I desired, viz. That they should make peace with the Sioux, deliver up their medals and flags; and that some of the chiefs should attend me to St. Louis. As a proof of their agreeing to the peace, I directed that they should smoke out of the wabasha's pipe, which lay on the table; they all complied, from the head chief to the young soldier. They generally delivered up their flags with a good grace, except the Flat-mouth, who said he had left his at his camp, three days' march distant, and promised to deliver them up to Mr. M'Gillis, to be forwarded: with respect to their accompanying me on my return, the old Sweet thought it most proper to return to the Indians of Red lake, Red river, and Rainy lake river; the Flat-mouth said it was necessary for him to restrain his young warriors. The other chiefs did not think themselves of consequence sufficient to offer any reason for not going with me to St. Louis, a journey of between two and three thousand miles, through hostile tribes of Indians. I then told them, "That I was sorry to find that the hearts of the Sauteurs of this quarter were so weak that the other nations would say,—What! are there no soldiers at Leech, Red and Rainy lakes, who had the heart to carry the calumet of their chief to their father?" This had the desired effect. The Buck and Beau, two of the most celebrated young warriors, rose and offered themselves to me for the embassy; they were accepted, and adopted as my children, and I was installed their father. Their example animated the others, and it would have been no difficult matter to have taken a company; two however were sufficient. I determined that it should be my care never to make them regret the noble confidence placed in me, for I would have protected their lives with my own. The Beau is brother to the Flat-mouth. I gave my new soldiers a dance and a dram; they attempted to get more liquor, but a firm and peremptory denial convinced them I was not to be trifled with.

Monday, 17th *February*.—The chief of the land brought in his flag, and delivered it up. I now made arrangements to march my party the next day. Instructed the Sweet how to send the parole to the Indians of Red river, &c. Put my men through the manual, and fired three blank rounds, all of which not a little astonished the Indians. I was obliged to give my two new soldiers each a blanket, a pair of leggings, scissors, and a looking-glass.

Tuesday, 18th *February.*—We began our march for Red Cedar lake about eleven o'clock, with a guide provided by Mr M'Gillis; we were all equipped with snow-shoes, and marched off amidst the acclamations and shouts of the Indians, who had remained to see us take our departure. Mr. Anderson promised to follow with letters; he arrived about twelve o'clock and remained all night. He concluded to go down with me, to see Mr. Dickson.

Wednesday, 19th *February.*—Bradley, Mr. Le Rone, the two young Indians and myself, left Mr. M'Gillis at ten o'clock, crossed Leech lake in a south-east direction, twenty-four miles. Mr. M'Gillis's hospitality deserves to be particularly noticed: he presented me with his dogs and cariole, valued in this country at two hundred dollars. One of the dogs broke out of his harness, and we were not able to catch him again; the other poor fellow was obliged to draw the whole load, at least a hundred and fifty pounds: this day's march was from lake to lake.

Thursday, 20th *February.*—I allowed my men to march at least three hours before me, notwithstanding which, as it was cold and the road good, my sledge dog brought me a-head of all by one o'clock. Halted for an encampment at half past two o'clock: our courses this day were first southeast six miles, then south eighteen miles; almost all the day over lakes, some of which were six miles across. Encamped at the bank of Sandy lake; the Indians were out hunting.

Friday, 21st *February.*—Traveled this day generally south, passed but two lakes; Sandy lake, which is of an oblong form, north and south four miles, and one other small one. The Indians, at the instigation of Mr. Le Rone, applied for him to accompany us; I consented that he should go as far as Red Cedar lake. I then wrote a note to Mr. M'Gillis upon the occasion: after Reale had departed with it, Le Rone disclosed to me that it was his wish to desert the North-Western Company entirely, and to accompany me. To have countenanced for a moment any thing of this kind, would I conceived have been inconsistent with every principle of honour; I therefore obliged him to return immediately. We then had no guide, our Indians not knowing the road : our course lay through woods and bad brush fifteen miles.

Saturday, 22d *February*.—Our course a little to the south of east, through woods not very thick : arrived at White-fish lake at eleven o'clock, and took an observation; my party crossed the lake, and encamped between the two lakes : this may be called the source of the Pine river. At this place has been one of the North-West Company's establishments, at the north-east side. It was a square stockade of about fifty feet, but at this time nearly all consumed by fire. There was one standing over the point on the eastern side.

Sunday, 23d *February*.— My two Indians, Boley, and myself, with my sledge and dog, left the party, under an idea that we should make Red Cedar lake. We marched hard all day, without arriving at the Mississippi. Our course was nearly due east until near night, when we changed more south. Took no provision nor bedding: my Indians killed fifteen partridges, some nearly black, with a red mark over their eyes, called the Savannah partridge. We were overtaken about noon by two of Mr. Anderson's men, Mr. Anderson himself not being able to come. Distance advanced, thirty miles.

Monday, 24th *February*.—We started early, and after passing over one of the worst roads in the world, found ourselves on a lake about three o'clock, took its outlet and struck the Mississippi about one mile below the canoes mentioned on the first of January, by which I knew where we were. Ascended the Mississippi about four miles, and encamped on the western side: our general course this day was nearly south, when it ought to have been south-east. My young warriors were still in good heart, singing and shewing every wish to keep me cheerful. The pressure of my racket-strings brought the blood through my socks and mockinsons, from which the pain I marched in may be imagined.

Tuesday, 25th *February*.—We marched and arrived at the Red Cedar lake before noon: found Mr. Grant and De Breche, (chief of Sandy lake) at the house. This gave me much pleasure, for I conceive Mr. Grant to be a gentleman of as much candour as any with whom I had made an acquaintance in this quarter; and the chief (De Breche,) is reputed to be a man of better information than any of the Sauteurs.

Wednesday, 26th *February.*— Sent one of Mr. Grant's men down, with a bag of rice to meet my people; he found them encamped on the Mississippi. Wrote a letter to Mr. Dickson on the subject of the Fols Avoins, also some orders to my sergeant. This evening had a long conversation with De Breche; he informed me that a string of wampum had been sent among the Chippeways, he thought by the British commanding officer at St. Joseph. He appeared to be a very intelligent man.

Thursday, 27th *February.*—The chief called the White-fisher and seven Indians, arrived at the house; my men also arrived at twelve o'clock.

Friday, 28th *February.*— We left Red Cedar lake about eleven o'clock, and went to where the canoes before-mentioned were seen. My young Indians remained behind under the pretence of waiting for the chief De Breche, who returned to Sandy lake for his flag and medals, and was to render himself at my fort with Mr. Grant, about the fifteenth of the following month.

Saturday, 1st *March.*— Departed early; passed our encampment of the 31st of December; at nine o'clock A. M., passed Pine river at twelve o'clock, our encampment of the 30th December, at three o'clock and our encampment of the 29th November, just before we came to our present, which we made on the point of the Pine ridge, below. Distance advanced, forty-three miles.

Sunday, 2d *March.*— Passed our encampment of the 28th of December, at ten o'clock, A. M.; that of the 27th of December, at one o'clock, P. M. and encamped at that of the 25th December. Found wood nearly sufficient for our use. This morning despatched Bradley to the last place at which we had buried a barrel of flour, to thaw the ground and hunt. This day a party of Indians struck the river behind Bradley, and before us, but left it ten miles above the Raven river.

Monday, 3d *March.*— Marched early; passed our Christmas encampment at sunrise. I was a-head of my party in my cariole. Soon afterwards I observed a smoke on the western shore; I hallooed, and some Indians appeared upon the bank. I waited until my interpreter came up, when we went to the camp: they proved to be a party of Chippeways, who had left the encampment the same day we had: they presented me with some roast meat, which I gave my sledge-dogs; they then left their camp, and accompanied us down the river. We passed our encampment of the 24th December, at nine o'clock, that of the 23d at ten o'clock, and of the 22d at eleven o'clock; here the Indians crossed on the western shore. We arrived at the encampment of the 21st December, where we had a barrel of flour, at twelve o'clock: I here found Corporal Meek, and another man from the fort, from whom I heard that the men were all well. They confirmed the account of a Sioux having fired at a sentinel and run off, but had promised to deliver himself up in the spring. The corporal informed me, that the sergeant had used all the fine hams and saddles of venison, which I had preserved to present to the commander in chief and other friends; that he had made away with all the whiskey, including a keg I had designed for my own use, having publicly sold it to the men, together with a barrel of pork; that he had broken open my trunk, and sold some articles out of it; traded with the Indians, given them liquor, &c., and this too, contrary to my most pointed and particular directions. Thus, after I had used, in going up the river with my party, the strictest economy, living upon two pounds of frozen venison a day, in order that we might have provision to carry us down in the spring; this fellow had been squandering away the flour, pork, and liquor, during the winter, while we were starving with hunger and cold. I had saved all our corn, bacon, and the meat of six deer, and left them at Sandy lake, with some tents, my mess-boxes, salt, tobacco, &c., all of which we were obliged to sacrifice, by not returning the same route we had ascended; and we had consoled ourselves under this loss, by the flattering idea, that we should find at our little fort, a handsome stock preserved: how mortifying the disappointment! We raised our barrel of flour, and came down to the mouth of a little river on the east, which we had passed on the 21st December. The ice was covered with water.

Tuesday, 4th *March.*—Proceeded early; passed our encampment of the 20th December, at sunrise, arrived at that of the 19th at nine o'clock; here we had buried two barrels: made a large fire to thaw the ground. Went on the prairie and found Sparks, one of my hunters, and brought him to the river at the Pine camp; passed on opposite to our encampment of the 13th December, and encamped where Sparks and some men had an old hunting camp, and where the Fresaie (a Chippeway chief) had surrounded them.

VOYAGE TO THE SOURCE

Wednesday, 5th *March.*—Passed all the encampments between Pine creek and the fort, at which we arrived about ten o'clock: I sent a man on a-head, to prevent the salute I had before ordered by letter; this I had done under the idea that the Sioux chiefs would accompany me. I found all well; confined my sergeant: about one o'clock Mr. Dickson arrived, with the Killeur Rouge, his son, and two other Sioux men, with two women, who had come up to be introduced to the Sauteurs, whom they expected to be with me.

Thursday, 6th *March.*—Thomas, the Fols Avoins' first chief, arrived with ten others of his nation; I made a serious and authoritative representation to him of my opinion of the conduct of the Shawonoes, another chief of his nation, who had behaved ill. I had also a conference with the Killeur Rouge and his people. At night, wrote to Messrs. Grant, M'Gillis and Anderson.

Friday, 7th *March.*—Held conversations with the Indians. Thomas the Fols Avoin chief assured me, that he would interest himself in obliging the Puants to deliver up the men who had recently committed murders on the Ouisconsin and Rock rivers; and if necessary would make it a national quarrel on the side of the Americans. This Thomas is a fine fellow, of a very masculine figure, noble and animated delivery, and appears to be very much attached to the Americans. The Sioux informed me that they would wait until I had determined my affairs in this country, and then bear my words to the River St. Peter's.

Saturday, 8th *March.*—The Fols Avoin chief presented me with his pipe, to give to the Sauteurs on their arrival, with assurances of their safety on their voyage, and his wish for them to descend the river. The son of the Killeur Rouge presented me with his pipe, to give to the Sauteur Indians, on their arrival; to make them smoke, and assure them of their friendly disposition, and that he would wait to see them at Mr. Dickson's. Thomas made a formal complaint against a Frenchman, by name Greignor, who resides at Green Bay; who he said abused the Indians, and beat them without provocation: I promised to write to the commanding officer or Indian agent at Michillimackinac, upon the subject. The Indians, with Mr. Dickson, all took their departure. Hitched my dogs in the sledge, who drew one of the Indian women down the ice to the no little amusement of the others. Went down the river in order to cut a mast; felled a pine mast thirty-five feet long, for my large boat at the prairie.

This day my little boy broke the cock of my gun : a few trifling misfortunes could have happened which I should have regretted more, as the wild fowl just began to return on the approach of spring.

Sunday, 9th *March.*—I examined into the conduct of my sergeant, and found that he was guilty of the offences charged to him, and punished him by reduction. Visited the Fols Avoins lodges, and received a present of some tallow. One of my men arrived from the hunting camp with two deer.

Monday, 10th *March.*—Was visited by the Fols Avoin chief and several others of the nation. This chief was an extraordinary hunter; to instance his power, he had killed forty elk and a bear in one day, chasing the former from dawn to eve. We were all busied in preparing oars, guns, masts, &c., against the breaking up of the ice which was opening fast.

Tuesday, 11th *March.*—In a long conversation with Reynard, he professed not to believe in an hereafter ; but he believed that the world would all be drowned by water, at some future period; he asked how it was to be re-peopled? In justice to his nation, however, I must observe, that his opinion was singular.

Wednesday, 12th *March.*—Continued our preparations; had a fine chase with deer on the ice; killed one. Since our return I had received eight deer from our camp.

Thursday, 13th *March.*—Received two deer from my hunting camp. Went out with my gun on the opposite side of the river; ascended the mountain which borders the prairie, and on the point of it found a stone, on which some Indians had sharpened their knives, and a war club half finished. From this spot you may extend the eye over vast prairies, with scarcely any interruption but clumps of trees which at a distance appeared like mountains. From two or three of which, the smoke rising in the air denoted the habitation of the wandering savage, and too often marked them out as victims to their enemies. From the cruelty of these I have had the pleasure, in the course of the winter, and through a wilderness of fifteen hundred miles extent, to preserve them, as peace has reigned through my mediation, from the Prairie des Chiens to the lower Red river. If a subaltern, with twenty men, at so great a distance from the seat of government, could effect so important a change in the minds of these savages, what might not a great

VOYAGE TO THE SOURCE

and independent power effect, if, instead of blowing up the flames of discord, it exerted its influence in the sacred cause of peace?

When I returned to the fort, I found the Fols Avoin chief, who intended to remain all night. He told me, that near the conclusion of the revolutionary war, his nation began to look upon him as a warrior; that they received a parole from Michillimackinac, on which he was despatched with forty warriors; that on his arrival he was requested to head them against the Americans. To which he replied, "We have considered you and the Americans as one people; you are now at war; how are we to decide who has justice on their side? Besides, you white people are like the leaves on the trees for numbers. Should I march with my forty warriors to the field of battle, they with their chief would be unnoticed in the multitude, and would be swallowed up as the big waters embosom the small rivulets which discharge themselves into them. No, I will return to my nation, where my countrymen may be of service against our red enemies, and their actions be renowned in the dance of our nation."

Friday, 14th *March*.—Took the latitude by an artificial horizon, and measured the river: received one deer and a half from my hunting camp. The ice thinner.

Saturday, 15th *March*.—This was the day fixed upon by Mr. Grant and the Chippeway warriors for their arrival at my fort, and I was all day anxiously expecting them; for I knew, should they not accompany me down, the peace, partially effected between them and the Sioux, would not be on a permanent footing: from this I take them to be neither so brave nor so generous as the Sioux, who, in all their transactions, appear to be candid and brave, whereas the Chippeways are suspicious, consequently treacherous, and of course cowards.

Sunday, 16th *March*.—Received three deer from our hunting camp; examined trees for canoes.

Monday, 17th *March*.—Left the fort with my interpreter, and Roy, in order to visit the Fols Avoin chief, who was encamped with six lodges of his nation, about twenty miles below us, on a little river which empties into the Mississippi on the western side, a little above Clear river. On our way down, killed one goose, wounded another, and a deer that the dogs had driven into an air hole; hung our game on the trees: arrived at the creek; took out on it; ascended three or four miles on the bank, and descended on the other: killed another goose; struck the Mississippi below: encamped at our encampment of the — of October, when we ascended the river; ate our goose for supper. It snowed all day, and at night a very severe storm arose. It may be imagined that we spent a very disagreeable night, without shelter, and with but one blanket each.

Tuesday, 18th *March*.—We marched, determined to find the lodges. Met an Indian, whose track we pursued through almost impenetrable woods, for about two miles and a half to the camp. Here there was one of the finest sugar camps I almost ever saw; the whole of the timber being sugar maples. We were conducted to the chief's lodge, who received us in the patriarchal style. He pulled off my leggings and mockinsons, put me in the best place in his lodge, and offered me dry clothes. He then presented us with syrups of the maple to drink, and asked whether I preferred eating beaver, swan, elk, or deer? Upon my giving the preference to the first, a large kettle was filled with it by his wife, of which soup was made. This being thickened with flour, we had what I then thought a delicious repast. After we had refreshed ourselves, he asked whether we would visit his people at the other lodges? Having complied, we were presented in each with something to eat; by some with a bowl of sugar, by others beavers' tails, and other esteemed delicacies. After making this tour, we returned to the chief's lodge, and found a berth provided for each of us, of good soft bear skins nicely spread, and on mine there was a large feather pillow. I must not here omit to mention an anecdote, which serves to characterize more particularly the manners of these people. This, in the eyes of the contracted moralist, would deform my hospitable host into a monster of libertinism; but by a liberal mind would be considered as arising from the hearty generosity of the wild savage. In the course of the day, observing a ring on one of my fingers, he enquired if it was gold? he was told it was the gift of one, with whom I should be happy to be at that time. He seemed to think seriously, and at night told my interpreter, "that perhaps his father (as they called me) felt much grieved for the want of a woman; if so, he could furnish him with one." He was answered, that with us each man had but one wife, and that I considered it strictly my duty to remain faithful to her. This he thought strange (he himself having three) and replied, "that he knew some Americans at his nation who had half a dozen wives during the winter." The interpreter observed, that they were men without character; but that all of our great men had each but one wife. The chief acquiesced, but said he liked better to have as many as he pleased. This conversation was without any appeal to me, as the interpreter knew my mind, and answered immediately; it did not therefore appear as a refusal of the chief's offer.

Wednesday, 19th *March.*—This morning purchased two baskets of sugar, for the amount of which I gave orders on Mr. Dickson. After feasting upon a swan, took our leave for camp: it had snowed all night, and still continued snowing. Finding my two companions unable to keep up, I pushed on and arrived at the river. When I reached the place where I had hung up my first goose, I found that the ravens and eagles had not left a feather, and there was at the time feasting upon the deer, a band sufficient to have carried it away; they had picked its bones nearly clean; what remained I gave to my dogs. I next stopped at the place where I expected to find the last goose, but could see nothing of it; at length I found it hidden under the grass and snow, where some animal had concealed it, after eating off its head and neck. I carried it to the fort, where I arrived about an hour before sunset. I despatched immediately two men with rackets to meet the interpreter and Le Roy. They arrived about two hours after dark; some men also arrived at the hunting camp with the deer. The snow ceased falling about one hour after dark: it was the deepest that had fallen so low down the river this winter, being nearly two feet thick.

Thursday, 20th *March.*—Despatched nine men to my hunting camp, from whence I received two deer. Cloudy almost all day, but the water rose fast over the ice.

Friday, 21st *March.*—Received a visit from the Fols Avoin chief, called the Shawonoes, and six young men. I informed him without reserve, the news I had heard of him at Red Cedar lake, and of the letter I had written to Mr. Dickson. He denied the accusation in toto, and on the contrary said, that he presented his flag and two medals to the Chippeways, as an inducement for them to descend in the spring, and gave them all the encouragement in his power. His party was much astonished at the language I held with him. But from his firm protestations, we finally parted friends. He informed me that a camp of Sauteurs were on the river, waiting for the chiefs to come down, from which it appears they were still expected. At night, after the others had gone, Thomas arrived and staid all night. We agreed upon a hunting party for the next day, and also promised to pay the old Shawonoes a visit. He informed me, that he had set out the other day to follow me, but finding the storm so very bad, had returned to his wigwam. The thermometer was lower this day than it had been at any time here, previously to my commencing my voyage

Saturday, 22d *March.*—Ten of my men arrived from my hunting camp, with four deer and a half. Thomas departed: sent a man with him to his traps, from which he sent me two beavers.

Sunday, 23d *March.*—Agreeably to my promise, after breakfast I departed with Miller and my interpreter, to pay a visit to the old chief Shawonoes. We arrived at his camp in about two hours. On our way we met the Fols Avoin, called the Chein Blanc, who had visited my post, previously to my starting up the river, at whose house we stopped when passing. We were received by the old Shawonoes at his lodge, with the usual Indian hospitality, but very different from the polite reception given us by Thomas. Charlevoix and others have all borne testimony to the personal beauty of this nation. From my own observation, I had sufficient reason to confirm their information as it respected the males; for they were all straight and well made, about the middle size; their complexions generally fair for savages, their teeth good, their eyes large, and rather languishing: they have a mild but independent expression of countenance, that charms at first sight: in short, they would be considered anywhere as handsome men. But their account of the women, I never before believed to be correct. In this lodge there were five very handsome females when we arrived; and about sundown, a pair arrived, whom my interpreter observed were the handsomest couple he had ever seen, and in truth they were; the man being about five feet eleven inches, and possessing in an eminent manner all the beauties of countenance which distinguish his nation. His companion was twenty-two years óld, having dark brown eyes, jet hair, and an elegantly proportioned neck, her figure by no means inclining to corpulency, as they generally are after marriage. The man appeared to attach himself particularly to me, and informed me his wife was the daughter of an American, who passing through their nation about twenty-three years before, remained a week or two possessed of her mother, and that she was the fruit of this amour, but his name they were unacquainted with. I had brought six biscuits with me, which I presented to her on the score of her being my countrywoman, which raised a loud laugh; and she was called the Bostonian during the rest of my stay. I found them generally extremely hard to deal with; my provision being only a little venison. I wished to procure some bear's oil; for a few gallons of which I was obliged to pay a dollar per gallon, and then they wanted to mix tallow with it. They also demanded ten dollars for a bear skin (the most beautiful, I confess, I ever saw), which I wanted to mount a saddle. Indeed I was informed that traders in this country sometimes give as much as sixteen dollars for rare skins, for they are eminently superior to any thing of the kind on the lower Mississippi, and sell in Europe for double the price.

In the evening we were entertained with the calumet and dog dance; also another dance, in which some of the men struck a post and told some of their war exploits; but as they spoke in *Menomene*, my interpreter could not explain it. After the dance we had the feast of the dead (as it is called) at which, every two or three were served with a pan or vessel full of meat, and when all were ready there was a prayer, after which the eating commenced; when it was expected we would eat up our portion entirely, being careful not to drop a bone, but to gather up all, and put them in the dish: we were then treated with soup. After the eating was finished, the chief again gave an exhortation, which concluded the ceremony. I am told they then gather up all the fragments, and throw them into the water, lest the dogs should get them. Burning them is considered sacrilegious. In this lodge were collected at one time forty-one persons, great and small, seventeen of whom were capable of bearing arms; besides dogs without number.

Monday, 24th *March.*—Rose early, and with my dog sledge arrived at the fort before ten o'clock. In the afternoon Mr. Grant arrived with De Breche and some of his young men : saluted him with fourteen rounds. I now found that my two young warriors of Leech lake had been brave enough to return to their homes. Mr. Grant and myself sat up late in conversation.

Tuesday, 25th *March.*—Sent an Indian to Thomas's lodge, and a letter to Mr. Dickson. It snowed and stormed all day.

Wednesday, 26th *March.*—Thomas, the Fols Avoin chief, arrived with seven of his men, and the old Shawonoes and six of his party. I had them all to feed as well as my own men. At night I gave them leave to dance in the gárrison, which they did until ten o'clock; but once or twice told me, that if I was tired of them the dance should cease. The old Shawonoes and the White Dog of the Fols Avoins rehearsed their exploits, which we could not understand; but De Breche arose and said " I once killed a Sioux and cut off his head with such a spear as I now present to this Winebago," at the same time presenting one to a Winebago, with whom the Chippeways were at war; this was considered by the latter as a great honour. My hunters went out, but killed nothing.

Thursday, 27th *March.*—In the morning the Chippeway chief made a speech, and presented his pipe to me to bear to the Sioux, on which were seven strings of Wampum, as authority from seven heads of the Chippeways, either to conclude peace or to make war: as he had chosen the former, he sent his pipe to the Sioux, and requested me to inform them, that he and his people would encamp at the mouth of the Raven river the ensuing summer, where he would see the United States flag flying, as a proof of his pacific disposition. The Fols Avoin chief then spoke and said, " His nation had been rendered small by its enemies; only a remnant was now left, but yet they could boast of not being slaves; for rather than suffer their women and children to be taken, they themselves killed them. But that their father (as they called me) had travelled far, and had taken much pains to prevent the Sioux and Chippeways from killing one another; that he thought none could be so ungenerous as to neglect listening to the words of their father: that he would report to the Sioux the pacific disposition of the Sauteurs, and hoped the peace would be firm and lasting." I then in a few words informed De Breche, " That I would report to the Sioux all he had said, and that I should ever feel pleased and grateful that the two nations had laid aside the tomahawk at my request. That I thanked the Fols Avoin chief for his good wishes and the parole which he had given the Sauteurs." After all this, each chief was furnished with a kettle of liquor, to drink each others health; and De Breche's flag (which I had presented to him) was displayed in the fort. The Fols Avoins then departed, at which I was by no means displeased; for they had already consumed all the dry meat I had laid aside for my voyage, and I was apprehensive that my hunters would not be able to provide another supply.

Friday, 28th *March.*—Late in the afternoon Mr. Grant and the Sauteurs took their departure, calculating that the Sioux had left the country. Taking with me one of my soldiers, I accompanied them to the lodge of the Shawonoes, where we stayed all night. The Fols Avoins and Sauteurs had a dance, at which I left them and went to sleep. Feasted on elk, sugar and syrup. Previously to the Indians' departure from my post, I demanded the chief's medal and flags; the former he delivered, but with a bad grace, the latter he said were in the lands where I left Lake de Sable, instructed I suppose, by the traders, and that he could not obtain them. It thundered and lightened this day.

Saturday, 29th *March.*—We all marched in the morning. Mr. Grant and party for Sandy lake, and I for my hunting camp. I gave him my spaniel dog: he joined me again after we had separated about five miles. I arrived at my hunting camp about eight o'clock in the morning, and was informed that my hunters had gone to bring in a deer; they shortly after arrived with it, and about eleven o'clock we all went out hunting: saw but few deer, out of which I had the good fortune to kill two. On our arrival at camp found one of my men at the garrison with a letter from Mr. Dickson. The soldier informed me that one Sioux had arrived with Mr. Dickson's men. Although much fatigued, as soon as I had eaten something, I took one of my men and departed for the garrison one hour before sundown. The distance was twenty-one miles, and the ice very dangerous, being rotten, and the water over it nearly a foot deep: we had sticks in our hands, and in many places run them through the ice: it thundered and lightened with rain. The Sioux, not finding the Sauteurs, had returned immediately.

Sunday, 30th *March.*—Wrote to Mr. Dickson and despatched his man. I found myself very stiff from my yesterday's march. We now caulked our boats, as the ice had every appearance of breaking up in a few days. Whilst thus on the wing of eager expectation, every day seemed an age.

Monday, 31st *March.*—Finished caulking my boats; the difficulty with me then, was, what I should get to pitch the seams with. We were all day as anxiously watching the ice, as a lover would be the arrival of the priest who was to unite him to his beloved. Sometimes it moved a little, but soon closed: an Indian and his woman crossed it, when the poles which they held in their hands were forced through in many places. The provision to which I was obliged to restrict myself and men, viz., two pounds of fresh venison per day, was scarcely sufficient to keep us alive. Though I had not an extraordinary appetite, yet I was continually hungry.

Wednesday, 2d *April.*—Went out and killed one deer and two partridges. The ice began to move opposite the fort at the foot of the rapids, but continued dammed up below. Received six bears from my hunting camp. Launched our canoe and brought her down.

Thursday, 3d *April.*—Sent one man down to examine the river, another to the camp, and took two men myself over the hills on the other side of the Mississippi to hunt. In the course of the day I killed a swan and a goose, and we certainly should have killed one or two elk, had it not been for the sledge-dogs; for we lay concealed on the banks of Clear river, when four of these animals came and threw themselves into it on the opposite shore, and were swimming directly towards us, when our dogs bounced into the water, and caused them to turn back: we then fired on them, but they carried off all the lead we gave them, and we could not cross the river, unless we rafted (it being bank full) which would have detained us too long a time. In the evening it became very cold, and we passed rather an uncomfortable night.

Friday, 4th *April.*—Took our course homewards; I killed one large buck and wounded another. We made a fire and ate our breakfast; arrived at the fort at two o'clock, P. M. when I was informed that the river was still shut below at the cluster of islands. Received some bear meat, and one deer from the camp.

Saturday, 5th *April.*—In the morning despatched two men down the river to see if it was open: my hunters arrived from the camps. Followed my boats with our canoes, and launched them; they made considerable water. The young Shawonoes arrived in my canoes from above, with about one thousand pounds of fur, which he deposited in the fort; then returned and informed me that the river was still shut about ten miles below.

Sunday, 6th *April.*—Sent my perroque with Sergeant Bradley and two men to descend the river, and see if it was yet open: they returned in the afternoon, and reported all clear. I had previously determined to load and embark the next day, and hoped to find it free by the time I arrived.

The Shawonoes arrived and encamped near the stockade; he informed me, that his nation had determined to send his son down in his stead, as he declined the voyage to St. Louis. All hearts and hands were now employed in preparing for our departure: in the evening the men cleared out their room, and danced to the violin and sang songs until eleven o'clock; so rejoiced was every heart at leaving this savage wilderness.

Monday, 7th *April*.—Loaded our boats, and departed at forty minutes past ten o'clock: at one o'clock arrived at Clear river, where we found my canoe and men. Although I had partly promised the Fols Avoin chief to remain one night, yet time was too precious, and we put off; passed the grand rapids, and arrived at Mr. Dickson's just before sundown; we were saluted with three rounds. At night he treated all my men with a supper and a dram. Mr. D., Mr. Paulize, and myself, sat up until four o'clock in the morning

Tuesday, 8th *April*.— Were obliged to remain this day, on account of some information to be obtained here. I spent the day in making a rough chart of St. Peter's, writing notes on the Sioux and other nations, settling the affairs of the Indian department with Mr. Dickson, for whose communications, and those of Mr. Paulize, I am infinitely indebted: made every necessary preparation for an early embarkation.

Wednesday, 9th *April*.— Rose early in the morning and commenced my arrangements. Having observed two Indians drunk during the night, and finding upon enquiry, that the liquor had been furnished them by a Mr. Gregnon or Mr. Yennesse, I sent my interpreter to them, to request they would not sell any strong liquor to the Indians, upon which Mr. Yennesse demanded the restrictions in writing which were given to him: on demanding his license from him it amounted to no more than merely a certificate that he had paid the tax required by a law of the Indian territory, on all retailers of merchandise; but it was by no means an Indian license; however, I did not think proper to go into a more close investigation. Last night was so cold, that the water was covered with floating cakes of ice of a strong consistence.

After receiving every mark of attention from Messrs. Dickson and Paulize, I took my departure at eight o'clock. At four P. M. arrived at the house of Mr. Paulize, twenty-five leagues distant, to whose brother I had a letter. I was received with politeness by him and a Mr. Veau, who had wintered along-side of him, on the very island at which we had encamped on the night of the —— of October, in ascending. Some time after having left this place, we discovered a bark canoe a-head; we gained on it for some time, when it turned a point about three hundred yards before us; and on our turning it also, it had entirely disappeared. This excited my curiosity. I stood up in the barge, and at last discovered it turned up in the grass of the prairie; but after we had passed a good gun shot, three savages made their appearance from under it, launched it in the river and followed, not knowing of my other boats which had just turned the point immediately upon them. They then came on, and upon my stopping for the night at a vacant trading house, stopped there also, and addressed me, "Saggo Commandant," or "your servant captain." I directed my interpreter to inquire their motives for concealing themselves. They replied, that their canoe leaked, and that they had turned her up to discharge the water. This I did not believe, and as their conduct was equivocal, I received them rather sternly; I gave them, however, a dram and a piece of bread; they then re-embarked and continued down the river. Their conduct brought to mind the visit of the Fils de Penichon to Mr. Dickson, during the winter; one principal cause of which was, that he wished to inform me, that the seven men whom I mentioned to have met when crossing the St. Anthony, had since declared that they would kill him, for agreeing to the peace between the Sioux and Sauteurs; and for being instrumental in preventing them from their revenge for their relations killed by the Sauteurs in August, 1805; and Thomas, the Fols Avoin chief, for the support he seemed disposed to give me. This information had not made the impression it ought to have done, coming from so respectable a source as the first chief of the village; but the conduct of those fellows made me take it into consideration, and I appeal to God and my country, whether self-preservation would not have justified me in destroying them wherever I found them? This my men would have done, if ordered, amidst a thousand of them, and I should have been supported by the chiefs of the St. Peter's, at the mouth of which were three hundred warriors awaiting my arrival. I dreaded the consequences of meeting the rascal who had fired at my sentinel last winter, for fear the impetuosity of my conduct might not be approved of by my government, who did not so intimately know the nature of these savages.

This day, for the first time, we saw the commencement of vegetation, yet the snow was a foot deep in some places.

Thursday, 10th *April.*—Sailed at half past five o'clock; about seven passed Rum river, and at eight were saluted by six or seven lodges of Fols Avoins, amongst whom was a clerk of Mr. Dickson's. These people had wintered on Rum river, and were waiting for their chiefs and traders to descend, in order to accompany them to the Prairie des Chiens. Arrived at the falls of St. Anthony at ten o'clock: carried over all our loading and the canoe to the lower end of the portage, and hauled our boats up on the bank. I pitched my tents at the lower end of the encampment, where all the men lodged except the guard, whose quarters were above. The appearance of the falls was much more tremendous than when we ascended: the increase of water occasioned the spray to rise much higher, and the mist appeared like clouds. How different my sensations now, from what they were when at this place before! At that time not having accomplished more than half my route, winter fast approaching, war existing between the most savage nations in the country I had to pass, my provisions greatly diminished, and having but a poor prospect of additional supplies; many of my men sick, and the others not a little disheartened, and our success in this arduous undertaking very doubtful; just upon the borders of the haunts of civilized man; about to launch into an unknown wilderness, for ours was the first canoe that had ever crossed this portage; were circumstances sufficient to rob my breast of contentment and ease: but now we have accomplished every wish, and peace reigns throughout this vast extent! We have returned thus far on our voyage without the loss of a single man, and have hopes of soon being blessed with the society of our relations and friends.

The river was this morning covered with ice, which continued floating all day. The shores still barricaded with it.

Friday, 11th *April.*—Although it snowed very hard, we brought over both boats, and descended the river to the island at the entrance of the St. Peter's. I sent to the chiefs and informed them, I had something to communicate to them. The Fils de Penichon immediately waited on me, and informed me that he would provide a place for the purpose: about sun-down I was sent for, and introduced into the council-house, where I found a great many chiefs of the Sussitongs, Gens de Feuille, and the Gens de Lac. The Yanctongs had not yet come down: they were all waiting for my arrival. There were in all about one hundred lodges, or six hundred people; we were saluted on our crossing the river with ball as usual. The council-house was formed of two large lodges, capable of containing three hundred men. In the upper were forty chiefs, and as many pipes, set against the poles, alongside of which I had the Sauteurs' pipe arranged. I then informed them, in a short detail, of my transactions with the Sauteurs, but my interpreters were not capable of making themselves understood; I was therefore obliged to omit mentioning every particular relative to the rascal who fired on my sentinel, and of the other delinquents who had broken the Fols Avoins' canoes, and threatened my life: the interpreters however informed them that I wanted some of their principal chiefs to go to St. Louis, and that those who thought proper might descend to the prairie, where we would give them more explicit information.

They all smoked out of the Sauteurs' pipes, excepting three, who were painted black, and were some of those who had lost their relations last winter. I invited the Fils de Penichon, and the son of the Killeur Rouge to come over and sup with me, when Mr. Dickson and myself endeavoured to explain what I intended to have said to them, could I have made myself understood; that at the prairie we would have all things explained; that I was desirous of making a better report of them than Captain Lewis could from their treatment of him. The former of these savages was the person who remained with his men around my post all last winter, and had treated my men so well.

Saturday, 12th April.—Embarked early: although my interpreter had been frequently up the river, he could not tell me where the cave, spoken of by Carver, could be found; we carefully sought for it, but in vain. At the Indian village a few miles above St. Peter's, we were about to pass a few lodges, but on receiving a very particular invitation to come on shore, we landed, and were received in a lodge where they presented us with sugar, and some other articles. I gave the proprietor a dram, and was about to depart, when he demanded a kettle of liquor: on being refused, and after

I had left the shore, he told me that he did not like the arrangements, and that he would go to war this summer. I directed the interpreter to tell him that if I returned to the St. Peter's with troops, I would settle that affair with him. On our arrival at the St. Croix, I found the Petit Corbeau with his people, and also Messrs. Frazer and Wood.

We had a conference; when the Petit Corbeau made many apologies for the misconduct of his people: he represented to us the different ways in which his young warriors had been inducing him to go to war; that he had been much blamed for dismissing his party last fall, but was determined to adhere as far as lay in his power to our instructions; that he thought it most prudent to remain here and restrain the warriors. He then presented me with a beaver robe and a pipe, and his message to the General, that he was determined to preserve peace and make the road clear, as a remembrance of his promised medal. I made him a reply calculated to confirm him in his good intentions, and assured him that he should not be the less remembered by his father, although not present.

I was informed that notwithstanding the instructions of license, and my particular request, Mr. Murdock Cameron had taken liquor and sold it to the Indians on the River St. Peter's, and that his partner below had been equally imprudent. I pledged myself to prosecute them according to law, for they have been the occasion of great confusion, and of much injury to the other traders. This day met a canoe of Mr. Dickson's, loaded with provision, under the charge of Mr. Anderson, brother of the Anderson at Leech lake.

He politely offered me any provision he had on board, (for which Mr. Dickson had given me an order,) but not now being in want, I did not accept of any. This day for the first time I observed the trees beginning to bud, and indeed the climate seemed to have changed very materially since we had passed the Falls of St. Anthony.

Sunday, 13th *April.*—We embarked after breakfast, accompanied by Messrs. Frazer and Wood, wind strong a-head; they outrowed us: theirs was the first boat or canoe we had met with on the voyage able to do this, but then they were doubly manned and light.

We arrived at the band of the Aile Rouge at two o'clock, when we were saluted as usual: we held a council here, when he spoke with more detestation of the conduct of the rascals, at the mouth of the St. Peter's, than any man I had yet heard. He assured me, speaking of the fellow who had fired on my sentinel, and threatened to kill me, that if I thought it requisite he should be put to death; but that as there were many chiefs above, with whom he wished to speak, he hoped I would remain one day, when all the Sioux would be down, and I might have the command of one thousand men of them; that I would probably think it no honour, but that the British used to flatter them they were proud of having them for soldiers. I replied in general terms, and assured him that it was not for the misconduct of two or three delinqents, that I meant to pass over all the good treatment I had received from the Sioux nation: and added, that in council I would explain myself: as to the Indian who fired at my sentinel, I stated that had I been near, the Sioux nation would never have been troubled with him, for I would have killed him on the spot; but that my young men did not do it, apprehensive that I might be displeased. I then gave him the news of the Sauteurs, and afterwards stated, that as to remaining one day, it would be of no service, that I was much pressed to arrive below, as my General expected me, my duty called me, and the state of my provisions demanded the utmost expedition; that I should be happy to oblige him, but that my men must eat. He replied, that Lake Pepin being yet shut with ice, if I went on and encamped on it, I should not be supplied with provisions; that he would send out all his young men the next day, and that if the other bands did not arrive he would depart the day after with me. In short, after much conversation, I agreed to remain one day, knowing that the lake was closed, and that we could proceed only nine miles if we went on.

This appeared to give general satisfaction; I was invited to different feasts, and entertained by one whose father was created a chief by the Spaniards.

At this feast I saw a man (called by the French, Nez Corbeau, and by the Indians, the Wind that Walks) who was formerly the second chief of the Sioux, but being the cause of the death of one of the traders, seven years since, he had voluntarily relinquished the dignity, and frequently requested to be given up to the whites. He had now determined to go to St. Louis and deliver himself up, where he said they might put him to death: his long repentance, and the great confidence which the nation reposed in him, would probably operate to protect him from the punishment which the crime merited; but as it had been committed long before the United States had assumed its authority over the district, and as no law of theirs could bear upon it, unless an ex post facto one were passed, I conceive it would not now be noticed: I did not think proper however to inform him of my opinion. I here received a letter from Mr. Rollet, partner of Mr. Cameron, with a present of some brandy, coffee and sugar: I hesitated about receiving these articles from the partner of the man I intended to prosecute.

Their amount being trifling however, I accepted of them, offering him payment. I assured him that the prosecution arose from a sense of duty, and not from any personal prejudice.

My canoe did not come up in consequence of the head wind: sent out two men in a canoe to set fishing lines; the boat overset, and had it not been for the timely assistance of the savages, who carried them into their lodges, undressed them, and treated them with the greatest humanity and kindness, the men must inevitably have perished. At this place I was informed that the Indian spoken of as having threatened my life had actually cocked his gun to shoot at me from behind the hills, but was prevented by the others.

Monday, 14th *April.*— Was invited to a feast by the Nez Corbeau; his conversation was interesting and shall be detailed hereafter: the other Indians had not yet arrived. Messrs. Wood, Frazer and myself, ascended a high hill called the Barn, from which we had a view of Lake Pepin, the valley through which the Mississippi by numerous channels wound itself as far as the St. Croix, the Cannon river, and the lofty hills on each side.

Tuesday, 15th *April.*— Arose very early and embarked about sunrise, much to the astonishment of the Indians, who were fully prepared for the council, when they heard I had put off. However after some conversation with Mr. Frazer, they acknowledged it was agreeably to what I had said, that I would sail early, and that they could not blame me. I was very positive in my word, for I found it by far the best way to treat the Indians. The Aile Rouge had a beaver robe and a pipe to present to me, but was obliged for the present to keep them.

We passed through Lake Pepin with the barges; the canoe being obliged to lay by did not come on: stopped at a prairie on the right bank, about nine miles below Lake Pepin: went out to view some hills which had the appearance of old fortifications. In these hollows I discovered a herd of elk; took out fifteen men, but we were not able to kill any. Mr. Frazer came up and passed on about two miles; we encamped together; neither Mr. Woods nor my canoe arrived. Snowed considerably.

Wednesday, 16th *April.*—Mr. Frazer's canoes and my boats sailed about one hour: waited some time, expecting Mr. Wood's barges and my canoe, but hearing a gun fired just above our encampment, we were induced to make sail. Passed the Aile prairie, also "the mountain that soaks in the water," and the Prairie de la Crosse, and encamped on the western shore, a few hundred yards below where I had before encamped in September in ascending: killed a goose flying; shot at some pigeons at our camp, and was answered from behind an island with two guns; we returned them, and were replied to by two more. This day the trees appeared in bloom: snow might still be seen on the sides of the hills. Distance descended seventy-five miles.

Thursday, 17th *April.*—Put off pretty early and arrived at Wabasha's band at eleven o'clock, where I remained all day for the Chief, but he alone of all the hunters remained out all night; left some powder and tobacco for him. The Sioux presented me with a kettle of boiled meat and a deer. I here received information that the Puants had killed some white men below. Mr. Woods and my canoe arrived.

Friday, 18th *April.*—Departed from our encampment very early: stopped to breakfast at the Painted Rock; arrived at the Prairie des Chiens at two o'clock, and were received by crowds on the bank. Took up my quarters at Mr. Fisher's; my men received a present of one barrel of pork from Mr. Campbell, a bag of biscuit, twenty loaves of bread, and some meat from Mr. Fisher. A Mr. Jearreau from Cahokia is here, who embarks to-morrow for St. Louis; I wrote to General Wilkinson by him. I was waited upon by a number of the Chiefs, Reynards, Sioux, Des Moines and others.

The Winebagoes were here, intending, as I was informed, to deliver up some of the murderers to me. Received a great deal of news from the states of Europe, both civil and military.

Saturday, 19th *April.*—Dined at Mr. Campbell's in company with Messrs. Wilmot, Blakely, Wood, Rollet, Fisher, Frazer, and Jearreau. Six canoes arrived from the upper part of the St. Peter's, with the Yanctong chiefs from the head of that river; their appearance was indeed savage, much more so than any nation I had yet seen. Prepared my boat for sail; gave notice to the Puants that I had business to transact with them the next day. A band of the Gens du Lac arrived. Took into my pay as interpreter, Mr. Y. Reinville.

Sunday, 20th *April.*—Held a council with the Puant chiefs, and demanded of them the murderers of their nation; they required till to-morrow to consider the subject.

This afternoon they had a great game of the cross on the prairie, between the Sioux on the one side, and the Puants and the Reynards on the other. The ball is made of some hard substance and covered with leather; the cross sticks are round, with net-work, and handles three feet long. The parties being ready, and bets agreed upon, (sometimes to the amount of some thousands of dollars,) the goals are erected on the prairie at the distance of half a mile; the ball is thrown up in the middle, and each party strives to drive it to the opposite goal; and when either party gains the first rubber, which is drawing it quite round the post, the ball is again taken to the centre, the ground changed, and the contest renewed; and this is continued until one side gains four times, which decides the bet.

It is an interesting sight to behold two or three hundred naked savages contending on the plain, who shall bear off the palm of victory; as he who drives the ball round the goal receives the shouts of his companions, in congratulation of his success. It sometimes happens, that one catches the ball in his racket, and depending on his speed, endeavours to carry it to the goal; and when he finds himself too closely pursued, he hurls it with great force and dexterity to an amazing distance, where there are always flankers of both parties ready to receive it: it seldom touches the ground, but is sometimes kept in the air for hours before either party can gain the victory. In the game which I witnessed the Sioux were victorious, more, I believe, from the superiority of their skill in throwing the ball, than from their swiftness, for I thought the Puants and Reynards the fleetest runners.

I made a written demand of the magistrates to take depositions concerning the late murders. Had a private conversation with Wabasha.

Monday, 21st *April.*—Was sent for by La Feuille, and had a long and interesting conversation with him, in which he spoke of the general jealousy of his nation towards their chiefs; and although he knew it might occasion some of the Sioux displeasure, he did not hesitate to declare that he looked on the Nez Corbeau as the man of most sense in their nation; and that he believed it would be generally acceptable, if he were reinstated in his rank. Upon my return, I was sent for by the Red Thunder, chief of the Yanctongs, the most savage band of the Sioux. He was prepared with the most elegant pipes and robes I ever saw. He briefly declared that white blood had never been shed in the village of the Yanctongs, even when rum was permitted: that Mr. Murdock Cameron had arrived at his village last autumn; that he had invited him to eat, given him corn as a bird; that he (Cameron) had informed him of the prohibition of rum, and was the only person who afterwards sold it in the village.

After this I had a council with the Puants. Spent the evening with Mr. Wilmot, one of the best informed, and most gentlemanly man in the place.

Tuesday, 22d *April.*—Held a council with the Sioux and Puants, the latter of whom delivered up their medals and flags: prepared to depart to-morrow.

Wednesday, 23d *April.*—After closing my accounts, and concluding other business, at half past twelve o'clock I left the prairie, and at the lower end of it was saluted by seventeen lodges of Puants. Met a barge, by which I received a letter from Mrs. Pike. Further on, met one batteau and one canoe of traders; passed one trader's camp; arrived at Mr. Dubuque's at ten o'clock at night: found some traders encamped at the entrance, with forty or fifty Indians. I obtained some information from Mr. D. and requested him to write to me on certain points. After we had boiled our victuals I divided my men into four watches, and put off; wind a-head: observed this day, for the first time, the half-formed leaves on the trees.

Thursday, 24th *April.*—In the morning used our oars until ten o'clock, and then floated while breakfasting: at this time two barges, one barque, and two wooden canoes, passed us under full sail; by one of which I sent back a letter to Mr. Dubuque, that I had forgotten to deliver. Stopped at dark to cook supper; after which, rowed under the windward shore, expecting we could make headway with four oars; but we were blown on the lee shore in a few moments, when all hands were summoned, and we again with difficulty made to windward: came to, placed one sentry on my bows, and all hands beside went to sleep.

It rained in the night, and before morning the water overflowed my bed in the bottom of the boat, having no cover, or any extra accommodations, as it might have retarded my voyage. The wind very hard a-head.

Friday, 25th *April.*—Obliged to unship our mast to prevent its rolling overboard with the swell. Passed the first Reynard village at twelve o'clock; counted eighteen lodges: stopped at the prairie in descending, on the left, about the middle of the rapids, where there is a beautiful cove or harbour. We found three lodges of Indians here, but none of them came near us. Shortly after we had left this place we observed a barge under sail, with the United States flag, which, upon our being seen, put to shore on the large island, about three miles above Stony river, where I also landed. It proved to be Captain Many, of the artillery, who was in search of some Osage prisoners amongst the Sacs and Reynards. He informed me that at the village of Stony Point the Indians had evinced a strong disposition to commit hostilities; that he was met at the mouth of the river by an old Indian, who said that all the inhabitants of the village were in a state of intoxication, and advised him to go up alone: this advice, however, he had rejected. That when they arrived there, they were saluted by the appellation of the Bloody Americans, who had killed such a person's father, and such a person's mother, brother, &c.; the women carried off the guns and other arms, and concealed them: that he had then crossed the river opposite to the village, and was followed by a number of Indians, with pistols under their blankets: that they would listen to no conference whatever relative to the delivery of the prisoners; but demanded, insolently, why he wore a plume in his hat; and declared that they looked upon it as a mark of war, and immediately decorated themselves with their ravens' feathers, worn only in cases of hostility. We regretted that our orders would not permit of our punishing the scoundrels, as by a *coup de main* we might easily have carried the village. Gave Captain Many a note of introduction to Messrs. Campbell, Fisher, Wilmot, and Dubuque, and every information in my power. We sat up late conversing.

Saturday, 26th *April.*—Captain Many and myself took breakfast, and embarked, wind directly a-head, and a most tremendous swell to combat with, which has been the case ever since we left the prairie. Captain

M. departed under full sail. We set off at the same time, and descended by all the sinuosities of the shore, to avoid the strength of the wind and force of the waves. I was confident he could sail much faster up than we could possibly down the stream. Encamped on Grant's prairie, where we had encamped on the 25th August, when ascending. There was one Indian and family present, to whom I gave some corn.

Sunday, 27th *April.*—It cleared off during the night; we embarked early, and by sun-set had come on to about eight to ten leagues above the River Iowa, to the establishment at the lower Sac village, a distance of nearly forty-eight leagues. Here I met with Messrs. Maxwell and Blondeau; took the deposition of the former on the subject of the Indians' intoxication at this place, for they were all drunk. They had stolen a horse from the establishment, and offered to bring it back for liquor; but laughed at them when offered a blanket and powder. Passed two canoes and two barges.

At the establishment received two letters from Mrs. Pike; took with us Corporal Eddy, and the other soldier, whom Captain Many had left behind. Rowed with four oars all night. A citizen took his passage with me.

Monday, 28th *April.*—In the morning passed a wintering ground, where, from appearance, there must have been at least seven or eight different establishments. At twelve o'clock arrived at the French house, mentioned in our voyage up on the 16th August; here we landed our citizen, who belonged to the settlement on Copper river. He informed me there were about twenty-five families in that settlement. About ten miles above Salt river we stopped at some islands where there were pigeon roosts, and in about fifteen minutes my men had knocked on the head, and brought on board, about three hundred. I had frequently heard of the fecundity of this bird, but never gave credit to what I then thought to approach the marvellous; but really the most fervid imagination cannot conceive their numbers. Their noise in the woods was like the continued roaring of the wind, and the ground may be said to have been absolutely covered with their excrement. The young ones which we killed were nearly as large as the old; they could fly about ten steps, and were one mass of fat; their craws were filled with acorns and the wild pea. They were still reposing on their nests, which were merely small bunches of sticks joined, with which all the small trees were covered.

Having proceeded on our voyage, we met four canoes of the Sacs, with wicker baskets filled with young pigeons. They made motions to exchange them for liquor, to which I returned the back of my hand.—Indeed the Indians had become so insolent through the instigation of the traders, that nothing but the lenity of our government, and humanity for the rogues, could have restrained me on my descent from carrying some of their towns by surprise, which I was determined to have done, had the information of their firing on Captain Many proved to be correct.—I put into the mouth of Salt river to cook our supper, after which, although raining, we put off, and set our watches, but so violent a gale and thunder storm came on about 12 o'clock that we put ashore: discovered that one of my sledge-dogs was missing.

Tuesday, 29th *April.*—In the morning still raining, the wind blowing right a-head, hoisted sail and returned to the mouth of the river; but neither here nor on the shore could we find my dog.—This was no little mortification, after having brought them so near home, as it broke the match whose important services I had already experienced. We continued on until 12 o'clock when it ceased raining for a little time, and we put ashore for breakfast, rowed till sun-down, when I set the watch; night fine and mild.

Wednesday, 30th *April.*—By day-light found ourselves at the Portage de Sioux. I here landed Captain Many's two men and ordered them across by land to the cantonment—as I had never seen the village, I walked up through it. The number of houses does not exceed twenty, they are built of square logs.—Met Lieutenant Hughes, about four miles above St. Louis, with between twenty and thirty Osage prisoners conveying them to the cantonment on the Missouri. He informed me my friends were all well. About 12 o'clock I arrived with my party at the town, after an absence of eight months and twenty-two days.

INDIAN NATIONS INHABITING THE DISTRICTS BORDERING ON THE UPPER MISSISSIPPI.

The first nation of Indians whom we met with in ascending the Mississippi from St. Louis were the Sacs, who principally reside in four villages. The first is situated at the head of the Rapids des Moines on the western shore, consisting of thirteen log lodges, the second on a prairie, on the eastern shore about sixty miles above, the third on Rock river, about three miles from the entrance, and the last on the River Iowa. They hunt on the Mississippi and its confluent streams from the Illinois to the River Iowa, and on the plains west of them which border on the Missouri. They are so perfectly consolidated with the Reynards, that they scarcely can be termed a distinct nation, but recently there appears to be a schism between them; the latter not approving of the insolence and ill will which has marked the conduct of the former to the United States on many late occurrences. They have for many years past made war, under the auspices of the Sioux, on the Sauteaux, Osages, and Missouries, but as at present, through the influence of the United States, a peace has been made between them and the nations of the Missouri, and by the same means between the Sioux and Sauteaux, their principal allies: it appears that it would be by no means a difficult matter to induce them to make a general peace, and pay still greater attention to the cultivation of the earth, as they now raise a considerable quantity of corn, beans, and melons. The character they bear with their savage brethren is, that they are much more to be dreaded for their deceit and disposition for stratagem, than for open courage.

The Reynards reside in three villages, the first situated on the western side of the Mississippi, six miles above the rapids of Rock river; the second about twelve miles in the rear of the lead mines; and the third on Turkey river, half a league from its entrance. They are engaged in the same wars, and have the same alliances as the Sacs, with whom they must be considered as indissolubly united. They hunt on both sides of the Mississippi from the River Iowa, below the Prairie des Chiens, to a river of that name above the said village. They raise a great quantity of corn, beans, and melons; the former of those articles in such abundance as to sell many hundred bushels per annum.

The Iowas reside on the Rivers des Moines and Iowa in two villages. They hunt on the western side of the Mississippi, the River des Moines, and westward to the Missouri; their wars and alliances are the same as those of the Sacs and Reynards, under whose special protection they conceived themselves to be. They cultivate some corn, but not so much in proportion as the two latter nations: their residence being on the small streams in the rear of the Mississippi, out of the high road of commerce, renders them less civilized. The Sacs, Reynards, and Iowas, since the treaty of the two former with the United States, claim the land from the entrance of the Jauflione on the western side of the Mississippi, up the latter river to the Iowa, above the Prairie des Chiens, and westward to the Missouri, but the limits between themselves are undefined. All the land formerly claimed by those nations east of the Mississippi is now ceded to the United States; but they reserved to themselves the privilege of hunting and residing on it as usual.

By killing the celebrated Sac chief Pontiac, the Illinois, Cahokias, Kaskaskias, and Priores, kindled a war with the allied nations of Sacs and Reynards, which has been the cause of the almost entire destruction of the former nations.

The Winebagoes, or Puants, are a nation who reside on the River Ouisconsin, Rock and Fox rivers, and Green bay, in seven villages, which are situated as follows, viz.: 1st, at the entrance of Green bay: 2d, at the end of Green bay: 3d, Wuckan: 4th, Lake Puckaway: 5th, portage of the Ouisconsin: 6th and 7th, both on Rock river. Those villages are so situated that the Winebagoes can embody the whole force of their nation, at one point of their territory, in four days. They hunt on the Ouisconsin, Rock river, and the eastern side of the Mississippi, from Rock river to the Prairie des Chiens, on Lake Michigan, Black river, and the countries between Lakes Michigan, Huron, and Superior. From a tradition amongst themselves, and their speaking the same language as the Ottoes of the River Plate, I am confident in asserting that they are a nation who have emigrated from Mexico, to avoid the oppression of the Spaniards; and the time may be fixed at one and a half centuries past; when they were taken under the protection of the Sioux, to whom they still profess to owe faith, and at least brotherly attention. They have formerly been at war with the nations west of the Mississippi, but appear recently to have laid down the hatchet. They are reputed brave, but from every circumstance their neighbours distinguish their bravery as the ferocity of a tiger, rather than the deliberate resolution of a man. Lately their conduct has been such as to authorize the remark made by a chief of a neighbouring nation, that a white man never should lie down to sleep in their villages without precaution.

The Menomene, or Fols Avoin nation, as it is termed by the French, reside in seven villages, situated as follows, viz.: 1st, at the River Menomene, fifteen leagues from Green bay, on the north side of the lake: 2d, at Green bay: 3d, at Little Kokalin: 4th, portage of Kokalin: 5th, Puant lake: 6th, entrance of a small lake on Fox river: and 7th, behind Les Buttes des Morts Their hunting grounds are the same as those of the Winebagoes, only that, owing to the very high estimation in which they are held both by the Sioux and Chippeways, they are frequently permitted to hunt near the Raven river on the Mississippi, which may be termed the battle ground between those two great nations.

The language which they speak is singular, for no white man has ever yet been known to acquire it. But this may probably be attributed to their all understanding the Algonquin, in which they and the Winebagoes carry on all conferences with the whites or other nations; and the facility with which that language is acquired is a further reason for its prevalence.

The Fols Avoin, although a small nation, are respected by all their neighbours for their bravery and independent spirit, and esteemed by the whites as their friends and protectors, when in their country.

The Sacs, Reynards, Puants, and Menomenes all reside, when not at their villages, in lodges in the form of an ellipsis, some of them thirty to forty feet in length, by fourteen or fifteen wide; which are sufficiently large to shelter sixty people from the storm, or for twenty to reside in. Their covering is formed of rushes plaited into mats, and carefully tied to poles. In the centre are fires, immediately over which is a small aperture in the lodge, which in fair weather is sufficient to give vent to the smoke, but in bad weather you must lie down on the ground to prevent being considerably incommoded by it.

We next came to that powerful nation the Sioux, the dread of whom is extended over all the savage tribes, from the confluence of the Mississippi and Missouri, to the Raven river on the former, and to the Snake Indians on the latter; but in those limits are many nations, whom they consider as allies, on a similar footing with the allies of ancient Rome, that is, humble dependents. But the Chippeway nation is an exception, who have maintained a long contest with them, owing to their country being intersected by numerous small lakes, watercourses, impenetrable morasses, and swamps; and they have hitherto bidden defiance to all the attacks of their neighbours. In order to have a correct idea of the Sioux nation, it is necessary to divide it into the different bands as distinguished by themselves. Agreeably to this plan, I shall begin with the Minowa Kantong, or Gens du Lac, who extend from the Prairie des Chiens to La Prairie des François, thirty-five miles up the St. Peter's. This band is again subdivided into four parts under different chiefs. The first of these most generally resides at their village on the upper Iowa river above the Prairie des Chiens, and is commanded by Wabasha, a chief whose father was considered as the first chief of all the Sioux nations. This subdivision hunts on both sides of the Mississippi, and its confluent streams, from the Prairie des Chiens to Buffalo river. The second subdivision resides near the head of Lake Pepin, and hunts from the Buffalo river to near the River St. Croix. The chief's name is Talangamane, a very celebrated warrior. The third subdivision resides between Cannon river and the entrance of St. Peter's. It is headed by Chatewaconamani; their principal hunting ground is on the St. Croix; they have a village at a place called the Grand Marais, fifteen miles below the entrance of the St. Peter's. It is situated on the eastern bank of the Mississippi, and consists of eleven log huts. The fourth subdivision is situated in the territory extending from the entrance of the St. Peter's to the Prairie des François; it is headed by a chief called Chatamutah, but a young man named Wagaganage has recently taken the lead in all its councils and affairs of state. It has one village nine miles up the St. Peter's, on the northeast side. This band, Minowa Kantong, are reputed the bravest of all the Sioux, and have for years been opposed to the Fols Avoin Sauteurs, who are reputed the bravest of all the numerous bands of the Chippeways. The second band of the Sioux are the Washpetong, or Gens des Feuilles, who inhabit the country from the Prairie des François, nearly to Roche Blanche, on the St. Peter's. Their first chief is Wasonquianni. They hunt on the St. Peter's, also on the Mississippi, up Rum river, and sometimes follow the buffalo on the plains. Their subdivisions I am unacquainted with.

The third band are the Sussitongs: they extend from the Roche Blanche to Lac de la Grosse Roche, on the River St. Peter's; they are divided into two subdivisions. The first band, called the Carreés, are headed by the chief Wuckieu Nutch, or the Tonnerre Rouge. The second, called the Sussitongs proper, are headed by Wacanto (or Esprit Bleu). These two sub-bands hunt eastward to the Mississippi, and up that river as far as Raven river. The fourth great band are the Yanctongs, who are dispersed from the Montagnes de la Prairie, which extend from St. Peter's to the Missouri, to the River des Moines. They are divided into two grand divisions, generally termed the Yanctongs of the north and the Yanctongs of the south. The former are headed by a chief, called Muckpeanutah, or Nuage Rouge, and those of Prairie by Petessung. This band are never stationary, but, with the Tetons, are the most erratic of all the Sioux; sometimes to be found on the borders of the lower Red river, sometimes on the Missouri, and on those immense plains which lie between the two rivers.

The fifth great band are the Tetons, who are dispersed on both sides of the Missouri. On the north, principally from the River Chien up, and on the south, from the Mahas to the Minetares or Gross Ventre. They may be divided into the Tetons of the north and south, but the immense plains over which they rove with the Yanctongs render it impossible to point out their places of habitation.

The sixth and smallest band of the Sioux, are the Washpeconte, who reside generally on the lands west of the Mississippi, between that river and the Missouri. They hunt most generally on the head of the River des Moines. They appeared to me to be the most stupid of all the Sioux.

The Minowa Kantongs are the only band of Sioux who use canoes, and are by far the most civilized, being the only ones who have ever built log huts, or cultivated any species of vegetables, and they but a very small quantity of corn and beans; for although I was with them in September or October, I never saw one kettle of either, always using the wild oats for bread. This production nature has furnished to all the most uncultivated nations of the north-west continent, who may gather a sufficiency in autumn. This, added to the productions of the chase, and the net, ensures them a subsistence through all the seasons of the year. This band is entirely armed with fire-arms, but is not considered by the other bands as anything superior on that account, especially on the plains.

The Washpetongs are a roving band; they leave the River St. Peter's in the month of April, and do not return from the plains until the month of August. The Sussitongs, of Roche Blanche, have the character of being the most evil disposed Indians on the River St. Peter's. They likewise follow the buffalo in the spring and summer months. The Sussitongs of the Lac de la Grosse Roche have the character of good hunters, and brave warriors, which may principally be attributed to their chief, the Tonnerre Rouge, who at the present day is allowed by both white people and savages of different bands (often their own chiefs) to be the first man in the Sioux nation. The Yanctongs and Tetons are the most independent Indians in the world; they follow the buffalo as chance directs, clothing themselves with the skin, and making their lodges, saddles, and bridles, of the same materials, the flesh of the animal furnishing their food. Possessing an innumerable stock of horses, they are here this day and five hundred miles off in ten days hence, and find themselves equally at home in either place, moving with a rapidity scarcely to be imagined by the inhabitants of the civilized world.

The trade of the Minowa Kantongs, Washpetongs, Sussitongs, and part of the Yanctongs, is all derived from the traders of Michillimackinac, and the latter supply the Yanctongs of the north and Tetons with the small quantities of iron-works which they require. Fire-arms are not in much estimation with them. The Washpecontes trade principally with the people of the Prairie des Chiens.

The claim of limits of the Sioux nation is allowed by all their neighbours to commence at the Prairie des Chiens, and to ascend the Mississippi on both sides the Raven river, up that river to its source, thence to the source of St. Peter's, from thence to the Montagnes de la Prairie, thence to the Missouri, down that river to the Mahas, bearing thence north-east to the source of the River des Moines, and from thence again to the Prairie des Chiens. They also claim a large territory south of the Missouri, but how far it extends is uncertain. The country east of the Mississippi from Rum river to Raven river is likewise in dispute between them and the Chippeways, and has been the scene of many a sharp encounter for near one hundred and fifty years past. From my knowledge of the Sioux, I do not hesitate to pronounce them the most warlike and independent nation of the Indians within the boundaries of the United States, their every passion being subservient to that of war, while at the same time the traders feel themselves perfectly secure from any combination being made against them. But it is extremely necessary to be careful not to injure the honour or feelings of an individual, which is certainly the principal cause of many broils that occur between them. Never was a trader known to suffer in the estimation of the nation by resenting any indignity offered him, even if he went so far as the taking of the life of the offender. Their gutteral pronunciation, high cheek bones, their visages, and distinct manners, together with their own traditions, supported by the testimony of neighbouring nations, put it in my mind beyond the shadow of a doubt, that they have emigrated from the north-west point of America, to which they had come across the narrow straits, which in that quarter divide the two continents, and are absolutely descendants of a Tartar tribe.

The only personal knowledge I have of the Chippeway nation, is restricted to the tribes of the south of Lake Superior; head waters of the Chippeway river and the St. Croix, and those who reside at Sandy lake, Leech lake, Rainy lake, Red lake, and the head of the Red river, the Mississippi, and Raven rivers. Like the Sioux they are divided into many bands, the names of only seven of which I am acquainted with. I shall begin with those who reside on the south side of Lake Superior, and on Sandy and Leech lakes, with the adjacent country. They are generally denominated by the traders by the name of Sauteaux, but those of the head waters of the Chippeway and St. Croix rivers are called Fols Avoin Sauteaux: I am unacquainted with the names of their chiefs. Those of Sandy lake are headed by a chief called Catawabata, or De Breche. They hunt on the Mille Lacs, Red lake, and the eastern bank of the Mississippi, from Rum river up to the Raven river, and from thence on both sides of the Mississippi to Pine river, on that river also, up the Mississippi again to Sandy lake, to nearly one hundred miles above that lake. Those of Leech lake hunt on its streams, Lake Winipic, upper Red Cedar lake, the Otter Tail lake, head of Raven river, and the upper part of lower Red river; their chief is La Gueule Plate, or Eskibugeckoge.

2d. The Crees reside on Red lake, and hunt in its vicinity, and on Red river; their first chief's name is Wiscoup, or Le Sucre.

3d. The Nepesangs reside on Lake Nippising, and on Lake St. Joseph.

4th. The Algonquins reside on the lake of the two mountains, and are dispersed along the north side of Lakes Ontario and Erie. From this tribe the language of the Chippeways derives its name, and the whole nation is frequently designated by the same appellation.

5th. The Ottoways reside on the north-western side of Lake Michigan and Lake Huron, and hunt between those lakes and Lake Superior.

6th. The Iroquois Chippeways are dispersed along the banks of all the great lakes from Ontario to the Lake of Woods.

7th. The Muscononges reside on the waters of lower Red river, near to Lake Winipic, and are the farthest band of the Chippeways. The Chippeways were the great and almost natural enemies of the Sioux, with whom they have been waging a war of extermination for near two centuries. On my arrival amongst them, I succeeded in inducing both sides to agree to a peace; and no blood was shed from September, 1805, to April, 1806, when I left the country. The object had frequently been, in vain, attempted by the British Government, who often brought the chiefs of the two nations together at Michillimackinac, made them presents, &c.; but the Sioux, still haughty and overbearing, spurned the proffered calumet, and returned to renew the scenes of slaughter and barbarity. It may then be demanded, how could a subaltern with twenty men, and no presents worthy of notice, effect that which the Governors of Canada with all the immense finances of the Indian department had attempted in vain, although they had frequently and urgently recommended it? I reply, that the British Government, it is true, requested, recommended, and made presents, but all this at a distance, and when the chiefs returned to their bands their thirst of blood soon obliterated from their recollection the lectures of humanity which they had heard in the councils of Michillimackinac. But when I appeared amongst them, the United States had lately acquired the jurisdiction over them, and the name of the Americans, as warriors, had frequently been sounded in their ears; and when I spoke to them on the subject, I recommended them, in the name of their great Father to make peace, and offered them the benefit of the mediation and guarantee of the United States, and spoke of the peace, not as a benefit to us, but a step taken to make themselves and children happy. This language, held up to both nations, with the assistance of the traders, a happy coincidence of circumstances, and, may I not add, the concurrence of the Almighty, effected that which had before been long attempted without success. But I am perfectly convinced, that unless troops are sent up between those two nations, with an agent whose business it should be to watch the rising discontents, and check the brooding spirit of revenge, the weapons of death will·again be raised, and the echoes of savage barbarity resound through the wilderness.

The Chippeways are uncommonly attached to spirituous liquors; but may not this be owing to their traders, who find it their interest to encourage their thirst after an article, which enables them to obtain their peltries at so low a rate as scarcely to be denominated a consideration, and have reduced the people near the establishment to a degree of degradation unparalleled?

The Algonquin language is one of the most copious and sonorous of all the savage dialects in North America, and is spoken and understood by the various nations (except the Sioux) from the gulf of St. Lawrence to Lake Winipic.

The Chippeways are much more mild and docile than the Sioux, and if we may judge from unprejudiced observers, more cool and deliberate in action; but the latter possess a much higher sense of the honour of their nation, while the former plan for self-preservation. The Sioux attack with impetuosity, the others defend with every necessary precaution. But the superior number of the Sioux would have enabled them to annihilate the Chippeways long since, had it not been for the nature of the country, which entirely precludes the possibility of an attack on horseback. It also gives them a decided advantage over an enemy, who being half armed with arrows, the least twig of a bush would turn the shaft of death out of its direction; a bullet holds its course, nor spends its force short of the destined victim. Thus we generally have found, that when engaged in a prairie, the Sioux came off victorious, but when in the woods, if not obliged to retreat, the carcasses of their slaughtered brethren have shown them how dearly they purchase victory.

The Sioux are bounded on the north-east and north by those two powerful nations the Chippeways and Knisteneaux, whose manners, strength, and boundaries, are ably described by Sir Alexander Mackenzie. The Assinniboins, or Stone Sioux, who border the Chippeways on the north-west and west, are a revolted band of the Sioux, and have maintained a war with the present nation for about a century, and rendered themselves their most violent enemies. They extend from Red river west, nearly to the Stony mountains, and are computed at one thousand five hundred warriors. They reside on the plains, and follow the buffalo, consequently they have very little occasion for traders or European productions.

VOYAGE TO THE SOURCE

Abstract of the Number, &c., of the Nations of Indians residing on the Mississippi and its confluent

	Names of the different nations, as pronounced in the English language.	Primitive names as given by the savages themselves.	Names given them by the French.	No. of Warriors.	No. of Women.	No. of Children.	No. of Villages.	Probable No. of Souls.	No. of Lodges of the Roving Bands.	No. of Fire Arms.	Primitive Language.	Traders or Bands with whom they traffic.	Amount of merchandise necessary for their annual consumption.	Annual return of Peltry in packs.	Species of Peltry.
													Dollars	Dols.	
	Sauks......	Sawkee......	Sac..........	700	750	1400	3	2850	....	700	Sauk..........	Of Michillimackinac, St.Louis, with the people of the Prairie des Chiens.	15000	600	Principally Deer-skins, some Bear, and a few Otter, Beaver and Rackoon.
	Foxes......	Ottagaumic..	Reynards ...	400	500	850	3	1750	....	400	Sauk, with a small difference in the idiom.......	Ditto	8500	400	Principally Deer, a few Bear, with a small proportion more of Furs.
	Iowas.......	Aiowais......	Ne Perce.....	300	400	700	2	1400	....	250	Missouries. ...	Of Michillimackinac.	10000	300	Deer-skins, Black Bear, Otter, Beaver, Mink, Rackoon, Grey Fox, and Musk-rat.
	Winebagoes..	Ochangras...	Puants.......	450	500	1000	7	1950	....	450	Missouries, or Zoto.	Of Ditto..........	9000	200	The same as the Fox's.
	Menomenes..	Menomene ..	Fols Avoin...	300	350	700	7	1350	....	300	Menomene ...	Of Ditto..........	9000	250	Beaver, Marten, Grey Fox, Mink, Muskrat, Otter, Deer-skins, Elk-skins, &c.
	Sues	Narcotah.....	Sioux.........	....	....	....	....	....	....	....	....	....	....	....	....
1st Band.	People of the Lakes	Minowa Kantong.	Gens du Lac.	305	600	1200	3	2105	125	305	Narcotah	Of Ditto..........	13500	230	Deer-skins, a few Bear, some Beaver, Rackoon, &c.
2nd Band.	People of the Leaves.	Washpetong..	Gens des Feuilles	180	350	530	.	1060	70	160	Ditto	Of Ditto..........	6000	115	Deer-skins, a few Buffalo Robes, some Beaver, Otter, Mink, &c.
			Sioux, carried forward ..	485	950	1730	3	3165	195	465					

OF THE MISSISSIPPI.

Streams, from St. Louis, Louisiana, to its Source, including Red Lake and Lower Red River.

The positions most proper for trading establishments.	Nations with whom at war.	Nations with whom at peace, or in alliance.	Names of the Chiefs or principal Men.			Remarks.
			Indian.	French.	English.	
At the head of the Rapid Des Moines.	Chippeways, ...	Reynards, Puants, Sioux, Osage, Potowatomies, Fols Avoin, Iowas, and all the nations of the Missouri.	Washione. Pockquinike	Bras Cassé........	Broken Arm.	
On a small stream called Giards river, nearly opposite the Prairie des Chiens, or at the confluence of the Mississippi and the Ouisconsin.	Chippeways	Ditto	Olopier .... Pecit............ Akaque.......	Le Petit Corbeau La Peau Blanche	Little Raven. White Skin.	First Fox Chief.
On the Rivers Des Moines and Iowa.	Chippeways .... ,..	Ditto.				
Portage de Kokalin, on Fox river, or at the Grand Calumet.	Since the peace was made between the Osages, Sacs, and Reynards, the Puants have tacitly ceased to make war on the former.	In alliance with the Sacs, Reynards, Fols Avoins, &c., and at peace with all other nations.	New Okat....... Sansamani Chenoway's Son,.. Karamone ...... Du Quarré ..... Macraragah....			First Chief of the nation—received a commission as first chief. Commissioned. Ditto. Ditto. Ditto.
Portage des Peres, on the Fox river.	None	Ottoway, Chippeway, and Ochangras; and at peace with all nations.	Tomaw .... Shawonoe. Neckech.	Thomas Carron..	Thomas Carron...	First chief of the nation—received a commission as first chief and a flag.
....	....	....	Wabasha.........	La Feuille......	The Leaf	First chief of the nation. Literally translated—received a commission and flag.
Entrance St. Croix........	Recently with the Chippeways, but now at peace with the Assiniboins, and some nations on the Missouri.	With the Sacs, Reynards, Iowas, and Fols Avoins.	Talangamane... Chatewaconamani. .... Tahamie........ Tatamane........	L'Aile Rouge Petit Corbeau... L'Orignal Levé. Nez Corbeau.....	The Red Wing....... Little Raven...... ... Rising Moose......... Raven Nose..........	Ditto. Ditto. Received a commission and flag. Literally translated. Literally, the wind that walks: commissioned.
Little Rapids............ Saint Peter's.	} Ditto	Ditto .... {	Wasonquianni ... Wakunsna.... Houho Otah.....	L'AraignéeJaune- Tonnerre qui sonne..........	Yellow Spider , The Rolling Thunder The Stone of Fruit...	First chief of the nation. Literally translated. Received a commission and flag.

VOYAGE TO THE SOURCE

nued.) Abstract of the Number, &c., of the Nations of Indians residing on the Mississippi and its confluer

nes of the fferent na-)ns, as pro-)unced in e English nguage.	Primitive names, as given by the savages themselves.	Names given them by the French.	No. of Warriors.	No. of Women.	No. of Children.	No. of Villages.	Probable No. of Souls.	No. of Lodges of the Roving Bands.	No. of Fire Arms.	Primitive Language.	Traders or Bands with whom they traffic.	Amount of merchandise necessary for their annual consumption.	Annual return of Peltry in packs.	Species of Peltry.
												Dollars	Dols.	
	Sioux, brought forward.		485	950	1730	3	3165	195	485					
iitons	Sussitongs	Sussitongs	360	700	1100		2160	155	260	Narcotah	Of Michillimackinac.	12500	160	Deer-skins and a large proportion of robes, with Furs gathered from the Raven river.
iktons	Yanctong	Yanctong	900	1600	2700		4300	270	350	Ditto	Of Ditto.	8000	130	Principally Buffalo robes.
ons	Titong	Titong	2000	3600	6000		11600	600	100	Ditto	With Yanctongs and part of the Sussitongs.			Buffalo robes.
ple of the saves detched.	Washpeconte	Gens des Féuilles tirées.	90	180	270		450	50	90	Ditto	People of the Prairie des Chiens and on the head of Des Molnes.	2000	30	Deer-skins, Beaver, Otter, Bear, &c.
	Total Sioux		3835	7030	11800	3	21675	1270	1285					
	This is merely a band of vagabonds who are formed by refugees from all the other bands, which they have left for some bad deed.													
ppeways	Ouchipawah.	Sauteurs.												
pers		Sauteurs proper.												
	Of Sandy Lake		45	70	224		334	24		Algonquin	N.-W. Company			Beaver, Muskrat, Otter, Marten, Black and Silver Fox, &c.
	Of Leech Lake	From actual estimate.	150	280	690		1120	65		Ditto	Ditto.			Ditto.
	Of Red Lake		150	260	610		1020	64		Ditto	Ditto			Ditto.
St. Croix and the Chippeway river			104	165	420		689	50		Ditto	Ditto			Ditto.
he other bands generally			1600	2400	4000		8000	400		Ditto	Ditto and others.	Uncertain.		Unknown.
	Total Chippeways		2049	3184	5944		11177	630	2049					

OF THE MISSISSIPPI.

Streams, from St. Louis, Louisiana, to its Source, including Red Lake and Lower Red River.

The positions most proper for trading establishments.	Nations with whom at war.	Nations with whom at peace, or in alliance.	Names of the Chiefs or principal Men.			Remarks.
			Indian.	French.	English.	
Lac de la Grosse Roche, Saint Peter's.	Recently with the Chippeways, but now at peace with the Asiniboins and some nations on the Missouri.	With the Sacs, Reynards, Iowas, and Fols Avoins.	Wacanto........	Esprit Bleu	Blue Spirit.........	First chief of his band.
			Waminisahah....	Killeur Noir.....	Black Eagle.....	Literally translated.
			Itoye	Gross Calumet...	Big Pipe.	
			Wuckieu Nutch..	Tonnerre Rouge.	Red Thunder.......	A literal translation—first chief of all the Sioux.
....	....	....	Petemung.......	La Vache Blanche	White Buffalo.......	Literally translated.
			Muckpesnutah...	Nuage Rouge....	Red Cloud.	Ditto. First Chief of the nation.
			Champanage.			
....	Various nations of the Missouri.	Ditto	Chantaoeteka....	Le Cœur Mauvais	The Bad Heart.......	Of Bois Brulé.
			Shenouskar ,.....	La Couverte Blanche.	White Blanket.......	Okandandas.
			Wamanoepenutah.	Le Cœur du Killeur Rouge.	The Heart of the Red Eagle.	
Prairie des Chiens.......	Ditto	Ditto	Tantangashatah .	Le Bœuf qui Joue	The Playing Buffalo.	Literal translation.
			Kachiwasigon ...	Le Corbean Français.	The French Raven...	Ditto.
Sandy Lake..............	Recently the Sioux; but now at peace. At war with the Sacs, Foxes, and Iowas.	With the Fols Avoins and all the nations of Canada.	Catawabata......	De Broche	Broken Teeth........	First chief of his band.
Leech Lake..............	Ditto	Ditto	Eskibugeckoge ..	Gueule Plate.....	Flat Mouth..........	First chief of his band.
			Obigouitte.	Chef de la Terre..	Chief of the land.	
			Oole	La Brulé....	The Burnt.	
Red Lake...............	Ditto	Ditto	Wisconp.........	Le Sucre.........	The Sweet..........	First chief of his band.
South side of Lake Superior.	Ditto	Ditto.				
....	....	....	Necktame........	Premier..........	Head Chief	Resides on Lac La Pluie river.

RECAPITULATION.

Names of Nations.	No. of Warriors.	No. of Women.	No. of Children.	No. of Villages.	Probable No. of Souls.	No. of Lodges of the Roving Bands.	No. of Fire Arms.
Sacs, - - - - -	700	750	1,400	3	2,850	....	700
Foxes, - - -	400	500	850	3	1,750	....	400
Iowas, - - - - -	300	400	700	2	1,400	....	250
Winebagoes, - -	450	500	1,000	7	1,950	....	450
Menomenes, - - -	300	350	700	7	1,350	....	300
Sioux, - - - - -	3,835	7,030	11,800	3	21,675	1,270	1,265
Chippeways, - -	2,049	3,184	5,944	....	11,177	603	2,049
Total, - - -	8,034	12,714	22,394	25	42,152	1,873	5,414

OBSERVATIONS

ON THE TRADE, VIEWS, AND POLICY OF THE NORTH-WEST COMPANY, AND THE NATIONAL OBJECTS CONNECTED WITH THEIR COMMERCE, AS IT INTERESTS THE GOVERNMENT OF THE UNITED STATES.

THE fur trade in Canada, has always been considered as an object of the first importance to that colony, and has been cherished by the respected governors of that province, by every regulation in their power, under both the French and English administrations. The great and almost unlimited influence, the traders of that country had acquired over the savages, was severely felt, and will long be remembered by the citizens on our frontiers.

Every attention was paid by the cabinet of St James in our treaty with Great Britain to secure to their Canadian subjects the privilege of the Indian trade within our territories, and with what judgment they have improved the advantages they obtained, time will soon unfold.

In the year 1766 the trade was first extended from Michillimackinac to the north-west, by a few desperate adventurers, whose mode of life on the voyage, and short residence in civil society, obtained for them the appellation of Coureurs des Bois   From this trifling beginning arose the present North-West Company, who, notwithstanding the repeated attacks made on their trade, have withstood every shock, and are now, by the coalition of the late X Y Company, established on so firm a basis, as to bid defiance to every opposition that can be made by private individuals. By a late purchase of the king's posts in Canada, they extended their lines of trade from Hudson's bay to the St. Lawrence, up that river on both sides to the lakes, from thence to Lake Superior, at which place the North-West Company have their head-quarters; from thence to the source of Red river, and on all its tributary streams, through the country to the Missouri, through the waters of Lake Winipic to the Saskashawin, on that river to its source, up Elk river to the Lake of the Hills; up Peace river to the Rocky Mountains; from the Lake of the Hills up Slave river to the Slave lake; and this year they have despatched a Mr. Mackenzie on a voyage of trade and discovery down Mackenzie's river to the North Sea, and also a Mr. M'Kay to cross the Rocky Mountains and proceed to the western ocean with the same objects.   They have had a gentleman by the name of Thompson, making a geographical survey of the north-west part of the continent; who for three years, with an astonishing spirit of enterprise and perseverance, passed over all that extensive and unknown country.   His establishment, although not splendid, (the mode of travelling not admitting it) was such as to allow of the most unlimited expenses in everything necessary to facilitate his inquiries, and he is now engaged in digesting the important results of his undertaking.   I find from the observations and suggestions of Mr. Thompson, that when at the source of the Mississippi, it was his opinion the line of limits between the United States and Great Britain must run such a course from the head of the Lake of the Woods, as to touch the source of the Mississippi, and this I discovered to be the opinion of the North-West Company, who, we may suppose, or reasonably conclude, speak the language held forth by their government. The admission of this pretension will throw out of our territory all the upper part of Red river, and nearly two-fifths of the territory of Louisiana, whereas, if the line is run due west from the head of the Lake of the Woods, it will cross Red river nearly at the entrance, and it is conjectured, strike the western ocean at Birch bay in Queen Charlotte Sound. These differences of opinion, it is presumed, might be easily adjusted between the two governments at the present day, but it is believed that delays, by unfolding the true value of the country, may produce difficulties which do not at present exist. The North-West Company have made establishments at several places on the south side of Lake Superior, and at the head waters of the Rivers Sauteaux and St. Croix, which discharge themselves into the Mississippi. The first I met with on the voyage up was at lower Red Cedar lake, about one hundred and fifty miles above the Isle de Corbeau, being on the eastern side of the river, and distant therefrom six miles; it is situated on the north point of the lake, and consists of log buildings flanked by picketed bastions on two right angles. The next establishment I met with was situated on Sandy lake.

The fort at this place is situated on the south side of the lake near the east end, and consists of a stockade of one hundred feet square with bastions, and the south-east and north-west angles pierced for small arms.

The pickets are squared on the outside, and round within, of about one foot in diameter, and are thirteen feet above ground.

There are three gates, the principal one fronts the lake on the north, and is ten feet by nine; the one on the west, six feet by four; the one on the east, six feet by five: as you enter by the main gate you have on the left a building of one story twenty feet square, the residence of the superintendent; opposite to this house on the left of the east gate is a house twenty-five feet by fifteen, the quarters of the men; on entering the west gate you will find the store house on the right, thirty feet by twenty, and on your left a building, forty feet by twenty, which contains rooms for clerks, a work shop and a provision store.

On the west and north-west is an enclosure of about four acres picketed in; in which last year they raised four hundred bushels of potatoes, cultivating no other vegetable; in this enclosure is a very ingeniously constructed vault to contain the potatoes, but which likewise has secret apartments to conceal liquors, dry goods, &c.

Midway between Sandy lake and Leech lake is a small house worthy of notice. On the south-west side of the latter lake from the outlet of the Mississippi, stand the head quarters of the Fond du Lac department.

The fort is situated on the western side of the lake in $47°\ 16'$, $13''$ north latitude; it is built near the shore on the declivity of a rising ground, having an enclosed garden of about five acres on the north-west. It is a square stockade of one hundred and fifty feet, the pickets being fifteen feet in length, three feet under, and thirteen above ground, and are bound together by horizontal bars, each ten feet long; pickets of ten feet are likewise driven into the ground on the inside of the work opposite the apertures between the large pickets. At the west and east angles are square bastions pierced for fire arms. The main building in the rear fronting the lake is sixty feet by twenty-five, one and a half stories high, the west end of which is occupied by the director of the Fond du Lac department: he has a hall eighteen feet square, bed room and kitchen, with an office. The centre is a trading shop of twelve and a half feet square, with a bed room in the rear of the same dimensions, the east end is a large store, twenty-five feet by twenty, under which there is an ice house well filled; the loft extends over the whole building, and contains bales of goods, packs of peltries, also chests containing wild rice; besides the ice house, there are cellars under all the other parts of the building. The door and window shutters are musket proof.

On the western side is a range of buildings, fifty-four by eighteen feet, fronting the parade, the first end of which is a cooper's shop, eighteen feet by fourteen with a cellar, adjoining to which is a room called the Indian hall, (expressly for the reception of the Indians, and in which the chiefs who met me in council were entertained): in this hall are two closed bunks for interpreters; its dimensions are twenty-two feet by eighteen: adjoining to this is a room, eighteen feet square, for the clerks, (in which my small party were quartered); under both of the latter rooms are cellars.

On the eastern side is a range of buildings, fifty feet by eighteen, which has one room twenty feet, and one of fifteen feet, for qarters for the men, also, a blacksmith's shop of fifteen feet, which is occupied by an excellent workman. On the left of the main gate fronting the river is a flag-staff of sixty feet in height.

Missing Page

Missing Page

authority in the country, it would not be in the least astonishing to see them revolt from the limited subjection which is claimed over them by the American government, and thereby be the cause of their receiving chastisement, although necessary, yet unfortunate, as they have been led astray by the policy of the traders of your country. I must likewise observe, Sir, that your establishments, if properly known, would be looked on with an eye of dissatisfaction by our government, for another reason, viz. there being so many furnished posts; in case of a rupture between the two powers, the English government would not fail to make use of these as places of deposit for arms, ammunition, &c. to be distributed to the savages who joined their arms, to the great annoyance of our territory, and the loss of the lives of many of our citizens. Your flags, Sir, when hoisted in enclosed works, are in direct contradiction to the laws of nations, and their practice in the like cases, which only admits of a foreign flag being expanded on board of vessels, and at the residence of ambassadors or consuls.

I am not ignorant of the necessity of your being in such a position as to protect you from the sallies of drunken savages, or the more deliberate plans of the intended plunderer, and under these considerations have I considered your stockades. You and the company to which you belong must be conscious from the foregoing statement, that strict justice would demand, and I assure you the law directs under similar circumstances, a total confiscation of your property, personal imprisonment, and fines; but having discretionary instructions, and no reason to think the conduct above noticed was dictated through ill will or disrespect to our government, and conceiving it in some degree departing from the character of an officer to embrace the first opportunity for executing those laws, I am willing to sacrifice my prospect of private advantage, conscious that the government looks not to interest but to its dignity in the transaction. I have therefore to request of you assurances on the following heads, which, setting aside the chicanéry of law, as gentleman you will strictly adhere to, viz.. That you will make representations to your agents at your head quarters on Lake Superior, of the quantity of goods wanting the ensuing spring for your establishment in the territory of the United States, time sufficient, or as early as possible, for them to enter them at the custom house of Michillimackinac, and obtain a clearance and licence to trade in due form, and that you will give immediate instruction to all your party in the said territory under your direction, at no time and under no pretence whatever, to hoist or suffer to be hoisted the English flag. If you conceive a flag necessary, you may make use of that of the United States, it is the only one which can be admitted. That you will on no future occasion present a flag or medal to an Indian, hold councils with them on political subjects, or others foreign from that of trade; but on being applied to on those heads, will refer them to the American agents, informing them that they are the only persons authorized to hold councils of a political nature with them. There are many other subjects, such as the distribution of liquor, &c., which would be too long to be treated of in detail; but the company will do well to furnish themselves with our

OF THE MISSISSIPPI. 145

laws, regulating the commerce with the savages, and regulate themselves in our territories accordingly. I embrace this opportunity to acknowledge myself and command under singular obligations to yourself and agents for the assistance which you have rendered us, and the polite treatment with which I have been honoured. With sentiments of high respect for the establishment and yourself,

I am, Sir,
Your most obedient servant,
Z. M. PIKE.

To Lieutenant Pike,
First Regiment United States Infantry.

Leech Lake, 15th *February,* 1806.

SIR,
YOUR address presented on the 6th instant, has attracted my most serious consideration to the several objects of duties on importations, of presents made to, and our consultations with the Indians; of enclosing our stores and dwelling houses; and finally, of the custom of hoisting the British flag on the territory belonging to the United States of America. I shall at as early a period as possible present the agents of the North-West Company with your representations regarding the payment of the duties on the importation of goods to be sent to our establishments within the boundaries of the territories of the United States, as also their being entered at the custom house at Michillimackinac; but I beg to be allowed to present for consideration, that the major part of the goods necessary to be sent to the said establishment for the trade of the ensuing winter, are now actually in our stores at Kamanitigua, our head quarters on Lake Superior, and that it would cause us vast expense and trouble to be obliged to convey those goods to Michillimackinac, to be entered at the custom house office: we therefore pray that the word of a gentleman with regard to the quantity and quality of the said goods to be sent to the said establishment, may be considered as equivalent to the certainty of a custom house register. Our intention has never been to injure your traders, paying the duties established by law, and hope those representations to your government respecting our concerns with the Indians may have been dictated with truth, and not exaggerated by envy, to prejudice our interests, and throw a stain upon our character which may require time to efface from the minds of a people to whom we must ever consider ourselves indebted for the lenity of procedure, of which the present is so notable a testimony. The inclosures to protect our stores and dwelling-houses from the insults and barbarity of savage rudeness, have been erected for the security of my property and person, in a country till now exposed to the wild will of the frantic Indians. We never formed the smallest idea that the said inclosures might ever be

useful in the event of a rupture between the two powers, nor do we now conceive that such poor shifts will ever be employed by the British Government: in a country overshadowed with wood, so adequate to every purpose, forts might in a short period of time be built far superior to any stockades we may have occasion to erect.

We were not conscious, Sir, of the error I acknowledge we have been guilty of, by exhibiting to view on your territories any standard of Great Britain. I will pledge myself to your government that I will use my utmost endeavours, as soon as possible, to prevent the future display of the British flag, or the presenting of medals, or the exhibiting to public view any other mark of European power, throughout the extent of the territory known to belong to the dominion of the United States. The custom has long been established, and we innocently and inoffensively (as we imagined) have conformed to it till the present day.

Be persuaded that on no consideration shall any Indian be entertained on political subjects, or on any affairs foreign to our trade, and reference shall be made to the American agents, should any application be made worthy such reference. And be assured that we, as a commercial company, must find it ever our interest to interfere as little as possible with affairs of government, in the course of trade, ignorant as we are in this rude and distant country, of the political views of nations.

We are convinced that the inestimable advantages arising from the endeavours of your government, to establish a more peaceful course of trade in this part of the territory belonging to the United States, are not acquired through the mere liberality of a nation, and are ready to contribute to the expense necessarily attending them. We are not averse to pay the common duties established by law, and shall ever be ready to conform ourselves to all rules and regulations of trade that may be established according to common justice.

I beg leave to be allowed to say, that we have reason to hope that every measure will be adopted to secure and facilitate the trade with the Indians; and these hopes seem to be confirmed beyond the smallest idea of doubt, when we see a man sent among us, who, instead of private consideration to pecuniary views, prefers the honour, dignity, and lenity of his government, and whose transactions are in every respect so conformable to equity.

When we behold an armed force ready to chastise or protect, as necessity or policy may direct, we know not how to express our gratitude to that people whose only view seems to be to promote the happiness of all, the savages that rove over the wild confines of their domain not excepted.

It is to you, Sir, we feel ourselves most greatly indebted, whose claim to honour esteem, and respect will ever be held in high estimation by myself and associates The dangers and hardships by your fortitude vanquished, and by your perseverance overcome, are signal, and will ever be preserved in the annals of the North-West Company. Were it solely from the consideration of those who have exposed their lives in a long and perilous march, through a country where they had every distress to suffer, and many dangers to expect, (and this with a view to establish peace in a savage country,) we should think ourselves under the most strict obligations to assist them; but we know we are in a country where hospitality and gratitude are to be esteemed above every other virtue, and therefore have offered for their relief what our poor means can allow.

And, Sir, permit me to embrace the opportunity to testify, that I feel myself highly honoured by your acceptance of such accommodations as my humble roof could afford.

With great consideration and high respect for the government of the United States, allow me to express my esteem and regard for you.
I am, Sir,
Your most obedient servant,
(Signed) H. M'GILLIS,
Of the North-West Company.

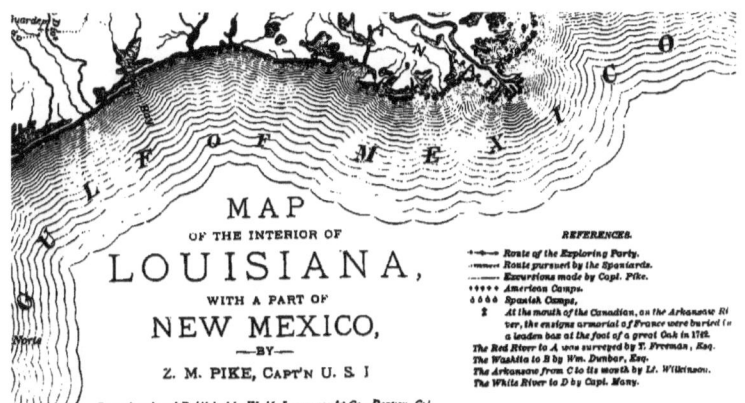

JOURNAL

OF AN

EXPEDITION THROUGH THE INTERIOR OF LOUISIANA, PERFORMED IN THE YEARS 1806 AND 1807.

ON *Tuesday*, the 15th of *July*, 1806, we sailed from the landing at Belle Fontaine, about three o'clock, P. M. in two boats. Our party consisted of two lieutenants, one surgeon, one sergeant, two corporals, sixteen privates, and one interpreter, We had also under our charge chiefs of the Osage and Pawnee nations, who, with a number of women and children, had been to Washington. These Indians had been redeemed from captivity among the Potowatomies, and were now to be restored to their friends at the Osage towns. The whole number of Indians amounted to fifty-one. We ascended the river about six miles, and encamped on the southern side behind an island. This day my boat swung round twice, once when we had a tow-rope on shore, which it snapped off in an instant. The Indians did not encamp with us at night. Distance advanced, six miles.

Wednesday, 16th *July* —We rejoined our red brethren at breakfast, after which we again separated, and with very severe labour arrived late in the evening opposite to the village of St. Charles, where the Indians joined us. Distance advanced, fifteen miles.

From the entrance of the Missouri, on the southern bank, the land is low, until you arrive at Belle Fontaine, four miles from its mouth. In this distance are several strata of soil one above the other. As the river is cutting off the north point and making land on the south, this part is well timbered with oak, walnut, ash, &c. &c. From Belle Fontaine to St. Charles, the northern side of the Missouri is low, bounded on its banks by timbered land extending from half a mile to a mile from the river. On the southern side the bottoms are narrow, the hills frequently coming in on the river. Six miles below St. Charles, on the south, in front of a village called Florissant, is a coal-hill, or as it is termed by the French, La Charbonniere; this is one solid stone hill, which would probably afford sufficient fuel for all the population of Louisiana.

St. Charles is situated on the western side of the Missouri, where the hill first joins the river, and is laid out parallel to the stream. The main street is on the first bank, the second on the top of the hill. In this street is situated a round wood tower, formerly occupied by the Spaniards as a fort or guard-house, but now converted into a prison; from this tower you have an extensive view of the river below. The town consists of about eighty houses, principally occupied by Indian traders or their engagees; it is the seat of justice for the district of St. Charles.

Thursday, 17th *July*.—We crossed the river to learn if any communications had arrived from St. Louis, and if there was any news of the Indian enemies of the Osages. Called at Mr. James Morrison's, and was introduced to a Mr. Henry (of New Jersey) about eight and twenty years of age; he spoke a little Spanish, and French tolerably well; he wished to go with me as a volunteer. From this place I wrote letters back to Belle Fontaine, whilst the Indians were crossing the river.*

A man of the name of Ramsay reported to the Indians that five hundred Sacs, Iowas, and Reynards, were at the mouth of big Manitou; this gave them considerable uneasiness, and it took me some time to do away the impression it made upon them, for I by no means believed it. We were about sailing when my interpreter was arrested by the sheriffs at the suit of Manuel De Liza for a debt of between three and four hundred dollars, and was obliged to return to St. Louis. This made it necessary for me to write another letter to the General. We encamped about three-fourths of a mile above the village.

Friday, 18th *July*.—Lieutenant Wilkinson and Dr. Robinson went with the Indians across the country to the village La Charrette. Mr. George Henry engaged under oath to accompany me on my tour.

Wrote to the General† and enclosed him one of Henry's engagements. After we had made our little arrangements, we marched by land and joined the boats (which had sailed early) at twelve o'clock. Two of the men being sick, I steered our boat, and Mr. Henry the other, by which means we were enabled to keep employed our full compliment of oars,

---
*See Appendix No. I. †See Appendix, No. II.

although we had put the sick men on shore. Encamped on the northern side, about eleven o'clock at night. A tremendous thunder storm arose, and it continued to blow and rain with thunder and lightning until day. Distance advanced, fifteen miles.

Saturday, 19th *July*.—In consequence of the rain, we did not put off until past nine o'clock; my sick men marched on shore. I had some reason to suspect that one of them intended never to join us again. At dinner time the sick man of my own boat came on board; I then went on board the other, and we continued to run races all day, and although this boat had hitherto kept behind, yet I arrived at the encamping ground with her nearly half an hour before the other. The current not generally so strong as below. Distance advanced, fourteen miles.

Sunday, 20th *July*.—Embarked about sun-rise. Wishing to ascertain the temperature of the water, I discovered my large thermometer to be missing, which probably had fallen into the river. Passed one settlement on the northern side, and after turning the point to the south, saw two warehouses on the southern shore. We encamped in a long reach, which bore north of west. The absentees had not yet joined us. Distance advanced, fifteen miles.

Monday, 21st *July*.—It commenced raining near day-break, and continued until four o'clock in the afternoon: the rain was immensely heavy, with thunder and lightning remarkably severe. This obliged me to lay by, for if we had proceeded with our boats, we should necessarily have exposed our baggage much more than when at rest, for the tarpaulin could then cover all.

We set sail at a quarter past four o'clock, and arrived at the village of La Charrette a little after dusk. Here we found Lieutenant Wilkinson and Dr. Robinson with the Indians: also Baroney; our interpreter, with letters from the General and our friends. The weather still continued cloudy, with rain. We were received into the house of a Mr. Chartron, and every accommodation in his power offered us. Distance advanced, six miles.

From St. Charles to the village of La Charrette, the western side we found to be generally low, but with hills running parallel at a great distance from the river: on the southern side more hilly with springs, scattering settlements seen on both sides. La Charrette is the last settlement we saw on the Missouri, although there is one above, at a saline on the western shore.

Tuesday, 22d *July.*—We arranged our boats, dried our loading, and wrote letters for Belle Fontaine

Wednesday, 23d *July.*—I despatched an express to the General with advertisements relative to Kennerman, the soldier who had deserted.*

We embarked after breakfast, and made good progress. Lieutenant Wilkinson steered one boat, and I the other, in order to detach all the men that we could spare on shore with the Indians. We crossed to the southern side a little below Shepherd river. Dr. Robinson killed a deer, which was the first killed by the party. Distance advanced, thirteen miles.

Thursday, 24th *July.*—We embarked at half past six o'clock; weather very foggy. The Indians proceeded on shore, accompanied by only three of my people. Lieutenant Wilkinson being a little indisposed, I was obliged to let Baroney steer his boat. We made an excellent day's progress, and encamped five miles from the Gasconade river: killed three deer, one bear, and three turkies. Distance advanced, eighteen miles. Only three or four of the Indians arrived; the others encamped a small distance below.

Friday, 25th *July.*—We embarked at half past six o'clock, and arrived at the entrance of the Gasconade river at half-past eight o'clock, at which place I determined to remain the day, as my Indians and foot people were yet in the rear, and had complained to me of being without shoes, leggings, &c. Distance advanced, five miles.

One of our Pawnees did not arrive until late, the other had communicated his suspicion to me, that the Otto, who was in company, had killed him; he acknowledged that he had proposed to him to take out their baggage, and return to St. Louis. The real occasion of his absence, however, was his having followed a large fresh trail up the Gasconade a considerable distance; but finding it lead from the Missouri he examined it, and discovered horses to have been on it; he then left it, joined ours and came in.

This being generally the route taken by the Potowatomies when they go to war against the Osage, it occasioned some alarm. Every morning

---
*See Appendix, No. III.

we were awakened by the mourning of the savages, who commenced crying about daylight, and continued their lamentation for the space of an hour. I made enquiry of my interpreter with respect to this practice, and was informed that it was a custom not only with those who had recently lost their relatives; but also with others, who recalled to mind the loss of some friend, dead long since, who joined the mourners purely from sympathy. They appeared extremely affected, tears ran down their cheeks, and they sobbed bitterly; but in a moment they dry their cheeks and cease their cries. Their songs of grief generally ran thus: "My dear father exists no longer, have pity on me, oh Great Spirit! you see I cry for ever; dry my tears and give me comfort." The warriors' songs are to the following effect: "Our enemies have slain my father, (or mother,) he is lost to me and his family; I pray to you, oh Master of Life! to preserve me until I revenge his death, and then do with me as Thou pleasest."

From La Charrette to the Gasconade river, you find on the north low land heavily timbered; on the south, hills, rivulets, and a number of small creeks, with very high cane. The Gasconade is two hundred yards wide at its entrance, and is navigable at certain seasons a hundred miles. At this time it was backed by the Mississippi, but was clear and transparent above their confluence. On the shore opposite to their junction, commences the line between the Sac Indians and the United States.

Saturday, 26th July.—We commenced at five o'clock to ferry the Indians over the Gasconade, and left the mouth of this river at half-past six o'clock in the afternoon. We met here five Frenchmen who informed us that they had just left the Osage river, and that it was so low they could not ascend it with their canoe. We wrote letters and sent them back by them.*

Dr. Robinson, Baroney, Sparks, and all the Indians encamped about one league above us. Killed one bear, two deer, one otter, three turkies, and one rackoon. Distance advanced, fifteen miles.

Sunday, 27th July.—We embarked at half-past five o'clock, and arrived at the Indians' camp at seven. They had been alarmed the day before, and in the evening sent men back in the trace, and some of the chiefs sat up all night. Breakfasted with them about half past three o'clock; encamped in sight of the Osage river, there being every appearance of rain. We halted thus early in order to give the Indians time to

---

* See Appendix, No. IV.

prepare temporary camps and to secure our baggage. I went out to hunt, and firing at a deer near two of the Indians who were in the woods, they knew the difference of the report of my rifle from their guns, were alarmed, and immediately retired to camp. Distance advanced, thirteen miles.

Monday, 28th *July.*—Embarked at half past five o'clock, and at half past ten arrived in the Osage river; where we stopped, discharged our guns, and bathed. We then proceeded on about six miles, when we waited for and conveyed the Indians across to the western shore; then proceeded to the first island and encamped on the west, Sans Oreille and four or five young men only coming up, the rest encamping some distance behind. Killed one deer, and one turkey: distance advanced, nineteen miles.

From the Gasconade to the entrance of the Osage river, the southern shore of the Missouri is hilly, but well timbered. On the north are low bottoms and heavy timber. In the whole of this space of the Missouri, from its entrance to the Osage river, we find it well timbered, the shores consisting of a rich soil, and very proper for the cultivation of all the productions of our middle and western States. It is timbered generally with cotton wood, ash, oak, pecan, hickory, with some elms; but the cotton wood predominates on all the made bottoms.

Tuesday, 29th *July.*—All the Indians arrived very early, and the Big Soldier, whom I had appointed the officer to regulate the march, was much displeased that Sans Oreille and the others had left him, and said that for that reason he would not suffer any woman to go in the boat, and would thus separate the party; but in truth it was from jealousy of the men whose women went in the boat. He began by flogging one of the young men, and was about to strike Sans Oreille's wife, but was prevented by him and told that he knew he had done wrong, but that the women were innocent. We then conveyed them over and embarked at half past eight o'clock. About twelve o'clock we found the Indians rafting the river, when the first chief of the little Osage, called Tuttasuggy, (or The Wind,) told me that the man whom the Big Soldier struck had not yet arrived with his wife. "But that he would throw them away." As I knew he was extremely mortified at the dissensions which appeared to reign amongst them, I told him by no means, that one of my boats should wait for the woman and her child, but that the man might go to the devil as a punishment for his insubordination.

THE INTERIOR OF LOUISIANA.

I then left Baroney with one boat and proceeded with the other. We were called ashore by three young Indians, who had killed some deer, and on putting them aboard I gave them about one or two gills of whiskey, which intoxicated them all. It commenced raining about one o'clock, and continued incessantly for three hours, which obliged us to stop and encamp. One of our men (Millar) lost himself, and did not arrive until after dark. Killed five deer, one turkey, and one rackoon. Distance advanced, fourteen miles.

Wednesday, 30th *July*.—After the fog dispersed, I left Lieutenant Wilkinson with the party to dry the baggage, and I went out with Dr. Robinson and Bradley. About two o'clock we returned, set sail, and having passed the first rapid about three miles, encamped on the eastern shore. Killed three deer. Distance advanced, five miles.

Thursday, 31st *July*.—We embarked early, and passed several rapids pretty well. Dined with the Indians; two of them left us in the morning for the village, and they all had an idea of doing the same, but finally concluded otherwise. One of the Osage, who had left the party for the village, returned, and reported that he had seen and heard strange Indians in the woods; this we considered as merely a pretext to come back. I this day lost my dog and the misfortune was the greater, as we had no other that would bring any thing out of the water; this was the dog Mr. Fisher presented to me at Prairie des Chiens. Killed three deer, and one turkey. Distance advanced, eighteen miles.

Friday, 1st *August*.—It having rained all night, the river appeared to have risen about six inches. We spread out our baggage to dry, but it continuing to rain by intervals all day, the things were wetter at sun-down than in the morning; we rolled them up and left them on the beach. We sent out two hunters in the morning, one of whom killed three deer: the Indians killed three more.

Saturday, 2d *August*.—The weather cleared up; the loading being spread out to dry, Dr. Robinson, myself, Bradley, Sparks and Brown, went out to hunt; we killed four deer, and the Indians two. Having reloaded the boats we embarked at five o'clock, and proceeded about two miles. The river rose in the last twenty-four hours four inches.

Sunday, 3d *August*.—Embarked early, and wishing to save the fresh I pushed hard all day. Sparks was lost and did not join us until night.

We encamped about twenty-five paces from the river on a sand-bar. Near daylight I heard the sentry observe that the boats had better be brought in; when I got up I found the water within a rod of our tent, and before we could get all our things out it had reached the tent. Distance advanced, eighteen miles. Killed nine deer, one wild cat, one goose, and one turkey.

Monday, 4th *August.*—We embarked early, and continued on for some time, not being able to find a suitable place to dry our things; but at length stopped on the eastern shore. Here we had to ferry the Indians over a small channel which we did not before observe; all of them however not arriving we put off, and continued our route. Finding our progress much impeded by our mast I unshipped it, and stripped it of its iron, and after Lieutenant Wilkinson had carved our names on it, set it adrift followed by the yards; this mast had been cut and made at Pine Creek, on the Upper Mississippi.

After proceeding some miles, we found the Indians on the western shore, they having rafted the river; we stopped for them to cook, after which we proceeded. The navigation had become very difficult from the rapidity of the current, occasioned by the rise of the water, which rose one foot in an hour: killed two deer. Distance advanced, ten miles; weather rainy.

Tuesday, 5th *August.*—We lay by this day, in order to give the Indians an opportunity to dry their baggage. Dr. Robinson and myself, accompanied by Mr. Henry, went out to hunt; we lost the latter about two miles from camp: after hunting some time on the western shore, we concluded to raft the river, which we effected with difficulty and danger, and hunted for some time, but without success: we then returned to the party, and found Mr. Henry had arrived one hour before us; he had met one of the soldiers, who brought him in. To-day, in our tour, I passed over a remarkably large rattle-snake as he lay coiled up, and trod so near as to touch it with my foot, it drawing itself up to make room for my heel; Dr. Robinson, who followed me, was on the point of treading on it, but by a spring avoided it: I then turned round and touched it with my ram-rod, but it shewed no disposition to bite, and appeared quite peaceable: the gratitude which I felt towards it for not having bitten me, induced me to save its life. Killed four deer: river risen thirteen inches; rain continued.

THE INTERIOR OF LOUISIANA. 157

Wednesday, 6th *August.*—We embarked at half past eight o'clock, the weather having cleared, and presenting the appearance of a fine day. Passed Gravel river, on the west; about three miles above this river, the Indians left us and informed me that by keeping a little to the south or west, they would make in fifteen miles what would be at least thirty-five miles for us along the course of the river. Dr. Robinson, Mr. Henry, and Sergeant Ballenger accompanied them. Killed two deer. Distance advanced, thirteen miles.

From the entrance of the Osage river to the Gravel river, a distance of one hundred and eighteen miles, the banks of the former are covered with timber, and consist of a very rich soil. Small hills with rocks alternately border the eastern and western shores: the bottoms being very excellent soil and the country abounding in game.

Thursday, 7th *August.*—Not being detained by the Indians we were for once enabled to embark at a quarter past five o'clock. The river having subsided since yesterday morning about four feet, we wished to improve every moment of time previously to its entire fall. We proceeded extremely well, passed the Saline river on the east, and encamped opposite La Belle Roche on the western shore. This day we passed many beautiful cliffs on both sides: saw a bear and a wolf swimming the river. I employed myself part of the day in translating into French a talk of Lieutenant Wilkinson's to the Cheveu Blanc. Distance advanced, twenty-one miles.

Friday, 8th *August.*—We embarked twenty minutes past five o'clock; found the river had fallen about two feet during the night. At the confluence of the Yungar with the Osage river we breakfasted; encamped at night on a bar. Distance advanced, twenty-one and a half miles.

From the Gravel river to the Yungar the Osage continues to exhibit the appearance of a rich, well timbered country. The Yungar (or Nehem-gar) as termed by the Indians, derives its name from the vast number of springs at its source: it is supposed to be nearly as extensive as the Osage river; is navigable for canoes one hundred miles, and is celebrated for the abundance of bears which are found on its branches. The Chasseurs du Bois of Louisiana hunt on it; they consist of Osage and Creeks, (or Muskogees) a wandering party of whom have established themselves in Louisiana, between whom and the French hunters frequent skirmishes have passed on the head of this river.

Saturday, 9th *August.*—We embarked at five o'clock, and at half past six met the Indians and our gentlemen. They had met with nothing extraordinary: they had killed in their excursion seven deer and three bears. We proceeded to an old wintering ground, where there were eight houses, which were occupied last winter by ———, who had not been able to proceed any higher for want of water. Passed the Old Man's rapid, below which, on the western shore, are some beautiful cliffs. Dined with the Indians, after which we passed Upper Gravel river on the west; Potatoe river on the east. Sparks went out to hunt and did not arrive at our encampment, nor did the Indians. Distance advanced, twenty-five miles.

Sunday, 10th *August.*—Embarked at quarter past five o'clock, when the sun shone out very clearly, but in fifteen minutes it began to rain, and continued to rain very hard until one o'clock. Passed the Indians, who were encamped on the western shore, about half a mile from the river, and halted for them; they all forded the river except Sans Oreille, who brought his wife up to the boats, and informed me that Sparks had encamped with them, but had left them to return in search of us. We proceeded after breakfast: Sparks arrived just at the moment we were embarking.

The Indians traversing the country on the east, had sent Sparks with Sans Oreille. About two o'clock, A. M. split a plank in the bottom of the batteau, unloaded and turned her up; repaired the breach, and continued on the route. By four o'clock found the Indians behind a large island; we made no stop and they followed us. We encamped together on a bar; where we proposed halting to dry our corn, &c. Killed four deer: distance advanced, eighteen and a half miles.

Monday, 11th *August.*—We remained here to dry our corn and baggage. This morning we had a match at shooting: the prize offered to the successful person was a jacket and a twist of tobacco, which I myself was so fortunate as to win; I made the articles, however, a present to the young fellow who waited on me. After this, taking Huddleson with me, I went out to hunt. Having travelled about twelve miles, we arrived at the river almost exhausted with thirst: I here indulged myself by drinking plentifully of the water, and was rendered so extremely unwell by it, that I was scarcely capable of pursuing my route to the camp. On arriving

THE INTERIOR OF LOUISIANA.

opposite to it, I swam the river, from which I experienced considerable relief. The party informed me that they had found the heat oppressive, and the mercury at sun-down was at 25° Reaumeur. This day I saw trout for the first time west of the Alleghany Mountains. Reloaded our boats, and finished two new oars which were wanted.

Tuesday, 12th *August*.—Previously to our embarkation, which took place at half past five o'clock, I was obliged to convince my red brethren, that, if I protected them, I would not suffer them to plunder my men with impunity: for the chief had got one of my lads' fur cap attached to his baggage, and notwithstanding it was marked with the initials of the soldier's name he refused to give it up; on which I requested the interpreter to tell him, "that I had no idea that he had purloined it, but supposed some other person had attached it to his baggage; but that knowing it to be my soldier's I requested him to deliver it up, or I should be obliged to take other measures to obtain it." This had the desired effect, or I certainly should have put my threats into execution, from this principle, formed by experience during my intercourse with Indians, that if you have justice on your side, and do not enforce it, they universally despise you.

When we stopped for dinner one of my men took his gun and went out: not having returned when we were ready to re-embark, I left him. Passed the Indians twice when they were crossing the river. Passed some very beautiful cliffs on the western shore; also, Vermillion and Grand rivers, the latter of which is a large stream.

Immediately after encamping, a thunder-squall came on, which blew overboard my flag-staff and a number of articles of my clothing, which were on the top of the cabin, and sunk them immediately. Being much fatigued, and the bank difficult of ascent, I lay down in the cabin without supper, and slept all night: it continued to rain. The man I left on shore arrived on the opposite bank in the night, having killed two deer, but was obliged to leave the largest behind; finding he was not to be sent for, he concealed his gun and deer and swam the river. Distance advanced twenty-four miles.

Wednesday, 13th *August*.—It continued to rain. In the morning sent a boat over for Sparks's gun and deer. Embarked at half past nine o'clock. Stopped to dine at two: during the time we halted, the river rose over the flat bar on which we were; this, if we had no other proof, would convince us we were near the head of the river, as the rain must have reached it. We made almost a perfect circle, so that at night I do not believe we were three miles from where we encamped last night. This day for the first time we saw prairie hills. Distance advanced, thirteen miles.

Thursday, 14th *August*.—Embarked at half past five o'clock; passed the park, which is ten miles round, and not more than three-quarters of a mile across, bearing from S. 5° E. to due N. At its head we breakfasted, and just as we were about to put off, we saw and brought to a canoe, manned with three engagees of Mr. ———, who informed us that the Little Osage had marched a war party against the Kanses, and the Grand Osage a party against our citizens on the Arkansaw river. Wrote by them to the General and all friends.*

Gave the poor fellows some whiskey and eight quarts of corn, they having had only two turkies for four days. We left them and proceeded very well in the afternoon, and encamped on an island above Turkey island. Distance advanced, twenty-eight miles.

Shortly after we left the Yungar river, the Osage became narrower, and evidently shewed the diminution occasioned by the loss of the waters of the former stream. On the eastern shore is a pond of water about twenty paces from the bank, half a mile in circumference; it is elevated at least twenty feet above the surface of the river: this appeared the more singular, as the soil seemed to be sandy, whence it might be concluded that the water of the pond would speedily discharge through the soil into the river; but there appeared to be no reason for any such deduction. From hence to a few miles below the park, the banks of the river continued as usual. We now, for the first time, were entertained with the sight of prairie land, but it was still interspersed with clumps of wood land, which diversified the prospect. In this district the cliffs, which generally bordered one of the sides of the river, were covered with the largest and most beautiful cedars I ever beheld.

Friday, 15th *August*.—We embarked at five o'clock, and at eight met the Indians and the gentlemen who accompanied them; found all well: they had been joined by their friends and relatives from the village, with horses to transport their baggage. Lieutenant Wilkinson informed me that their

---

* See Appendix, No. V.

THE INTERIOR OF LOUISIANA.   161

meeting was very tender and affectionate. "Wives throwing themselves into the arms of their husbands; parents embracing their children, and children their parents; brothers and sisters meeting, one from captivity, the others from the towns; at the same time returning thanks to the GOOD GOD for having brought them once more together." In short, the *tout ensemble* was such as might have made polished society blush, when compared with these savages, in whom the passions of the mind, either joy, grief, fear, anger, or revenge, have their full scope. Why can we not correct the baneful passions, without weakening the good? Sans Oreille made them a speech, in which he remarked, "Osage, you now see your wives, your brothers, your daughters, your sons, redeemed from captivity. Who did this? Were they the Spaniards? No! The French? No! Had either of those people been governors of the country, your relatives might have rotted in captivity, and you never would have seen them more. But the Americans stretched forth their hands, and they are restored to you! What can you do in return for all this goodness? Nothing. All your lives would not suffice to repay their bounty." This man had children in captivity, not one of whom were we able to obtain for him!

The chiefs then requested that Lieutenant Wilkinson and Dr. Robinson might be permitted to accompany them by land, which I consented to. Wrote a letter to the Cheveu Blanc by Mr. Wilkinson. When we parted (after delivering the Indians their baggage) Sans Oreille put an Indian on board to hunt, or obey any other commands I might have for him. We stopped at eleven o'clock to dry our baggage; found our biscuit and crackers almost all ruined. Put off at half past four o'clock, and encamped at three quarters past five. Distance advanced, fifteen and a half miles.

Saturday, 16th *August*.—We embarked at five o'clock, and proceeded extremely well in the barge to a French hunting camp (evacuated) twelve miles to breakfast: the batteau coming up late, we exchanged hands. About twelve o'clock passed the Grand Fork, which is equal in size to the branch of the river on which we pursued our route. Waited to dine at the rocks called the Swallow's Nest on the western shore, above the Forks. The batteau having gained nearly half an hour, the crews are convinced that it is not the boat but the men who make the difference. Each took their own boat, after which we proceeded very well, the water being good and the men in spirits. Saw one elk on the shore, also met an old man alone hunting, from whom we obtained no information of consequence Encamped on the western shore at Mine river: passed the place where the chief called the Belle Oiseau and others were killed.* Distance advanced, thirty-seven miles.

Sunday, 17th *August.*—We embarked at five o'clock, and proceeded twelve miles to breakfast; at four o'clock arrived at ten French houses on the eastern shore, where then resided a Sac, who was married to an Osage woman, and spoke French only. We afterwards passed the position where Mr. Chouteau formerly had his fort, not a vestige of which was remaining; the spot being only marked by the superior growth of vegetation. Here the river bank is one solid bed of stone coal; just below which is a very shoal and rapid ripple. From hence to the village of the Grand Osage the distance is nine miles across a large prairie, but by water fifty. We came about two miles above, and encamped on the western shore. This day the river has been generally bounded by prairies on both sides. Distance advanced forty-one and a half miles.

Monday, 18th *August.*—We put off at half past five o'clock. Stopped at nine o'clock to breakfast. Passed the second fork of the river at twelve o'clock, the right hand fork bearing north, about thirty yards wide, the left (the one we pursued) N. 60° W. and not more than fifty or sixty feet in width, very full of old trees, &c., but having plenty of water. Observed the road where the chiefs and Lieutenant Wilkinson had crossed. We proceeded till one o'clock, when we were halted by a large drift quite across the river. Despatched Baroney to the village of the Grand Osage, to procure horses to take our baggage nearer to the towns. Unloaded our boats, and in about two hours Lieutenant Wilkinson with Tattassuggy arrived at our camp: the former of whom presented me with an express

---

* The Belle Oiseau was killed by the Sacs in the year 1804, in a boat of Manuel de Liza, when on his way down to St. Louis, in order to join the first deputation of his nation, who were forwarded to the seat of government by Governor Lewis. A particular relation of the event has no doubt been given by that gentleman. This chief had a son who accompanied me to the Pawnee nation, who for his honourable deportment, attachment to our government, amiableness of disposition, and the respect and esteem with which he was held by his compeers, is entitled to the attention of our agents to his nation.

THE INTERIOR OF LOUISIANA.

from the General,* and letters from my friends. The chiefs remained at our camp all night. I was attacked by a violent head-ache. It commenced raining, and continued with great force until day. Distance advanced, nineteen miles and a quarter.

Tuesday, 19th *August.*—We commenced very early to arrange our baggage, but had not finished at one o'clock, when the chief of the Grand Osage and forty or fifty men of his village arrived with horses. We loaded and took our departure for the place where Manuel de Liza had his establishment, at which we arrived about four o'clock, and commenced pitching our encampment near the edge of the prairie. I was here informed that three men had arrived from St. Louis, sent by Manuel de Liza: I despatched Lieutenant Wilkinson to the village with Baroney, who brought to camp the man who had charge of the others from St. Louis; he having no passport, I detained him for farther consideration.

Our reception by the Osage was flattering, and particularly by the Cheveu Blanc or *White Hair*, and our fellow travellers. This evening there arrived in the village of the Grand Osage an express from the Arkansaw; who brought intelligence, that a boat ascending that river had been fired on, and had had two white men killed and two wounded, and that the brother-in-law of the Cheveu Blanc, who happened to be on board, was also killed. This put the whole village in mourning.

Wednesday, 20th *August.*—About twelve o'clock I despatched Baroney for the chiefs of the Grand village, in order to give the General's parole to the Cheveu Blanc; also a young man to the village of the Little Osage. The Cheveu Blanc and his people arrived about three o'clock, and after waiting some time for The Wind and his people, I just informed the chiefs that I had merely assembled them to deliver the parole of the General, and present marks of distinction intended for the Cheveu Blanc and his son; at the same time hanging a grand medal round the neck of the latter. The packets committed to my charge for the relations of the deceased Osages were then delivered to them; the widows making the distribution. It must be remarked, that I had merely requested the Cheveu Blanc to come with his son and receive the General's message; but instead of coming with a few chiefs, he was accompanied by one hundred and eighty-six men, to all of whom we are obliged to give something

---
*See Appendix, No VI.

to drink. When the council was over we mounted our horses and rode to the village: I halted at the quarters of the chief, where we were regaled with boiled pumpkins; we then went to two different houses, and were invited to many others, but declined, promising to pay them a visit previous to my departure and to spend the whole day with them; we then returned to camp. After enquiring of the Cheveu Blanc if the men of Manuel de Liza had any ostensible object in view, he informed me that they had only said to him that they expected Manuel would be up to trade in the autumn. I concluded to take the deposition of Babtiste Larme as to the manner in which he was employed by Manuel de Liza, and forward the same to Dr. Brown and the Attorney-General of Louisiana, and permitted the men to return to St. Louis, as it was impossible for me to detach a party with them as prisoners.

Thursday, 21st *August.*—In the morning the Cheveu Blanc paid us a visit, and brought a present of corn, meal, and grease: we invited him, his son, and son-in-law to breakfast with us, and gave his companions something to eat. I then wrote a number of letters to send by express, and enclosed the deposition of Larme. In the afternoon we rode to the village of the Little Osage, and were received by our fellow travellers with true hospitality. Returned in the evening, when a tremendous storm of rain, thunder, and lightning commenced, and continued with extraordinary violence until half-past nine o'clock. It was with great difficulty we were enabled to keep our tents from blowing down. The place prepared for an observatory was carried away.

Friday, 22d *August.*—Preparing in the morning for the council, and committing to paper the heads of the subjects on which I intended to speak. The chiefs of the Little Osage arrived about one o'clock; also the interpreter of the Grand Osage, who pretended to say that the Grand Osage had expected us at their village with the Little Osage. The Cheveu Blanc arrived with his chiefs. The ceremony of the council being arranged, I delivered them the General's *parole* which I had received by express. My reason for not delivering it until this time was that I might have the two villages together, as it equally concerned both. After this I explained at large the will, wishes, and advice of their *Great Father;* and the mode which I conceived to be the most proper for carrying them into effect. The Cheveu Blanc replied in a few words, and promised to give me a full answer to-morrow: The Wind spoke to the same purport. After which the Cheveu Blanc addressed himself to The Wind as follows: "I am shocked at your conduct Tuttassuggy, you who have lately come from the States, and should have been wise; but you led the redeemed captives, with an officer of the United States, to your village, instead of bringing them through my town in the first instance." To this The Wind made no reply, but left his seat shortly after, under pretence of giving some orders to his young men. I conceived this reprimand intended barely to show us the superiority of the one, and inferiority of the other; and to have originated from an altercation of Lieutenant Wilkinson with the Cheveu Blanc, in which allusions were made by the former, to the more friendly conduct of the Little Chief (or The Wind) when compared with that of the latter.

I must here observe, that when the chiefs and prisoners left me, accompanied by Lieutenant Wilkinson, I did not know the geographical situation of the two villages, but conceived, that in going to the Little village, they would pass by the Grand village, and of course that Lieutenant Wilkinson and the chief would arrange the affair properly.

Saturday, 23d *August.*—I expected to have received from the chiefs their answers to my demands, but had an express from both villages informing me that they wished to defer them until to-morrow. I then adjusted my instruments, took equal altitudes, and a meridianal altitude of the sun; but owing to flying clouds missed the immersions of Jupiter's Satellites.

Sunday, 24th *August.*—Was nearly half the day in adjusting the line of culmination in the telescope sights of my theodolite. It began to grow cloudy before evening, and although the sky was not entirely covered, I was so unfortunate as to miss the time of an immersion, and (although clear in the intermediate period) an emersion also. I was informed by Baroney that the Little village had made up eleven horses for us. In the evening, however, the interpreter accompanied by the son-in-law and son of the Cheveu Blanc came to camp, and informed me, that there were no horses to be procured in the village of the Great Osage.*

---

* The following is the substance of the conversation held on this occasion:
The son-in-law spoke as follows: "I am come to give you the news of our village, which is unfortunate for us; our chief having assembled his young men and warriors,

Monday, 25th *August.*—In the morning we were visited by the Cheveu Blanc and three or four of his chiefs, who were pleased to accede to my demands. He found much difficulty in informing me that in all his village he could only raise four horses, but said that we should be accompanied by his son and son-in-law. I then expressed to him the difference of our expectations from the reality.

We remained until after twelve o'clock, when I went to the Little Osage village, and was received with great friendship by the chief. Remained all night at the house of Tuttassuggy. Took the census.

Tuesday, 26th *August.*—Rose early, and found my friends in council, which was merely relative to our horses. The Chief then declared their determination to me, and said that he himself gave me one horse, and lent me eight more to carry our baggage to the Pawnees.

Sold the old batteau for one hundred dollars in merchandize, which I conceived infinitely preferable to leaving her to the uncertain safe-guard of the Indians. About this time we received the news that the party of Potowatomies were discovered to be near the towns; I gave them the best advice I could, and then returned to our camp.

Wednesday, 27th *August.*—Spent in arranging our baggage for the horses. Received four horses from the Little village, and two from the

---

and proposed to them to furnish horses, &c., they have generally refused him, but I, who am the principal man after the Cheveu Blanc, will accompany you."

The son, "Our young men and warriors will not take pity on my father, nor on me, nor on you, and have refused to comply with your request. But I will accompany you with two horses to carry provision for your voyage."

The interpreter: "The Cheveu Blanc was ashamed to bring you this answer, but will again assemble his village, and to-morrow will come himself and give you the answer."

I replied: "That I had made the demand without explanation, merely to let the Osage act agreeably to their inclination, in order that we might see what disposition they would manifest towards us. But why do I ask of their chiefs to follow me to the Pawnees; is it for our good or their own? Is it not to make peace with the Kanses, to put their wives and children out of danger? As to the horses which they may furnish us, I will pay them for their hire; but it is uncertain whether I can pay them here, or give them an order on the superintendent of Indian affairs at St. Louis; but this I do not now wish them to be made acquainted with."

THE INTERIOR OF LOUISIANA.

Grand village. In the evening Lieutenant Wilkinson rode to the latter. I observed two immersions of Jupiter's Satellites.

Thursday, 28th *August.*—Wrote to the Secretary at War, and the General; and made arrangements for our departure. Visited by The Wind, and Sans Oreille.

Friday, 29th *August.*—Forenoon occupied in writing letters. In the afternoon Dr. Robinson and myself went to the Grand village, at which we saw the great medicine dance. Remained at the village all night.

Saturday, 30th *August.*—Returned to the camp after settling all my affairs at the town. Sealed up our despatches, and sent off the General's express.*

In the afternoon we were visited by the principal men of the Little village, and the chief, to whom I presented a flag, and made the donations which I conceived requisite to the different Indians, on account of horses, &c.

Sunday, 31st *August.*—Arranging our packs, and loading our horses, in order to fit our loads, as we expected to march on the morrow. Up late writing letters.

Monday, 1st *September.*—Struck our tents early in the morning, and commenced loading our horses. We now discovered that an Indian had stolen a large black horse, which the Cheveu Blanc had presented to Lieutenant Wilkinson. I mounted a horse to pursue him, but the interpreter went to town, and the Chief's wife sent another in its stead. We left this place about twelve o'clock, with fifteen loaded horses. Our party, consisting of two lieutenants, one doctor, two sergeants, one corporal, fifteen privates, two interpreters, three Pawnees, and four chiefs of the Grand Osage, amounting in all to thirty warriors and one woman. We crossed the Grand Osage fork, and a prairie, N. 80° W. five miles to the fork of the Little Osage: distance, eight miles. Joined by Sans Oreille and seven Little Osages, all of whom I equipped for the march.

The country round the Osage villages is one of the most beautiful that the eye ever beheld. The three branches of the river, viz., the large eastern fork, the middle one, (up which we ascended,) and the northern, all winding round and past the villages, giving the advantages of wood and water, and at the same time the extensive prairie, crowned with rich and

---
*See Appendix, No. VII.

luxuriant grass and flowers, gently diversified by rising swells and sloping lawns, presenting to the warm imagination the future seats of husbandry, the numerous herds of domestic animals, which are no doubt destined to crown with joy these happy plains. From the last village on the Missouri to the prairie on the Osage river, we found plenty of deer, bears, and some turkies; from thence to the towns are some elk and deer, but near the villages they become scarce.

The Osage Indians appear to have emigrated from the north and west, and from their speaking the same language with the Kanses, Ottoes, Missouries, and Mahaws, together with one great similarity of manners, morals, and customs, there is left no room to doubt that they were originally the same nation; but separated by those great laws of nature, self-preservation, the love of freedom, and the ambition of various characters, so inherent in the breast of man. As nations purely erratic must depend solely on the chase for subsistence, (unless pastoral, which is not the case with our savages,) it requires large tracts of country to afford food for a very limited number of souls; consequently self-preservation obliges them to expand themselves over a large and extensive district. The power of certain chiefs becoming unlimited, and their rule severe, added to the passionate love of liberty, and the ambition of their young, bold, and daring characters, who step forward to head the mal-contents, and like the tribes of Israel, to lead them through the wilderness to a new land, the land of promise, which flowed with milk and honey (alias, abounding with deer and buffalo); these characters soon succeeded in leading forth a new colony, and in process of time establishing a new nation. The Mahaws, Missouries, and Ottoes, remained on the banks of the Missouri river, such a distance up as to be within the reach of that powerful enemy, the Sioux, who, with the aid of the small-pox, which the former nations unfortunately contracted by their connection with the whites, have reduced the Mahaws, formerly a brave and powerful nation, to a mere cypher, and obliged the Ottoes and Missouries, who now form but one nation, to join their forces. The Kanses and Osages came farther to the east, and thereby avoided the Sioux, but fell into the hands of the Iowas, Sacs, Kickapoos, Potowatomies, Delawares, Shawonoes, Chreokees, Chickasaws, Choctaws, Arkansaws, Chaddoes, and Ietans; and what astonished me extremely, was, that they have not been entirely destroyed by those nations: but this must be

THE INTERIOR OF LOUISIANA.

attributed only to their ignorance of the enemy's force, their want of concert, wars between themselves, and the great renown the invaders always acquire by the boldness of the enterprise, on the mind of the invaded.

The government of the Osages is oligarchical, but still partakes of the nature of a republic; for although the power is nominally vested in a small number of chiefs, yet they never undertake any matter of importance without first assembling the warriors, and proposing the subject in council, there to be discussed and decided on by a majority. Their chiefs are hereditary in most instances, but there are many men who have risen to more influence than those of illustrious ancestry, by their activity and boldness in war. Although there is no code of laws, yet there is a tacit acknowledgment of the right which some have to command on certain occasions; whilst others are bound to obey, and even to submit to corporal punishment, as was instanced in the affair related in my diary of the 29th of July, when Has-ha-ke-da-tungar (or the Big Soldier) whom I had made a partizan to regulate the movements of the Indians, flogged a young Indian with arms in his hands. On the whole, the government may be termed an oligarchical republic, where the chiefs propose, and the people decide on all public acts.

The manners of the Osage are different from those of any nation I ever saw, (except those before mentioned of the same origin,) having their people divided into classes, all the bulk of the nation being warriors and hunters, the terms being almost synonymous with them; the rest are divided into two classes, cooks and doctors, the latter of whom likewise exercise the functions of priests or magicians, and have great influence on the councils of the nation, by their pretended divinations, interpretations of dreams, and magical performances, an illustration of which will be better given by the following incident, which took place during my stay: Having had all the doctors, or magicians, assembled in the lodge of Ca-ha-ga-tonga, (or Cheveu Blanc,) and about five hundred spectators, they had two rows of fires prepared, around the spot where the sacred band was stationed. They commenced the tragic comedy, by putting a large butcher's knife down their throats, the blood appearing to run during the operation very naturally. The scene was continued by putting sticks through their noses, swallowing bones, and taking them out of the nostrils, &c.: at length one fellow demanded of me what I would give if he would run a stick through his tongue, and let another person cut off the piece? I replied, a shirt; he then apparently performed his promise seemingly with great pain, forcing a stick through his tongue, and then giving a knife to a by-stander, who appeared to cut off the piece, which he held to the light for the satisfaction of the audience, then joined it to his tongue, and by a magical charm healed the wound immediately. On demanding of me what I thought of the performance? I replied, I would give him twenty shirts, if he would let me cut off the piece from his tongue. This disconcerted him a great deal, and I was sorry I made the observation.

The cooks are either for the general use, or attached particularly to the family of some great man; and what is more singular is, that frequently persons who have been great warriors, and brave men, having lost all their families by disease or in war, and themselves becoming old and infirm, frequently take up the profession of a cook, in which they do not carry arms, and are supported by the public, or by their particular patron. They likewise exercise the functions of town criers, calling the chiefs to council, or to feasts; and if any particular person is wanted, you employ a crier, who goes through the village calling his name, and informing him he is wanted at such a lodge.

When received into the Osage village, you immediately present yourself at the lodge of the chief, who receives you as his guest, where you generally eat first, after the old patriarchal style; you are then invited to a feast by all the great men of the village, and it would be a great insult not to comply, at least so far as to taste of their victuals. In one instance I was obliged to taste of fifteen different entertainments in the same afternoon. You will hear the cooks crying, come and eat, such a one gives a feast, come and eat of his bounty. Their dishes were generally boiled sweet corn in buffalo grease, or boiled meat and pumpkins; but Sans Oreille (or Tetobah) treated me with some tea in a wooden dish, new horn spoons, boiled meat and crullers; he had been in the United States.

Their towns hold more people in the same space of ground than any place I ever saw; their lodges being posted with scarcely any regularity, each individual building in the manner, direction and dimensions that suit him best; by which means they frequently leave only room for a single man to squeeze between them. Added to this, they have pens for their

THE INTERIOR OF LOUISIANA.

horses, all within the village, into which they always drive them at night, in case they think there is any reason to believe an enemy to be lurking in the vicinity. The Osage lodges are generally constructed with upright posts, put firmly in the ground, about twenty feet in height, with a crotch at the top. They are generally about twelve feet distant from each other. In the crotch of these posts are put the ridge poles, over which are bent small poles, the ends of which are brought down and fastened to a row of stakes, of about five feet in height; these are fastened together with three horizontal bars, and form the flank walls of the lodge. The gable ends are generally broad slabs, and rounded off to the ridge pole. The whole of the building and sides are covered with matting made of rushes of two or three feet in length, and four feet in width, which are joined together, and entirely exclude the rain. The doors are in the side of the building, and there is generally one on each side; the fires are made in holes in the centre of the lodge, the smoke ascending through apertures left in the roof for the purpose. At one end of the dwelling is a raised platform about three feet from the ground, which is covered with bear skins, and generally holds all the little choice furniture of the master, and on this repose his honourable guests. In fact, with neatness and a pleasing companion, they compose a very comfortable and pleasant summer habitation; but they are left in the winter for the woods: they vary in length from thirty-six to one hundred feet.

The Osage nation is divided into three villages, and in a few years you may say nations, viz., the Grand Osage, the Little Osage, and those of the Arkansaw. The Little separated from the Grand Osage about two years since; and their chiefs, on obtaining permission to lead forth a colony from the grand council of the nation, moved on to the Missouri; but after some years, finding themselves too hard pressed by their enemies, they again obtained leave to return and put themselves under the protection of the Grand village, and settled down about six miles off. The Arkansaw schism was effected by Mr. Pierre Chouteau, ten or twelve years ago, in revenge of Mr. Manuel de Liza, who had obtained from the Spanish government the exclusive trade of the Osage nation by the way of the Osage river, after it had been in the hands of M. Chouteau for nearly twenty years; the latter leaving the trade of the Arkansaw, thereby nearly rendered abortive, the exclusive privilege of his rival. He has been vainly promising to the government, that he would bring them back to join the Grand village, but his reception at the Arkansaw village must have nearly cured him of that idea. And in fact every reason induces a belief, that the other villages are much more likely to join the Arkansaw, which is daily becoming more powerful, than the latter return to its ancient residence; for the Grand and Little Osage are both obliged to proceed to the Arkansaw every winter to kill the summer provision: all the nations with whom they are now at war are besides situated to the westward of that river, from whence they get all their horses. These inducements are such, that the young, the bold, and the enterprising are daily emigrating from the Osage village to the Arkansaw village. In fact it would become the interest of our government to encourage that emigration, if they intended to promote the extension of the settlement of Upper Louisiana; but their true policy is to use every method to prevent their elongation from the Missouri.

They are considered by the nations to the south and west of them as a brave and warlike people, but are by no means a match for the northern nations, who make use of the rifle, and can combat them two for one, whilst they again may fight those armed with bows, arrows, and lances, at the same disproportion. The humane policy which the United States have held forth to the Indians of accommodating their differences, and acting as mediators between them, has succeeded to a miracle with the Osage of the Grand village and the Little Osage. They have by this means become a nation of quakers, as it respects the nations to the north and east of them, at the same time that they continue to make war on the naked and defenseless savages of the west. An instance of their forbearance was exhibited by an attack made on a hunting party of the Little Osage some time since, on the Grand river of the Osage, by a party of Potowatomies, who crossed the River Missouri by the Saline, and found the women and children alone and defenceless. The men, fifty or sixty in number, having found plenty of deer the day before, had encamped out all night. The enemy struck the camp about ten o'clock in the morning, killed all the women and boys who made resistance, also some infants, the whole number amounting to thirty-four, and led into captivity near sixty, forty-six of whom were afterwards recovered by the United States, and sent under my protection to the village. When the men returned to the camp, they found their families all destroyed or taken prisoners; my narrator had his wife and four children killed on the spot! and yet in obedience to the injunction of their "Great Father" they forebore to revenge the blow! As an instance of the great influence the French formerly had over this nation, the following anecdote may be interesting: Chtoka (or Wet Stone), a Little Osage, said, "he was at Braddock's defeat, with all the warriors who could be spared from both villages; that they were engaged by Mr. M'Cartie, who commanded at Fort Chartres, and who supplied them with powder and ball; that the general place of rendezvous was near a lake and large fall, (suppose Niagara,) the Kanses did not arrive until after the battle, but that the Ottoes were present; they were absent from their villages seven months,. and were obliged to eat their horses on their return."

The Osage raise large quantities of corn, beans, and pumpkins, which they manage with the greatest economy, in order to make them last from year to year; all the agricultural labour is done by women.

If the government think it expedient to establish factories for the Grand and Little villages, equi-distant from both, which would answer for either, the other establishment should be on the Arkansaw, near the entrance of the Verdigrise river,* for the Arkansaw Osage.

Tuesday, 2d September.—Marched at six o'clock, halted at ten, and at two o'clock on the side of the Creek, our route having been all the time on its borders. I was here informed by a young Indian, that Mr. Chouteau had arrived at the towns. I conceived it proper for me to return, which I did, accompanied by Baroney, first to the Little village, whence we were accompanied by The Wind to the Grand village, where we remained all night at the lodge of the Cheveu Blanc. Mr. Chouteau gave us all the news; after which I scrawled a letter to the General and my friends.

Wednesday, 3d September.—Rose early and went to the Little village to breakfast. After giving my letters to Mr. Henry, and arranging my affairs, we proceeded and overtook our party at two o'clock. They had advanced from their first camp about four miles. Our horses being much fatigued, we concluded to remain all night: sent out our red and white hunters, who, together, only killed two turkies. Distance advanced, four miles.

---

* As stated by Lieutenant Wilkinson. See Appendix, No. X.

Thursday, 4th *September*.—When about to march in the morning, one of our horses was observed to be missing; we left Sans Oreille with the two Pawnees to search for him, and proceeded till about nine o'clock, then stopped until twelve, and afterwards marched again; in about half an hour I was overtaken and informed that Sans Oreille had not been able to find our horse; upon which we encamped and sent two horses back for the load. One of the Indians being jealous of his wife, sent her back for the village.

After making the necessary notes, Dr. Robinson and myself took our horses, and followed the course of the little stream, until we arrived at the Grand river, which was distant about six miles. We here found a most delightful basin of clear water, of twenty-five paces diameter, and about one hundred in circumference, in which we bathed;· found it deep and delightfully pleasant. Nature scarcely ever formed a more beautiful place for a farm. We returned to camp about dusk, when I was informed that some of the Indians had been dreaming, and wished to return. Killed one deer, one turkey, and one rackoon. Distance advanced, thirteen miles.

Friday, 5th *September*.—In the morning our Little Osage Indians all came to a determination to return; and, much to my surprise, Sans Oreille amongst the rest. I had given an order on the chiefs for the lost horse to be delivered to Sans Oreille's wife, previously to my knowing that he was going back, but I took his gun from him, and from all the others. In about five miles we struck a beautiful hill, which bears south on the prairie; its elevation I supposed to be one hundred feet. From its summit the view is sublime, to the east and south-east. We waited on this hill to breakfast, and had to send two miles for water. Killed a deer on the rise, which was soon roasting before the fire. Here another Indian expressed his wish to return; and take his horse with him; which, as we had so few, I could not allow; for he had already received a gun for the use of it. I told him he might return, but his horse would go to the Pawnees. We marched, leaving the Osage trace which we had hitherto followed, and crossed the hills to a creek which was almost dry; descended it to the main river, where we dined. The discontented Indian came up, and put on an air of satisfaction and content. We again marched about six miles further, and encamped at the head of a small creek, about half a mile from the water. Distance advanced, nineteen miles.

THE INTERIOR OF LOUISIANA. 175

Saturday, 6th *September.*—We marched at half past six o'clock, and arrived at a large fork of the Little Osage river, where we breakfasted. In the holes in the creek we discovered many fish, which, from the stripes on their bellies and their spots, I supposed to be trout and bass; they were twelve inches long. This brought to mind the necessity of a net, which would have frequently afforded subsistence to the whole party. We halted at one o'clock, and remained until four. Being told that we could not arrive at any water, we here filled our vessels. At five o'clock arrived at the dividing ridge between the water of the Osage and Arkansaw, or White river; the dry branches of which intersect within twenty yards of each other. The prospect from the dividing ridge, to the east and south-east, is sublime. The prairie rising and falling in regular swells, as far as the sight can extend, produces a very beautiful appearance. We left our course, and struck down to the south-west, on a small creek, or rather a puddle of water. Distance advanced, twenty miles.

Sunday 7th, *September.*—We killed one deer at half past six o'clock, before which we had a difficulty with the son of the chief, which was accommodated. At nine o'clock we came on a large fork, and stopped for breakfast, Proceeded on, and encamped on a fine stream, where we swam our horses, and bathed ourselves. Distanced advanced fifteen miles. Killed four deer.

Monday, 8th *September.*—Marched early, and arrived at a grand fork of the White river. The Indians were all discontented, we had taken the wrong ford; but, as they were dispersed through the woods, we could not be governed by their movements. Previously to our leaving the camp, the son of the Cheveu Blanc proposed returning, and offered no other reason than that he felt too lazy to perform the route. The reasons I urged were ineffectual to prevent his going; and he departed with his hunter, who deprived us of one horse. His return left us without any chief or man of consideration, except the son of the Belle Oiseau, who was but a lad. The former appeared to be a discontented young fellow; and filled with self-conceit; he certainly ought to have considered it an honour to be sent on so respectable an embassy as he was. Another Indian, who owned one of our horses, wished to return with him, which was positively refused him; but fearing he might steal the horse, I contented him with a present. We marched and made the second branch, crossing one prairie, for twelve miles of which we suffered much from drought. Distance advanced, twenty-two miles.

Tuesday, 9th *September*.—Marched at seven o'clock, and struck a large creek at eleven miles distance. On holding a council it was determined to ascend this to the highest point of water, and then strike across to a large river of the Arkansaw. We proceeded four miles and a half, and encamped. Distanced advanced in all twelve miles. Killed one cabrie, two deer, and two turkies.

From the Osage towns to the source of the Osage river, there is no difference in the appearance of the country from that of their vicinity, except that on the south and east, the view on the prairies becomes unbounded. The waters of the White river and the Osage, as above remarked, are divided merely by a small ridge in the prairie, and the dry branches appear to interlock at their head. From thence to the main branch of the said river the country appeared high, with gravelly ridges of prairie land. On the main White river is found large timber and fine ground for cultivation. Hence a doubt arises as to the disemboguing of this stream.—Lieutenant Wilkinson, from some authority, has drawn the conclusion, that it discharges itself into the Arkansaw, a short distance below the Vermillion river; but from the voyage of Captain Many on the White river, the information of hunters, Indians, &c., I am rather induced to believe it to be the White river of the Mississippi, as at their mouths there is not so great a difference between their magnitude; and all persons agree in asserting that the White river heads between the Osage river, Arkansaw, and Kanses rivers, which would still leave the Arkansaw near eight hundred miles longer than the White river. From these proofs I am pretty confident in asserting that this was the White river of the Mississippi which we crossed.* At the place where we traversed it, the stream was amply navigable for canoes, even at this dry season of the year.

Wednesday, 10th *September*.—Marched early, struck and passed the dividing ground between the Grand and the Verdigrise rivers. Stopped to breakfast on a small stream of the latter; after which we marched and

---

*On comparing this passage with the map, Lieutenant Wilkinson appears to have been rightly informed, for the sources of what is here called the White river, of the Mississippi, are laid down, agreeably to Captain Many's survey, considerably farther to the southward.   E.

THE INTERIOR OF LOUISIANA.

encamped on the fourth small stream. Distance advanced, twenty-one miles. Killed one elk and one deer.

Up the Grand river to the dividing ridges between it and the Verdigrise, the bottom is of some magnitude and importance; but the latter river is bounded here by a narrow bed of prairie hills, affording not more than sufficient timber for fire-wood for a limited number of inhabitants for a few years.

Thursday, 11th *September.*—Passed four more branches, and encamped at night on a large branch of Grand river. Killed one cabrie and one deer. Distance advanced, seventeen miles.

Friday, 12th *September.*—Commenced our march at seven o'clock, and passed some very rough flint hills; my feet blistered, and were very sore, Standing on a hill, I beheld in one view below me, buffaloes, elks, deer, cabrie, and panthers. Encamped on the main branch of Grand river, which had very steep banks, and was deep. Dr. Robinson, Bradley and Baroney, arrived after dusk, having killed three buffaloes, which, with one I had killed, and two by the Indians, made in all six. The Indians alleging it was the Kanses hunting ground, said they would destroy all the game they possibly could. Distance advanced, eighteen miles.

Saturday, 13th *September.*—Late in marching, it having every appearance of rain. Halted to dine on a branch of Grand river. Marched again at half-past two o'clock, and halted at five, intending to despatch Dr. Robinson and one of our Pawnees to the village to-morrow. Distance advanced, nine miles. Killed six buffaloes, one elk, and three deer.

Sunday, 14th *September.*—The Doctor, and Frank (a young Pawnee), marched to the village at daylight, and we pursued our route at half-past six o'clock. Halted at one o'clock. On the march we were continually passing through large herds of buffaloes, elk, and cabrie; and I have no doubt but one hunter could support two hundred men.' I prevented the men shooting at the game, not merely because of the scarcity of ammunition, but as I conceived the laws of morality also forbade it. Encamped at sunset on the main branch of White river, hitherto called Grand river.* Distance advanced, twenty-one miles. Killed one buffalo and one cabrie.

---

* On the map they clearly appear as very distinct streams, the latter being a tributary branch of the Arkansaw.   E.

Monday, 15th *September*.—Marched at seven o'clock; passed a very large Kanses encampment evacuated, which had been occupied last summer. Proceeded on to the dividing ridge, between the waters of the White river and the Kanses. Halted at one o'clock very much against the inclination of the Osage; who, from the running of the buffaloes, conceived a party of the Kanses to be near. Distance advanced, eighteen miles. Killed two buffaloes.

From the Verdigrise river our course had lain over gravelly hills, and a prairie country, but well watered by the branches of the Verdigrise, and White or Grand river. From the dividing ridge, which parts these streams, to the source of the latter, there is very little timber. The grass is short, the prairies high and dry; from the head of White river over the dividing ridge between that and the eastern branch of the Kanses river, the land is high and dry, and exhibits many appearances of iron ore; and on the western side some spa springs. Here the country is very deficient of water.

Tuesday, 16th *September*.—Marched late, and in about four miles and a half distance came to a very handsome stream of water, at which we stopped, and remained until after two o'clock, when we pursued our march and crossed two branches, and encamped on the third. At the second creek, a horse was discovered on the prairie, when Baroney went in pursuit of him on a horse of Lieutenant Wilkinson's, but arrived at our camp without success. Distance advanced, thirteen miles.

Wednesday, 17th *September*.—Marched early, and struck the main south-east branch of the Kanses river at nine o'clock; it appeared to be twenty-five or thirty yards wide, and is navigable in the flood seasons. We passed, and proceeded six miles, to a small stream, to breakfast. Game getting scarce, our provisions began to run low. Marched about two o'clock, and encamped at sun down, on another large branch. Killed one buffalo. Distance advanced, twenty-one miles.

Thursday, 18th *September*.—Marched at our usual hour, and at twelve o'clock halted at a large branch of the Kanses, which was strongly impregnated with salt. This day we expected the people of the village to meet us. We marched again at four o'clock, our route being over a continued series of hills and hollows, we were until eight at night before we arrived at a small dry branch; it was nearly ten before we found any water. Commenced raining a little before day. Distance advanced, twenty-five miles.

THE INTERIOR OF LOUISIANA.

Friday, 19th *September.*—It having commenced raining early, we secured our baggage, and pitched our tents. The rain continued without any intermission the whole day; during which we employed ourselves in reading, and in pricking on our arms with India ink some characters which will frequently bring to mind our forlorn and dreary situation, as well as the happiest days of our lives. In the rear of our encampment was a hill, on which there was a large rock where the Indians kept a continual sentinel, as I imagine, to apprise them of the approach of any party, friends or foes, as well as to see if they could discover any game on the prairies.

Saturday, 20th *September.*—It appearing as if we might possibly have a clear day, I ordered our baggage to be spread abroad, but it shortly after clouded up, and commenced raining. The Osage sentinel discovered a buffalo on the prairies; upon which we despatched a hunter on horseback in pursuit of him. Sent also some hunters out on foot, and before night they killed three buffaloes; some of the best of which we brought in, and jirked or dried by the fire. It continued showery until the afternoon, when we put our baggage again in a position to dry, and remained encamped. The detention of the Doctor and our Pawnee ambassador, began to be a matter of serious consideration to us.

Sunday, 21st *September.*—We marched at eight o'clock, although the weather exhibited every appearance of rain; and at eleven o'clock passed a large creek remarkably salt. Stopped at one o'clock on a fresh branch of the salt creek. Our interpreter having killed an elk, we sent out for some meat, which detained us so late that I concluded it best to encamp where we were, in preference to running the risk of finding no water. Lieutenant Wilkinson was attacked with a severe head-ache, and slight fever. One of my men had been attacked with a touch of the pleurisy on the 18th, and was still ill. We were informed by an Osage woman, that two of the Indians, one of whom was her husband, were conspiring to desert us in the night, and to steal some of our horses. We engaged her as our spy. Thus were we obliged to keep ourselves on our guard against our own companions and fellow travellers, men of a nation highly favoured by the United States, but whom I believe to be a faithless set of poltroons, incapable of a great and generous action. Amongst them, indeed, there may be some exceptions.

In the evening, finding the two Indians above mentioned had made all preparations to depart, I sent for one of them who owned a horse, and had received a gun and other property for his hire, and told him, "I knew his plans, and that if he was disposed to desert, I should take care to retain his horse; that as for himself, he might leave me if he pleased, as I only wanted *men* with us." He replied, "that he was a *man*, and that he always performed his promises; that he had never said he would return, but that he would follow me to the Pawnees' village, which he intended to do." He then brought his baggage, and put it under charge of the sentinel, and slept by my fire; but notwithstanding I had him well watched. Distance advanced, ten miles. Killed one elk.

Monday, 22d *September*.—We did not march until eight o'clock, owing to the indisposition of Lieutenant Wilkinson. At eleven waited to dine. Light mists of rain, with flying clouds. We marched again at three o'clock, and continued our route for twelve miles, to the first branch of the Republican fork. Met a Pawnee hunter, who informed us, that the Chief had left the village the day after the Doctor arrived, with fifty or sixty horses and many people, and had taken his course to the northward of our route, consequently we had missed each other. He likewise informed me that the Ietans had recently killed six Pawnees; the Kanses stolen some horses; and that a party of three hundred Spaniards had lately been as far as the Saline, but for what purpose was unknown. Distance advanced, twenty-one miles.

Tuesday, 23d *September*.—Marched early, and passed a large fork of the Kanses river, which I supposed to be the one generally called Solomon's fork. One of our horses fell into the water, and wetted his load. Halted at ten o'clock on a branch of this fork. We marched again at half past one o'clock, and encamped at sun down, on a dry river course where we had great difficulty to find water. We were overtaken by a Pawnee, who encamped with us. He offered his horse for our use. Distance advanced, twenty-one miles.

Wednesday, 24th *September*.—We could not find our horses until late, when we marched. Before noon met Frank (who had accompanied Dr. Robinson to the village), and three other Pawnees, who informed us that the Chief and his party had only arrived at the village yesterday, and had despatched them out in search of us. Before three o'clock we were joined by several Pawnees; one of them wore a scarlet coat, with a small medal of General Washington, and a Spanish medal also. We encamped at sun-set, on a middle-sized branch, and were joined by several Pawnees in the evening, who brought us some buffalo meat. Here we saw some mules, horses, bridles, and blankets, which they had obtained of the Spaniards. Few only had breech cloths, most being wrapped in buffalo robes; otherwise quite naked. Distance advanced, eighteen miles.

Thursday, 25th *September*.—We marched at a good hour, and in about eight miles struck a very large road, along which the Spanish troops had returned; and on which we could yet discover the grass beaten down, in the direction they had taken.

When we arrived within about three miles of the village, we were requested to remain, as the ceremony of receiving the Osage into the towns was to be performed here. There was a small circular spot, clear of grass, before which the Osage sat down. We were a small distance in advance of the Indians. The Pawnees then advanced within a mile of us, and halted; divided into two troops, and came on each flank at full charge, making all the gestures and performing the manœuvres of a real war charge. They then encircled us around, and the Chief advanced in the centre and gave us his hand. His name was Characterick. He was accompanied by his two sons, and a chief by the name of Iskatappe. The Osage were still seated; but the Belle Oiseau then rose, and came forward with a pipe, and presented it to the Chief, who took a whiff or two from it. We then proceeded on; the Chief, Lieutenant Wilkinson, and myself, in front; my sergeant, on a white horse, next, with the colours; then our horses and baggage, escorted by our men; with the Pawnees on each side, running races, &c. When we arrived on the hill above the town, we were again halted, and the Osage seated themselves in a row, when each Pawnee, who intended so to do, presented a horse, and gave a pipe to smoke to the Osage to whom he had made the present. In this manner were eight horses given. Lieutenant Wilkinson then proceeded on with the party to the river above the town, and encamped. As the Chief had invited us to his lodge to eat, we thought it proper for one of us to go. At the lodge he gave me many particulars, which were interesting to us, relative to the late visit of the Spaniards.*

---

*I will here attempt to give some memoranda of this expedition, which was the most important ever sent out of the province of New Mexico; and in fact the only.

I went up to our camp in the evening, having a young Pawnee with me loaded with corn for my men. Distance advanced, twelve miles.

---

one directed to the north-eastward, except that mentioned by the Abbé Raynal, in his History of the Indies, to the Pawnees.

In the year 1806 our affairs with Spain began to wear a very serious aspect, and the troops of the two governments almost came to actual hostilities on the frontiers of Texas and the Orleans territory; at this time, when matters bore every appearance of coming to a crisis, I was fitting out for my expedition from St. Louis, when some of the Spanish emissaries in that country transmitted the information to Major Merior, and the Spanish council at that place, who immediately forwarded the information to Captain Sebastian Roderiques, the then commandant of Nacogdoches, who forwarded it to Colonel Cordero, by whom it was transmitted to the seat of government. This information was personally communicated to me, as an instance of the rapid means they possessed of conveying intelligence relative to the occurrences transacting on our frontiers. The expedition was then determined on; and had three objects in view; first, to descend the Red river, in order if they met our expedition to intercept and turn it back; or should Major Sparks and Mr. Freeman have missed the party from Nacogdoches, under the command of Captain Viana, to oblige them to return, and not penetrate further into the country, or make them prisoners of war.

Secondly, to explore and examine all the internal parts of the country, from the frontiers of the province of New Mexico to the Missouri, between the La Plate and Kanses rivers.

Thirdly, to visit the Ietans, Pawnee republic, Grand Pawnees, Pawnee Mahaws, and Kanses. To the head chief of each of these nations, the commanding officer bore flags, a commission, grand medal, four mules: and with all of them he had to renew the chains of ancient amity, which was said to have existed between their father, his most catholic majesty, and his children, the red people.

The commanding officers also bore positive orders to oblige all parties or persons in the above specified countries, either to retire from them into the acknowledged territories of the United States, or to make prisoners of them, and conduct them into the province of New Mexico.

Lieut. Don Facundo Malgares, the officer selected from the five internal provinces to command this expedition, was an European, and his uncle was at that time one of the royal judges of the kingdom of New Spain. He had distinguished himself in several long expeditions against the Appaches and other Indian nations, with whom the Spaniards were at war; added to these circumstances, he was a man of immense fortune, and generous in its disposal, almost to profusion; possessed a liberal education, a high sense of honour, and a disposition formed for military enterprize.

This officer marched from the province of Biscay, with one hundred dragoons of the regular service, and at Santa Fe, the place where the expedition was fitted out, he was joined by five hundred of the mounted militia of that province, and completely

THE INTERIOR OF LOUISIANA. 183

From the eastern branch of the Kanses river (by our route), to the Pawnee republic, on the Republican fork, the prairies are low, the grass high, the country abounding with salines, and the earth appearing to be impregnated with nitrous and common salts. The immediate borders of the Republican fork near the village consist of high ridges, but this is an exception to the general face of the country. All the territory between the forks of the Kanses river, for a distance of one hundred and sixty miles, may be called prairie, notwithstanding the borders of woodland which ornament the banks of those streams, but are no more than a line traced on a sheet of paper when compared to the immense tract of meadow country. For some distance from the Osage villages, you only find deer, then elk, then cabrie, and finally, buffalo. But it is worthy of remark, that although the male buffaloes were in great abundance, yet in all our route from the Osage to the Pawnees, we never saw one female. I acknowledge myself at a loss to determine, whether this is to be attributed to the decided preference the savages give to the meat of the female, and that consequently they are almost exterminated in the hunting grounds of the nations, or to some physical causes, for I afterwards discovered the

---

equipped with ammunition, &c., for six months; each man leading with him (by order) two horses and one mule. The whole number of their beasts was two thousand and seventy-five. They descended the Red river two hundred and thirty-three leagues. Met the grand bands of the Ietans, held councils with them; then struck off to the north-east, and crossed the country to the Arkansaw, where Lieut. Malgares left two hundred and forty of his men, with the lame and tired horses, whilst he proceeded on with the rest to the Pawnee republic. Here he was met by the chiefs and warriors of the Grand Pawnees; held councils with the two nations, and presented them the flags, medals, &c., which were designed for them. He did not proceed on to the execution of his missions with the Pawnee, Mahaws, and Kanses, as he represented to me, from the poverty of their horses, and the discontent of his own men; but as I conceive, from the suspicion and discontent which began to arise between the Spaniards and the Indians. The former wishing to revenge the death of Villeneuve and his party, whilst the latter possessed all the suspicions of conscious villany, deserving punishment.

Malgares took with him all the traders he found there from our country, some of whom being sent to Natchitoches, were in abject poverty at that place on my arrival, and applied to me for means to return to St. Louis. Lieutenant Malgares returned to Santa Fé in October, when his militia was disbanded; but he remained in the vicinity of that place until we were brought in, when with his dragoons he became our escort to the seat of government.

females with young in such immense herds, as gave me no reason to believe they yielded to the males in numbers.

The Pawnees are a numerous nation of Indians, residing on the rivers Plate and Kanses. They are divided into three distinct nations, two of them being now at war; but their manners, language, customs, and improvements, are in the same degree of advancement. On the La Plate reside the Grand Pawnee village, and the Pawnee Loups on one of its branches, with whom the Pawnee republicans are at war. Their language is guttural, and approaches nearer to that of the Sioux than the Osage; their figure is slim, and their high cheek bones clearly indicate their Asiatic origin; but their emigration south, and the ease with which they live on the buffalo plains, have probably been the cause of a degeneracy of manners; for they are neither so brave nor so honest as their more northern neighbours. Their government is the same as that of the Osage, an hereditary aristocracy; the father handing his dignity of chieftain down to his son: but their power is extremely limited, notwithstanding the long life they have to establish their authority and influence; they merely recommend and give council in the great assemblage of the nation. They are not so cleanly, neither do they carry their internal police so far, as the Osage; but out of the bounds of the village, it appeared to me that they exceeded them, as I have frequently seen two young soldiers come out to my camp and by the strokes of long whips instantly disperse a hundred persons, who were assembled there to trade with my men. In regard to the cultivation of the soil, they are about equal to the Osage, raising a sufficiency of corn and pumpkins to afford a little thickening to their soup during the year. Their pumpkins they cut into thin slices, and dry in the sun, which reduces them to a small size, and not more than a tenth of their original weight. With respect to raising horses, the Pawnees are far superior to the Osage, having vast numbers of excellent cattle, which they are daily increasing by their attention to their breeding mares, which they never use for labour; and in addition, they frequently purchase some from the Spaniards. Their houses are a perfect circle, excepting where the door is placed, from whence there is a projection of about fifteen feet, the whole being constructed after the following manner: There is first an excavation of a circular form, made in the ground, of about four feet deep and sixty in diameter, where there is a row of posts, about five feet high, with crotchets

THE INTERIOR OF LOUISIANA.

at the top, set firmly in all round, and horizontal poles from one to another; there is then a row of posts forming a circle of about ten feet width in the diameter of the others, and ten feet in heighth. The crotchets of these are so directed that horizontal poles are also laid from one to another, long poles are then laid slanting from the lower poles over the upper, and meeting nearly at the top, leaving only a small aperture for the smoke of the fire, which is made on the ground in the middle of the lodge. A number of small poles are then put up round the circle, so as to form the wall, and wicker-work ran through the whole. The roof is thatched with grass and earth, thrown up against the wall. Until a bank is made to the eaves; the thatch is also covered with earth, one or two feet thick, and rendered so tight as entirely to exclude any storm whatsoever, and make the lodge extremely warm. The entrance is about six feet wide, with walls on each side, and roofed like our houses in shape, but of the same materials as the main building. Inside there are numerous little apartments, constructed of wicker-work, against the wall, with small doors, having a great appearance of neatness; in these the members of the family sleep, and have their little deposits.

Their towns are by no means so much crowded as the Osage, giving much more space; but they have the same practice of introducing all the horses into the village at night which makes it extremely crowded, they keeping guard with them during the day. They are extremely addicted to gaming, and have for that purpose a smooth piece of ground cleared out on each side of the village, for about one hundred and fifty yards in length, at which they play the following games: One is played by two players at a time, and in the following manner: they have a large hoop, of about four feet diameter, in the centre of which is a small leather ring attached to leather thongs, which are extended to the hoop, so as to keep it in its central position; they also have a pole, of about six feet in length, the player holding this in one hand, rolls the hoop from him, and immediately slides the pole after it, and the nearer the head of the pole lies to the small ring within the hoop, when they both fall, the greater is the cast. But I could not ascertain their mode of counting sufficiently to decide when the game was won. Another game is played with a small stick, with several hooks, and a hoop about four inches diameter, which is rolled along the ground, and the forked stick darted after it, when the value of the cast is estimated by the hook on which the ring is caught; this game is gained at a hundred. The third game alluded to is that of La Plate, described by various travellers, and is played by the women, children, and old men, who, like grass-hoppers, crawl out to the circus, to bask in the sun, probably covered only with an old buffalo robe.

The Pawnees, like the Osage, quit their villages in the winter, making concealments under ground of their corn, in which it keeps perfectly sound until spring. The only nations with whom the Pawnees are now at war are the Ietans, Utahs, and Kyaways; the two latter of whom reside in the mountains of North Mexico; the former generally inhabiting the borders of the Upper Red River, Arkansaw, and Rio del Norte. The war has been carried on by those nations for years, without any decisive action being fought, although they frequently march with two or three hundred men. The Pawnees have much the advantage of their enemies in point of arms, having at least one half fire-arms, whilst their opponents have only bows, arrows, lances, shields, and slings. The Pawnees always march to war on foot, their enemies are all cavalry. This nation may be considered as the one equi-distant between the Spanish population and that of our settlements of Louisiana, but are at present decidedly under Spanish influence, and should a war commence to-morrow, would all be in their interests. This circumstance does not arise from their local situation, because they are all situated on the navigable waters of the Missouri; nor from their interests, because from the Spaniards they obtain nothing, except horses and a few coarse blankets of West Mexico, whilst from us they receive all their supplies of arms, ammunition, and clothing; but all these articles in very small quantities, not more than half having a blanket, many being without breech cloths to cover their nakedness. But the grand principle by which the Spaniards keep them in their influence is fear, frequently chastising their small parties on their frontiers. To this may be added, their sending out the detachment of six hundred horsemen, which had visited them just before our arrival. This has made such an impression that they may safely calculate on them in case of war. This detachment took some of the Pawnees to Chihuahua, at the time I entered the provinces. But by withholding their supplies of arms, ammunition, and clothing, one or two years, bringing on their backs the Osage and Kanses, they would be in great distress, and feel the necessity of a good understanding with the United States.

THE INTERIOR OF LOUISIANA. 187

If there should ever be factories established for their accommodation, they should be at the entrance of the La Plate and Kanses rivers, as those waters are of so uncertain navigation, being navigable only in freshes, that it would be folly to attempt any permanent establishments high up; and to make those establishments useful to the Pawnees, we must pre-suppose our influence sufficient to guarantee to them peace, and a safe passage through the nations of the Kanses, Ottoes, and Missouries; the first on the Kanses river, the two latter on the River Plate.

Friday, 26th *September.*—Finding our encampment not eligible as to situation, we moved down the prairie hill, about three-quarters of a mile nearer the village. We pitched our camp upon a beautiful eminence, from whence we had a view of the town, and all transacting in it. We sent our interpreter to town, to trade for provisions. About three o'clock in the afternoon twelve Kanses arrived at the village, and informed Baroney that they had come to meet us, hearing we were to be at the Pawnee village.

The Kanses are a small nation, situated on the river of that name; and are in language, manners, customs, and agricultural pursuits, precisely similar to the Osage, with whom, I believe them, as before observed, to have one common origin. It may be said, however, that their language differs in some degree, but not more than the dialect of our eastern states differs from the southern. But in war they are yet more brave than their Osage brethren; being, although not more than one-third their number, their most dreaded enemies, and frequently make the Pawnees tremble.

Saturday, 27th *September.*—Baroney arrived from the village about one o'clock, with Charaterick and three other chiefs, to all of whom we gave a dinner. I then made an appropriate present to each; after which Lieutenant Wilkinson and myself accompanied them to town, where we remained a few hours, and afterwards returned. . Appointed to-morrow for the interview with the Kanses and Osages.

Sunday, 28th *September.*—Held a council of the Kanses and Osage, and made them smoke of the pipe of peace.*

---

* The following is the form of a convention of peace, we forwarded to the Kanses and Osage nation.

In council held by the subscribers at the village of the Pawnee republic, appeared Wahonsongay, with eight principal soldiers of the Kanses nation on the one part, and

TRAVELS THROUGH

Two of the Kanses agreed to accompany us. We received a visit from the Chief of the village. Made an observation on an emersion of one of Jupiter's satellites.

Monday, 29th *September*.—Held our grand council with the Pawnees; at which were present not less than four hundred warriors. The circumstances of which were extremely interesting.*

Shinga-Wasa, a chief of the Osage nation, with four of the warriors of the Grand and Little villages on the other part; after having smoked the pipe of peace, and buried past animosities, they individually and jointly bound themselves in behalf of and for their respective nations, to observe a friendly intercourse, and keep a permanent peace, and mutually pledge themselves to use their every influence to further the commands and wishes of their great father.

We, therefore, American chiefs, do require of each nation, a strict observance of the above treaty, as they value the good will of their great father, the President of the United States.

Done at our council-fire, at the Pawnee republican village, the 28th September, 1806, and the 31st year of American independence.

Signed   Z. M. PIKE,
J. B. WILKINSON.

* The notes I took at my grand council held with the Pawnee nation were seized by the Spanish Governor, together with all my speeches to the different nations. But it may be interesting to observe here (in case they should never be returned), that the Spaniards had left several of their flags in this village; one of which was unfurled at the chief's door the day of the grand council; and amongst the various demands and charges I made was, that the said flag should be delivered to me, and one of the United States' flags be received and hoisted in its place. This probably was carrying the pride of nations a little too far, as there had so lately been a large force of Spanish cavalry at the village, which had made a great impression on the minds of the young men, as to their power, consequence, &c., which my appearance with twenty infantry was by no means calculated to remove. After the chiefs had replied to various parts of my discourse, but were silent as to the flag, I again reiterated the demand for the flag, adding that it was impossible for the nation to have two fathers; that they must either be the children of the Spaniards or acknowledge their American father. After a silence of some time, an old man rose, went to the door, and took down the Spanish flag, and brought it and laid it my feet; and then received the American flag, and elevated it on the staff, which had lately borne the standard of his catholic majesty. This gave great satisfaction to the Osage and Kanses, both of whom decidedly avow themselves to be under the American protection. Perceiving that every face in the council was clouded with sorrow, as if some great national calamity was about to befall them, I took up the contested colours, and told them, that as they had

THE INTERIOR OF LOUISIANA.

Tuesday, 30th *September*.—Remained all day at the camp, but sent Baroney to town, who informed me on his return, that the Chief appeared to wish to throw obstacles in our way. A great disturbance had taken place in the village, owing to one of the young Pawnees (who had lately come from the United States), Frank, having taken the wife of an Osage and run away with her. The Chief, in whose lodge the Osage had put up, was extremely enraged; considering it a breach of hospitality to a person under his roof, and threatened to kill Frank, if he caught him.

Wednesday, 1st *October*.—Paid a visit to town, and had a very long conversation with the Chief, who urged every thing in his power to induce us to turn back. He finally very candidly told us that the Spaniards wished to have gone further into our country, but he had induced them to give up the idea; that they had listened to him, and he wished us to do the same: that he had promised the Spaniards to act as he now did, and that we must proceed no further, or he must stop us by force of arms. My reply was, "That I had been sent out by our great Father to explore the western country, to visit all his red children, to make peace between them, and turn them from shedding blood; that he had seen how I had caused the Osage and Kanses to meet to smoke the pipe of peace together, and take each other by the hand like brothers: that as yet my road had been smooth with a blue sky over our heads. I had not seen any blood in our paths. But that he must know that the young warriors of his great American Father were not women, to be turned back by words; that I should therefore proceed, and if he thought proper to stop me, he might attempt it, but we were *men*, well armed, and would sell our lives at a dear rate to his nation: that we knew our great Father would send other young warriors there to gather our bones, and revenge our deaths on his people, when our spirits would rejoice in hearing our exploits sung in the warsongs of our chiefs."

---

now shewn themselves dutiful children in acknowledging their great American father, I had no desire to embarrass them with the Spaniards, for it was the wish of the Americans, that their red brethren should remain peaceably round their own fires, and not embroil themselves in any disputes between the white people: and that for fear the Spaniards might return there in force again, I gave them back their flag; but with an injunction that it should never be hoisted during our stay. At this there was a general shout of applause, and the charge was particularly attended to.

I then left his lodge and returned to camp, in considerable perturbation of mind.

Thursday, 2d *October*.—We received advice from our Kanses, that the Chief had given publicity to his idea of stopping us by force of arms; this caused me some serious reflections, and was productive of many singular expressions from my brave lads; which called for my esteem at the same time that they excited my laughter.

I attempted to trade for horses, but could not succeed. In the night we were alarmed by some savages coming near our camp in full speed; but they retreated equally expeditiously, on being hailed with fierceness by our sentinels. This created some degree of indignation in my little band, as we had noticed that all the day had passed without any traders presenting themselves, which appeared as if all intercourse were interdicted! Wrote to the Secretary at War, the General, &c.

Friday, 3d *October*.—The intercourse again commenced. Traded for some horses. Writing for my express.

Saturday, 4th *October*.—Two French traders arrived at the village in order to procure horses, to transport their goods from the Missouri to the village : they gave us information that Captains Lewis and Clarke, with all their people, had descended the river to St. Louis; this diffused general joy throughout our party. Our trade for horses did not proceed this day.

Sunday, 5th *October*.—Buying horses, preparing to march, and finishing my letters.*

Monday, 6th *October*.—Marched off my express, purchased horses, and prepared to resume my journey on the morrow.

Tuesday, 7th *October*.—In the morning found two of our newly purchased horses missing; sent in search of them: the Indians brought in one pretty early. Struck our tents and commenced loading our horses: finding there was no probability of our obtaining the other that was missing, we marched at two o'clock P. M., and as the Chief had threatened to stop us by force of arms, we had made every arrangement to make him pay as dearly for the attempt as possible. The party was kept compact, and marched on by a road round the village, in order that if attacked the savages might not have their houses to retreat to for cover. I had given orders not to fire until within five or six paces, and then to charge with

---

* See Appendix, No. VIII.

PIKE'S PEAK.

bayonet and sabre; when I believe it would have cost them at least one hundred men to have exterminated us (which would have been necessary). The village appeared to be all in motion. I galloped up to the lodge of the Chief attended by my interpreter and one soldier; but soon saw there was no serious attempt to be made, although many young men were walking about with their bows, arrows, guns and lances. After speaking to the Chief with apparent indifference, I told him that I calculated on his justice in obtaining the horse, and that I should leave a man until the next day at twelve o'clock to bring it after me. We then joined the party and pursued our route. When I was once on the summit of the hill which overlooks the village, my mind felt as if relieved from a heavy burthen. Yet all the evil I wished the Pawnees was, that I might be the instrument in the hands of our government to open their ears and eyes, and with a strong hand, to convince them of our power.

Our party now consisted of two officers, one doctor, eighteen soldiers, one interpreter, three Osage men and one woman, making twenty-five warriors. We marched out and encamped on a small branch. Distance advanced, seven miles, along the same route by which we had come in. Rain in the night.

Wednesday, 8th *October*.—I conceived it best to send Baroney back to the village with a present, to be offered for our horse; the Chief having suggested the propriety of the measure. On his way he met his son and Sparks with the horse. Marched at ten o'clock, and at four came to the place where the Spanish troops had encamped the first night after they had left the village of the Pawnees. Their encampment was circular, and having only small fires round the circle for the purpose of cooking. We counted fifty-nine fires; so that allowing six men to each, the party must have comprised three hundred and fifty-four persons. We encamped on a large branch of the second fork of the Kanses river. Distance advanced, eighteen miles.

Thursday, 9th *October*.—Marched at eight o'clock, being detained until that time by our horses being at a great distance. At eleven o'clock we found the forks of the Spanish and Pawnee roads, and when we halted at twelve o'clock, we were overtaken by the second chief (Iskatappe) and the American chief, with one-third of the village. They presented us with a piece of bear meat. When we were about to proceed we discovered that Dr. Robinson's dirk had been stolen from behind his saddle. After marching the men, the Doctor and myself with the interpreter went to the Chief and demanded that he should cause a search to be made. This was done, but when the dirk was found the possessor asserted that he had found it on the road. I told him that he did not speak the truth; and informed the Chief that we never suffered a thing of ever so little value to be taken without permission: at this time the prairie was covered with his men, who began to encircle us, and Lieutenant Wilkinson with the troops had gained half a mile on the road. The Indian demanded a knife before he would deliver up the dirk; but as we refused to give one, the Chief took one from his belt and gave him. I took the dirk and presented it to the Doctor, who immediately returned it to the Chief as a present, and desired Baroney to inform him that he might now see it was not the value of the article, but the act, we took into consideration; we then galloped off. After proceeding about a mile we discovered a herd of elk, which we pursued: they took back in sight of the Pawnees, who immediately mounted fifty or sixty young men and joined in the pursuit; then, for the first time in my life, I saw animals slaughtered by the true savages with their original weapons, bows and arrows. They buried the arrow up to the plume in the animal. We took a piece of meat and followed our party; overtook them, and encamped within the Grand or Solomon's Fork, which we had crossed lower down, on the 23d September, on our route to the Pawnees. This had been the Spanish camping ground. In the evening two Pawnees came to our camp who had not eaten for three days: they had been carrying a sick companion, whom they had left that day; we gave them supper, with some meat and corn, and they immediately departed, in order to carry this seasonable supply to their friend. As they were coming into the camp, the sentinel challenged, it being dark: on seeing him bring his piece to the charge, supposing he was about to fire on them, they approached to give him their hands, he however not well descrying their motions, was on the point of firing, but being a cool, collected little fellow, called out that there were two Indians on him, and asked if he should fire; this drew out the guard, when the poor affrightened savages were brought in, very much alarmed, for they had not heard of a white man being within their country, and thought they were entering one of the camps of their own people. Distance advanced, eighteen miles.

THE INTERIOR OF LOUISIANA.

Friday, 10th *October*.—Marched at seven o'clock, and halted at twelve to dine. Were overtaken by the Pawnee chief, whose party we had left the day before, who informed us the hunting party had taken another road, and that he had come to bid us good bye. We left a large ridge on our left, and at sun-down crossed it. From this place we had an extensive view to the south-west; we observed a creek at a distance, for which I meant to proceed. The Doctor, interpreter, and myself arrived at eight o'clock at night; found water and wood, but had nothing to eat. Kindled a fire, in order to guide the party; but they not being able to find the route, and not knowing the distance, encamped on the prairie without wood or water.

Saturday, 11th *October*.—Ordered Baroney to return to find the party and conduct them to our camp. The Doctor and myself went out to hunt, and on our return found all our people had arrived except the rear guard, which was in sight. Whilst we halted, five Pawnees came to us and brought some bones of a horse which the Spanish troops had been obliged to eat at their encampment. On this creek we took up our line of march at twelve o'clock, and at sun-down the party halted on the Saline. I was in pursuit of buffalo, and did not make the camp until near ten o'clock at night: killed one buffalo: distance advanced, twelve miles.

Sunday, 12th *October*.—Here the Belle Oiseau and one Osage left us, and there remained only one man and woman of that nation. Their reason for leaving us was, that our course bore too much west, and they desired to bear more for the hunting ground of the Osage. In the morning sent out to obtain the buffalo meat, and laid by until after breakfast. Proceeded at eleven o'clock, and crossing the river two or three times we passed two camps where the Spanish troops had halted. Here they appeared to have remained some days. Their roads being so much blinded by the traces of the buffalo, we lost them entirely. This was a mortifying circumstance, as we had reason to calculate that they had good guides and were on the best route for wood and water. We took a south-west direction, and before night were fortunate enough to strike their road on the left, and at dusk much to our surprise struck the eastern fork of the Kanses, or la Fourche de la côte Boucaniere: killed one buffalo: distance advanced, eighteen miles.

Monday, 13th *October*.—The day being rainy, we did not march until two o'clock, when there being an appearance of the weather clearing, we raised our camp; after which we marched seven miles, and halted at the head of a branch of the river we had left. Had to go two miles for water: killed one cabrie.

Tuesday, 14th *October*.—Drizzling rain having fallen all night, and the atmosphere being entirely obscured, we did not march until a quarter past nine o'clock, and then commenced crossing the dividing ridge between the Kanses and Arkansaw rivers. Arrived on a branch of the latter at one o'clock; continued down it in search of water until after dusk, when we found a pond on the prairie, which induced us to halt. Sparks did not come up, being scarcely able to walk from rheumatic pains: wounded several buffaloes, but could get none of them: distance advanced, twenty-four miles.

Wednesday, 15th *October*.—In the morning rode out in search of the Spaniards' trace, and crossed the low prairie, which was nearly all covered with ponds, but could not discover it. Finding Sparks did not arrive, sent two men back in search of him, who rejoined us with him about eleven o'clock. At twelve we commenced our line of march, and at five Dr. Robinson and myself left the party at a large creek, having pointed out to Lieutenant Wilkinson a distant wood for our encampment, in order to search some distance up it for the Spaniards' trace. Killed two buffaloes, and left part of our clothing with them, to scare away the wolves. Went afterwards in pursuit of the party. On our arrival at the creek appointed for the encampment, we did not find them. Proceeded down it for some miles, and not discovering them, we encamped, struck fire, and then supped on the tongue of one of our buffaloes.

Thursday, 16th *October*.—Early on horseback: proceeded up the creek some distance, in search of our party, but at twelve o'clock crossed to our two buffaloes. Found a great many wolves at them, notwithstanding the precaution taken to keep them off. Cooked some marrow bones, and again mounted our horses, and proceeded down the creek. Finding nothing of the party, I began to be seriously alarmed for their safety. Killed two more buffaloes, made our encampment, and feasted sumptuously on the marrow bones. Rain in the night.

Friday, 17th *October*.—Rose early, determined to search the creek to its source. Very hard rain accompanied by a cold north wind all day. Encamped near night, without being able to discover any signs of the

THE INTERIOR OF LOUISIANA.   195

party. Our sensations now became excruciating, not only on account of their personal safety, but the fear of the failure of the national objects intended to be accomplished by the expedition; and our own situation was not the most agreeable, not having more than four rounds of ammunition each; and being four hundred miles in the nearest direction from the first civilized inhabitants. We however concluded to search for them on the morrow, and if we did not succeed in finding them, to strike for the Arkansaw, where we were in hopes of discovering some traces of them, if they were not cut off by the savages.

Saturday, 18th *October.*—Commenced our route at an early hour, and about ten o'clock discovered two men on horseback in search of us, one my attendant. They informed us the party was encamped on the Arkansaw, about three miles south of where we then were. This surprised us very much, as we had no conception of that river being so near. On our arrival we were met by Lieutenant Wilkinson, who, with all the party, was greatly concerned for our safety.

In the afternoon the Doctor and myself took our horses and crossed the Arkansaw, in order to search for some trees which might answer the purpose to make canoes; found but one and returned at dusk. It commenced raining at twelve o'clock at night.

Sunday, 19th *October.*—Finding the river rising rapidly, I thought it best to secure our passage over; we consequently made it good by ten o'clock A. M.: rain all day. Prepared our tools and arms for labour and the chase on the morrow.

From the Pawnee town on the Kanses river to the Arkansaw, the country may almost be termed mountainous; but a want of timber gives the hills less claim to the appellation of mountains; they are watered and created as it were by the various branches of the Kanses river. One of those branches, a stream of considerable magnitude, say twenty yards, which I have designated on the chart by the name of the Saline, was so salt at the place where we crossed it, on our route to the Arkansaw, that it salted sufficiently the soup of the meat which my men boiled in it. We were at this place very eligibly situated, had a fresh spring issuing from a bank near us; plenty of the necessaries of life all around, viz., buffalo, a beautiful little sugar loaf hill, for a look-out post, fine grass for our horses, and a saline in front of us. As you approach the Arkansaw, on this route, within fifteen or twenty miles, the country appears to be low and swampy, or the land is covered with ponds extending out from the river some distance. The river at the place where we struck it, is nearly five hundred yards wide, from bank to bank; those banks not more than four feet high, thinly covered with cotton wood. The north side is a swampy low prairie, and the south a sandy sterile desert.

Monday, 20th *October.*—We commenced our labour at two trees for canoes, but one proved too much doated. Killed two buffaloes and one cabrie. Discharged our guns at a mark, the best shot a prize of one vest and a pair of shoes. Our only dog was standing at the root of the tree, in the grass, and one of the balls struck him on the head, and killed him. Ceased raining about twelve o'clock.

Tuesday, 21st *October.*—Dr. Robinson and myself mounted our horses in order to go down the river to the entrance of the three last creeks we had crossed in our route, but meeting with buffaloes, we killed four. Returned to camp and sent for the meat. Killed also one cabrie.

Wednesday, 22d *October.*—Having sat up very late the last evening, expecting the sergeant and party, who did not arrive, we became very anxious on their account; but about ten o'clock Bradley arrived and informed us that they could not find the buffalo which we had killed on the prairie. They all arrived however before noon, and in the afternoon we scaffolded some meat, and nearly completed the frame of a skin canoe, which we had resolved to build. Overhauled my instruments, and made some rectifications preparatory to taking an observation.

Thursday, 23d *October.*—Dr. Robinson and myself, accompanied by one man, ascended the river with an intention of searching for the Spanish trace. At the same time we despatched Baroney and our two hunters to kill some buffaloes, to obtain the skins for canoes. We ascended the river about twenty miles to a large branch on the right. Just at dusk gave chase to a buffalo; and were obliged to shoot nineteen balls into him before we killed him. Encamped in the fork.

Friday, 24th *October.*—We ascended the right hand branch about five miles, but could not see any signs of the Spanish trace; this is not surprising as the river bears south-west, and they no doubt kept more to the west, from the head of one branch to another. We returned, and on our

THE INTERIOR OF LOUISIANA. 197

way killed some prairie squirrels, or wish-ton-wishes, and nine large rattlesnakes, which frequent their villages.*

---

* The wish-ton-wish of the Indians, the prairie dogs of some travellers, or squirrels, as I should be inclined to denominate them, reside on the prairies of Louisiana in towns or villages, having an evident police established in their communities.

The sites of their towns are generally on the brow of a hill, near some small creek or pond, in order to be convenient for water, and that the high ground which they inhabit may not be subject to inundation. Their residence, being under ground, is burrowed, and the earth brought out is made to answer the double purpose of keeping out the water and affording an elevated place in wet seasons to repose on, and to give them a further and more distinct view of the country. Their holes descend in a spiral form, on which account I could never ascertain their depth; but I once had a hundred and forty kettles of water poured into one of them, in order to drive out the occupant, but without effect. In the circuit of the villages they clear off all the grass, and leave the earth bare of vegetation; but whether this be from an instinct they possess inclining them to keep the ground thus cleared, or whether they make use of the herbage as food, I cannot pretend to determine. The latter opinion I think is entitled to a preference, as their teeth designate them to be of the granivorous species, and I know of no other substance which is produced in the vicinity of their stations, on which they could subsist; for they never extend their excursions more than half a mile from the burrows. They are of a dark brown colour, except their bellies, which are white; their tails are not so long as those of our grey squirrels, but are shaped precisely the same. Their teeth, head, nails, and body are those of the perfect squirrel, except that they are generally fatter than that animal. Their villages sometimes extend over two and three miles square, in which there must be innumerable hosts of them, as there is generally a burrow every ten steps, containing two or more inhabitants, and you see new ones partly excavated on all the borders of the town. We killed great numbers of these animals with our rifles, and found them excellent meat after they were exposed a night or two to the frost, by which means the rankness acquired by their subterraneous dwelling is corrected. As you approah their towns you are saluted on all sides by the cry of wish-ton-wish, from which they derive their name with the Indians, uttered in a shrill and piercing manner. You then observe them all retreating to the entrance of their burrows, where they post themselves and watch even the slightest movement that you make. It requires a very nice shot with a rifle to kill them, as they must be shot dead, for as long as life exists they continue to work into their cells. It was extremely dangerous to pass through their towns, as they abounded with rattle-snakes, both of the yellow and black species, and, strange as it may appear, I have seen the wish-ton-wish, the rattle-snake, the horn-frog with which the prairie abounds (termed by the Spaniards the camelion, from their taking no visible sustenance), and a land tortoise, all take refuge in the same hole. I do not pretend to assert, that it was their common place of resort, but I have witnessed the fact in more than one instance.

On our arrival found the hunters had come in about one hour with two buffalo skins and one elk skin.

Saturday, 25th *October*.—Took an observation. Passed the day in writing and preparing for the departure of Lieutenant Wilkinson.

Sunday, 26th *October*.—Delivered out a ration of corn by way of distinction of the Sabbath. Prepared for our departure.

Monday, 27th *October*.—Delivered to Lieutenant Wilkinson letters for the General* and our friends, with other papers, consisting of his instructions, traverse tables of our voyage, and a draft of our route to that place complete, in order that if we were lost, and he arrived in safety, we might not have made the tour without some benefit to our country. He took with him in corn and meat twenty-one days' provision, and all the necessary tools for building canoes or cabins. Launched his canoes. We concluded we should separate in the morning; he to descend the river, and we to ascend it to the mountains.

Tuesday, 28th *October*.—All was in motion as soon as possible, my party crossing the river to the north side, and Lieutenant Wilkinson launching his canoes of skins and wood. We breakfasted together, and then filed off. I suffered my party to march, and remained myself to see Lieutenant Wilkinson sail, which he did at ten o'clock, having one skin canoe made of four buffalo skins, and two elk skins, which held three men besides himself, and one Osage; and a wooden canoe, in which were one soldier, one Osage, and their baggage: one other soldier marched on shore. We parted with "God bless you," from both parties; they appeared to sail very well.†

In the pursuit of our party, Dr. Robinson, Baroney, one soldier, and myself killed a blaireau, and a buffalo; of the latter we took only his marrow bones and liver. Arrived where our men had encamped about dusk. Distance advanced, fourteen miles.

Wednesday, 29th *October*.—March after breakfast, and during the first hour passed two fires, where twenty-one Indians had recently encamped, in which party, as appeared by their paintings on the rocks, there were seven guns. Killed a buffalo. Halted, made a fire, and feasted on the

---

* See Appendix, No. IX.
† For an account of Lieutenant Wilkinson's voyage down the Arkansaw, see Appendix, No. X.

THE INTERIOR OF LOUISIANA.

choicest pieces of meat. About noon discovered two horses feeding with a herd of buffaloes; we attempted to surround them, but they soon outstript our fleetest coursers; one appeared to be an elegant animal. These were the first wild horses we had seen.

Two or three hours before night struck the Spanish road, and as it was snowing, halted, and encamped the party at the first wood on the bank of the river. The Doctor and myself forded it (the ice running very thick), in order to discover the course the Spaniards had taken, but owing to the many buffalo roads, we could not ascertain it; but it evidently appeared that they had halted here some time, as the ground was covered with horse dung for miles around. Returned to camp. The snow fell two inches deep, and then it cleared up. Distance advanced, twelve miles.

Thursday, 30th *October.*—In the morning sent out to kill a buffalo, to have his marrow bones for breakfast, which was accomplished. After breakfast the party marched upon the north side, and the Doctor and myself crossed with considerable difficulty, on account of the ice, to the Spaniards' course, when we took a large circuit, in order to discover the Spaniards' trace, and came in at a point of wood, south of the river, where we found our party encamped. We discovered also, that the Spanish troops had marched up the river, and that a party of savages had been there not more than three days before. Killed two buffaloes. Distance advanced, four miles.

Friday, 31st *October.*—Fine day. Marched at three-quarters past nine o'clock on the Spanish road. Encamped, sun an hour high, after having made sixteen miles. We observed this day a species of congelation on the road, when the sun was high, in low places where there had been water settled: on tasting, found it to be salt; this, in my estimation, gave some authority to the report of the prairie being covered for leagues. Discovered the trace of about twenty savages, who had followed our road; and horses going down the river. Killed one buffalo, one elk, and one deer.

Saturday, 1st *November.*—Marched early: just after commencing our line, heard a gun on our left. The Doctor, Baroney, and myself being in advance, and lying on the ground waiting for the party, a band of cabrie came up amongst our horses, to satisfy their curiosity. We could not resist the temptation of killing two, although we had plenty of meat. At the report of the guns they appeared astonished, and stood still until we hallooed at them to drive them away. Encamped in the evening on an island. Upon using my glass to view the adjacent country, I observed on the prairie a herd of horses. Dr. Robinson and Baroney accompanied me to go and examine them; when within about quarter of a mile, they discovered us, and immediately approached, making the earth tremble under them; they brought to my recollection a charge of cavalry. They stopped and gave us an opportunity to view them. Amongst them there were some very beautiful bays, blacks, and greys, and indeed of all colors. We fired at a black horse with an idea of creasing him, but did not succeed; they flourished round and returned again to view us. We then returned to camp.

Sunday, 2d *November*.—In the morning, for the purpose of trying the experiment, we equipped six of our fleetest coursers with riders, and ropes to noose the wild horses, if in our power to come amongst the herd. They stood until we approached within forty yards, neighing and whinnying, when the chase began, which we continued two miles without success. Two of our horses ran up with them, but we could not take them. Returned to camp. I have since laughed at our folly for endeavouring to take the wild horses in that manner, which is scarcely ever attempted even with the fleetest animals and most expert ropers.*

Marched late. The river turned to north by west; hills changed to the north side. Distance advanced, thirteen miles and a half. Killed one buffalo.

Monday, 3d *November*.—Marched at ten o'clock. Passed several herds of buffalo, elk and some horses, and other animals, all travelling south. The river bottoms were observed full of salt ponds, and the grass to be similar to that of our salt meadows. Killed one buffalo. Distance advanced, twenty-five miles and a half.

Tuesday, 4th *November*.—This day brought to our recollection the fate of our countrymen at Recovery, when defeated by the Indians in the year 1791. In the afternoon discovered the north side of the river to be covered with animals, which, when we came to them, proved to be cows and calves, and buffaloes. I do not think it an exaggeration to say there were three thousand in one view. It is worthy of remark, that in all the extent of country yet crossed, we never saw one cow, and that now the

---
*Some account of these animals will be given in a subsequent part of this work.

THE INTERIOR OF LOUISIANA.

face of the earth appeared to be covered with them. Killed one buffalo. Distance advanced, twenty-four miles and a half.

Wednesday, 5th *November.*—Marched at our usual hour. After proceeding two miles, shot a buffalo and two deer, and halted, which detained us so long, that we foolishly concluded to halt the remainder of the day and kill some cows and calves, which lay on the opposite side of the river. I took post on a hill, and sent some horsemen over, when a scene took place which gave a lively representation of an engagement. The herd of buffaloes being divided into separate bands, covered the prairie with dust, and first charged on the one side, then to the other, as the pursuit of the horsemen impelled them; the report and smoke from the guns added to the pleasure of the scene, which in part compensated for our detention.

Thursday, 6th *November.*—Marched early, but were detained two or three hours by the cows which we had killed. The cow buffalo was equal to any meat I ever saw, and we feasted sumptuously on the choice morsels. I will not attempt to describe the droves of animals we now saw on our route, suffice it to say, that the face of the prairie was covered with them on both sides of the river; their numbers exceeded imagination. Distance advanced, sixteen miles.

Friday, 7th *November.*—Marched early. The herbage being very poor, concluded to lay by on the morrow, in order to recruit our horses. Killed three cow buffaloes, one calf, two wolves and one blaireau. Distance advanced, eighteen miles.

Saturday, 8th *November.*—Our horses being very much jaded, and our situation very eligible, we halted all day. Jerked meat, mended our mockinsons, &c.

Sunday, 9th *November.*—Marched early. At twelve o'clock struck the Spanish road, which had been on the outside of us; it appeared to be considerably augmented, and on our arrival at the Spanish camp, found it to consist of ninety-six fires, from which a reasonable conclusion might be drawn that there were from six to seven hundred men.

We this day found the face of the country considerably changed, being hilly, with springs. Passed numerous herds of buffaloes and some horses. Distance advanced, twenty-seven miles.

Monday, 10th *November.*—The hills increased; the banks of the river were covered with groves of young cotton wood; the river itself much narrower and crooked. Our horses growing weak, two gave out, which we brought along unloaded. Cut down trees at night for them to browse on. Killed one buffalo. Distance advanced, twenty miles.

Tuesday, 11th *November.*—Marched at the usual hour. Passed two old camps, and one of last summer, which had belonged to the savages, and we supposed Ietans.* Passed a Spanish camp, where it appeared the party had remained some days, as we conjectured, to lay up meat, previously to entering the Ietan country, as the buffalo evidently began to grow much less numerous. Finding the impossibility of performing the tour in the time proposed. I determined to spare no pains to accomplish every object I had in contemplation, even should it oblige me to spend

---

* The Ietans, or Camanches, as the Spaniards term them, or Padoucas as they are called by the Pawnees, are a powerful nation which are entirely erratic, without the least species of cultivation, subsisting solely by the chase. Their wanderings are confined to the frontiers of New Mexico on the west, the nations on the Lower Red river on the south, the Pawnees and Osage on the east, and the Utahs, Kyaways and various unknown nations on the north. This nation, although entirely in our territories, is claimed exclusively by the Spaniards, and may be said to be decidedly in their interest, notwithstanding the few who lately paid a visit to Natchitoches. They are the only nation who border on the Spanish settlements, which that government treats as an independent people. They are by the Spaniards reputed brave; indeed they have given them some very strong evidences of this.

When I first entered the province of New Mexico, I was shewn various deserted villages and towns beaten down, which had been destroyed by the Ietans in an invasion of that province, when they were at war with the Spaniards about ten years since. From the village of Agua Caliente they carried off at one time two hundred head of horses, but they are now on an excellent understanding with the Spaniards, which Don Faciendo Malgares's late expedition has served very much to strengthen. He personally related his rencontre with the Ietans in the following manner:—Having been previously apprised of each other's approximation, and appointed a time for the Indians to receive him on an extensive prairie, he sallied forth from his camp with five hundred men all on white horses, excepting himself and his two principal officers, who rode jet black ones, and was received on the plain by one thousand five hundred of those savages, dressed in their gay robes and displaying their various feats of chivalry. I leave this subject to the judicious, whether the circumstance would not be handed down to the latest posterity, as an instance of the good will and respect which the Spaniards paid their nation, as no doubt Malgares had policy sufficient to induce them to believe that the expedition was fitted out principally with the view of paying them a visit.

THE INTERIOR OF LOUISIANA. 203

another winter in the desert. Killed one buffalo and one blaireau. Distance advanced, twenty-four miles.

Wednesday, 12th *November.*— Was obliged to leave two horses which entirely gave out. Missed the Spanish road. Killed one buffalo. Distance advanced, twenty miles.

Thursday, 13th *November.*— We marched at the usual hour. The river banks began to be entirely covered with woods on both sides, but no other species than cotton wood. Discovered very fresh signs of Indians, and one of our hunters informed me he had seen a man on horseback ascending a ravine on our left. Discovered signs of war parties ascending the river. Wounded several buffaloes; killed one turkey, the first we had seen since we left the Pawnees.

Friday, 14th *November.*— In the morning Dr. Robinson, one man, and myself, went up the ravine on which the Indian was supposed to have been seen, but could make no important discovery. Marched at two o'clock, and passed a point of red rocks, and one large creek. Distance advanced, ten miles.

Saturday, 15th *November.*— Marched early. Passed two deep creeks, and many high points of rocks; also, large herds of buffaloes. At two o'clock in the afternoon, I thought I could distinguish a mountain to our right, which appeared like a small blue cloud; viewed it with the spy glass, and was still more confirmed in my conjecture, yet only communicated it to Dr. Robinson, who was in front with me, but in half an hour it appeared in full view before us. When our small party arrived on the hill, they with one accord gave three cheers to the Mexican mountains. Their appearance can easily be imagined by those who have crossed the Alleghany, but their sides were white as if covered with snow, or a white stone. These proved to be a spur of the grand western chain of mountains, which divide the waters of the Pacific from those of the Atlantic Ocean, and divided the waters which empty into the bay of the Holy Spirit, from those of the Mississippi, as the Alleghany do those that discharge themselves into the latter river, and the Atlantic. They appeared to present a boundary between the province of Louisiana and North Mexico, and would be a defined and natural limit. Before evening we discovered a fork on the south side, bearing S. 25° W. and as the Spanish troops appeared to have borne up it, we encamped on its banks, about one mile from its confluence, that we might make further discoveries on the morrow. Killed three buffaloes. Distance advanced, twenty-four miles.

Sunday, 16th *November.*—After ascertaining that the Spanish troops had ascended the right branch or main river, we marched at two o'clock P. M. The Arkansaw appeared at this place to be much more navigable than below where we had first struck it, and for any impediment I have yet discovered in the river, I would not hesitate to embark in February at its mouth, and ascend to the Mexican mountains, with crafts properly constructed. Distance advanced, eleven miles and a half.

Monday, 17th *November.*—Marched at our usual hour: pushed on with an idea of arriving at the mountains, but found at night no visible difference in their appearance from what we had observed yesterday. One of our horses gave out and was left in a ravine, not being able to ascend the hill; but I sent back for him, and had him brought to the camp. Distance advanced, twenty-three miles and a half.

Tuesday, 18th *November.*—As we discovered fresh signs of the savages, we concluded it best to stop and kill some meat, for fear we should get into a country where we could not obtain game. Sent out the hunters. I walked myself to an eminence, from whence I took the courses to the different mountains, and a small sketch of their appearance. In the evening found the hunters had killed without mercy, having slain seventeen buffaloes, and wounded at least twenty more.

Wednesday 19th *November.*—Having several carcasses brought in, I gave out sufficient meat to last this month. I found it expedient to remain and dry the meat, for our horses were getting very weak, and the one died which was brought in yesterday. Had a general feast of marrow bones; one hundred and thirty-six of them furnishing the repast.

Thursday, 20th *November.*—Marched at our usual hour, but as our horses' loads were considerably augmented by the death of one, and the addition of nine hundred pounds of meat, we moved slowly, and made only eighteen miles. Killed two buffalo cows, and took some choice pieces.

Friday, 21st *November.*—Marched at our usual hour: passed two Spanish camps within three miles of each other. We again discovered the tracks of two men who had ascended the river yesterday. This caused us to move with caution, but at the same time increased our anxiety to discover them. The river was certainly as navigable here, and I think much

THE INTERIOR OF LOUISIANA.

more so, than some hundred miles below, which I suppose to arise from its flowing through a long course of sandy soil, which must absorb much of the water, and render it shoaler below than above near the mountains. Distance advanced, twenty-one miles.

Saturday, 22d November.—Marched early, and with rather more caution than usual. After having proceeded about five miles on the prairie, and as those in front were descending into the bottom, Baroney cried out, "Voila un sauvage," when we observed a number of Indians running from the woods towards us. We advanced towards them, and on turning my head to the left, I observed several running on the hill, as it were to surround us; one of them bearing a stand of colours. This caused a momentary halt, but perceiving those in front reaching out their hands, and without arms, we again advanced. They met us with open arms, crowding round to touch and embrace us. They appeared so anxious, that I dismounted from my horse, and in a moment a fellow had mounted him and driven off. I then observed the Doctor and Baroney in the same predicament. The Indians were embracing the soldiers. After some time tranquillity was so far restored, they having returned our horses all safe, as to enable us to learn they were a war party from the Grand Pawnees, who had been in search of the Ietans, but not finding them, were now on their return. An unsuccessful war party on their way home are always ready to embrace an opportunity of gratifying their disappointed vengeance on the first persons they meet.

We made for the woods and unloaded our horses, when the two leaders endeavoured to arrange the party; it was with great difficulty they got them tranquil, and not until there had been a bow or two bent on the occasion. When in some order, we found them to be sixty warriors, half with fire arms, and half with bows, arrows, and lances. Our party was in all sixteen. In a short time they were arranged in a ring, and I took my seat between the two leaders: our colours were placed opposite each other; the utensils for smoking, &c., being prepared on a small seat before us. Thus far all was well. I then ordered half a carrot of tobacco, one dozen knives, sixty fire steels, and sixty flints to be presented to them. They demanded corn, ammunition, blankets, kettles, &c., all of which they were refused, notwithstanding the pressing instances of my interpreter to accede to some points. The pipes yet lay unmoved, as if they were undetermined whether to treat us as friends or as enemies; but after some time we were presented with a kettle of water, drank, smoked, and ate together. During this time Dr. Robinson was standing up to observe their actions, in order that, if necessary, we might be ready to commence hostilities as soon as they. The Indians now took their presents and commenced distributing them, but some malcontents threw them away, as if out of contempt. We began to load our horses, when they encircled us and commenced stealing every thing they could. Finding it was difficult to preserve my pistols, I mounted my horse, when I found myself frequently surrounded, during which some were endeavouring to steal the pistols. The Doctor was equally engaged in another quarter, and all the soldiers at their several posts, taking things from them. One having stolen my tomahawk, I informed the Chief, but he paid no respect to my remonstrance, except to reply, that "they were pitiful." Finding this, we determined to protect ourselves as far as was in our power, and the affair began to wear a serious aspect. I ordered my men to take their arms, and separate themselves from the savages; at the same time declaring to them I would kill the first man who touched our baggage, on which they commenced filing off immediately. We marched about the same time, and found after they had left us, that they had contrived to steal one sword, a tomahawk, a broad ax, five canteens, and sundry other small articles. When I reflected on the subject I felt sincerely mortified, that the smallness of my number obliged me thus to submit to the insults of lawless banditti, it being the first time a savage had ever taken any thing from me with the least appearance of force.

After encamping at night, the Doctor and myself went about one mile back, and waylaid the road, determined, in case we discovered any of the rascals pursuing us to steal our horses, to kill two at least; but after waiting behind some logs until some time in the night, and discovering no person, we returned to camp. Distance advanced, seventeen miles. Killed two buffaloes, and one deer.

Sunday, 23d November.—Marched at ten o'clock. At one, came up to the third fork on the south side, and encamped at night on the point of the Grand Forks. As the river appeared to be dividing itself into several small branches, and of course must be near its extreme source, I concluded to put my party in a defensible situation, and ascend the north fork to the high point of the Blue Mountain, which we conceived would be one day's march; in order to be enabled from its summit, to lay down the various branches of the river, and the positions of the country. Distance advanced, nineteen miles. Killed five buffaloes.

Monday, 24th *November.*—Early in the morning cut down fourteen logs, and put up a breast-work five feet high on three sides, and the other was thrown on the river. After giving the necessary orders for the government of my men, during my absence, in case of our not returning, we marched at one o'clock with an idea of arriving at the foot of the mountain, but found ourselves obliged to take up our lodging this night under a single cedar, which we found in the prairie, without water, and extremely cold. Our party, besides myself, consisted of Dr. Robinson, and privates Miller and Brown. Distance advanced, twelve miles.

Tuesday, 25th *November.*—Marched early, with the expectation of ascending the mountain, but was only able to encamp at its base, after passing over many small hills covered with cedars and pitch pines. Our encampment was on a creek; we found no water for several miles from the mountain, but near its base found springs sufficient. Took a meridional observation, and the altitude of the mountain. Killed two buffaloes. Distance advanced, twenty-two miles and a half.

Wednesday, 26th *November.*—Expecting to return to our camp that evening, we left all our blankets and provision at the foot of the mountain. Killed a deer of a new species, and hung his skin on a tree with some meat. We commenced ascending; found the way very difficult, being obliged to climb up rocks sometimes almost perpendicular; and after marching all day we encamped in a cave without blankets, victuals, or water. We had a fine clear sky, whilst it was snowing at the bottom. On the side of the mountain we found only yellow and pitch pine; some distance up we saw buffalo; and higher still, the new species of deer and pheasants.

Thursday, 27th *November.*—Arose hungry, thirsty, and extremely sore, from the unevenness of the rocks on which we had lain all night; but were amply compensated for our toil by the sublimity of the prospects below. The unbounded prairie was overhung with clouds, which appeared like the ocean in a storm, wave piled on wave, and foaming, whilst the sky over our heads was perfectly clear. Commenced our march up the mountain, and in about one hour arrived at the summit of this chain ; here we found the snow middle deep, and discovered no sign of beast or bird inhabiting this region. The thermometer which stood at 9° above 0 at the foot of the mountain, here fell to 4° below. The summit of the Grand Peak, which was entirely bare of vegetation, and covered with snow, now appeared at the distance of fifteen or sixteen miles from us, and as high again as that we had ascended; it would have taken a whole day's march to have arrived at its base, when I believe no human being could have ascended to its summit. This, with the condition of my soldiers, who had only light overhauls on, and no stockings, and were every way ill provided to endure the inclemency of this region, the bad prospect of killing any-anything to subsist on, with the further detention of two or three days which it must occasion, determined us to return. The clouds from below had now ascended the mountain, and entirely enveloped the summit on which rest eternal snows. We descended by a long deep ravine with much less difficulty than we had contemplated. Found all our baggage safe, but the provision all destroyed. It began to snow, and we sought shelter under the side of a projecting rock, where we all four made a meal on one partridge, and a pair of deer's ribs, which the ravens had left us, being the first food we had eaten for forty-eight hours.

Friday, 28th November.—Marched at nine o'clock. Kept straight down the creek to avoid the hills. At half past one o'clock shot two buffaloes, when we made the first full meal we had eaten for three days. Encamped in a valley under a shelving rock. The land here was very rich, and covered with old Ietan camps.

Saturday, 29th November.—Marched after a short repast, and arrived at our camp before night. Found all well.

From the entrance of the Arkansaw into the mountains to its source, it is alternately bounded by perpendicular precipices, or small narrow prairies, on which the buffalo and elk have found means to arrive, and are almost secure from danger, and from their destroyer, man. In many places the river precipitates itself over rocks, so as to be at one moment visible only in the foaming and boiling of its waters, at the next disappearing in the chasms of the over-hanging precipices.

The Arkansaw river, taking its meanders, is one thousand nine hundred and eighty-one miles from its junction with the Mississippi to the mountains, and from thence to its source one hundred and ninety-two

CHART
OF THE
INTERNAL PART
—OF—
LOUISIANA,
INCLUDING ALL THE HITHERTO UNEXPLORED COUNTRIES,

lying between the River La Platte of the Missouri on the N. and the Red River on the S; the Mississippi East and the Mountains of Mexico West; with a part of New Mexico and the Province of Texas, by Z. M PIKE, Capt. U.S I.

The grass of this bottom is Similar to our Salt meadow grass, from the great quantity of Salt.

Here commences the congelation of particles of Salt, on the surface of the Earth.

Above the first Fork of the Arkansaw the bank becomes very rough, which although narrow * carries a quality of water, of a red color, and is the left branch of the Arkansaw, which connects with the Red River of the Mississippi, which is extremely easy distinguishable in ascending; as from a few miles above, nearly in a parallel line, is a high Ridge bearing off at right angles from the main River.

*The Fork.

Benedict & Co., Engr's, Chicago.

THE INTERIOR OF LOUISIANA. 209

miles, making its total length two thousand one hundred and seventy-three miles, all of which may be navigated with proper boats, constructed for the purpose; except the one hundred and ninety-two miles in the mountains. It receives several small rivers, which are navigable for one hundred miles and upwards. Boats bound up the whole length of the navigation should embark at its entrance on the first of February, when they would have the fresh quite to the mountains, and meet with no detentions; but if later, they will find the river one thousand five hundred miles up, nearly dry. It has one singularity which struck me very forcibly at first view, but on reflection I was induced to believe the case to be the same with all rivers whose courses lie through a low, dry, and sandy soil in warm climates. For the extent of four or five hundred miles before you arrive at the mountains, the bed of the river is extensive, and a perfect sand bar, which at certain seasons is dry, at least the water is standing in ponds, not affording sufficient to procure a running course from one to the other: when you come nearer the mountains, you find the river contracted, with a gravelly bottom, and a deep navigable stream. From which circumstances it is evident, that the sandy soil imbibes all the waters, which the sources project from the hills, and renders the river, in dry seasons, less navigable at the distance of five hundred than at two hundred miles from its source.

The borders of the Arkansaw may be termed the paradise terrestrial of our territories for wandering savages. Of all the countries visited by the footsteps of civilized man, there never was one probably that produced game in greater abundance, and we know that the manners and morals of the erratic nations are such (the reasons I leave to be given by Ontologists) as never to give them a numerous population, and I believe that there are buffalo, elk, and deer sufficient on the borders of the Arkansaw alone, if used without waste, to feed all the savages of the United States territory for one century.

By the route of the Arkansaw, and the Rio Colorado of California, I am confident in asserting (if my information be correct) there can be established the best communication on this side the Isthmus of Darien, between the Atlantic and Pacific oceans; as, admitting the utmost, the land carriage would not be more than two hundred miles, and the route may be made quite as eligible as our public highways over the Alleghany

Mountains. The Rio Colorado is to the great gulph of California, what the Mississippi is to the Gulph of Mexico, and is navigable for ships of considerable burthen, opposite to the upper part of the province of Senora.

Sunday, 30th *November.*—We commenced our march at eleven o'clock, it snowing very fast, but my impatience to be moving would not permit me to lie still at our present camp. The Doctor, Baroney, and myself went to view an Ietan encampment, which appeared to be about two years old, and from the occupiers having cut down so large a quantity of trees to support their horses, we concluded there must have been at least one thousand souls. Past several more in the course of the day, also one Spanish camp. Distance advanced, fifteen miles. Killed two deer. This day came to the first cedar and pine, except the few we had seen in the mountains.

Monday, 1st *December.*—The storm still continuing with violence, we remained encamped; the snow by night was one foot deep, our horses being obliged to scrape it away to obtain their miserable pittance. To increase their misfortune, the poor animals were attacked by the magpies, which attracted by the scent of their sore backs, alighted on them, and in defiance of their whinnying and kicking, picked many places quite raw; the difficulty of procuring food rendered these birds so bold as to light on our men's arms, and eat meat out of their hands. One of our hunters was out, but killed nothing.

Tuesday, 2d *December.*—It cleared off in the night, and in the morning the thermometer stood at 17° below 0 (Reaumeure), being three times as cold as any morning we had yet experienced. We killed an old buffalo on the opposite side of the river, which here was so deep as to swim horses. Marched, and found it necessary to cross to the north side, about two miles up, as the ridge joined the river. The ford was a good one, but the ice ran very bad, and two of the men had their feet frozen, before we could get accommodated with fire, &c. Secured some of our old buffalo, and continued our march. The country being very rugged and hilly, one of our horses took a freak in his head and turned back, which occasioned three of our rear guard to lie out all night. I was very apprehensive they might perish in the open prairie. Distance advanced, thirteen miles.

Wednesday, 3d *December.*—The weather moderating at 3° below 0, our absentees joined us, one with his feet frozen, but they were not able

THE INTERIOR OF LOUISIANA.

to bring up the horse; sent two men back on horseback. The hardships of my last voyage now began to be again experienced, and had the climate been as severe as that to which I was then exposed, some of the men must have perished, for they had no winter clothing. I wore myself cotton overhauls, for I had not calculated on being out in this inclement season of the year. Dr. Robinson, and myself, with assistants, went out and took the altitude of the north mountain on the base of a mile;* after which, together with Sparks, we endeavoured to kill a cow, but without effect. Killed two bulls, that the men might take pieces of their hides for mockinsons. Left Sparks out. On our return to camp, found the men had got back with the strayed horse, but too late to march.

Thursday, 4th *December.*—Marched about five o'clock. Took up Sparks, who had succeeded in killing a cow. Killed two buffaloes and six turkies. Distance advanced, twenty miles.

Friday, 5th *December.*—Marched at our usual hour. Passed one very bad place of falling rocks, where we had to carry our loads. Encamped on the main branch of the river, near the entrance of the South Mountain. In the evening, walked up to the mountain. Heard fourteen guns at camp, during my absence, which alarmed me considerably; returned as quickly as possibly, and found that the cause of my alarm arose from their shooting turkies. Killed two buffaloes and nine turkies. Distance advanced, eighteen miles.

Saturday, 6th *December.*—Sent out three different parties to hunt the Spanish trace, but without success. The Doctor and myself followed the river into the mountain, which was bounded on each side by rocks two hundred feet high, leaving a small valley of fifty or sixty feet. Killed two buffaloes, two deer, and one turkey.

---

* The perpendicular height of the mountain from the level of the prairie, we found to be ten thousand five hundred and eighty-one feet, and admitting the prairie to be eight thousand feet above the level of the sea, it would make the elevation of this peak eighteen thousand five hundred and eighty-one feet, equal to that of some, and surpassing the calculated height of others for the peak of Teneriffe, and falling short of that of Chimborazo only one thousand seven hundred and one feet. Indeed, it was so remarkable as to be known to all the savage nations for hundreds of miles round, and to be spoken of with admiration by the Spaniards of New Mexico, and formed the bounds of their travels to the N. W. In our wandering in the mountains from the 14th November to the 27th January, it was never out of our sight, except when we were in a valley.

Sunday, 7th *December.*—We again despatched parties in search of the Spanish trace. One party discovered it on the other side of the river, and followed it into the valley of the stream at the entrance of the mountains, where they met two parties who were returning from exploring the two branches of the river; of which they reported, that they had ascended until the river was merely a brook, bounded on both sides with perpendicular rocks, impracticable for horses ever to pass. Then they recrossed the river to the north side and discovered, as they supposed, that the Spanish troops had ascended a dry valley to the right. On their return they found some rock salt, samples of which were brought me. We determined to march on the morrow to the entrance of the valley, there to examine the salt and the road. Killed one wild cat.

Monday, 8th *December.*—On examining the trace found yesterday, conceived it to have been only that of a reconnoitring party despatched from the main body; and on analysing the rock salt, found it to be strongly impregnated with sulphur, and there were some very strong sulphurated springs at its base. Returned to camp, took with me Dr. Robinson and Miller, and descended the river, in order to discover certainly if the whole party had come by this route. Descended about seven miles on the south side. Saw great numbers of turkies, and deer. Killed one of the latter.

Tuesday, 9th *December.*— Before we marched, killed a fine buck at our camp, as he was passing. I found the Spanish camp, about four miles below, and from every observation we could make conceived they had ascended the river. Returned to camp, where we arrived about two o'clock, and found all well; would have moved immediately, but four men were out reconnoitring. Killed three deer.

Wednesday, 10th *December.*— Marched, and found the road over the mountain to be excellent. Encamped on a dry ravine. Obliged to melt snow for ourselves and horses. And as there was nothing else for the latter to eat, gave them one pint of corn each. Killed one buffalo.

Thursday, 11th *December.*—Marched at ten o'clock, and after proceeding one mile, struck a branch of the Arkansaw, on which the supposed Spaniards had encamped, where there were both water and grass. Kept along this branch, but was frequently embarrassed as to the trace. At three o'clock, P. M. having no sign of it, halted and encamped, and went out to search for it; found it about one mile to the right. Distance advanced, fifteen miles.

THE INTERIOR OF LOUISIANA.

Friday, 12th *December.*—Marched at nine o'clock; continued up the same branch as yesterday. The ridges on our right and left appeared to grow lower, but mountains appeared on our flanks through the intervals covered with snow. Owing to the weakness of our horses made only twelve miles.

Saturday, 13th *December.*—Marched at the usual hour, and passed large springs and the supposed Spanish camp; at twelve o'clock passed a dividing ridge, and immediately fell on a small branch running N. 20° W. There being no appearance of wood we left it, together with the Spanish trace, to our right, and made for the hills to encamp. After the halt I took my gun, and went out to see what discovery I could make. After marching about two miles north, fell on a river forty yards wide frozen over, which after some investigation I found ran north-east. This was the occasion of much surprise, as we were taught to expect to meet with the branches of the Red river, which should have run south-east. Query, must it not be the head water of the River Plate? If so, the Missouri must run much more to the west than is generally represented. For the Plate is a small river, by no means calculated to excite an expectation of so extensive a course.* Distance advanced, eighteen miles. One horse gave out and was left.

Sunday, 14th *December.*—Struck the river upon our march; ascended it four miles and encamped on the northern side. The prairie being about two miles wide, was covered for at least six miles along the banks of the river, with horse dung and the marks of Indian camps, which had been stationed here since the cold weather had set in, as was evident by the fires which were in the centre of the lodges. The signs made by their horses were astonishing, and must have taken one thousand cattle some months to have left them. As it was impossible to say which course the Spaniards had pursued amongst the multiplicity of signs which now appeared, we halted early, and discovered that they or the savages, had

---

* Much light has been thrown on the geography of the countries adjacent to the Missouri, by the journey of Captains Lewis and Clarke, to the source of that river, and across the dividing ridge of the Stony Mountains to the Pacific. There seems little doubt of the correctness of Mr. Pike's suggestion, that this stream composed a main branch of the Plate, and it is accordingly so laid down in his own large chart. E.

ascended the river. We determined to pursue the route. As the geography of the country had turned out to be so different from our expectations, we were somewhat at a loss which course to pursue, unless we attempted to cross the snow-capt mountains to the south-east of us, which appeared almost impossible. On this day burst one of our rifles, which was a great loss, as it was the third gun that had burst, and, the fifth broken on the march. One of my men was now armed with my sword and pistols. Killed two buffaloes.

Monday, 15th *December*.—After repairing the guns, we marched, but were obliged to leave another horse. Ascended the river, both sides of which were covered with old Indian camps, at which we found corn cribs; we were induced to believe that these savages, although erratic, must remain long enough in one place to cultivate grain; or must obtain it of the Spaniards. From their sign they must have been extremely numerous, and have possessed vast numbers of horses.

My poor fellows now suffered extremely from the cold, being almost naked. Distance advanced, ten miles.

Tuesday, 16th *December*.—Marched up the river about two miles and killed a buffalo. When, finding no road up the stream, we halted, and despatched parties in different directions. The Doctor and myself ascending high enough to enable me to lay down the course of the river into the mountains. From a high ridge we reconnoitred the adjacent country, and resolved to put the Spanish trace out of the question, and to shape our course south-west for the head of Red river. One of our party found a large camp, which had been occupied by at least three thousand Indians, with a large cross in the middle. Are these people Catholics?

Wednesday, 17th *December*.—On striking a left hand fork of the river we had left, found it to be the main branch, and ascended it some distance; but finding it to bear too much to the north, we encamped about two miles from its banks for the purpose of benefiting by its water. Distance advanced, fifteen miles.

Thursday, 18th *December*.—Crossed the mountain which lay south-west of us. In a distance of seven miles arrived at a small spring. Some of our men observed, they supposed it to be the Red river, to which I then gave very little credit. On entering a gap in the next mountain, came to an excellent spring which formed a fine creek: this we followed through narrows in the mountain for about six miles. Found many evacuated camps of Indians, the latest yet seen. After pointing out the ground for the encampment, the Doctor and myself went on to make discoveries, as was our usual custom, and in about four miles march, struck what we supposed to be Red river, which here was about twenty-five yards wide: ran with great rapidity, and was full of rocks. We returned to the party with the news, which gave general pleasure. Determined to remain a day or two in order to examine the source. Distance advanced, eighteen miles. Snowy weather.

Friday, 19th *December.*—Marched down the creek, near the opening of the prairie, and encamped. Sent out parties hunting, but had no success. Still snowing and stormy. Making preparations to take an observation.

Saturday, 20th *December.*—Having found a fine place for pasture on the river, sent our horses down to it with a guard. Also, three parties out a hunting, all of whom returned without success. Took an observation. As there was no prospect of killing any game, it was necessary that the party should leave this place. I therefore determined that the Doctor and Baroney should descend the river in the morning; that myself and two men would ascend, and the rest of the party descend after the Doctor, until they obtained provision, and could wait for me.

Sunday, 21st *December.*—The Doctor and Baroney marched; the party remained for me to take a meridional observation, after which we separated. Myself, and the two men who accompanied me (Mountjoy and Miller), ascended for twelve miles; and encamped on the north side of the river, continuing close to the north mountain, and running through a narrow rocky channel, in some places not more than twenty feet wide, and at least ten feet deep. Its banks bordered with yellow pine, cedar, &c.

Monday, 22d *December.*—Marched up thirteen miles farther, to a large point of the mountain, whence we had a view of at least thirty-five miles, to where the river entered the mountain, it being at that place not more than ten or fifteen feet wide; and, properly speaking, only a *brook*. From this place, after taking the course and estimating the distance, we returned to our camp of last evening. Killed a turkey and a hare.

Tuesday, 23d *December.*—Marched early, and at two o'clock P. M. discovered the trail of the party on the opposite side of the river; forded it, although extremely cold, and marched until some time in the night, when we arrived at the second night's encampment of the party. Our clothing was frozen stiff, and we ourselves were considerably benumbed.

Wednesday, 24th *December.*—The parties' provision extending only to the 23d, and their orders being not to halt until they killed some game, and then wait for us, they might have been considerably advanced. About eleven o'clock met Dr. Robinson on a prairie, who informed me that he and Baroney had been absent from the party two days, without killing anything, also without eating; but that over night they had killed four buffaloes, and that he was in search of the men. I suffered the two men who were with me to go to the camp where the meat was, as we had also been nearly two days without eating. The Doctor and myself pursued the trail, and found them encamped on the river's bottom. Sent out horses for the meat; shortly after, Sparks arrived, and informed us he had killed four cows. Thus, from being in a starving condition, we had at once eight beeves in our camp. We now again found ourselves all assembled together on Christmas eve, and appeared generally to be content, although all the refreshment we had to celebrate the day with was buffalo flesh, without salt, or any other thing whatever.

My little excursion up the river had been undertaken with a view of establishing the geography of the sources of the (supposed) Red river, as I well knew the indefatigable researches of Dr. Hunter, Dunbar, and Freeman, had left nothing unnoticed in the extent of their voyage up that stream. I determined that its upper branches should be equally well explored, as in this voyage I had already ascertained the sources of the Osage and *White rivers, been round the head of the Kanses river, and on the head waters of the Plate.

Thursday, 25th *December.*—The weather being stormy, and having some meat to dry, I concluded to lie by this day. Here I must take the liberty of observing that in this situation the hardships and privations we underwent, were on this day brought more fully to our minds than at any time previously. We had before been occasionally accustomed to some degree of relaxation, and extra enjoyments; but the case was now far different: eight hundred miles from the frontiers of our country, in the most

---
* Comparing Mr. Pike's map with his journal, it certainly does not appear that he saw the White river, having mistaken for it a branch of the Arkansaw. E.

inclement season of the year; not one person properly clothed for the winter, many without blankets, having been obliged to cut them up for socks and other articles; lying down too at night on the snow or wet ground, one side burning whilst the other was pierced with the cold wind; this was briefly the situation of the party: whilst some were endeavouring to make a miserable substitute of raw buffalo hide for shoes, and other covering. I will not speak of diet, as I conceive that to be beneath the serious consideration of a man on a journey of such a nature. We spent this day as agreeably as could be expected from men in our circumstances. Caught a bird of a new species, by a trap made for him.*

Friday, 26th *December.*—Marched at two o'clock and made seven miles and a half to the entrance of the mountains. On this piece of prairie the river spread considerably, and formed several small islands. A large stream enters from the south. As my boy and some others were unwell, I omitted pitching our tent, in order that they might have it; in consequence of which we were completely covered with snow, as well as having it for our bed.

Saturday, 27th *December.*—Marched over an extremely rough road, our horses frequently fell and cut themselves considerably on the rocks. From there being no roads of buffaloes, or sign of horses, I am convinced that neither these animals, nor the Aborigines of the country ever take this route to go from the source of the river out of the mountains; but that they must cross one of the chains to the right or left, and find a smoother tract to the lower country. We were obliged to unload our horses and carry the baggage at several places. Distance advanced, twelve miles and a half.

Sunday, 28th *December.*—Marched over an open space, and from the appearance before us concluded we were going out of the mountains, but at night encamped at the entrance of most perpendicular precipices on both

---

* This bird was of a green colour, almost the size of a quail, and had a small tuft on its head like a pheasant, and was one of the carnivorous species; it differed from any bird we ever saw in the United States. We kept it with us in a small wicker cage, feeding it on meat, until I left the interpreter on the Arkansaw, to whose care I committed it. We at one time took a companion of the same species, and put him in the same cage, when the first resident never ceased attacking the stranger, until he had killed him.

sides, through which the river ran and our course lay. Distance advanced, sixteen miles.

Monday, 29th *December.*—Owing to the extreme ruggedness of the road, we made but five miles march. Saw an animal of a new species on the mountain, ascended to kill him, but did not succeed. Finding the impossibility of getting along with the horses, made one sledge, which with the men attached to three horses, carried their load.

Tuesday, 30th *December.*—At half past one o'clock were obliged to halt on our march and send back for the sledge loads, as they had broken it, and could not proceed owing to the waters running over the ice. Distance advanced, eight miles. Crossed our horses twice on the ice.

Wednesday, 31st *December.*—Marched. Had frequently to cross the river on the ice, during our march; the horses falling down, we were obliged to pull them over on the ice. The river turned so much to the north, as almost to induce us to believe it was the Arkansaw. Distance advanced, ten miles and three-quarters.

Thursday, 1st *January*, 1807.—The Doctor and one man marched early, in order to precede the party until they should kill a supply of provision. We had great difficulty in getting our horses along, some of the poor animals having nearly killed themselves by falling on the ice. Found on the way one of the mountain rams which the Doctor and Brown had killed and left on the road. Skinned it with horns, &c. At night ascended a mountain, and discovered a prairie ahead about eight miles; the news of which gave great joy to the party.

Friday, 2d *January.*—Laboured all day, but advanced only one mile, many of our horses being much wounded in falling on the rocks. Provisions growing short, left Stout and Miller with two loads to come on with a sledge on the ice, which covered the water in some of the coves. Finding it almost impossible to proceed any further with the horses by the lead of the river, ascended the mountain, and immediately after were again obliged to descend an almost perpendicular side, in effecting which, one horse fell down the precipice, and bruised himself so miserably that I conceived it mercy to cause the poor animal to be shot. Many others were nearly killed by falls. Left two men with loads and tools to make sledges. The two men we had left in the morning had passed us.

THE INTERIOR OF LOUISIANA.

Saturday, 3d *January.*—Left two more men to make sledges, and to follow us. We pursued the river, and with great difficulty made six miles, by frequently cutting roads on the ice, and covering it with earth, in order to go round precipices that projected into the course.

The men left in the morning encamped with us at night, but we saw nothing of those of the day before. This day two of the horses became senseless from the bruises received on the rocks, and we were obliged to leave them.

Sunday, 4th *January.*—We made the prairie about three o'clock, when I detached Baroney and two soldiers with the horses, in order to find some practicable way for them to get out of the mountains without their loads. I then divided the others into two parties of two men each, to make sledges, and bring on the baggage. I determined to continue down the river alone, until I could kill some provision, and find the two men who had left us on the second, or the Doctor and his companion, for we had now no food left, and every one had to depend on his own exertions for safety and subsistence. Thus we were divided into eight different parties, viz., first, the Doctor and his companion; second, the two men with the first sledge; third, the interpreter and the two men with the horses; fourth, myself; fifth, sixth, seventh and eighth, two men each, with sledges, at different distances; all of whom, except the last, had orders, if they killed any game, to secure some part in a conspicuous place for their companions in the rear. I marched on about five miles on the river, which was one continued fall through a narrow channel, and immense cliffs on both sides. Near night I came to a place where the rocks were perpendicular on both sides, and no ice, except a narrow border on the water. I began to look about, in order to discover which way the Doctor and his companion had managed, and to find what had become of the two men with the first sledge; when I discovered one of the latter climbing up the side of the rocks; I called to him, and he and his companion immediately joined me. They said they had not known whether we were before, or in the rear; that they had eaten nothing for the last two days; and that this night they intended to have boiled a deer's skin to subsist on. We at length discovered a narrow ravine, where we observed the trace of the Doctor and his companion; as the water had run over it and frozen hard, it was one continued sheet of ice; we ascended with the utmost difficulty and danger, loaded with the baggage. On the summit of the first ridge we found an encampment of the Doctor's, where they had killed a deer, but they had now no meat. He afterwards informed me that they had left the greatest part of it hanging on a tree, but supposed the birds had destroyed it. I left the men to bring up the remainder of the baggage and went out in order to kill something for subsistence; wounded a deer but the darkness of the night approaching could not find him; when I returned hungry, weary, and thirsty, and had only snow to supply the calls of nature. Distance advanced, eight miles.

Monday, 5th *January*.—I went out in the morning to hunt, whilst the two men were bringing up some of their loads still left at the foot of the mountain. Wounded several deer, but was surprised to find I killed none, and on examining my gun found it bent; owing as I suppose to some fall on the ice or rocks. I shortly after received a fall on the side of a hill which broke it off by the breech; this put me into despair, as I calculated on it, as my grandest resource for a great portion of my party. Returned to my companions sorely fatigued and hungry. I then took a double-barrelled gun, and left them, with assurances that the first animal I killed I would return with part of for their relief. About ten o'clock rose the highest summit of the mountain, when the unbounded extent of the prairies again presented itself to my view, and from some distant peaks, I immediately recognized our situation to be one outlet of the Arkansaw, which we had left nearly one month since. This was a great mortification, but at the same time, I consoled myself with the knowledge I had acquired of the source of the Plate and Arkansaw rivers, with the river to the north-west, supposed to be the Pierre Jaun,* which scarcely any person but a madman would ever purposely attempt to trace any further than the entrance of these mountains, which had hitherto secured their sources from the scrutinizing eye of civilized man.

---

* The Yellow Stone river branch of the Missouri. This rises a few miles to the northward of the Plate river, nearly as high up as the sources of the Arkansaw, but on the other side of a chain of mountains, about lat. 41 42′. It is remarkable that no mention is made in the proper place in the journal of the discovery of this stream. From Mr. Pike's large chart, it appears to have been seen by an exploring detachment of his party. E.

I arrived at the foot of the mountain and the bank of the river in the afternoon, and at the same time discovered on the other shore Baroney with the horses. They had found quite an eligible pass; they had killed one buffalo and some deer. We proceeded to our old camp, which we had left the tenth of December, and re-occupied it. Saw the traces of the Doctor and his companion, but could not discover the place of their retreat.

This was my birth day, and most fervently did I hope never to pass another so miserably. Distance advanced, seven miles. Fired a gun as a signal for the Doctor.

Tuesday, 6th *January*.— Despatched the two soldiers back with some provision to meet the first men and assist them on; and sent the interpreter to hunt. About eight o'clock the Doctor arrived, having seen some of the men. He had been confined to the camp for one or two days, by a vertigo, which proceeded from some berries he had eaten on the mountains. His companion brought down six deer which they had at their camp; thus we again began to be out of danger of starving. In the afternoon, some of the men arrived, and part were immediately sent back with provisions, &c. Killed three deer.

Wednesday, 7th *January*.—Sent more men back to assist in the rear, and to carry the poor fellows provision: at the same time kept Baroney and one man hunting. Killed three deer.

Thursday, 8th *January*.— Some of the different parties arrived. Put one man to stocking my rifle. Others sent back to assist up the rear. Killed two deer.

Friday, 9th. *January*. — The whole party was once more joined together, when we felt comparatively happy, notwithstanding the great mortifications I had experienced at being so egregiously deceived as to the Red river. I now felt at considerable loss how to proceed, as any idea of service at that time from my horses was entirely preposterous. Thus, after various plans formed and rejected, and the most mature deliberation, I determined to build a small place for defence and deposit, and leave part of the baggage, horses, my interpreter, and one man; and with the remainder, with our packs of Indian presents, ammunition, tools, &c., on our backs, to cross the mountains on foot, find the Red river, and then send back a detachment to conduct the horses and baggage after us, by the most eligible route we could discover; by which time we calculated our horses would be so far recovered as to be able to endure the fatigue of the march. In consequence of this determination, some were put to constructing block houses, some to hunting, some to take care of horses, &c., &c. I myself made preparations to pursue a course of observations, that would enable me to ascertain the latitude and longitude of the situation, which I conceived to be an important one. Killed three deer.

Saturday, 10th *January*.— Killed five deer. Took equal altitudes, angular distances of two stars, &c., but now do not recollect which. Killed three more deer.

Sunday, 11th *January*.— Ascertained the latitude, and took the angular distances of some stars. Killed four deer.

Monday, 12th *January*.— Preparing the baggage for a march, by separating it, &c. Observations continued.

Tuesday, 13th *January*.— Weighed out each man's pack. This day I obtained the angle between the sun and moon, which I conceived the most correct way I possessed of ascertaining the longitude, as an immersion or emersion of Jupiter's satellites could not now be obtained. Killed four deer.

Wednesday, 14th *January*.— We marched our party, consisting of eleven soldiers, the Doctor, and myself, each of us carrying forty-five pounds, and as much provision as he thought proper; which, with arms, &c., made on an average seventy pounds, leaving Baroney and one man, Patrick Smith, behind. We crossed the first ridge, leaving the main branch of the river to the north of us, and struck on the south fork, on which we encamped, intending to pursue it through the mountains, as its course was more southerly. The Doctor killed one deer. Distance advanced, thirteen miles.

Thursday, 15th *January*.— Followed up this branch and passed the main ridge of what I term the Blue Mountains. Halted early ; the Doctor, myself, and one hunter went out with our guns, each killed a deer and brought them into a camp. Distance advanced, nineteen miles.

Friday, 16th *January*.— Marched up the creek all day. Encamped early, as it was snowing. I went out to hunt, but killed nothing. Deer on the hills and mountains lessening. Distance advanced, eighteen miles.

THE INTERIOR OF LOUISIANA.

Saturday, 17th *January*.—Marched about four miles when the great White Mountain presented itself before us: in sight of which we had been for more than a month, and through which we supposed lay the long sought Red river. We now left the creek on the north of us, and bore away more east to a low place in the mountains. About sunset we came to the edge of a prairie, which bounded the foot of the mountain, and as there was no wood or water where we were, and the wood from the skirts of the mountain appeared to be at no great distance, I thought proper to march for it. In the middle of the prairie crossed the creek which now bore almost east. Here we all got our feet wet. The night commenced extremely cold. When we halted at the woods at eight o'clock for encampment, after getting fires made, we discovered that the feet of nine of our men were frozen, and to add to the misfortune, of both of those whom we called hunters among the number. This night we had no provision. Distance advanced, twenty-eight miles. Reaumeure's thermometer stood at 18½° below 0.

Sunday, 18th *January*.—We started out two of the men least injured; the Doctor and myself (who fortunately were untouched by the frost) also went out to hunt for something to preserve existence. Near evening we wounded a buffalo with three balls, but had the mortification to see him run off notwithstanding. We concluded it was useless to go home to add to the general gloom, and went amongst some rocks, where we encamped, and sat up all night, as from the intense cold it was impossible to sleep: also, hungry and without cover.

Monday, 19th *January*.—We again took the field, and after crawling about one mile in the snow, got to shoot eight times among a gang of buffaloes, and could plainly perceive two or three to be badly wounded, but by accident they took the wind of us, and to our great mortification were all able to run off. By this time I was become extremely weak and faint, being the fourth day since we had received sustenance, the whole of which time we were marching hard, and the last night had scarcely closed our eyes to sleep. We were then inclining our course to a point of wood, determined to remain absent and die by ourselves rather than return to our camp and behold the misery of our poor companions; when we discovered a gang of buffaloes coming along at some distance. With great exertion I made out to run and place myself behind some cedars, and by the greatest good luck the first shot stopped one, which we killed in three more shots, and by the dusk had cut each of us a heavy load, with which we determined immediately to proceed to the camp in order to relieve the anxiety of our men, and carry them some relief. We arrived there about twelve o'clock, and when I threw my load down, it was with difficulty I prevented myself from falling: I was attacked with a giddiness which lasted for some minutes. On the countenances of the men was not a frown, nor was there a desponding eye; all seemed happy to hail their officer and companions; yet not a mouthful had they eaten for four days. On demanding what were their thoughts, the sergeant replied, the most robust had determined to set out on the morrow in search of us; and not return unless they found us, or killed something to preserve the lives of their starving companions.

Tuesday, 20th *January*.—The Doctor and all the men able to march, returned to the buffalo to bring in the remainder of the meat.

On examining the feet of those who were frozen, we found it impossible for two of them to proceed. And two others only without loads by the help of a stick. One of the former was my waiter, a promising young lad of twenty, whose feet were so badly frozen as to present every probability of his loosing them.

The Doctor and party returned towards evening loaded with the buffalo meat.

Wednesday, 21st *January*.—This day separated the four loads we intended to leave, and took them at some distance from the camp, where we secured them. I went up to the foot of the mountain, to see what prospect there was of being able to cross it, but had not more than fairly arrived at its base when I found the snow four or five feet deep; this obliged me to determine to proceed and cotoyer the mountains to the south, where it appeared lower, and until we found a place where we could cross.

Thursday, 22d *January*.—I furnished the two poor fellows who were to remain with ammunition, and made use of every argument in my power to encourage them to have fortitude to resist their fate, and gave them assurances of my sending relief as soon as possible.

We parted, but not without tears. We pursued our march, taking merely sufficient provision for one meal, in order to leave as much as possible for the two poor fellows who remained (who were Thomas Dougherty and John Sparks). We went on eight miles and encamped on a little creek, which came down from the mountains. At three o'clock went out to hunt, but found nothing. Little snow.

Friday, 23d *January*.—After shewing the sergeant a point to steer for, the Doctor and myself proceeded on a-head, in hopes of killing something, as we were again without victuals. About one o'clock it commenced snowing very hard. We retreated to a small copse of pine, where we constructed a camp to shelter us, and as it was time the party should arrive, we sallied forth to search for them.

We separated, and had not marched more than one or two miles, when I found it impossible to keep any course without the compass continually in my hand, and then not being able to see more than ten yards. I began to perceive the difficulty even of finding the way back to our camp; and I can scarcely conceive a more dreadful idea than that of remaining on the wild, where inevitable death must have ensued. It was with great pleasure I again reached the camp, where I found the Doctor had arrived before me. We lay down and strove to dissipate the ideas of hunger and our misery, by the thoughts of our far distant homes and relatives. Distance advanced, eight miles.

Saturday, 24th *January*.—We sallied out in the morning, and shortly after perceived our little band marching through the snow, then about two feet and a half deep, silent and with downcast countenances. We joined them, and learnt that finding the snow to fall so thickly that it was impossible to proceed, they had encamped about one o'clock the preceding day. As I found all the buffaloes had left the plains, I determined to attempt the traverse of the mountains, in which we persevered, until the snow became so deep as to render it impossible to proceed; when I again turned my face to the plain, and for the first time in the journey found myself discouraged; and it was the first time I heard a man express himself in a seditious manner. One had exclaimed, "that it was more than human nature could bear to march three days without sustenance, through snows three feet deep, and carry burdens only fit for horses."

As I knew very well the fidelity and attachment of the majority of the men, and even of this poor fellow, only he could not endure fasting, and that it was in my power to chastise him when I thought proper, I passed it over for the moment, determined to notice it at a more auspicious time.

We dragged our weary and emaciated limbs along, until about ten o'clock. The Doctor and myself, who were in advance, discovered some buffaloes on the plain, when we left our loads and orders on the snow to proceed to the nearest woods to encamp. We went in pursuit of the buffaloes which were on the move.

The Doctor, who was then less reduced than myself, ran and got behind a hill and shot one down, which stopped the remainder. We crawled up to the dead one, and shot from him as many as twelve or fourteen times among the herd; when they removed out of sight. We then proceeded to butcher the one we had shot, and after procuring each of us a load of the meat, marched for the camp, the smoke of which was in view. We arrived there to the great joy of our brave lads, who immediately feasted sumptuously. After our repast, I sent for the man who had presumed to speak discontentedly in the course of the day, and addressed him to the following effect:

"Brown, you this day presumed to make use of language which was seditious and mutinous; I then passed it over, pitying your situation and attributing your conduct to your distress, rather than your inclination to sow discontent amongst the party. Had I reserved provisions for ourselves, whilst you were starving; had we been marching along light and at our ease, whilst you were weighed down with your burden, then you would have had some pretext for your observations; but when we were equally hungry, weary, emaciated and charged with burdens which I believe my natural strength is less able to bear than any man's in the party; when we are always foremost in breaking the road, reconnoitring and enduring the fatigues of the chase, it was the height of ingratitude in you to let an expression escape which was indicative of discontent. Your ready compliance and firm perseverance I had reason to expect, as the leader of men who are my companions in misery and danger. But your duty as a soldier called on your obedience to your officer, and a prohibition of such language, which for this time I will pardon; but assure you, should it ever be repeated, by instant *death* I will revenge your ingratitude and punish your disobedience. I take this opportunity likewise to express to you, soldiers, generally, my thanks for your obedience, perseverance, and ready contempt of every danger, which you have in common evinced; and assure you nothing shall be wanting on my part, to procure you the rewards of our government and the gratitude of your countrymen."

They all appeared very much affected, and retired with assurances of perseverance in their duty. Distance advanced, nine miles.

Sunday, 25th *January*.—I determined never again to march with so little provision on hand; for had the storm continued one day longer, the animals would have continued in the mountains, and we should have become so weak as not to be able to hunt, and of course have perished.

The Doctor went out with the men, and secured three of the buffaloes, and commenced bringing in the meat, at which we continued all day.

Monday, 26th *January*.—Got in all the meat and dried it on a scaffold; intending to take as much as possible along and leave one of my frozen lads with the remainder, as a deposit for the parties who might return for them with the baggage, &c., on their way to Baroney's camp.

Tuesday, 27th *January*.—We proceeded on our march, determining to cross the mountains, leaving Menaugh encamped with our deposit. After a bad day's march through snows, some places three feet deep, we struck on a brook that led west, which I followed down, and shortly came to a small stream, running in the same direction. This we hailed with fervency, as the waters of the Red river. Saw some sign of elk. Distance advanced, fourteen miles.

Wednesday, 28th *January*.—Followed down the ravine, and discovered after some time that there had been a road cut out, and on many trees were various hieroglyphics painted. After marching some miles we discovered, through the lengthy vista at a distance, another chain of mountains, and nearer to us at the foot of the White Mountains, which we were then descending, sandy hills.

We marched on to the outlet of the mountain and left the sandy desert to our right; kept down between it and the mountain. When we encamped I ascended one of the largest hills of sand, and with my glass could discover a large river, flowing nearly north by west and south by east through the plain which came out of the third chain of mountains about north $75°$ west. The prairie between the two chains of mountains bore nearly north and south: I returned to camp with the news of my discovery. The sand hills extended up and down at the foot of the White

Mountains about fifteen miles, and appeared to be about five miles in width. Their appearance was exactly that of the sea in a storm, except as to colour, not the least sign of vegetation existing on them. Distance advanced, fifteen miles.

Thursday, 29th *January*.— Finding the distance too great to attempt crossing immediately to the river in a direct line, we marched obliquely to a copse of woods which made down a considerable distance from the mountain. Distance advanced, seventeen miles. Saw sign of horses.

Friday, 30th *January*.— We marched hard and in the evening arrived on the banks of the Rio del Norte, then supposed to be the Red river. Distance advanced, twenty-four miles.

Saturday, 31st *January*.— As there was no timber here, we determined on descending until we found some, in order to make transports to descend the river with; where we might establish a position that four or five might defend against the insolence, cupidity or barbarity of the savages; whilst the others returned to assist on the poor fellows who were left behind at different points. We descended eighteen miles, when we met a large west branch, emptying into the main stream; up which, about five miles, we took our station. Killed one deer. Distance advanced, eighteen miles.

Sunday, 1st *February*.— Laid out the plan for our works, and went out hunting.

Monday, 2d *February*.— The Doctor and myself went out to hunt, and with great difficulty by night killed one deer, at the distance of seven or eight miles from camp, which we carried in.

Tuesday, 3d *February*.— Spent this day in reading, &c.

Wednesday, 4th *February*.— Went out hunting, but could not kill anything. One of my men killed a deer.

Thursday, 5th *February*.— The Doctor and myself went out to hunt, and after chasing some deer several hours without success, we ascended a high hill, which lay south of our camp, from whence we had a view of all the prairie and rivers to the north of us: it was one of the most sublime and beautiful inland prospects ever presented to the eyes of man. The prairie lying nearly north and south, was propably sixty miles by forty-five.

THE INTERIOR OF LOUISIANA.

The main river bursting out of the western mountains and meeting from the north-east a large branch which divides the chain, proceeds down the prairie, making many large and beautiful islands, one of which I judge contains one hundred thousand acres of land, all meadow ground, covered with innumerable herds of deer.) About six miles from the mountains which cross the prairie, at the south end, a branch of twelve steps wide pays its tribute to the main stream from the western course. Due W. 12. N. 75. W. 6. Four miles below is a stream of the same size, which enters on the east; its general course is N. 65 E., up which was a large road; down from the entrance of this, was about three miles to the junction of the western Fork, which waters the foot of the hill on the north, whilst the main river wound along in meanders on the east. In short, this view combined the sublime and beautiful.

The great and lofty mountains covered with eternal snow, seemed to surround the luxuriant vale crowned with perennial flowers, like a terrestrial paradise, shut out from the view of man.

The country we had traversed from the Arkansaw to the Rio del Norte was covered with mountains and small prairies, but the game becomes gradually much more scarce, owing to the vicinity of the Spanish Indians, and the Spaniards themselves. In this western traverse of Louisiana, the following general observations may be made: from the Missouri to the head of the Osage river, a distance in a straight line probably of three hundred miles, the country will admit of a numerous, extensive, and compact population; from thence on the rivers Kanses, La Plate, Arkansaw, and their various branches, it appears to me to be only possible to introduce a limited population. The inhabitants would find it most to their advantage to pay attention to the rearing of cattle, horses, sheep and goats: all of which they can raise in abundance, the earth producing spontaneously sufficient for their support, both in winter and summer, by which means their herds might become immensely numerous; but the wood now in the country would not be sufficient for a moderate population more than fifteen years, and then it would be out of the question to think of using any of it in manufactories, consequently their houses would be built entirely of mud bricks (like those in New Spain), or of the brick manufactured with fire; but possibly time may make the discovery of coal mines, which would render the country habitable. (The source of the La

Plate, as before observed, is situated in the same chain of mountains as the Arkansaw, and comes from that grand reservoir of snows and fountains, which gives birth on its north-eastern side to the Red river, the Yellow Stone river of Lewis, and of the Missouri (its great south-western branch), and the Platte; on its south-western side, it produces the Rio Colorado of California, on its eastern the Arkansaw, and on its southern the Rio del Norte of North Mexico. I have no hesitation in asserting I can take a position in the mountains from whence I can visit either of those rivers in one day.*

Numerous have been the hypotheses formed by various naturalists, to account for the vast tract of untimbered country which lies between the waters of the Missouri, Mississippi and the western ocean, from the mouth of the Mississippi to the 48° north latitude. Although not flattering myself to be able to elucidate what numbers of highly scientific characters have acknowledged to be beyond their depth of research, still I would not think I had done my country justice, did I not give publicity to what few lights my examination of those internal deserts has enabled me to acquire. In that vast country of which we speak, we find the soil generally dry, sandy, with gravel; and discover that the moment we approach a stream, the land becomes more humid with small timber: I therefore conclude that this country never was wooded, as from the earliest age the aridity of the soil, having so few water-courses running through it, and they being principally dry in summer, has never afforded moisture sufficient to support the growth of timber. In all timbered land the annual discharge of the leaves, with the continual decay of old trees and branches, creates a manure and moisture, which are preserved from the heat, the sun not being permitted to direct his rays perpendicularly, but only to shed them obliquely through the foliage. But here a barren soil, parched and dried up for eight months in the year, presents neither moisture nor nutriment sufficient for the growth of wood. These vast plains of the western hemisphere may become in time equally celebrated with the sandy deserts of Africa, for I saw in my route, in various places, tracts of many leagues where the wind had thrown up the sand, in all the fanciful forms of the ocean's rolling waves, and on which not a speck of vegetation existed. But from these immense prairies may arise one great

* This must evidently be a mistake so far as it relates to the Red river, which rises far to the southward. E.

THE INTERIOR OF LOUISIANA.

advantage to the United States, viz., the restriction of our population to some certain limits, and thereby a continuation of the union. Our citizens being so prone to rambling, and extending themselves on the frontiers, will, through necessity, be constrained to limit their extent on the west to the borders of the Missouri and Mississippi, while they leave the prairies, incapable of cultivation, to the wandering and uncivilized Aborigines of the country.

Friday, 6th *February*.—The Doctor having some pecuniary demands on the Province of New Mexico, conceived this to be the most eligible point for him to set out from, in order to return previously to all my party having joined me from the Arkansaw, and before I could be prepared to descend to Natchitoches. He therefore this day made his preparations for proceeding on the morrow. I went out hunting, and killed a deer at three miles' distance; which with great difficulty I brought in whole.

We continued to go on with our stockade or breast-work, which was situated on the north bank of the western branch, about five miles from its junction with the main river.

The stockade was situated in a small prairie, on the west fork of the Rio del Norte. The south flank joining the edge of the river, (which at that place was not fordable,) the east and west curtains were flanked by bastions in the N. E. and N. W. angles, which likewise flanked the curtain of the north side of the work. The stockade from the centre of the angles of the bastions was thirty-six feet square. There were heavy cottonwood logs about two feet diameter, laid up all round about six feet, after which lighter ones until we made it twelve feet in height; these logs were joined together by a lap of about two feet at each end. We then dug a small ditch on the inside all round, making it perpendicular on the internal side, and sloping next the work: in this ditch we planted small stakes of about six inches diameter, sharpened at the upper end to a nice point, slanted them over the top of the work, giving them about two and a half feet projection. We then secured them below and above in that position, which formed a small pointed frieze, which must have been removed before the works could have been scaled. Lastly, we had dug a ditch round the whole four feet wide, and let the water into it; the earth taken out being thrown against the work, formed an excellent rampart against small arms, three or four feet high. Our mode of getting in was to crawl over the ditch on a plank, and into a small hole sunk below the level of the work near the river for that purpose. Our port-holes we pierced about eight feet from the ground, and a platform prepared to shoot from.

Thus fortified, I should not have had the least hesitation in putting the hundred Spanish horse at defiance until the first and second night, and then to have made our

Saturday, 7th *February*.—The Doctor marched alone for Santa Fé.†
In the evening I despatched Corporal Jackson with four men to recross the mountains, in order to bring in the baggage left with the frozen men, and to see if they were yet able to proceed. This detachment left me with four men only, two of whom had their feet frozen: they were

---

escape under cover of the darkness; or made a sally and dispersed them, when resting under a full confidence of our being panic struck by their numbers and force.

† The demands which Dr. Robinson had on persons in New Mexico, although originally legitimate, were in some degree spurious in his hands : the circumstances were as follows : In the year 1804, William Morrison, Esq., an enterprising merchant of Kaskaskias, sent a man by the name of Babtiste Lalande, a Creole of the country of Missouri and of La Plate, directing him if possible to push into Santa Fé. He sent in Indians, and the Spaniards came out with horses and carried him and his goods into the province. Finding that he sold the goods high, had land offered him, and that the women were kind, he concluded to expatriate himself, and convert the property of Morrison to his own benefit. When I was about to sail, Morrison conceiving that it was possible I might meet some Spanish factors on the Red river, intrusted me with the claim, in order if they were acquainted with Lalande, I might negotiate the affair with some of them. When on the frontiers, the idea suggested itself to us of making this claim a pretext for Robinson to visit Santa Fé. We therefore gave it the proper appearance, and he marched for that place. Our views were to gain a knowledge of the country, the prospect of trade, force, &c., whilst at the same time our treaties with Spain guaranteed to him, as a citizen of the United States, the right of seeking the recovery of all just debts, dues, or demands, before the legal and authorized tribunals of the country, as a franchised inhabitant of the same, as specified in the 22d article of the treaty.

As it was uncertain whether this gentleman would ever join me again, I at that time committed the following testimonial of respect for his good qualities to paper, which I do not at this time feel any disposition to efface.

He has had the benefit of a liberal education, without having spent his time as too many of our gentlemen do in colleges, in skimming over the surfaces of science, without ever endeavouring to make themselves masters of the solid foundations; but he had studied and reasoned. With these qualifications he possessed a liberality of mind too great ever to reject an hypothesis, because it was not agreeable to the dogmas of the schools; or adopt it, because it had all the eclat of novelty. His soul could conceive great actions, and his hand was ready to achieve them: in short, it may truly be said, that nothing was above his genius, nor anything so minute that he conceived it entirely unworthy of consideration. As a gentleman and companion in dangers, difficulties and hardships, I, in particular, and the expedition in general, owe much to his exertions.

THE INTERIOR OF LOUISIANA.

employed in finishing the stockade, and myself in supporting them by the chase.

Sunday, 8th *February*.—Refreshing my memory as to the French grammar, and observing the work.

Monday, 9th *February*.—Hunting, &c.

Tuesday, 10th *February*.—Read, and laboured at our works.

Wednesday, 11th *February*.—Hunting. Killed three deer.

Thursday, 12th *February*.—Studying.

Friday, 13th *February*.—Hunting. Killed two deer.

Saturday, 14th *February*.—Crossed the river, and examined the numerous springs which issued from the foot of the hill opposite to our camp, which were so strongly impregnated with mineral qualities as not only to keep clear of ice, previously to their joining the main branch, but to keep open the west Fork until its junction with the main river, and for a few miles afterwards; whilst all the other branches in the neighbourhood were bound in the adamantine chains of winter.

Sunday, 15th *February*.—Reading, and works going on, &c.

Monday, 16th *February*.—I took one man and went out hunting; about six miles from the post shot and wounded a deer. Immediately afterwards discovered two horsemen rising the summit of a hill, about half a mile to our right. As my orders were to avoid giving alarm or offence to the Spanish government of New Mexico I endeavoured to shun them at first, but when we attempted to retreat, they pursued us at full charge flourishing their lances, and when we advanced, they would retire as fast as their horses could carry them. Seeing this we got into a small ravine, in hopes to decoy them near enough to oblige them to come to a parley, which happened agreeably to our desires. As they came on, hunting us with great caution, we suffered them to get within forty yards, where we had allured them, but were about running off again, when I ordered the soldier to lay down his arms and walk towards them, at the same time standing ready with my rifle to kill either who should lift an arm in a hostile manner. I then hallooed to them, that we were Americans and friends, which were almost the only two words I knew in the Spanish language: after which, with great signs of fear, they came up, and proved to be a Spanish dragoon and a civilized Indian; armed after their manner, of which we see a description in the Essai Militaire. We were jealous of our arms on both sides, and acted with great precaution. They informed me, that was the fourth day since they had left Santa Fé; that Robinson had arrived there, and had been received with great kindness by the Governor. As I knew them to be spies, I thought it proper merely to inform them that I was about to descend the river to Natchitoches. We sat here on the ground a long time, and finding they were determined not to leave me, we arose and bade them adieu; but they demanded where our camp was, and finding they were not about to depart, I thought it most proper to take them with me, thinking we were on Red river, and of course in the territory claimed by the United States.

We took the road to my fort, and as they were on horseback, they travelled rather faster than myself. They were halted by the sentinel, and immediately retreated much surprised. When I came up I took them in and then explained to them as well as I was able, my intentions of descending the river to Natchitoches; but at the same time told them that if Governor Allencaster would send out an officer with an interpreter, who spoke French or English, I would do myself the pleasure to give his Excellency every reasonable satisfaction as to my intentions in coming on his frontiers. They informed me that on the second day they would be in Santa Fé, but were careful never to suggest an idea of my being on the Rio del Norte. As they concluded I did not think as I spoke, they were very anxious to ascertain our number, &c. Seeing only five men here, they could not believe we came without horses; to this I did not think proper to afford them any satisfaction, giving them to understand we were in many parties.

Tuesday, 17th *February*.—In the morning our two Spanish visitors departed, after I had made them some trifling presents, with which they seemed highly delighted. After their departure we commenced labouring at our little work. As I thought it probable the Governor might dispute my right to descend the Red river, and send out Indians or some light party to attack us, I determined to be as much prepared to receive them as possible. This evening the corporal and three of the men arrived, who had been sent back to the camp of their frozen companions. They informed me that two more would arrive the next day, one of whom was Menaugh, who had been left alone on the 27th January; but the other two, Dogherty and Sparks, were unable to come. They said that they had hailed them with tears of joy, and were in despair when they again left them with the chance of never seeing them more. They sent on to me some of the bones taken out of their feet, and conjured me by all that was sacred, not to leave them to perish far from the civilized world. Oh! little did they know my heart, if they could suspect me of conduct so ungenerous! No, before they should be left, I would for months have carried the end of a litter, in order to secure them the happiness of once more seeing their native homes, and being received in the bosom of a grateful country.

Thus, these poor fellows are to be invalids for life, made infirm at the commencement of manhood, and in the prime of their course; doomed to pass the remainder of their days in misery and want. For what is the pension? not sufficient to buy a man his victuals! What man would even lose the smallest of his joints for such a trifling pittance!

Wednesday, 18th *February*.—The other two men arrived: in the evening I ordered the sergeant and one man to prepare to march on the morrow for the Arkansaw, where we had left our interpreter, horses, &c., to conduct them to us, and on his return to bring the two invalids, who were still on the mountains.

Thursday, 19th *February*.—Sergeant Meek marched with one man, whose name was Theodore Miller, and I took three others to accompany him some distance, in order to point out to him a pass in the mountain, which I conceived more eligible for horses than the one we had penetrated.

I must here remark the effect of habit, discipline, and example, in two soldiers soliciting a command of more than one hundred and eighty miles, over two great ridges of mountains covered with snow, inhabited by bands of unknown savages in the interest of a nation with whom we were not on the best understanding: and to perform this journey, each had about ten pounds of venison! Only let me ask, what would our soldiers generally think on being ordered on such a tour, thus equipped? Yet those men volunteered with others, and were chosen, for which they thought themselves highly honoured.

We accompanied them about six miles, pointed out the pass alluded to in a particular manner; but the corporal reported that the new one which I had obliged him to take was impassable, having been three days in snows nearly middle deep.

We then separated, and having killed a deer, sent one of the men back to the fort with it. With the other two I kept on my exploring trip down the river on the eastern side, at some leagues from its banks, intending to return. At nine o'clock at night, encamped on a small creek which emptied into the river by nearly a due east course.

Friday, 20th *February*.—We marched down the river for a few hours, but seeing no fresh sign of persons, or any other object to attract our attention, took up our route for the fort; discovered the sign of horses and men on the shore. We arrived after a night's absence, and found all well.

Saturday, 21st *February*.—As I was suspicious that possibly some party of Indians might be harbouring round, I gave particular orders to my men, if they discovered any people to endeavour to retreat unobserved; but if not, never to run, and not to suffer themselves to be disarmed or taken prisoners, but conduct whatever party discovered them, if they could not escape, to the fort.

Sunday, 22d *February*.—As I began to think it was time we received a visit from the Spaniards, or their emissaries, I established a look-out guard on the top of a hill all day, and at night a sentinel in a bastion on the land side. Studying, reading, &c. Working at our ditch to bring the river round the work.

Monday, 23d *February*.—Reading, writing, &c.; the men at the usual work.

Tuesday, 24th *February*.—Took one man with me and went out on the Spanish road hunting. Killed one deer and wounded several others, and as we were a great distance from the fort, we encamped near the road all night. Saw several signs of horses.

Wednesday, 25th *February*.—Killed two more deer, when we marched for out post. Took all three of the deer with us, and arrived about nine o'clock at night, as much fatigued as ever I was in my life. Our arrival dissipated the anxiety of the men, who began to be apprehensive we were taken or killed by some of the savages.

Thursday, 26th *February*.—In the morning was apprised by the report of a gun from my look-out guard, of the approach of strangers; immediately after two Frenchmen arrived.

My sentinel halted them, and I ordered them to be admitted after some questions. They informed me that his excellency Governor Allencaster, hearing it was the intention of the Utah Indians to attack me, had

THE INTERIOR OF LOUISIANA.

detached an officer with fifty dragoons to come out and protect me, and that they would be with me in two days. To this I made no reply, but shortly after the party hove in sight, as I afterwards learnt; fifty dragoons and fifty mounted militia of the province, armed in the same manner with lances, escopates, and pistols. My sentinels halted them at the distance of about fifty yards. I had the works manned: I thought it most proper to send out the two Frenchmen to inform the commanding officer, that it was my request he should leave his party in a small copse of wood where he halted, and that I would meet him myself in the prairie, in which our work was situated; this I did, with my sword on me only. I was thus introduced to Don Ignatio Saltelo and Don Bartholemew Fernandez, two lieutenants; the former the commander of the party: I gave them an invitation to enter the works, but requested the troops might remain where they were. This was complied with: but when they came round and discovered that to enter they were obliged to crawl on their bellies over a small drawbridge, they appeared astonished; they however entered without further hesitation.

We first breakfasted on some deer, meal, goose, and some biscuit, which the civilized Indian who came out as a spy had brought me. After breakfast the commanding officer addressed me as follows:

"Sir, the Governor of New Mexico, being informed that you had missed your route, ordered me to offer you in his name, mules, horses, money, or whatever you may stand in need of, to conduct you to the head of Red river; as from Santa Fé, to where it is sometimes navigable, is eight days' journey, and we have guides and the routes of the traders to conduct us."

"What," interrupted I, "is not this the Red river?" "No, sir, it is the Rio del Norte." I immediately ordered my flag to be taken down and rolled up, feeling how sensibly I had committed myself in entering their territory, and was conscious that they must have positive orders to take me in. He now added, "that he had provided one hundred mules and horses to take in my party and baggage, and stated how anxious his excellency was to see me at Santa Fé." I stated to him the absence of my sergeant, the situation of the rest of the party; and that my orders would not justify my entering into the Spanish territories. He urged still further, until I began to feel myself a little heated in the argument, and told him in a peremptory style, I would not go until the arrival of my sergeant, with the remainder of my party. He replied, that there was not the least restraint to be used, only that it was necessary His Excellency should receive an explanation of my business on his frontier; that I might go now, or on the arrival of my party; but that if none went at present he should be obliged to send in for provisions. He added, that if I would now march, he would leave an Indian interpreter and an escort of dragoons to conduct the sergeant into Santa Fé. His mildness induced me to tell him that I would march, but must leave two men in order to meet the sergeant and party to instruct him as to coming in, as he would never do so without a fight, unless ordered.

I was induced to consent to the measure, by conviction that the officer had a positive command to convey me in; and as I had no orders to engage in hostilities, and indeed had committed myself, although innocently, by violating their territory, I conceived it would appear better to shew a will to come to an explanation, rather than be any way constrained. Yet my situation was so eligible, and I could so easily have put them to defiance, that it was with great reluctance I suffered all our labour to be lost, without once trying the efficacy of it.

My compliance seemed to spread general joy through the Spanish party as soon as it was communicated. But it appeared to be different with my men, who wished to have had a little *dust*, (as they expressed themselves,) and were likewise fearful of Spanish treachery.

My determination being once taken, I gave permission for the lieutenant's men to come to the outside of the works and some of mine to go out and see them. Immediately the hospitality and goodness of the Creoles and Mestis began to be manifested by their producing their provision and giving it to my men; at the same time covering them with their blankets.

After writing orders to my sergeant, and leaving them with my corporal and one private who were to remain, we sallied forth, mounted our horses, and went up the river about twelve miles to a place where the Spanish officers had made a camp deposit, from whence we sent down mules for our baggage.

THE INTERIOR OF LOUISIANA.

Abstract of the number of the Indian Nations on the preceding Route.

Names of Nations.	No. of Warriors.	No. of Women.	No. of Children.	No. of Villages.	Probable No. of Souls.	No. of Lodges of the Roving Bands.	No. of Fire Arms.
Osage, - - - - -	1,252	1,793	74	3	4,019	516	1,200
Kanses, - - - -	465	500	600	1	1,565	204	450
Pawnees, - - - -	1,993	2,170	2,060	3	6,223	174	700
Ietans, - - - -	2,700	3,000	2,500	....	8,200	1,020	270
Total, - -	6,410	7,463	6,134	7	20,007	1,914	2,620

JOURNAL

OF A

TOUR THROUGH THE INTERIOR PROVINCES OF NEW SPAIN, IN THE YEAR 1807, IN CONTINUATION OF THE PRECEDING NARRATIVE.

FRIDAY, 27th *February*.—In the morning I discovered that the lieutenant was writing letters, addressed to the Governor and others, on which I demanded if he was not going on with me to Santa Fé. He appeared confused, and said no ; that his orders were so positive as to the safe conduct and protection of my men, that he durst not go and leave any behind ; that his companion would accompany me to Santa Fé, with fifty men, whilst he, with the others, would wait for the sergeant and the remainder of my party. I replied that he had deceived me, and had not acted with candour: but it was now too late for me to remedy the evil.

We marched about eleven o'clock, ascending the Rio del Norte five miles more, south, 60° west, when we went round through a chain of hills, and bore off to the south. We proceeded nine miles further, when we crossed the main branch of that stream, which was now bearing nearly west, towards the main chain of the third chain of mountains. We encamped on the opposite shore, after having proceeded fifteen miles. The weather was intensely cold, and we were obliged to stop frequently to make fires. Snow deep.

Saturday, 28th *February*.—We marched late. One of the Frenchmen informed me that the expedition which had been at the Pawnees had descended the Red river two hundred and thirty-three leagues, and had then crossed to the Pawnees, expressly in search of my party (this was afterwards confirmed by the gentleman who commanded the troops); he then expressed great regret at my misfortunes, as he termed them, in being taken, and offered his services in secreting papers, &c. I easily saw his design, but for my amusement I thought I would try him, and accordingly gave him a leaf or two of my journal, (copied,) which mentioned the time of our sailing from Belle Fontaine, and our force. This I charged him to guard very carefully, and return to me after the investigation of my papers at Santa Fé. This day we saw a herd of wild horses; the Spaniards pursued them, and caught two colts, one of which the Indians killed and ate, the other was liberated. We continued our journey over some hills, where the snow was very deep, and encamped at last on the top of a pretty high hill, among some pines. Distance advanced, thirty-six miles. We left the river, which in general ran about six, eight, and ten miles to the left or eastward of us. Saw great sign of elk.

Sunday, 1st *March*.—We marched early, and although we rode very hard, only got to the village of Agua Caliente or Warm Springs, sometime in the afternoon, which was about forty-five miles. The difference of the climate was here astonishing; after we left the hills and deep snows, we found ourselves on plains where there was no snow, and where vegetation was sprouting. The village of the Warm Springs, or Agua Caliente, (in their language,) is situated on the eastern branch of a creek of that name; and at a distance, presents to the eye a square enclosure of mud walls, the houses forming the wall. They are flat on the top, or with extremely little ascent to one side, where there are spouts to carry off the water of the melting snow and rain when it falls, which, we were informed, had not been the case but once in two years, previously to our entering the country. Inside of the enclosure were the different streets, formed of houses of the same fashion, all of one story; the doors were narrow, the windows small, and in one or two houses we observed talc lights. This village had a mill near it, on the little creek, which made very good flour. The population consisted of civilized Indians, but much mixed blood, and may comprise about five hundred souls. Here we had a dance, which in general terms is called the fandango; but there was one which was copied from the Mexicans, and is now danced in the first societies of New Spain, and had even been introduced at the court of Madrid.

The greatest natural curiosity are the warm springs, which are two in number, about ten yards apart, and each affording sufficient water for a mill seat. They appeared to be impregnated with copper, and were more than $33°$ above blood heat. From this village the Ietans drove off two thousand horses at one time, when at war with the Spaniards.

THE INTERIOR OF NEW SPAIN.

Monday, 2d *March.*—We marched late, and passed several little mud-walled villages and settlements, all of which had round mud towers, of the ancient shape and construction, to defènd the inhabitants from the intrusions of the savages. I was this day shewn the ruins of several old villages, which had been taken and destroyed by the Ietans.

We were frequently stopped on our march by the women, who invited us into their houses to eat, and in every place where we halted a moment, there was a contest who should be our hosts. My poor lads who had been frozen were conducted home by old men, who would cause their daughters to dress their feet, provide their victuals and drink, and at night give them the best bed in the house. The whole of their conduct brought to my recollection the hospitality of the ancient patriarchs, and caused me to sigh with regret at the corruption of that noble principle by the polish of modern ages.

We descended the creek of Agua Caliente about twelve miles, to where it joined the river of Conejos from the west. This river was about thirty yards wide, and was settled for twelve miles above its junction with the Agua Caliente, as the latter was for its whole course from the village of that name. From their junction, the distance was about five miles to the Rio del Norte, on the eastern branch of which was situated the village of St. John's, which was the residence of the president priest of the province, who had dwelt there forty years.

The tops of the houses, as well as the streets, were crowded when we entered; and at the door of the public quarters we were met by the priest. My companion, who commanded the escort, received him in a street and embraced him, and all the poor creatures who stood round strove to kiss the ring or hand of the holy Father; for myself, I saluted him in the usual style. My men were conducted into the quarters, and I went to the house of the priest, where we were treated by him with politeness: he offered us coffee, chocolate, and whatever we thought proper, and desired me to make myself at home.

As I was going sometime after to the quarters of my men, I was addressed at the door by a man in broken English: "My friend, I am very sorry to see you here; we are all prisoners in this country, and can never return; I have been a prisoner for nearly three years, and cannot get away." I replied, "that as for his being a prisoner, it must be for some crime; that with respect to myself I felt no apprehension, and requested him to speak French, as I hardly understood his English." He then began to demand of me so many different questions on the mode of my getting into the country, my intentions, &c., that by the time I arrived in the room of my men I was perfectly satisfied of his being ordered by some person to endeavour to obtain a confession or acknowledgment of sinister designs in my appearing on the frontiers, and some confidential communications which might implicate me. As he had been rather insolent in his enquiries, I ordered my men to shut and fasten the door. I then told him that I believed him to be an emissary sent on purpose by the Governor, or some other person, to endeavour to betray me; that all men of that description were scoundrels, and should never escape punishment whilst I possessed the power to chastise them, cautioning him at the same time, if he cried or made the least resistance, I should be obliged to make use of the sabre which I had in my hand : on which he was so much alarmed that he begged of me for God's sake not to hurt him; and said that he had been ordered by the Governor to meet me, and endeavour to trace out what and who I was, and what were my designs, after gaining my confidence by exclaiming against the Spaniards, and complaining of the tyranny which they had exercised towards him. After this confession, I told him that I looked upon him as too contemptible for further notice, but that he might tell the Governor the next time he employed emissaries, to choose those of more abilities and sense, and that I questioned if His Excellency would find the sifting of us an easy task. This man's name was Baptiste Lalande; he had come from the Illinois to the Pawnees to trade with goods furnished him by William Morrison, a gentleman of the Illinois, and from thence with his merchandize to North Mexico, where he had established himself; he was the man on whom Robinson had a claim. He returned to the priest's house with me, and instead of making any complaint, in reply to their inquiries of who I was, &c., informed them that when he left Louisiana I was governor of the Illinois. This, I presume, he took from my having commanded for some time at Kaskaskias, the first military post the United States established in that country after the peace. The report served but to add to the respect with which my companions and host treated me. This being the first place at

THE INTERIOR OF NEW SPAIN.

which I had partaken of a good meal, wine, &c., the house too being warm, and having made perhaps rather an immoderate use of the refreshments, I was attacked by something like the cholera morbus, which alarmed me considerably, and made me determine to be more guarded in future.

I found that this Father was a great naturalist, or rather a florist. He had large collections of flowers, and plants, and several works on his favourite studies, the margin and bottoms of which were filled by his own notes in the Castilian language. As I had not a natural turn for botany sufficient to induce me to puzzle my head with the Latin, and did not understand the Castilian, I enjoyed but little of his pedantic lectures, which he continued to give me for nearly two hours; but by this small degree of patience, I entirely acquired the esteem of the worthy Father, who called me his son, and lamented extremely that my fate had not made me one of the Holy Catholic Church.*

St. John was enclosed with a mud wall, and probably contained one thousand souls; its population consisted principally of civilized Indians, and indeed all the villages of North Mexico are the same, the whites not forming the one-twentieth part.

Tuesday, 3d March.—We marched after breakfast, Baptiste Lalande accompanying us, and in about six miles came to a village containing, I suppose, more than two thousand souls. Here we halted at the house of the priest, who, understanding that I would not kiss his hand, did not pre-

---

* The Father being informed that I had some astronomical instruments, expressed a desire to see them: all that I had with me was my sextant, and a large glass which magnified considerably, calculated for the day or night, the remainder being with my sergeant and party. On examining the sextant, and shewing him the effect of it, in the reflection of the sun, he appeared more surprised, as well as hundreds who surrounded us, at the circumstance than any nation of savages I was ever among. It struck me as extraordinary, how a man who appeared perfect master of the ancient languages, a botanist, mineralogist and chemist, should be so ignorant of the powers of reflection, and the first principles of mathematics: but my friend explained the enigma, by informing me of the care the Spanish government took to prevent any branch of science being made a pursuit, which would have a tendency to extend the views of the subjects of the provinces to the geography of their country, or any other subject which might bring to view a comparison of their local advantages and situations with those of other countries.

sent it to me. The conduct and behaviour of a young priest who came in, was such as in our country would have been amply sufficient forever to have banished him from the clerical association, strutting about with a dirk in his boot, a cane in his hand, whispering to one girl, chucking another under the chin, and going out with a third, &c., yet this holy and reverend father would not give his hand to a Protestant, for fear of contamination!

From this to another small village of five hundred inhabitants the distance is seven miles; at each of these there is a small stream sufficient for the purpose of watering their fields: at the father's house we took coffee; and here was the first bedstead seen in the country. From this village we travelled seventeen miles to another of civilized Indians, containing four hundred inhabitants. Here we changed horses and prepared for entering the capital, which we came in sight of in the evening. Santa Fé is situated along the banks of a small creek, which comes down from the mountains, and runs west to the Rio del Norte. The length of the town on the creek may be estimated at one mile, and it is but three streets in width. Its appearance from a distance, struck my mind with the same effect as a fleet of flat bottomed boats, such as are seen in the spring and fall seasons descending the Ohio river. There are two churches, the magnificence of whose steeples forms a striking contrast to the miserable appearance of the other buildings. On the north side of the town is the square of soldiers' houses, one hundred and twenty, or one hundred and forty on each flank. The public square is in the centre of the town, on the north side of which is situated the palace, as they term it, or government house, with the quarters for guards, &c., the other is occupied by the clergy, and public officers. In general, the houses have a shed before their front, some of which have a flooring of brick; this occasions the streets to be very narrow, being, in general, about twenty-five feet. The supposed population is four thousand five hundred souls.*

On our entering the town, the crowd was great and followed us to the government-house: here we dismounted, and were ushered in through various rooms, the floors all covered with the skins of buffalo, bear, or some other animal. We waited in a chamber for some time until His

---

* Humboldt states the population at 3,600. Pol. Ess. on N. Spain, vol. ii. p. 317. Eng. Tran. E.

THE INTERIOR OF NEW SPAIN.

Excellency appeared, when we rose, and the following conversation took place in French:
Governor.—Do you speak French?
Pike.—Yes, Sir.
Governor.—You come to reconnoitre our country, do you?
Pike.—I marched to reconnoitre our own.
Governor.—In what character are you?
Pike.—In my proper character, an officer of the United States army.
Governor.—And this Robinson, is he attached to your party?
Pike.—No.
Governor.—Do you know him?
Pike.—Yes, he is from St. Louis.*
Governor.—How many men have you? A. Fifteen.
Governor.—And this Robinson makes sixteen? A. I have already told your Excellency that he does not belong to my party, and shall answer no more interrogatories on that subject.
Governor.—When did you leave St. Louis?
Answer.—15th July.
Governor.—I think you marched in June?
Answer.—No, Sir.
Governor.—Well, return with Mr. Bartholomew to his house, and come here again at seven o'clock and bring your papers. On which we returned to the house of my friend Bartholomew, who seemed much hurt at the interview. At the door of the government-house I met the old Frenchman to whom I had given the scrap of paper, on the 27th February. He had left us in the morning, and, as I supposed, hurried in to make his report, and I presume had presented this paper to His Excellency. I demanded, with a look of contempt, if he had made his report; to which he replied in a humble tone, and began to excuse himself, but I did not wait to hear him.

---

* I had understood the Doctor had been sent forty-five leagues from Santa Fé under a strong guard, and the haughty and unfriendly reception of the Governor induced me to believe war must have been declared, and that if it were known Doctor Robinson accompanied me, he would be treated with great severity. I was correct in saying he was not attached to my party, for he was only a volunteer, and could not properly be said to be one of my command.

At the hour appointed we returned, when the Governor demanded my papers. I told him I understood my trunk was taken possession of by his guard. He expressed surprise, and immediately ordered it in; he also sent for Solomon Colly, formerly a sergeant in our army, and one of the unfortunate company of Nolan. When we were seated he ordered this man to demand my name, to which I replied; he then asked in what province I was born? I answered in English, and then addressed His Excellency in French, and told him I did not think it necessary to enter into such a catechising; that if he would be at the pains of reading my commission from the United States, and my orders from my General, it would be all that I presumed would be necessary to convince His Excellency that I came with no hostile intentions towards the Spanish government; that on the contrary I had express instructions to guard against giving them offence or alarm, and that His Excellency would be convinced, that myself and party were to be considered as objects on which the so much celebrated generosity of the Spanish nation might be exercised, rather than subjects to occasion opposite sentiments. He then requested to see my commission and orders, which I read to him in French, on which he got up and gave me his hand (for the first time) and said, that he was happy to be acquainted with me as a man of honour and a gentleman; that I might retire in the evening, and take my trunk with me; that on the morrow he would make further arrangements.

Wednesday, 4th *March*.—I was desired by the Governor to bring up my trunk in order that he might make some observations on my route, &c.

When he had ordered me to take my trunk with me over night, I had conceived the examination of papers was over, and as many of my documents were entrusted to the care of my men, and I found that the inhabitants were treating them with liquor, I was fearful they would become intoxicated, and through inadvertency betray or discover the papers. I therefore obtained several of them and had put them in the trunk. When an officer arrived for myself and it in the morning, I had no opportunity of taking them out again before I was conducted to the palace. I discovered instantly that I was deceived, but it was too late to remedy the evil.

After examining the contents of my trunk, the Governor informed me I must with my troop go to Chihuahua in the Province of Biscay, to appear before the commandant general; he added, "You have the key of your trunk in your own possession, the trunk will be put under charge of the officer who commands your escort." The following conversation then took place:

Captain Pike.—If we go to Chihuahua we must be considered as prisoners of war?

Governor.—By no means.

Pike.—You have already disarmed my men without my knowledge; are their arms to be returned, or not?

Governor.—They can receive them any moment.

Pike.—But, Sir, I cannot consent to be lead three or four hundred leagues out of my route, without its being by force of arms.

Governor.—I know you do not go voluntarily, but I will give you a certificate from under my hand, of my having obliged you to march.

Pike.—I will address you a letter on the subject.*

Governor.—You will dine with me to-day, and march afterwards to a village about six miles distant, escorted by Captain Anthony D'Almansa, with a detachment of dragoons, who will accompany you to where the remainder of your escort is now waiting for you, under the command of the officer who commanded the expedition to the Pawnees.

Pike.—I would not wish to be impertinent in my observations to your Excellency, but pray, Sir, do you not think it was a greater infringement of our territory to send six hundred miles into the Pawnees country, than for me, with our small party, to come on the frontiers of yours, with an intent to descend Red river?

Governor.—I do not understand you.

Pike.—No, Sir! any further explanation is unnecessary.

I then returned to the house of my friend, Bartholomew, and wrote my letter to His Excellency, which I had not finished before we were hurried to dinner. In the morning I had received from the Governor by the hands of his private secretary, twenty-one dollars, notifying to me that it was the amount of the King's allowance for my party to Chihuahua, and that it would be charged to me on account of my subsistence: from this I clearly understood that it was calculated the expenses of the party to Chihuahua were to be defrayed by the United States. I also received by

---

*See Appendix, No. XI.

the same hands, from His Excellency, a shirt and neckcloth, with his compliments, wishing me to accept them as they were made in Spain by his sister, and never had been worn by any person; for which I returned him my sincere acknowledgments.

It may not be deemed impertinent, if I explain at this period the miserable appearance we made, and the situation we were in, with the reasons for it. After we left our interpreter and one man on the Arkansaw, we were obliged to carry all our baggage on our backs; consequently that which was the most useful was preferred to the few ornamental articles of dress we possessed. The ammunition claimed our first care, tools secondary, leather leggins, boots and mockinsons were the next in consideration: consequently I left behind all my uniform clothing, trunks, &c., and the men also did the same, except what they had on, conceiving that which would secure the feet and legs from the cold to be preferable to any other. Thus, when we presented ourselves at Santa Fé, I was dressed in a pair of blue trowsers, mockinsons, blanket coat, and a red cap, made of scarlet cloth, lined with fox skins; and my poor fellows in leggins, breech cloths, and leather coats; and not a hat in the whole party. This appearance was extremely mortifying to us all, especially as soldiers; and although some of the officers used frequently to observe to me, "that worth made the man," with a variety of adages to the same amount, yet the first impression made on the ignorant is hard to eradicate; and a greater proof cannot be given of the ignorance of the common people than their asking if we lived in houses, or in camps like the Indians, or if we wore hats in our country These observations are sufficient to shew the impression our savage appearance made among them.

The dinner at the Governor's was rather splendid, consisting of a variety of dishes, and wines of the Southern Provinces, and when His Excellency was a little warmed with the influence of the cheering liquor, he became very sociable, and expressed his opinion freely. It must be understood that no person at the table could understand our conversation. He informed me that there existed a serious difficulty between the commandant general of the internal provinces and the Marquis Casa Calva, who had given permission to Mr. Dunbar to explore the Ouchata contrary to the general principles of their government, in consequence of which the former had made representations against the latter to the court of Madrid.

After dinner His Excellency ordered up his coach, Captain D'Almansa, Bartholomew and myself entered with him and drove out three miles. He was drawn by six mules, and attended by a guard of cavalry. When we parted his adieu was, Remember Allencaster in peace or war.

I left a note for my sergeant, with instructions to keep up good discipline, and not be alarmed or discouraged. As I was about leaving the public square, poor Colly, the American prisoner, came up with tears in his eyes, and expressed his hope I would not forget him when I arrived in the United States. After we left the Governor, we rode on about three miles to a defile, where we halted for the troops, and I soon found that the old soldier who accompanied us, and commanded our escort, was fond of a drop of the cheering liquor, as his boy carried a bottle in his cochmelies (a small leather case attached to the saddle for the purpose of carrying small articles). We were accompanied by my friend Bartholomew. We ascended a hill and galloped on until about ten o'clock, snowing hard all the time, when we came to a precipice, which we descended, meeting with great difficulty from the obscurity of the night, to a small village, where we put up in the quarters of the priest, he being absent.

After supper Captain D'Almansa related to me, that he had served His Catholic Majesty forty years to arrive at the rank he then held, which was that of first lieutenant in the line and a captain by brevet, whilst he had seen various young Europeans promoted over his head. After the old man had taken his *quantum sufficit*, and gone to sleep, Bartholomew and myself sat up for some hours; he explaining to me their situation, and the great desire they felt for a change of affairs, and an open trade with the United States. I pointed out to him with chalk on the floor, the geographical connection and route from North Mexico and Louisiana, and finally gave him a certificate addressed to the citizens of the United States, stating his being friendly disposed and a man of influence. This paper he seemed to estimate as a very valuable acquisition, as he was decidedly of opinion we should invade that country the ensuing spring, and not all my assurances to the contrary could eradicate that idea.

Thursday, 5th *March.*—It snowing very badly in the morning, we did not march until eleven o'clock. In the meantime, Bartholomew and myself paid a visit to an old invalid Spaniard, who received us in the most hospitable manner, giving us chocolate and other refreshments. He made many enquiries as to our government and religion, and of * * * * who did not fail to give them the brightest colouring, he being enthusiastic in their favour, from his many conversations with me, and drawing comparisons with his own country. What appeared most extraordinary to the old veteran was, that we ever changed our president, (whose powers I was obliged to draw on a nearer affinity with those of a monarch than they really are, in order that they might comprehend his station,) and that there was a perfect freedom of conscience permitted in our country. He expressed his warm approbation of the measure. In the priest's house in which we put up were a couple of orphan girls, who were adopted by him in their infancy, and at this time constituted his whole family.

I bade adieu to my friend Bartholomew, and could not avoid shedding tears; he embraced me and all my men.

We arrived at two o'clock at the village of St. Domingo, which I apprehend to be nine miles to the eastward of the Rio del Norte. Its population may be about one thousand natives, generally governed by their own chief. The chiefs of the villages were distinguished by a cane, with a silver head and black tassel. On our arrival at the public house, Captain D'Almansa was waited on by the Governor, cap in hand, to receive his orders for furnishing our quarters, and ourselves with wood, water, provisions, &c., for the house itself contained nothing but bare walls, and small grated windows; and brought to my mind a lively idea of the representation of the Spanish inhabitants, made by Dr. Moore in his travels through Spain, Italy, &c. This village, as well as that of St. Philip and St. Bartholomew, are of the nation of Keres, many of whom do not yet speak good Spanish.

After we had refreshed ourselves a little, the Captain sent for the keys of the church, when we entered it. I was much astonished to find, inclosed in mud brick walls, many rich paintings, and the Saint (Domingo) as large as life, elegantly ornamented with gold and silver. The Captain made a slight inclination of the head, and intimated to me that this was the patron of the village. We then ascended into the gallery where the choir are generally placed. In an outside hall was placed another image of the Saint, less richly ornamented, where the populace repaired daily, and knelt to return thanks for benefactions received, or to ask new favours.

THE INTERIOR OF NEW SPAIN.

Many young girls made choice of the time of our visit to be on their knees before the holy patron. From the flat roof of the church, we had a delightful view of the village, the Rio del Norte on the west, the mountains of St. Dies to the south, and the valley round the town, on which were numerous herds of goats, sheep and asses : upon the whole, this was one of the finest views in New Mexico.

Friday, 6th *March.*—Marched down the Rio del Norte, on the eastern side; snow one foot deep; passed large flocks of goats. At the village of St. Philip crossed a bridge of eight arches, constructed as follows, viz.: the pillars made of neat wood work, something similar to a crate, and in the form of a keel boat, the sharp end (or bow) to the current; this crate or butment filled with stone, in which the river had lodged sand, clay, &c., until it had become of a tolerably firm consistence. On the top of the pillars were laid pine logs, length ways, squared on two sides, and being joined pretty close, made a tolerable bridge for horses, but would not have been very safe for carriages, as there were no hand rails.

On our arrival at the house of the priest, we were received in a very polite and friendly manner, and before my departure we seemed to have been friends for years. During our dinner, at which we had a variety of wines, we were entertained with music, consisting of bass drums, French horns, violins and cymbals. We also entered into a long and candid detail of the injustice done to the Creoles, wherein the Father neither spared the government nor its administrators. Both as to government and religion he displayed a liberality of opinion and a fund of knowledge which astonished me. He shewed me a statistical table, on which he had in a regular manner taken the whole province of New Mexico by villages, beginning at Taos on the northwest, and ending with Valencia on the south; giving their latitude, longitude, population, whether savages or Spaniards, civilized or barbarous, Christians or Pagans; numbers, name of the nation, when converted, how governed, military force, clergy, salary, &c., &c., in short a complete geographical and historical sketch of the province. Of this I wished to obtain a copy, but perceived that the Captain was somewhat surprised at the Father's having shewn it me. When we parted we promised to write to each other, which I performed from Chihuahua. Here was an old Indian who was extremely inquisitive to know if we were Spaniards; to which an old gentleman, who appeared to be an inmate of the Father's, replied in the affirmative: but the Indian observed, they do not speak Castilian? True, replied the other, but you are an Indian of the nation of Keres, are you not? Yes. Well, the Utahs are Indians also? Yes. But still you do not understand them, they speak a different language. True, replied the Indian. Well, said the old gentleman, these strangers are likewise Spaniards, but do not speak the same language with us. This reasoning seemed to satisfy the poor savage, and I could not but smile at the ingenuity displayed to make him believe there was no other nation of whites but the Spaniards.

Whilst at dinner, the Father was informed one of his parishioners was at the point of death, and wished his attendance to receive his confession.

We took our departure, but were shortly after overtaken by our friend, who after giving me another hearty shake of the hand, left us at full speed. Crossed the river, and passed two small hamlets and houses on the road, to the village of St. Dies, opposite the mountain of the same name, where we were received in a house of the Father's, this making part of his domains.

✗ *Saturday*, 7th *March.*—Marched at nine o'clock, through a country better cultivated and inhabited than any I had yet seen. Arrived at Albuquerque, a village on the eastern side of the Rio del Norte. We were received by Father Ambrosio Guerra in a very flattering manner, and led into his hall, from thence, after taking some refreshment, into an inner apartment, where he ordered his adopted children of the female sex to appear, when they came in by turns. They were Indians of various nations—Spanish, French, and finally two young girls who, from their complexion, I conceived to be English: on perceiving I noticed them, he ordered the rest to retire, many of whom were beautiful, and directed these two to sit down on the sofa beside me. Thus situated, he told me that they had been taken to the east by the Ietans, passed from one nation to the other until he purchased them, (at that time infants) but they could recollect neither names nor language. Concluding they were my country women, he ordered them to embrace me as a mark of their friendship, to which they appeared nothing loath. We then sat down to dinner, which consisted of various dishes, excellent wines, and to crown all, we were waited upon by half a dozen of those beautiful girls, who like Hebe at the

THE INTERIOR OF NEW SPAIN.

feast of the gods, converted our wine into nectar, and with their ambrosial breath shed incense on our cups. After the cloth was removed, the priest beckoned to me to follow him, and led me into his sanctum sanctorum, where he had the rich and majestic images of various saints, and in the midst the crucified Jesus, crowned with thorns, but with rich rays of golden glory surrounding his head. The room being hung with black silk curtains, served to augment the gloom and majesty of the scene. When he conceived my imagination sufficiently wrought up, he put on a black gown and mitre, kneeled before the cross, took hold of my hand, and endeavoured gently to pull me down beside him: on my refusal, he prayed fervently for a few minutes, and then rose, laid his hands on my shoulders, and as I conceived blessed me; he then said to me, "You will not be a Christian. Oh, what a pity! oh, what a pity!" He then threw off his robes, took me by the hand, led me out to the company, smiling; but the scene I had gone through, made too serious an impression on my mind to be eradicated, until we took our departure an hour after, having received great marks of favour from the Father.

At Father Ambrosio's was the only chart I saw in the province; and it gave the near connection of the sources of the Rio del Norte, and the Rio Colorado of California, with their ramifications.

Both above and below Albuquerque the citizens were beginning to open the canals, to let in the water of the river to fertilize the plains and fields which border its banks on both sides: we saw men, women, and children of all ages and both sexes, at the joyful labour, which was to crown with rich abundance their future harvest, and ensure them plenty for the ensuing year. These scenes brought to my recollection the bright descriptions given by Savary, of the opening of the canals of Egypt. The cultivation of the fields was now commencing, and everything appeared to give life and gaiety to the surrounding scenery. We crossed the Rio del Norte, a little below the village of Albuquerque, where it was four hundred yards wide, but not more than three feet deep, and excellent fording. On our arrival at the next village, a dependency of Father Ambrosio's, we were invited into the house of the commandant. When I entered, I saw a man sitting by the fire, reading a book, with blooming cheeks, fine complexion, and a genius speaking eye. He arose from his seat; it was Robinson!

not that Robinson who had left my camp on the head waters of the Rio del Norte, pale, emaciated, with uncombed locks and beard of eight months' growth, but with fire, unsubdued enterprise and fortitude; the change was indeed surprising. I started back, and exclaimed, Robinson! yes, but I do not know you, I replied; but I know you, he exclaimed, and I would not be unknown to you here, in this land of tyranny and oppression, to avoid all the pains they dare to inflict. Yet, my friend, I grieve to see you here, and thus, for I presume you are a prisoner? I replied, No! I wear my sword you see, and all my men have their arms, and the moment they dare to ill-treat us, we will surprise their guards in the night, carry off some horses, and make our way to Apaches, and then set them at defiance. At this moment, Captain D'Almansa entered, and I introduced Robinson to him, as my *companion de voyage* and friend. Having before seen him at Santa Fé, he did not appear much surprised, and received him with a significant smile, as much as to say I knew this. We then marched out to the place where the soldiers were encamped, not one of whom would recognize him, agreeably to my orders, until I gave them the sign; then it was a joyful meeting, as the whole party was enthusiastically fond of him. He gave me the following relation of his adventures after he left me:

"I marched the first day up the branch on which we were situated (as you know we had concluded it would be the most proper to follow it to its source, and then cross the mountains west, when we had conceived we should find the Spanish settlements). At night I encamped on its banks: the second day I left it a little and bore more south, and was getting up the side of the mountain, when I discovered two Indians, for whom I made. They were armed with bows and arrows, and were extremely shy of my approach; but after sometime, confidence being somewhat restored, I signified a wish to go to Santa Fé, when they pointed due south down the river on which I had left you. As I could not believe them, I reiterated the inquiry, and received the same reply. I then concluded that we had been deceived, and that you were on the Rio del Norte, instead of Red river, and was embarrassed whether I should not immediately return and apprise you of it, but concluded it to be too late, as I was discovered by the Indians. If I had not met them, or some others, I should have continued on and crossed the mountain to

THE INTERIOR OF NEW SPAIN.

the waters of the Colorado and descended them, until from their course I should have discovered my mistake. I therefore offered the Indians some presents to conduct me in: they agreed, conducted me to their camp, where their women were, and in five minutes we were on our march. That night we encamped in the woods: I slept very little, owing to my distrust of my companions. The next day at three o'clock, P. M. we arrived at the village of Agua Caliente, where I was immediately taken into the house of the commandant, and expresses were despatched to Santa Fé; that night I was put to sleep on a mattress on the floor. The next day we departed early, leaving my arms and baggage at the commandant's, he promising to have them forwarded to me at the city. On our arrival at Santa Fé, the Governor received me with great austerity at first, entered into an examination of my business, and took possession of all my papers. After all this was explained, he ordered me to a room where the officers were confined when under arrest, and commanded a non-commissioned officer to attend me when I walked into the city, which I had free permission to do. I was supplied with provision from the Governor's table, who had promised he would write to Baptiste Lalande, whose circumstances I had apprised myself of, to come down and answer to the claim I had against him. The second day the Governor sent for me, and informed me that he had made enquiry as to the abilities of Lalande to discharge the debt, and found that he possessed no property, but that at some future period he would secure the money for me. To this I made a spirited remonstrance, as an infringement of our treaties, and a protection of a refugee citizen of the United States against his creditors; which had no other effect than to obtain me an invitation to dinner, and rather more respectful treatment than I had hitherto received from his excellency. Being slightly afflicted with the dropsy, he requested my advice as to his case. On which I prescribed a regimen and mode of treatment, which happening to differ from the one adopted by a monk and practising physician of the place, brought on me his enmity and ill-offices. The ensuing day I was ordered by the Governor to hold myself in readiness to proceed to the internal parts of the country: to which I agreed, determining not to attempt to leave the country in a clandestine manner, unless they offered to treat me with indignity or hardship, and conceiving it in my power to join you, on your retreat, or find Red river and descend it, should you not be brought in, but in that case to share your destiny: added to this, I felt a desire to see more of the country, for which purpose I was willing to run the risk of future consequences. We marched the ensuing day, I having been equipped by a friend with some small articles of which I stood in need, such as I would receive out of numerous offers. The fourth day I arrived at the village of St. Fernandez, where I was received and taken charge of by Lieutenant Don Faciendo Malgares, who commanded the expedition to the Pawnees, and whom you will find a gentleman, a soldier, and one of the most gallant men you ever knew. With him I could no longer keep the disguise, and when he informed me (two days since) that you were on the way in, I confessed to him I belonged to your party, and we have been ever since anticipating the pleasures we shall enjoy in our journey to Chihuahua, for he is to command the escort, his dragoons being now encamped in the field. Since I have been with him I have practiced physic in the country, in order to have an opportunity of examining the manners, customs, &c. of the people, and to endeavour to ascertain their political and religious feelings, with every other species of information which would be necessary to our country or ourselves. I am now here on a visit to this man's wife, attended by a corporal of dragoons as a guard, who answered very well as a waiter and guide in my excursions through the country, but I will immediately return with you to Malgares."

Thus ended Robinson's relation; and I in return recounted what had occurred to the party and myself. We agreed upon our future line of conduct, and then joined my old captain in the house, who had been persuaded to tarry all night, provided it was agreeable to me, as our host wished Robinson to remain until next day. With this proposition I complied, in order that Robinson and myself might have a further discussion before we joined Malgares, who I suspected would watch us closely. The troops proceeded on to the village of Tousac that evening.

Sunday, 8th *March.*—Marched after taking breakfast, and halted at the little village of Tousac, three miles distant, situated on the western side of the Rio del Norte. The men informed me that on their arrival over night they had been all furnished with an excellent supper, and after supper wine and a violin, with an assemblage of the young people to a dance. When we left this village, the priest sent a cart down to ferry us over, as the river was nearly four feet deep. When we approached the village of

St. Fernandez, we were met by Lieutenant Malgares, accompanied by two or three other officers: he received me with the most manly frankness and the politeness of a man of the world, yet my feelings were such as almost overpowered me, and obliged me to ride alone for a short period, in order to recover myself. My sensations arose from my knowledge, that he had now been absent from Chihuahua ten months, and it had cost the King of Spain more than ten thousand dollars to do that which a mere accident, and the deception of the Governor, had affected. Malgares, perceiving I did not find myself at ease, took every means in his power to banish my reserve, which made it impossible on my part not to endeavour to appear cheerful. We conversed as well as we could, and in two hours were as well acquainted as some people would be in the same number of months. Malgares possesses none of the haughty Castilian pride, but much of the urbanity of the Frenchman; and I will add my feeble testimony to his loyalty, by declaring that he was one of the few officers or citizens whom I found loyal to their King, felt indignation at the degraded state of the Spanish monarchy, and deprecated a revolution or separation of Spanish America from the mother country, unless France should usurp the government of Spain. These are the men who possess the heads to plan, the hearts to feel, and the hands to carry this great and important work into execution.

In the afternoon our friend wrote the following notification to the Alcaldes of several small villages around us: "Send this evening six or eight of your handsomest young girls to the village of St. Fernandez, where I propose giving a fandango, for the entertainment of the American officers arrived to-day."

(Signed)   Don Faciendo.

This order was punctually obeyed, and pourtrays more clearly than a chapter of observations the degraded state of the common people. In the evening, when the company arrived, the ball began after their usual manner, and there was really a handsome display of beauty.

It will be proper to mention here, that when my small paper trunk was brought in, Lieutenant Malgares struck his foot against it, and said, " the Governor informs me, this is a prisoner of war, or that I have charge of it; but, Sir, only assure me that you will hold the papers therein contained sacred, I will have nothing to do with it " I bowed assent, and I will only add, that the condition was scrupulously adhered to, as I was bound by every tie of military and national honour, and let me add gratitude, not to abuse his high confidence in the honour of a soldier. He further added, "Dr. Robinson being now acknowledged one of your party, I shall withdraw his guard, and consider him as under your parole of honour." These marks of politeness and friendship caused me to endeavour to evince to my brother soldier that we were capable of appreciating his honourable conduct towards us.

Monday, 9th *March*.—The troops marched about ten o'clock. Lieutenant Malgares and myself accompanied Captain D'Almansa about three miles back on his route to Santa Fé, to the house of a citizen, where we dined; after which we separated. I wrote by the Captain to the Governor in French,* respecting Robinson. D'Almansa presented me with his cap and whip, and gave me a letter of recommendation to an officer at Chihuahua. We returned to our old quarters, and being joined by our escort commenced our route. Passed a village called St. Thomas, one mile distant from the camp. The camp was formed in an ellipsis, the two long sides presenting a breastwork, composed of the saddles and loads of the mules, each end of the ellipsis having a small opening to pass and repass at. In the centre was the commandant's tent. Thus in case of an attack upon the camp there were ready formed works to fight from. Malgares's mode of living was superior to anything we have an idea of in our army, having eight mules loaded with his common camp equipage, wines, confectionary &c. But this only served to evince the corruption of the Spanish discipline, for if a subaltern indulged himself, with such a quantity of baggage, what would be the cavalade attending an army? Dr. Robinson had been called over the river to a small village to see a sick woman, and did not return that night. Distance advanced, twelve miles.

Tuesday, 10th *March*.—Marched at eight o'clock and arrived at the village of Sibilleta; having passed on the way the villages of Sabinez and Xaxales on the western side. Sibilleta is situated on the eastern side, and is a regular square, appearing like a large mud wall on the outside, the doors, windows, &c. facing the square, and is the neatest and most regular village I have yet seen. It is governed by a sergeant, at whose quarters I put up.

---

* See Appendix, No. XII.

THE INTERIOR OF NEW SPAIN.

Wednesday, 11th *March.*—Marched at eleven o'clock; came twelve miles and encamped, the troops having preceded us. The village at which we passed the night being the last of the inhabited country, we now entered the wilderness, and the road became rough, small hills running into the river forming vallies, but the bottoms appeared richer than those to the north.

Thursday, 12th *March.*—Marched at seven o'clock, and passed on the western side of the river the mountains of Magdalen, and the Black Mountains on the east. Passed the encampment of the caravan, going out with about fifteen thousand sheep for the other provinces, for which they bring back merchandize. This expedition consisted of about three hundred men, chiefly citizens, escorted by an officer and thirty-five or forty troops; they are collected at Sibilleta, and separate on their return; they go out in February and return in March. A similar expedition goes out in the autumn; during the other parts of the year no citizen travels the road. The couriers meet at the pass of the Rio del Norte and exchange packets, when each returns to his own province. Met a caravan of fifty men and probably two hundred horses, loaded with traffic for New Mexico. Halted at twelve o'clock and marched at three. Lieutenant Malgares shewed me the place where he had been in two affrays with the Apaches, in one he commanded himself, and in the other was commanded by Captain D'Almansa; in the former there was one Spaniard killed and eight wounded, and ten Apaches made prisoners; in the latter fifty-two Apaches wounded, and seventeen killed, they being surprised in the night. Malgares killed two himself, and had two horses killed under him.

Friday, 13th *March.*—Marched at seven o'clock; saw many deer; halted at eleven, and marched again at four o'clock. This day one of our horses threw a young woman, and ran off (as was the habit of all the Spanish horses, if by chance they threw their rider) when many of the dragoons and Malgares himself pursued him. I being mounted on an elegant horse of Malgares's, joined in the chase, and notwithstanding their superior horsemanship overtook the horse, caught his bridle and stopped him, when both the horses were nearly at full speed. This act procured me the applause of the Spanish dragoons, and it is astonishing how it operated on their good will.

TRAVELS THROUGH

Saturday, 14th *March*.—Marched at ten o'clock, and halted at a mountain, distant ten miles. This is the point at which the road leaves the river for two days' journey, bearing due south, the river taking a turn southwest, it being five days' journey along its course to where the roads again meet. We marched at four o'clock, and eight miles below crossed the river to the western side. Two mules fell in the water, and as our stars would have it, with the loads containing the stores of Lieutenant Malgares, by which means we lost all our bread, and an excellent assortment of biscuits, &c. Distance advanced, eighteen miles.

Sunday, 15th *March*.—Marched at half past ten o'clock; made twenty-eight miles; the route rough and stony; course S. 20° W.

Monday, 16th *March*.—Marched at seven o'clock, and halted at twelve; passed on the eastern side the Horse Mountain, and the Mountain of the Dead: came on the trail of the appearance of two hundred horses, supposed to be that of an expedition from the Province of Biscay against the Indians.

Tuesday, 17th *March*.—Marched at ten o'clock, and at four in the afternoon crossed the river to the eastern side; saw several fresh Indian tracks, also the trail of a large party of horse, supposed to be Spanish troops in pursuit of the Indians: marched down the river twenty-six miles. Perceived fresh sign of Indians, and of a party of horse. Country mountainous on both sides of the river.

Wednesday, 18th *March*.—Marched down the river twenty-six miles; observed fresh sign of Indians, and of a party of horse; country still mountainous on both sides of the river.

Thursday, 19th *March*.—Struck out eastward about three miles, and fell into the main road, (or a large flat prairie) which we left at the mountain of the Friar Christopher.

Friday, 20th *March*.—Halted at ten o'clock at a salt lake; marched until two o'clock, when we halted for the day. Vegetation began now to be discoverable; on the seventeenth and this day the weeds and grass were quite high.

Saturday, 21st *March*.—Marched in the morning and arrived at the Passo del Norte at eleven o'clock, the road leading through a hilly and mountainous country. We put up at the house of Don Francisco Garcia, who was a merchant and a planter; he possessed in the vicinity of the

THE INTERIOR OF NEW SPAIN.

town twenty thousand sheep, and one thousand cows. We were received in a most hospitable manner by Don Pedro Roderique Rey, the lieutenant governor, and Father Joseph Prado, the vicar of the place. This was by far the most flourishing town we had been in.

Sunday, 22d *March.*—Remained at the Passo.

Monday, 23d *March.*—Attended mass. Left the Passo at three o'clock for St. Eleazaro, accompanied by the Lieutenant-Governor, the vicar, and Allencaster, a brother of the Governor. Malgares, myself, and the Doctor took up our quarters at the house of Captain ———, who was then at Chihuahua; but his lady and sister entertained us in a very elegant and hospitable manner. They began playing cards, and continued until late the third day. Malgares, who won considerably, would send frequently fifteen or twenty dollars from the table to the lady of the house, her sisters, and others, and beg their acceptance of them, in order that fortune might still continue propitious; in this manner he distributed five hundred dollars.

Round this fort were a great number of Apaches, who were on a treaty with the Spaniards: these people appeared to be perfectly independent in their manners, and were the only savages I saw in the Spanish dominions whose spirit was not humbled, and whose neck was not bound to the yoke of their invaders. With these people Malgares was extremely popular, and I believe he sought popularity with them, and with all the common people, for there was no man so poor or so humble under whose roof he would not enter; and when he walked out I have seen him put a handful of dollars in his pocket, and give them all before he returned to quarters, to the old men, women, and children; but to his equals he was haughty and overbearing. This conduct he pursued through the whole provinces of North Mexico and Biscay, when at a distance from the seat of government. But I could plainly perceive he was cautious of his conduct as he approached the capital. I here left a letter for my sergeant.

Tuesday, 24th *March.*—Very bad weather.

Wednesday, 25th *March.*—The troops marched, but Lieutenant Malgares and myself remained.

Thursday, 26th *March.*—Divine service was performed in the morning at the garrison, at which all the troops attended under arms. At one part of their mass they present arms; at another, sink on one knee, and rest the muzzle of the gun on the ground, in signification of their submission to their Divine Master. At one o'clock we bade adieu to our friendly hostess, who was one of the finest women I had seen in New Spain. At dusk arrived at a small pond, made by a spring which arose in the centre, called the *Ojo Malalka*, and seemed formed by Providence to enable the human race to pass that route, as it was the only water for sixty miles of the road. Here we overtook Sergeant Belardie, with the party of dragoons from Senora and Biscay, who had left us at St. Eleazaro, where we had received a new escort. Distance advanced, twenty miles.

Friday, 27th *March*.—Arrived at Carracal at twelve o'clock; distant twenty-eight miles. The road was well watered, and the situation pleasant. The father-in-law of our friend commanded six or seven years here. When we arrived at the fort, the commandant, Don Pedro Rues Saramende, received Robinson and myself with a cold bow, and informed Malgares that we might repair to the public quarters: to this Malgares indignantly replied, that he should accompany us, and turned to depart, when the commandant took him by the arm, made many apologies to him and us, and we at length reluctantly entered his quarters. Here for the first time I saw the Gazette of Mexico, which gave rumours of Colonel Burr's conspiracies, the movements of our troops, &c. &c.; but which were stated in so vague and undefined a manner as only to excite our anxiety, without throwing any light on the subject.

Saturday, 28th *March*.—Marched at half past three o'clock, and arrived at the warm springs at sun-down; crossed one little fosse on the route.

Sunday, 29th *March*.—Marched at ten o'clock, and continued our route with but a short halt until sun-down, when we encamped without water. Distance advanced, thirty miles.

Monday, 30th *March*.—Marched before seven o'clock; the front arrived at water at eleven o'clock, the mules at twelve. The spring on the side of the mountain to the eastward of the road is in a beautiful situation. I here saw the first ash timber I observed in the country. This water is fifty-two miles from the warm springs. Yesterday and to day saw much cabrie. Marched fifteen miles further, and encamped without wood or water; passed two other small springs to the eastward of the road.

Tuesday, 31st *March*—Marched early, and arrived at a delightful spring at ten o'clock. The road from Senora, Tanos and Buenaventura, &c. joins about four hundred yards before you arrive at the spring. Arrived at the village of ———— at night, containing a large and elegant house for the country. Here were various labours carried on by criminals in irons. We here met with a Catalonian who was but a short time from Spain, and whose dialect was such that he could scarcely be understood by Malgares, and his manners were much more like those of a citizen of our western frontiers than a subject of a despotic prince.

Wednesday, 1st *April.*—In the morning Malgares despatched a courier with a letter to the commanding general, to inform him of our approach; also to his father-in-law ————.

Thursday, 2d *April.*—When we arrived at Chihuahua, we pursued our course through the town to the house of the General. I was much astonished to see with what anxiety Malgares anticipated the meeting with his military chief, after having been on the most arduous and enterprising expedition ever undertaken by any of his majesty's officers from these provinces, and having executed it with equal spirit and judgment; yet was he fearful of his meeting him with an eye of displeasure, and appeared to be much more agitated than ourselves, although we may be supposed to have had our sensations likewise; as on the will of this man depended our future destiny, at least until our country could interfere in our behalf. On our arrival at the General's, we were halted in the hall of the guard, until word was sent to him of our presence, when Malgares was first introduced, and remained with him some time. During this interval, a Frenchman came up and endeavoured to enter into conversation with us, but was soon frowned into silence, as we conceived him to be only some authorized spy. Malgares at last came out and asked me to walk in. I found the General sitting at his desk; he was a middle sized man, apparently about fifty-five years of age, with a stern countenance; but he received me graciously and beckoned to a seat: he then observed, "you have given us and yourself a great deal of trouble."

Capt. Pike.—On my part, entirely unsought, and on that of the Spanish government voluntary.

General.—Where are your papers?

Capt. Pike.—Under charge of Lieutenant Malgares. Malgares was then ordered to have my small trunk brought in; which being done, a Lieutenant Walker entered: he is a native of New Orleans, his father an Englishman, his mother a French-woman, and he spoke both languages equally well, also the Spanish; he was a lieutenant of dragoons in the Spanish service, and master of the military school at Chihuahua. This young gentleman was employed by Mr. Andrew Ellicot, as a deputy surveyor in the Florida line, between the United States and Spain, in the years 1797 and 1798.

General Salcedo desired him to assist me in taking out my papers, and requested me to explain the nature of each. Such as he conceived to be relevant to the expedition he caused to be laid on one side, and those which were not of a public nature on the other; the whole either passing through the hands of the General or Walker, except a few letters from Mrs. Pike. On my taking up these and saying they were letters from a lady, the General gave a proof, that if the ancient Spanish bravery had degenerated in their nation generally, their gallantry still existed, by bowing; I then put them in my pocket. He now informed me that he would examine the papers, but that in the meanwhile he wished me to make, and present him a short sketch of my voyage, which might probably be satisfactory. This I would have positively refused, had I had an idea that it was his determination to keep the papers; which I could not at that time conceive from his urbanity, and the satisfaction which he appeared to exhibit on the event of our interview. He then told me that I should take up my quarters with Walker, in order, as he said, to be better accommodated by having a person with me who spoke the English language; but, as I suspected, that he might be a spy on our actions, and on those who visited us. Robinson all this time had been standing in the guard-room boiling with indignation at being so long detained there, subject to the observations of the soldiery and the gaping curiosity of the vulgar. He was now introduced by some mistake of one of the aids-de-camp; when he appeared he made a slight bow to the General, who demanded of Malgares who he was; he replied, a doctor who accompanied the expedition. " Let him retire," and he went out: the General then invited me to return and dine with him. We now went to the quarters of Walker, where we received several different invitations to take quarters at houses where we might be better accommodated; but understanding that the General had designated our quarters, all were silent. We returned to dine at the palace, where we met Malgares, who, with ourselves, was the only guest. At the table were the treasurer Truxillio and a priest called Father Rocus. The dinner was mean, and by no means more splendid than many of our subalterns give when they have company, but it was in character with our host.

Friday, 3d *April.*—Employed in giving a sketch of our voyage, for the General and commandant of these provinces. Introduced to Don Bernardo Villamil, Don Alberto Mayner, Lieut.-Colonel and father-in-law to Malgares, Don Manuel Zuloaga, a member of the secretary office, to whom I am under obligations of gratitude, and whom I shall remember with esteem. Visited his house in the evening.

Saturday, 4th *April.*—Visited the hospital where were two fine looking men, who were severely afflicted with the lues venerea, and there was not a physician in his majesty's hospital who was able to cure them, but after repeated attempts, had given them up to perish. This shews the extreme impaired state of the medical science in the provinces. I endeavoured to get Robinson to undertake to cure these poor fellows, but the jealousy and envy of the Spanish doctors made it impracticable.

Sunday, 5th *April*—Visited by Lieutnant M. with a very polite message from His Excellency, and delivered in the most impressive terms of offers of assistance, with money, &c., for which I returned my respectful thanks. Accompanied Malgares to the public walk, where we found the secretary, Captain Villamil, Zuloaga, and other officers of distinction. We here likewise met with the wife of my friend Malgares, to whom he introduced us. She was like all the other ladies of New Spain, a little gross in her form, but possessed the national beauty of eye in a superior degree. There was a large assemblage of ladies, amongst whom were two of the most celebrated in the capital. They were the only two ladies who had spirit sufficient, and whose husbands had generosity enough to allow them to think themselves rational beings, to be treated on an equality, to receive the visits of their friends, and give way to the hospitality of their dispositions, without constraint: they were therefore the envy of the ladies, and the subject of scandal to prudes. Their houses were the rendezvous of all the fashionable male society; and every man who was conspicuous for science, arts or arms, was sure to meet a welcome. We as unfortunate strangers were consequently not forgotten. I returned with Malgares to the house of his father-in-law, who was originally from Cadiz, a man of good information, and much in favour of an emancipation of that country from the French t——y, and took every opportunity when his son-in-law was not present, to converse with Robinson and myself on that subject, as to the means to be pursued by Spanish America, and what probable assistance we would give, &c.

Monday, 6th *April.*—Dined with the General. In the evening visited Malgares and the secretary : after dinner wine was put on the table, and we were entertained with songs in the French, Italian, Spanish, and English languages. Accustomed as I was to sitting some time after dinner, I forgot their *siesta*, or afternoon repose, until Walker hinted the subject to me and we retired. Wrote to the General on the subject of a loan of money.*

Tuesday, 7th *April.*—Dined at Don Antonio Cabraries in company with Villamil, Zuloaga, Walker, &c. Sent in a sketch of my voyage to the General; spent the evening at Colonel Minors' with Malgares.

Wednesday, 8th *April.*—Visited the treasurer, who shewed me a double-barrelled gun given him by Governor Claiborne, and another, formerly the property of Nolan.

Thursday, 9th *April.*—In the evening was informed that David Pharo was in town, and wished to speak to me. This man had formerly been my father's ensign, and was taken with Nolan's party at the time the latter was killed. He possessed a brave soul, and had borne every oppression since his being made prisoner with astonishing fortitude; although his leaving the place of his confinement (the village of Jeronime) without the knowledge of the General, was in some measure clandestine, yet a countryman, an acquaintance, and formerly a brother soldier, in a strange land in distress, had ventured considerably to see me; could I deny him the interview from any motives of delicacy ? no, forbid it humanity, forbid it every sentiment of my soul! Our meeting was affecting. With tears standing in his eyes, he informed me of the particulars of their being taken and many other circumstances since their being in the country. I promised to do all I could for him, consistently with my character and honour, and with the circumstance of their having entered the country without the authority of the United States. As he was obliged to leave the town before

---

* See Appendix, No. XIII.

THE INTERIOR OF NEW SPAIN.

day, he called on me at my quarters, when I bade him adieu, and gave him what my purse afforded, not what my heart dictated.

Friday, 10th *April.*—In the evening at Colonel Minors', Captain Roderiquas arrived from the Province of Texas. He had been under arrest one year, for going to Natchetoches with the Marquis Casabalvo.

Saturday, 11th *April*—Rode out in the coach with Malgares; was hospitably entertained at the house of one of the Vallois; here we drank London porter. Visited the Secretary Vallamil.

Sunday, 12th *April.*—Dined with the Doctor at Don Antonio Cabraries', with our usual guests; in the evening at the public walks.

Monday, 13th *April.*—Nothing extraordinary.

Tuesday, 14th *April.*—Spent the forenoon in writing, the afternoon at Don Antonio Cabraries'.

Wednesday, 15th *April.*—Spent the evening at Colonel Minors' with our friend Malgares; wrote a letter to the General on the subject of my papers.*

Thursday, 16th *April.*—Spent the evening at Secretary Don Vallamil's.

Friday, 17th *April.*—Sent my letter to His Excellency; spent the evening with my friend Malgares.

Saturday, 18th *April.*—Spent the evening at Cabraries', &c. Wrote to Governor Allencaster.

Sunday, 19th *April.*—In the evening at a fandango.

Monday, 20th *April.*—We this day learned that an American officer had gone on to the City of Mexico: this was an enigma to us inexplicable, as we conceived that the jealousy of the Spanish government would have prevented any foreign officer from penetrating the country; and what the United States could send an authorized agent to the Vice-royalty for, when the Spanish government had at the seat of our government a *charge des affaires* served but to darken our conjectures.† We likewise received an account of a commercial treaty having been entered into between Great Britain and the United States, which by the Dons was only considered as the preliminary step to an alliance offensive and defensive between the two nations.

---

*See Appendix, No. XIV.

† The person alluded to was Mr. Bueling, a citizen of Mississippi territory, whose mission is now known to the government.

Tuesday, 21st April.—Presented the commanding General with a letter for General Wilkinson, which he promised to have forwarded to the Governor of Texas.*

Wednesday, 22d April.—Spent the day in reading and studying Spanish, the evening at Captain Vallamil's.

Thursday, 23d April.—Dined at Don Pedro Vallois'; in the evening with Colonel Minors; bade him adieu as he was to march the next day. In the evening received a letter from the commanding General, informing me my papers were to be detained, and giving a certificate of their numbers, contents, &c., &c.†

Friday, 24th April.—Spent the evening at * * * * with his relations, and gave him a hint as to the following circumstances: About sun-down an officer of the government called on me, and told me that the government had been informed, that in conversation in all societies Robinson and myself had held forth political maxims and principles, which, if *just*, I must be conscious would, if generally disseminated, in a very few years be the occasion of a revolt of those kingdoms. That these impressions had taken such effect, that it was no uncommon thing in the circles in which we associated, to hear the comparative principle of a republican and monarchical government discussed; and even the allegiance due, in case of certain events, to the court called in question; that various characters of consideration had indulged themselves in these conversations, all of whom were noted, and would be taken care of; but that as it respected myself and companion, it was the desire of His Excellency, that whilst in the dominions of Spain, we would not hold any conversations whatsoever either on the subjects of religion or politics. I replied, that it was true I had held various and free conversations on the subjects complained of, but only with men high in office, who might be supposed to be firmly attached to the king, and partial to the government of their country: that I had never gone among the poor and illiterate, preaching up republicanism or a free government; that as to the Catholic religion, I had only combated some of what I had conceived to be its illiberal dogmas; but that I had spoken of it in all instances as a respectable branch of the Christian religion, which, as well as all others, was tolerated in the United

---
* See Appendix, No. XV. † See Appendix, No. XVI.

THE INTERIOR OF NEW SPAIN.

States: that, had I come to that kingdom in a diplomatic character, delicacy towards the government would have sealed my lips; had I been a prisoner of war, personal safety might have had the same effect, but being there in the capacity I was, not voluntarily, but by coercion of the Spanish government, which at the same time had officially notified to me that they did not consider me under *any restraint whatever;* I should, when called on, always give my opinion freely, either as to politics or religion, but at the same time with urbanity and a proper respect to the legitimate authorities of the country. He replied, "well, you may then rest assured your conduct will be represented in no very favourable point of view to your government." I answered, "to my government I am certainly responsible, but to no other." He then left me, and I immediately waited on some of my friends, and notified them to the threat; at which they appeared much alarmed, and we went immediately to consult * * *, who to great attachment to his friends joined the most incorruptible loyalty and the confidence of the government. Our consultation ended in a determination to be silent and watch events.

Saturday, 25th *April.*—At eleven o'clock called on His Excellency, but was informed he was engaged: about three o'clock I received a message from him by Lieutenant Walker, informing me that he was surprised I had not returned, and requesting me to call without ceremony in the evening, which I did, and presented him with a letter on the subject of Nolan's men.* He then candidly informed me my party would not join me in the territory of the King of Spain, but that they should be attended to punctually, and forwarded immediately after me. He requested that I would leave orders with my sergeant to deliver up all his ammunition, and dispose in some measure of the horses of which he had charge. I stated in reply, that with respect to the ammunition, I would give orders to my sergeant to deliver (if demanded) all they possessed, above what was necessary to fill their horns; but that as to the horses, I considered their loss to be a charge which must be adjusted between the two governments, that therefore I should not give any directions respecting them, except as to bringing them on as far and as long as they were able to travel. He then gave me an invitation to dine with him on the morrow.

---

*See Appendix, No. XVII.

Sunday, 26th April. Dined at the General's; in the evening went to Zuloaga's, and to others. * * * * took me out from the party and addressed me : " We are both Americans, are we not? Yes ; and we will yet see the time when those who tyrannize over us as they now do, will be on a level. I hope so, my friend. Yes, and so do most of the true Spaniards." This gentleman proposed to send one of his sons to the United States with me for education, and carried the idea so far as to ask permission, which was positively refused, and he was told that the request was considered heretical and disloyal. Wrote to my sergeant and Pharo, to the latter of whom I sent ten dollars, and to the other some money to purchase clothes for the party. We had been for some time suspicious that the Doctor was to be detained, but this evening he likewise obtained permission to pursue his voyage with me, which diffused general joy throughout the party.

Monday, 27th April.—Spent this day in making arrangements for our departure.

* * * had living with him an old negro, (the only one I saw on that side of St. Antonio,) who had been the property of some person residing near Natchez, and had been taken with Nolan. Having been acquainted with him in the Mississippi country, he solicited and obtained permission for Cæsar to live with him. I found him very communicative and extremely useful the day I arrived : when we were left alone, he came in, and looked around at the walls of the room, and exclaimed, "What, all gone ?" I demanded an explanation, and he informed me that the maps of the different provinces taken by * * *, and other surveyors, had been hung up against the walls, but the day we arrived they had all been taken down and deposited elsewhere.

In the evening it was notified to me to be ready to march the next day at three o'clock.

Tuesday, 28th April.—In the morning Malgares waited on us, and informed us he was to accompany us some distance on the route. After bidding adieu to all our friends, marched at a quarter past three o'clock, and encamped at nine o'clock at night at a spring. Passed near Chihuahua a small ridge of mountains, and then encamped in a hollow. This day, as we were riding along, Malgares rode up to me and informed me the General had given orders that I should not be permitted to make any

THE INTERIOR OF NEW SPAIN.

astronomical observations. To this I replied, he well knew I never had attempted, since in the Spanish dominions, to make any observations whatever.

Wednesday, 29th *April.*—Arrived at a settlement at eight o'clock; plenty of milk, &c. When about to make my journal, Malgares changed colour, and informed me his orders were, I should not take notes. At first I felt considerably indignant, and was on the point of refusing to comply, but thinking for a moment of the many politenesses I had received from him, I was induced to bow assent with a smile, and we proceeded on our route; but had not gone far before I made a pretext to halt, established my boy as a videt, and sat down peaceably under a bush and made my notes. This course I pursued ever after, not without a considerable degree of trouble to separate myself from the party. Arrived at the fort of St. Paul at eleven o'clock, situated on a small river of the same name, whose course is north-east, and south-west, at that time not more than a mill stream, but sometimes it is three hundred yards wide and impassable. Distance advanced, thirty miles.

Thursday, 30th *April.*—Marched at six o'clock, and at eleven arrived at the River Conchos, twenty-four miles; beautiful green trees on its banks. I was taken very sick at half past ten o'clock. Arrived at night at a small station on the River Conchos, garrisoned by a sergeant and ten men from the Fort Conchos, fifteen leagues up the river. Distance advanced, forty-three miles.

Friday, 1st *May.*—Marched up the Conchos to its confluence with the River Florida, fifteen leagues from whence we left the former river entirely, and took up the latter, which bears from the Conchos, south 80°, and 50° east. On its banks are very flourishing settlements, and the land is well timbered. There is a poor miserable village at the confluence. Came ten miles up the Florida to dinner, and rested at night at a private house. This property or plantation was valued formerly at three hundred thousand dollars, and extended on the Florida from the small place at which we slept on the last of April thirty leagues up the river. Distance advanced, forty-five miles.

Finding that a new species of discipline had taken place, and that the suspicions of my friend M. were much more acute than ever, I conceived it necessary to take some steps to secure the notes I had taken, which were clandestinely written. In the night I arose, and after making my men charge all their pieces well, I took my small books, and made them up in small rolls; then tearing a fine shirt to pieces I wrapped it round the papers and put them down in the barrels of the guns, until we just left room for the tompions, which were then carefully put in; the remainder we secured about our bodies under our shirts. This occupied about two hours, but was effected without discovery, and without suspicion.

Saturday, 2d *May.*—Marched early, and in four hours and a quarter arrived at Guaxequillo, situated on the River Florida, where we were to exchange our friend Malgares for Captain Barelo. He was a Mexican by birth, born near the capital, and entered as a cadet at Guaxequillo near twenty years past, and by his extraordinary merits (being a Creole) had been promoted to the rank of captain, which was even by himself considered as his ultimate promotion. He was a gentleman in his manners, generous and frank, and I believe a good soldier.

Sunday, 3d *May.*—At Guaxequillo, the Captain gave up his command to Malgares. At night the officers gave a ball, at which appeared at least sixty women, ten or a dozen of whom were very handsome.

Monday, 4th *May.*—Don Hymen Guleo arrived from Chihuahua, accompanied by a citizen and the friar, who had been arrested by order of the commandant general, on his way to Mexico for trial.

Tuesday, 5th *May.*—The party marched with all the spare horses and baggage.

Wednesday, 6th *May.*—Marched at five o'clock; ascended the river four miles, when we left it to our right, and directed our course south 60° east, for eight miles. Our friend Malgares accompanied us a few miles, after which we bade an eternal adieu, unless war bring us together in the field of battle, opposed as the most deadly enemies, when our hearts acknowledge the greatest friendship. Halted at ten o'clock, and marched again at four. No water on the road. Detached a Spanish soldier in search of some, who did not join us until twelve o'clock at night. Encamped on the open prairies; no wood or water except what the soldier brought us in gourds. The mules came up at eleven o'clock at night. Distance advanced, thirty miles.

THE INTERIOR OF NEW SPAIN. 275

Thursday, 7th *May.*—Marched very early; wind fresh from the south. The punctuality of Captain Barelo as to hours was remarkable. Arrived at half-past nine o'clock at a spring, the first water from Guaxequillo. The mules did not unload, but continued on nine miles to a spring at the foot of a mountain, with warm and good pasturage round it. Mountains on each side all day. Distance advanced, twenty-eight miles.

Friday, 8th *May.*—Marched five miles due west, through a gap in the mountain, then turned south 20° east, and more south to a river about twenty feet wide, with high steep banks. It was now dry, except in holes, but sometimes it is full and impassable. Halted at seven o'clock, and sent on the loaded mules. Marched at five o'clock; proceeded ten miles, and encamped without water. Distance advanced, eighteen miles.

Saturday, 9th *May.*—Marched between four and five o'clock, and arrived at Pelia at eight. This is only a station for a few soldiers, but is surrounded by mines. At this place are two large warm springs, strongly impregnated, and this is the water used by the party who are stationed here. We remained here all day. Captain Barelo had two beeves killed for his and my men, and charged nothing to either. He received orders at this place from the General, to lead us through the wilderness to Montelovez, in order that we might not approximate to the frontiers of Mexico, which we should have done by the usual route of Paras, &c.

Sunday, 10th *May.*—Marched past one copper mine, now diligently worked. At this place the proprietor had one hundred thousand sheep, cattle, horses, &c. Arrived at the Cadena, a house built and occupied by a priest. It is situated on a small stream at the pass of the mountains, called by the Spaniards the Door of the Prison, from its being surrounded by mountains. The proprietor was at Sumbraretta, six days' march distant. This Hacienda was obliged to furnish accommodations to all travellers. Marched at five o'clock, and passed the chain of mountains due east twelve miles, and encamped without water. Distance advanced, thirty-one miles.

Monday, 11th *May.*—Marched at eight o'clock, and arrived at Mauperne, a village situated at the foot of mountains of minerals, where they worked eight or nine mines; but the mass of the people were naked and starved wretches. The proprietor of the mines gave us an elegant repast. Here the orders of Salcedo were explained to me by the Captain.

I replied, that they excited my laughter, as there were disaffected perso[n] sufficient to serve as guides, should an army ever come into the countr[y] We pursued our march three miles further, to a station where were f[ig] trees and a fruit called by the French, le grain, situated on a little strea[m] which flowed through the gardens, and formed a terrestrial Paradise; he[re] we remained all day sleeping in the shade of the fig trees, and at nig[ht] continued our residence in the garden. We obliged the inhabitants wi[th] a ball. Several persons expressed great anxiety for a relief from the present distressed state, and a change of government.

Tuesday, 12th *May.*—I was awakened in the morning by the singin[g] of the birds and the perfumes of the trees around. I attempted to sen[d] two of my soldiers to town, but they were overtaken by a dragoon, an[d] ordered back; they returned, when I again ordered them to go, and if [a] soldier attempted to stop them, to take him off his horse, and flog hi[m]. This I did, conceiving it to be the duty of the Captain to explain his orde[r] relative to me, which he had not done, and I thought this would bring [on] an explanation. They were pursued by a dragoon through the town, wh[o] rode after them, making use of ill language. They attempted to cat[ch] him, but could not succeed. As I had mentioned my intentions of sendi[ng] my men to town after some stores to Captain Barelo, and he had n[ot] made any objections, I conceived it was acting with duplicity to send me[n] to watch the motions of my messengers. I determined therefore th[ey] should punish the dragoon, unless he had candour sufficient to explain t[he] reasons for his not wishing the men to go to the town, to which I shou[ld] undoubtedly have acquiesced; but as he never mentioned the circumstanc[e] I remained equally silent, and the affair never interrupted our harmony.

We marched at five o'clock; came on fifteen miles, and encampe[d] without water. One mile on this side of the little village the road branch[es] out into three, the right hand one leads by Paras, Saltello, &c., being t[he] main road to Mexico and St. Antonio. The centre which we took, leav[es] all the villages a little to the right, passing only some plantations; the le[ft] hand one goes immediately through the mountains to Montelovez, but [is] dangerous for small parties on account of the savages. This road is call[ed] the route by the Bolson of Mauperne, and was first travelled by Monsie[ur] de la Croix (afterwards Vice-roy of Peru). In passing from Chihuahua [to] Texas by this route, you make in seven days what takes fifteen or twen[ty] by the ordinary road, but it is very scarce of water, and your guards must either be so strong as to defy the Apaches, or calculate to escape them by swiftness; for they fill these mountains, from whence they continually carry on a predatory war against the Spanish settlements and caravans. We this day passed on to the territories of the Marquis de San Miguel, who owns the land from the mountains of the Rio del Norte to some distance into the Kingdom of Old Mexico, and his annual income is immense.

Wednesday, 13th *May*.—Came on to the River Nasas Rancho de St. Antonio, part of the Marquis's estate. My boy and self halted at the River Nasas to water our horses, having ridden on a-head. We took the bridles from their mouths, in order to enable them to drink freely, which they cannot do with the Spanish bridles on. The one I rode had been accustomed to be held by his master in a peculiar manner when bridled, and would not let me put it on again for a long time: in the meanwhile my boy's horse ran away, and it was out of our power to catch him, but when we arrived at the station we soon had out a number of boys who brought him in with all his different equipments, which were scattered on the road. This certainly was a strong proof of their honesty, and did not go unrewarded. In the evening we gave the inhabitants a ball, according to custom. We here learnt that one peck of corn per week was the allowance given to a grown person, with three pounds of meat. They expressed to Robinson their anxious hope that the day would ere long arrive, when the earth would be divided among their children, and their sweat and toil no longer be thrown away on others.

Thursday, 14th *May*.—Did not march until half past four o'clock, and about nine o'clock an officer arrived from Sta. Rosa with twenty-four men and two Apaches in irons; they were noble looking fellows, of large stature, and appeared by no means cast down by their misfortunes, although they knew their fate was transportation beyond the sea, never more to see their friends and relations. Knowing as I did the cruelty of the Spaniards to these people, I would have liberated them, had this been in my power. I went near them and gave them to understand we were friends, and conveyed to them some articles which would be of service to them. This day the thermometer stood at 30′ Reaumeur, and 99° 30′ Fahrenheit. The dust and dryness of the road obliged us to march in the night, when we proceeded fifteen miles and encamped without water. Indeed this road which the General obliged us to take, is almost impassable at this season for want of water, whilst the other affords it plentifully.

Friday, 15th *May.*—Marched early and came on five miles, when we arrived at a pit dug in a hollow, which afforded a poor pittance of muddy water for ourselves and beasts; and here we were again obliged to remain all day in order to travel in the night, as our beasts could now enjoy the benefit of water. Left this place at half past five o'clock, and proceeded fifteen miles by eleven o'clock, when we encamped without water or food for our beasts. Passed a miserable burnt up soil. Distance advanced, twenty miles.

Saturday, 16th *May.*—Marched two hours, and arrived at a miserable house, where we drew water from a well for all the beasts; marched in the evening and made fifteen miles further. We had left the right hand road on this side of Mauperne, but joined it about four miles back. Distance advanced, fifteen miles.

Sunday, 17th *May.*—Marched, and at about seven o'clock came in sight of Paras, which we left on the right, and halted at the Hacienda of St. Lorenzo, a short league to the north of Paras. At the Hacienda of St. Lorenzo was a young priest who was extremely anxious for a change of government, and came to our beds and conversed for hours on the subject.

Monday, 18th *May.*—Marched early, and came through a mountainous tract of country, but well watered, with houses situated here and there among the rocks. Joined the main road at the Hacienda of —— belonging to the Marquis de San Miguel; good gardens and fruit, also a small stream. The mules did not arrive until late at night, when it had commenced raining.

Tuesday, 19th *May.*—Did not march until three o'clock, the Captain not being very well. He here determined to take the main road, notwithstanding the orders of General Salcedo. Proceeded ten miles. Met an Irishman, a deserter from Captain Johnston's company; he returned and came to the camp, begging of me to take him back to his company, but I would not give him any encouragement; I presented him with a little change, as he was without a farthing.

THE INTERIOR OF NEW SPAIN.

Wednesday, 20th *May*.—Proceeded to the Hacienda of Polloss by nine o clock. This is a handsome place, and the Marquis de San Miguel frequently spends his summer at it, coming out from Mexico in his coach in ten days. Here we met the Mexican post going to Chihuahua. Don Hymen, who had left us at Paras, rejoined us here in a coach and six, in which we came out to a little settlement called the Florida, one league from Polloss, due north. Distance advanced, eighteen miles.

The Hacienda of Polloss is a square inclosure of about three hundred feet, the building being one story high, but some of the apartments are very elegantly furnished. In the centre of the square is a *jet d'eau*, which casts forth water from eight spouts, extended from a colossal female form; from this fountain all the population procure their supply of water. The Marquis had likewise a very handsome church, which, with its ornaments, cost him at least twenty thousand dollars; to officiate in this, he maintained a little stiff superstitious priest. In the rear of the palace (for so it might be called) was a fish-pond, furnished with immense numbers of fine fish. The population was about two thousand souls. This was our nearest point to the City of Mexico.

Thursday, 21st *May*.—Marched down a water-course, over a rough and stony road about ten miles, when we left it on the right, and proceeded eight miles further to a horse range of the Marquis, where he had four of his soldiers as a guarda cabello. Halted at half past nine o'clock, and afterwards pursued our journey.

Friday, 22d *May*.—Marched at three o'clock, and proceeded sixteen miles to a small shed, and in the afternoon to a rancho,* eight miles to the left of the main road, near the foot of the mountain, where was a pond of water, but no houses; some of the Marquis's soldiers were here. We left Polloss Mountains on our right and left, but here there was a cross one which we were to traverse in the morning. The Marquis maintains fifteen hundred troops, to protect his vassals and property from the savages. They are all cavalry, and are as well dressed and armed as the king's, but are treated by the latter as if vastly their inferiors.

Saturday, 23d *May*.—Marched early, and came on to the mountain to a spring. Distance advanced, fifteen miles.

---
* A rancho is a solitary farm. E.

Sunday, 24th *May*.—Marched at a good hour, ana passed through the mountain, having scarcely any road; it is called the Mountain of the Three Rivers. At the thirteenth mile joined the main road, left to our right on the 22d instant, and in one hour after the main Mexican road from the eastern provinces. From thence we proceeded north-west to a rancho, nine miles from Montelovez, from whence the Captain sent in an express to announce our approach.

Monday, 25th *May*.—In the afternoon Lieutenant Adams, commandant of the company of Montelovez, arrived in a coach and six to escort us into the town, where we arrived about five o'clock, P. M. In the evening visited Captain de Fereda, the commandant of the troops of Cogquilla, inspector and captain of the five internal provinces. He was a tall thin man with a very military appearance, and presenting an extraordinary instance of garrulity in a Spaniard. Lieutenant Adams, who commanded the place, was the son of an Irish engineer in the service of Spain; he had married a rich girl of the Passo del Norte, and they lived here in an elegant style for the country. We put up at his quarters, and were very hospitably entertained.

Tuesday, 26th *May*.—Made preparations for marching the next day. I arose early before any of our people were up, and walked nearly round the town, and from the hill took a small survey with my pencil and a pocket compass; which I always carried with me. Returned and found the family at breakfast, they having sent three or four of my men to search for me. The Spanish troops at this place were remarkably polite; always fronting and saluting when I passed; this I attributed to their commandant, Lieutenant Adams.

Wednesday, 27th *May*.—Marched at seven o'clock, after taking an affectionate leave of Don Hymen, and at half past twelve arrived at the Hacienda of Don Melcher, situated on the same stream as Montelovez.

Don Melcher was a man of very large fortune, polite, generous and friendly. He had in his service a man who had deserted from Captain Lockwood's first regiment of infantry, by the name of Pratt. From this man he had acquired a considerable portion of crude undigested information relative to the United States, and when he met with us, his thirst after a knowledge of our laws and institutions appeared to be insatiable. He caused a fine large sheep to be killed and given to my men.

Thursday, 28th *May.*—Marched early and arrived at Encina Hacienda at ten o'clock; this place was owned by Don Barigo. When we arrived at the Hacienda of Encina, I found a youth of eighteen sitting in the house genteely dressed, whom I immediately recognized from his physiognomy to be an American, and entered into conversation with him. He expressed great satisfaction at meeting a countryman, and we had a great deal of conversation. He sat at a table with us, and partook of a cold collation prepared of fruits and confectionary, but I was much surprised to learn shortly after we quitted the table, that he was a deserter from our army. On which I questioned him, and he replied, that his name was Griffith; that he had enlisted in Philadelphia, arrived at New Orleans, and deserted as soon as possible; that the Spaniards had treated him much better than his own countrymen, and that he should never return. I was extremely surprised at his insolence, and mortified that I should have been betrayed into any polite conduct towards him. I told him it was astonishing he should have the impertinence to address himself to me, knowing I was an American officer. He muttered something about being in a country where he was protected, &c.; on which I told him if he again opened his mouth to me I would instantly chastise him, notwithstanding his supposed protection. He was silent, and I called up one of my soldiers and told him in his hearing, that if he attempted to mix with them, to turn him out of company, which they executed by leading him to the door of their room a short time after, when he was about to enter it.

When dinner was nearly ready I sent a message to the proprietor, stating, that we assumed no right to say whom he should introduce to his table, but that we should think it a great indignity offered to a Spanish officer to attempt to set him down at the same board with a deserter from their army; and that if the man who was at the table in the morning was to make his appearance again, we should decline eating in his company. He replied that it was accident which produced the incident of the morning; that he was sorry our feelings had been offended, and that he would take care he did not appear again whilst we were there.

This day was the feast of God; we of course staid to partake of it, but as it has been frequently described by travellers in Catholic countries, I shall not add to the many repetitions of this class.

This day we passed the last mountains, and again entered the great Mississippi Valley, it being six months and thirteen days since we had first come in sight of them. Distance advanced, twenty miles.

Friday, 29th *May.*—Marched at seven o'clock, and came to the River Millada to a rancho.

Saturday, 30th *May.*—Marched at five o'clock, and arrived at the River Sabine at eight; forded it: marched in the evening at four o'clock, and at ten encamped at the second ridge without water. Distance advanced, twenty-seven miles.

Sunday, 31st *May.*—Marched early, and at nine o'clock arrived at a rancho and fine running water, course east and west. Marched eight miles further to a point of woods and encamped. No water. Distance advanced, twenty-seven miles.

Monday, 1st *June.*—Arrived at the Presidio Rio Grande at eight o'clock. This place was the position to which our friend Barelo was ordered, and which had been very highly spoken of to him; but he found himself miserably mistaken, for it was with the greatest difficulty we obtained anything to eat, which mortified him extremely.

When at Chihuahua, General Salcedo had asked me if I had not lost a man by desertion, to which I replied in the negative. He then informed me that an American had arrived at the Presidio of Rio Grande in the last year; that he had at first confined him, but that he was now released and practising physic, and that he wished me to examine him on my arrival; I therefore had him sent for. The moment he entered the room I discovered he had never received a liberal education, or been accustomed to polished society. I told him the reason I had requested to see him was, that I had it in my power to serve him, if I found him a character worthy of interference. He then related the following story: His name was Martin Henderson; he was born in Rockbridge county, state of Virginia; had been brought up a farmer, but, coming early to the states of Kentucky and Tennessee, he had acquired the taste for a frontier life, and in the spring of 1806, himself and four companions had left the saline in the district of Saint Genevieve, Upper Louisiana, in order to penetrate through the woods to the Province of Texas; his companions had left him on the White river, but he had continued on. In swimming some western branch his horse sunk under him, and it was with difficulty he made the shore with his gun. Here he waited three or four days until his horse rose, and he then got his saddlebags, but all his notes on the country, courses, &c. were destroyed. He then proceeded on foot for a few days, when he was met by thirty or forty Osage warriors, who, on his telling them he was going to the Spaniards, were proceeding to kill him, but on his saying he would go to the Americans, they held a consultation over him; and afterwards seized on his clothes, and divided them between them; then his pistols, dirk, compass, and watch, which they took to pieces and hung on their noses and ears. They then stripped him naked, and round his body they found a belt with gold pieces sewed in it; this they also took, and finally seized on his gun and ammunition. As they were marching off to leave him in this condition, he followed them, thinking it better to be killed, than be left in such a state to die of hunger and cold The savages after some time halted, and one pulled off an old pair of leggings, and gave him, others mockinsons, and a third a buffalo robe, and the one who had carried his heavy rifle, had by this time become tired of his prize (they never using rifles). They counted him out twenty-five charges of powder and ball, then sent two Indians with him, who put him on a war trace, which they said led to American establishments. As soon as the Indians left him he directed his course, as he supposed, for Saint Antonio: he killed deer and made himself some clothes. He proceeded on and expended all his ammunition three days before he struck the grand road, nearly at the Rio Grande. He further stated, that he had discovered two mines, one of silver and the other of gold, the situation of which he particularly described; but that the General had taken the samples from him. He said he would not attempt to'pass himself upon us for a physician, and hoped as he only used simples, and was careful to do no harm, we would not betray him. He concluded by saying since his being here he had made (from information) maps of all the adjacent country, which had been taken from him.

I had begun strongly to suspect that he was an agent of Burr's, and was revolving in my mind whether I should denounce him as such to the commandant, but felt reluctant from an apprehension that he might be innocent, when one of my men came in and informed me, that he was Trainer, who had killed Major Bashier in the wilderness between Natchez and Tennessee, when he was his servant. He had shot him through the head with his own pistòls while taking a nap at noon. The Governor of the State and the major's friends offered a very considerable reward for his apprehension, which obliged him to quit the neighbourhood; and with an Amazonian woman, who handled arms and hunted like a savage, he retreated to the source of the White river, but being routed thence by Captain Many, of the United States army, and a party of Cherokees, he and his female companion bore west. She proving to be pregnant, was left by him in the desert, and (I was informed) arrived at the settlement of Red river, but by what means is to me unknown. The articles and money taken from him by the Osages were the property of the deceased major.

I reported the circumstance to Captain Barelo, who had him immediately confined, until the will of Governor Cordero was known, who informed me, when at St. Antonio, he would have him sent to some place of perpetual confinement in the interior. Thus vengeance has overtaken the ingrate and homicide, when he least expected it.

In the evening we went to see some dancers on the slack rope, who were nowise extraordinary in their performances except in language, which would almost bring a blush on the cheek of the most abandoned of the female sex in the United States; but here appeared to be the greatest part of the entertainment, as every sally was attended with loud and repeated bursts of laughter from the female part of the audience.

Tuesday, 2d *June*.—In the day time, while I was endeavouring to regulate our watches by my compass, the instant my back was turned, some person stole it, and I could by no means recover it. I had strong suspicions that the theft was approved, as the instrument occasioned great dissatisfaction. This day the Captain went out to dine with some monks, who would have thought it profanation to have us for their guests, notwithstanding the priest of the place had escorted us round the town, and to all their missions; and we had found him a very communicative, liberal, and intelligent man. We saw no resource for dinner, but in the inventive genius of the little Frenchman, who had accompanied us from Chihuahua, where he had been officiating one year as cook to the General, and of whom he gave us many interesting anecdotes. He went off, and in a very short time returned with table-cloth, plates, and a dinner of three or four courses, a bottle of wine, and a pretty girl to wait at table.

THE INTERIOR OF NEW SPAIN. 285

We enquired by what magic he had brought this about, and found that he had gone to one of the officers, and notified, that it was the wish of the Commandant he should supply the two Americans with a decent dinner, (this we explained to Barelo in the evening, and he laughed heartily,) which was done, but we took care to compensate them for their trouble. At five o'clock we parted from the captains with regret and assurances of remembrances, and proceeded, escorted by an ensign and guard: came to the Rio Grande, which we passed, and encamped at a rancho on the other side. Distance advanced, seven miles.

Wednesday, 3d *June*.—The mosquettoes, which had commenced the first night on this side Montelovez, had now become very troublesome. This day saw the first horse-flies, and some wild horses. Proceeded to the open plain, where there was no water. Distance advanced, thirty miles.

Thursday, 4th *June*.—Came on sixteen miles to a pond and dined: great sign of wild horses in the afternoon. Proceeded to a river. Distance advanced, thirty-six miles.

Friday, 5th *June*.—After losing two horses in ferrying, we crossed and continued our route. Passed two herds of wild horses, which merely left the road for us. Halted at a pond, on the left of the road fifteen miles on, where we saw the first oak since we entered Mexico, and this was of the scrub kind. Passed many deer yesterday and to-day. Came to a small creek at night, where we met a party of the company of St. Fernandez, returning from the line. Distance advanced, thirty-one miles.

Saturday, 6th *June*.—Marched early, and met several parties of troops returning from Texas, where they had been sent to reinforce, when our troops were near the line. Observed immense numbers of cross roads made by the wild horses. Killed a wild hog, which on examination I found to be very different from the tame breed, being smaller, of a brown colour, long hair, and short legs; they are to be found in all parts between Red river and the Spanish settlements. Passed an encampment made by the Lee Panis. Met one of that nation with his wife. In the afternoon struck the wood land, which was the first we had been in from the time we had left the Osage nation. Distance advanced, thirty-nine miles.

Sunday, 7th *June.*—Came on fifteen miles to the River Mariana, the line between Texas and Bogquilla, a pretty little stream; from thence in the afternoon to St. Antonio. We halted at the mission of St. Joseph, and were received in a friendly manner by the priest of the mission and others. We were met out of the town about three miles by Governors Cordero and Herrara, in a coach. We repaired to their quarters, where we were received like their children. Cordero informed me that he had discretionary orders as to the manner of my going out of the country: that he therefore wished me to chose my time, mode, &c., and that any sum of money I might want was at my service; that in the mean time Robinson and myself would make his quarters our residence; and that he had caused to be vacated a house immediately opposite for my men. In the evening his levee was attended by a crowd of officers and priests. After supper we went to the public square, where might be seen the two governors joined in a dance with people who in the day time would approach them with reverence and awe. We were here introduced to the sister of Lieutenant Malgares's wife, who was one of the finest women we saw, and was married to a Captain Ugarte, to whom we had letters of introduction.

Monday, 8th *June.*—Remained at St. Antonio.

Tuesday, 9th *June.*—A large party dined at the Governor Cordero's, who gave as his first toast, The President of the United States. I returned the compliment by toasting, His Catholic Majesty: these were followed by General Wilkinson, and one of the company then gave, These Gentlemen, their safe and happy arrival in their own country, their honourable reception, and the continuation of the good understanding which exists between the two countries.

Wednesday, 10th *June.* — A large party at the Governor's to dinner; he gave as a toast his companion Herrara.

Thursday, 11th *June.*—Preparing to march to-morrow. We this evening had a conversation with the two Governors, wherein they exhibited an astonishing knowledge of the political character of our executive; the local interests of the different parts of the union, and the military disposition of General Wilkinson; and concluded with a high coloured picture of * * * *, to whose querulous disposition they attributed the late disputes between the two governments on the frontiers. As I did not know that gentleman, I could only reply generally, that I thought it impossible an agent of our government, standing in the situation of the * * * *, would dare to blow up the flames of hostility between the two countries, knowing as he must the general disposition which the United States has always exhibited to pacific measures.

Friday, 12th *June*.—One of the captains from the kingdom of Leon having died, we were invited to attend the burial: accompanied the two Generals in their coach, where we had an opportunity of viewing the solemnity of the interment, agreeably to the ritual of the Spanish church, attended with the military honours, which were conferred on the deceased by his late brethren in arms. Governor Cordero gave the information of my intended expedition to the Commandant General as early as July, the month I took my departure; he had received his intelligence via Natchez.

Saturday, 13th *June*.—This morning there were marched two hundred dragoons for the sea-coast to look out for the English, and that evening Colonel Cordero was to have proceeded to join them. We marched at seven o'clock, Governor Cordero taking us out in his coach about two leagues, accompanied by Father M'Guire, Dr. Zerbon, &c. It may not be improper to mention here something of the two latter gentlemen, who certainly treated us with all imaginable attention while at St. Antonio. The former was an Irish priest, who formerly resided on the coast above Orleans, and was noted for his hospitality and social qualities. On the cession of Louisiana, he followed the standard of the "king his master," who never suffers an old servant to be neglected. He received at Cuba an establishment, as chaplain of the mint at Mexico, from whence the instability of human affairs carried him to St. Antonio. He was a man of chaste classical taste, observation, and research. Dr. Zerbon formerly resided at Natchez, but in consequence of pecuniary embarrassments emigrated into the Spanish territories. Being a young man of a handsome person and insinuating address, he had obtained the good will of Governor Cordero, who had conferred on him an appointment in the King's hospital, and many other advantages by which he might have made a fortune. But he had recently committed many great indiscretions, by which he had nearly lost the favour of Colonel Cordero; but whilst we were there he was treated with attention. We took a friendly adieu of Governor Herrara, and our other friends at St. Antonio.

I will here attempt to pourtray a faint resemblance of the characters of the two governors, whom we found at St. Antonio; but to whose superexcellent qualities it would require the pen of a master to do justice. Don Antonio Cordero was fifty years of age, about five feet ten inches in height, fair complexion, and blue eyes: he wore his hair turned back, and in every part of his dress was eligibly written "the soldier." He yet possessed an excellent constitution, and a body which appeared to be neither impaired by the fatigues of the various campaigns he had made, nor disfigured by the numerous wounds received from the enemies of his king. He was one of the select officers who had been chosen by the court of Madrid, to be sent to America about thirty-five years since, to discipline and organize the Spanish provincials, and had been employed in all the various kingdoms and provinces of New Spain, and through the parts which we explored. He was universally beloved and respected, and when I pronounce him by far the most popular man in the internal provinces, I risk nothing by the assertion. He spoke the Latin and French languages well, was generous, gallant, brave, and sincerely attached to his King and country. These numerous qualifications have advanced him to the rank of colonel of cavalry, and governor of the Provinces of Bogquilla and Texas. His usual residence was Montelovez, which he had greatly embellished; but since our taking possession of Louisiana, he had removed to St. Antonio, in order to be nearer the frontier, to be able to apply the remedy to any evil which might arise from the collision of our lines.

Don Simon de Herrara is about five- feet eleven inches high, has a sparkling black eye, dark complexion and hair. He was born in the Canary Islands, served in the infantry in France, Spain, and Flanders, and speaks the French language well, and a little of the English. He is engaging in his conversation with his equals; polite and obliging to his inferiors, and in all his actions one of the most gallant and accomplished men I ever knew. He possesses a great knowledge of mankind, from his experience in various countries and societies, and knows how to employ the genius of each of his subordinates to advantage. He had been in the United States during the presidency of General Washington, and had been introduced to that hero, of whom he spoke in terms of exalted veneration. He is now lieutenant-colonel of infantry and governor of the kingdom of New Leon. His seat of government is Montelrey; and probably if ever a chief was adored by his people it is Herrara. When his time expired last he immediately repaired to Mexico, attended by three hundred of the most respectable people of his district, who carried with them the sighs, tears, and prayers of thousands that he might be continued in that government. The Vice-roy thought proper to accede to their wishes pro-tempore, and the King has since confirmed his nomination. When I saw him he had been about one year absent, during which time the citizens of rank in Montelrey had not suffered a marriage or baptism to take place in any of their families, waiting until their common father could be there to consent, and give joy to the occasion by his presence. What greater proof could be given of their esteem and love? In drawing a parallel between the two friends. I should say, that Cordero was the man of the greatest reading, Herrara of the world. Cordero has lived all his life a bachelor, Herrara married an English lady in early youth at Cadiz, who, by her suavity of manners, makes herself as much beloved and esteemed by the ladies as her noble husband is by the men. By her he has several children, one now an officer in the service of his royal master. But the two friends agree perfectly in one point, their hatred of tyranny of every kind, and in a secret determination never to see that flourishing part of the new world subject to any European lord, except *him*, whom their honour and loyalty bind them to defend with their lives and fortunes.

Before I close this subject, it may not be improper to state, that we owe to Governor Herrara's prudence, that we are not now engaged in a war with Spain. This will be explained by the following anecdote, which he related in the presence of his friend Cordero, and was confirmed by him: When the difficulties commenced on the Sabine, the Commandant General and the Vice-roy consulted each other, and they mutually determined to maintain (what they demanded) the dominions of their master inviolate. The Vice-roy therefore ordered Herrara to join Cordero with thirteen hundred men, and both the Vice-roy and General Salcedo ordered Cordero to cause our troops to be attacked, should they pass the Rio Onde. These orders were positively reiterated to Herrara, the actual commanding officer of the Spanish army on the frontiers, and gave rise to the many messages which he sent to Genera Wilkinson, when he was advancing with our troops; but finding they were not attended to, he called a council of war on the question, to attack or not ;. when it was given as their opinion, that they should immediately commence a predatory warfare, but avoid a general engagement. Yet, notwithstanding the orders of the Vice-roy, the Commanding General, Governor Cordero, and the opinion of his officers, he had the firmness or temerity to enter into the agreement with General Wilkinson, which at present exists relative to our boundaries on that frontier. On his return he was received with coolness by Cordero, and they both made their communication to their superiors. Until an answer was received (said Herrara) I experienced the most unhappy period of my life, conscious I had served my country faithfully, at the same time I had violated every principle of military duty. At length the answer arrived, and what was it, but the thanks of the Vice-roy and the Commandant General, for having pointedly disobeyed their orders, with assurances that they would represent his services in exalted terms to the King. What could have produced this change of sentiment is to me unknown, but the letter was published to the army, and confidence again restored between the two chiefs and the troops.

Our company now consisted of Lieutenant John Echararria, who commanded the escort, Captain Eugene Marchon, of New Orleans, and Father Jose Angel Cabaso, who was bound to the camp at or near the Trinity, with a suitable proportion of soldiers. We proceeded sixteen miles to a place called the Beson, where we halted until the loads came up. Marched again at four o'clock, and arrived at the River of Guadelupe at eight o'clock at night. Distance advanced, thirty miles.

Sunday, 14th *June*.—When we left St. Antonio, everything appeared to be in a flourishing and improving state, owing to the examples and encouragement given to industry, politeness, and civilization by their excellent Governor, Cordero, and his colleague Herrara ; and also to the large body of troops maintained at that place, in consequence of the difference existing between the United States and Spain. Came on to the St. Mark in the morning ; in the afternoon, proceeded fifteen miles further, but were late, owing to our having taken the wrong road. Distance advanced, thirty miles.

Monday, 15th *June*.—Marched twenty miles in the morning to a small pond, which, in dry seasons, has no water, where we halted. Here commenced the oak timber, having seen only musqueet from St. Antonio.

THE INTERIOR OF NEW SPAIN.

Prairie like the Indian territory. In the afternoon, came on six miles further to a creek, where we encamped early. Distance advanced, twenty-six miles.

Tuesday, 16th *June.*—Marched early, and at eight o'clock arrived at Red river; here was a small Spanish station, and several lodges of Tancards, tall, handsome men, but without exception the most naked savages I ever yet saw. They complained much of their situation. In the afternoon, passed over hilly, stony land, with pine timber; encamped on a small run. Distance advanced, twenty-six miles. Killed one deer.

Wednesday, 17th *June.*—Came on at nine o'clock to a large encampment of Tancards, containing more than forty lodges; their poverty was as remarkable as their independence, although possessing immense herds of horses, &c. I gave a Camanche and Tancard each a silk handkerchief, and a recommendation to the commandant at Natchitoches. In the afternoon, marched for three hours, and encamped on a hill, at a creek on the right hand side of the road. Met a large herd of mules, escorted by four soldiers. The Lieutenant took some money from them, which they had in charge. Distance advanced, thirty miles.

Thursday, 18th *June.*—Rode on until half-past ten o'clock, when we arrived at the River Brassos, after having travelled twenty-five miles. Here is a stockade guard of one corporal and six men, and a ferry boat. Swam our horses over; one was drowned, and several others near it, owing to their striking each other with their feet. After having crossed the river, we proceeded about two miles on this side of a bayou, called the Little Brassos, which is only a branch of the other, and makes an impassable swamp at certain seasons between them. Distance advanced, thirty-one miles.

Friday, 19th *June.*—Came on through prairies and woods alternately twenty miles, to a small creek, Corpus Christi; well wooded, rich land. In the afternoon, proceeded ten miles, and passed a creek, which in high water is nearly impassable for four miles. Encamped about one mile on this side, on high land to the right of the road; met the mail, Indians, and others. Distance advanced, thirty miles.

Saturday, 20th *June.*—Came on sixteen miles in the morning; passed several herds of mustangs or wild horses. Good land, with occasionally ponds and small dry creeks, prairie and woods alternately. It rained considerably: we halted to dry our baggage long before night. Distance advanced, twenty miles.

Sunday, 21st *June.*—Came on to the River Trinity by eight o'clock. Here were stationed two captains, two lieutenants, and three ensigns, with nearly one hundred men, all sick, one scarcely able to assist the other. Met a number of runaway negroes, and also some French and Irishmen. Received information of Lieutenant Wilkinson's safe arrival. Crossed all our horses and baggage without much difficulty. Distance advanced, twenty miles.

Monday, 22d *June.*—Marched the mules and horses in the forenoon, but did not depart ourselves until three o'clock P. M. Father Jose Angel Calosos separated from us at this place, for the post to which he was destined. Passed thick woods, and a few small prairies with high rich grass. Sent a despatch to Nacogdoches. Distance advanced, twenty-two miles.

Tuesday, 23d *June.*—Came on twenty miles in the forenoon, to a small creek of standing water; good land and well timbered. Met a sergeant from Nacogdoches. In the afternoon made twenty miles, and crossed the River Natchez, running north-west and south-east twenty yards wide. It was belly deep to the horses at that time, but sometimes it is impassable. Two miles on this side, encamped on a hill in a little prairie. Mules and loads arrived at twelve o'clock. The sandy soil and pine timber began again to appear this afternoon, but the land near the river is good. Distance advanced, forty miles.

Wednesday, 24th *June.*—The horses came up this morning ; lost six over night. We marched early, and after proceeding fifteen miles came to the River Angelina, about the width of the Natchez, running north and south, with good land on its banks. Two miles farther was a settlement of Barr and Davenport, where were three of our deserters. One mile further, two houses, where we halted for dinner. Marched at four o'clock, and half past eight arrived at Nacogdoches, where we were politely received by the adjutant and inspector, and Captains Herrara, Davenport, &c. This part of the country is well watered, but a sandy, hilly soil, with pine, scrub oak, &c. Distance advanced, thirty-seven miles.

THE INTERIOR OF NEW SPAIN.

Thursday, 25th *June*.— Spent in reading gazettes from the United States, &c. A large party at the adjutant and inspector's to dinner. First toast, "The President of the United States. Second, The King of Spain. Third, Governors Herrara and Cordero."

Friday, 26th *June*.—Made preparations to march the next day. Saw an old acquaintance; also Lorrieniers's son-in-law, from the district of Cape Jerardeau. Dined at the commandant's and spent the evening at Davenport's.

Saturday, 27th *June*.—Marched after dinner, but proceeded only twelve miles. Was escorted by Lieutenant Guodiana and a military party. Mr. Davenport's brother-in-law, who was taking in some money, also accompanied us. Don Francis Viana, adjutant and inspector of the internal provinces, who commanded at Nacogdoches, is an old and veteran officer, and was one of those who came to America at the same time with Colonel Cordero; but possessing a mind of frankness, he unfortunately spoke his opinions too freely in some instances, which, finding its way to court, prevented his promotion. But he is highly respected by his superiors, and looked up to as a model of military conduct by his inferiors. He unfortunately does not possess flexibility sufficient to be useful in the present *corrupted* state of the Spanish kingdoms. He is the officer who caused Major Sparks and Mr. Freeman to return from their expedition on the Red river.

Sunday, 28th *June*.—Marched early, and at nine o'clock crossed the river called Toyac, from whence we pushed on, in order to arrive at the house of a Frenchman,—— miles distant from the Sabine. We stopped at a house on the road, where the Lieutenant informed me an American, by the name of Johnson, lived, but was surprised to find he had crossed the line with his family, together with a French family from his neighbourhood. When we began conversing with them, they seemed much alarmed, thinking we had come to examine them, and expressed great attachment to the Spanish government, but were somewhat astonished to find I was an American officer; and on my companion stepping out, expressed themselves in strong terms of hatred of his nation. I excused them for their weakness, and gave them a caution.

The land here is fine, and well watered and timbered, with hickory, oak, sugar maple, &c. Distance advanced, forty miles.

Monday, 29th *June*.—Our baggage and horses came up about ten o'clock, when we despatched them on: marched ourselves at two o'clock, and arrived at the River Sabine by five. Here we saw the cantonment of the Spanish troops, when commanded by Colonel Herrara, in the late affair between the two governments. Crossed the Sabine river, and proceeded about one league on this side to a little prairie, where we encamped. Parted with Lieutenant Guodiana, and our Spanish escort. And here I think proper to bear testimony to the politeness, civility, and attention of all the officers, who at different periods, and in different provinces, commanded my escort; but in a particular manner, to Malgares and Barelo, who appeared studious to please, and accommodate as much as lay in their power; and also to the obliging mild dispositions evinced in all instances by their rank and file.

On this side of the Sabine, I went up to a house, where I found ten or fifteen Americans hovering near the line, in order to embrace an opportunity of carrying on some illicit commerce with the Spaniards, who, on their side, were equally eager. Here we found Thorpe and Sea, who had been old sergeants in General Wayne's army. Distance advanced, fifteen miles.

Tuesday, 30th *June*.—Marched early, and came on fifteen miles to a house on a small creek, where lived a Dutch family, named Faulk, where we left a small roan horse which had given out. Marched twelve miles further to a large bayou, where there had been an encampment of our troops, which I recognized by its form, and took pleasure in imagining the position of the General's marque, and the tents of my different friends and acquaintances. Distance advanced, twenty-eight miles.

Wednesday, 1st *July*.—Finding that a horse of Dr. Robinson's, which had come all the way from Chihuahua, could not proceed, I was obliged to leave him here. Yesterday and to-day passed many Choctaws, whose clothing, furniture, &c., evidently marked the superiority of the situation of those who bordered on our frontiers, to those of the naked half-starved Indians whom we found hanging round the Spanish settlements. Came on, passed a string of huts, supposed to be built by our troops; and at a small run, a fortified camp, but a half mile from the hill, where anciently stood the village Adyes. We proceeded on to a spring, where we halted for our loads; and finding the horses much fatigued, and not able to proceed, left them and the baggage, and continued our journey. We arrived at Natchitoches about four o'clock P. M., and were affectionately received by Colonel Freeman, Captains Stony and Woolstoncraft, Lieutenant Smith, and all the officers of the post.

Language cannot express the gaiety of my heart, when I once more beheld the standard of my country waved aloft! All hail, cried I, the ever-sacred name of country, in which is embraced that of kindred, friends, and every other tie which is dear to the soul of man!

Z. M. PIKE.

GEOGRAPHICAL, STATISTICAL, AND GENERAL

OBSERVATIONS

ON THE

INTERIOR PROVINCES OF NEW SPAIN, FROM LOUISIANA TO THE VICE-ROYALTY, AND BETWEEN THE PACIFIC OCEAN, THE GULPH OF CALIFORNIA, AND THE ATLANTIC OCEAN.

THE Kingdom of New Spain lies between the 16° and 44° N. latitude, and 86° and 119° W. longitude: it is divided into two separate and independent governments, and these again into various subdivisions.

In the Vice-Royalty is included the Administration of Guadalaxara, which lies between 18° 30′ and 24° 30′ N. latitude, and 104° and 109° W. longitude, and is bounded on the south and west by the South Sea; on the north by the Province of Biscay, and Sinaloa; on the north-east, by the Administration of Zacatecas; on the east, by the Administration of Guanaxuato; and on the south-east, by that of Valladolid; extending three hundred and fifty miles in length, from north-west to south-east, and two hundred and fifty in width east and west. The population may be estimated at one hundred thousand. This is one of the most luxuriant and rich administrations in the Vice-Royalty. It is intersected from east to west by the great River de Santiago, which receives most of its waters from Lake Chapala. Guadalaxara the capital, situated in latitude 20° 50′ N., longitude 105 W., was built by one of the German family in 1551, and in 1570, the bishopric was removed from Campostella to that place. It is the seat of the audience of Guadalaxara, which includes the Administrations of Guadalaxara and of Zacatecas. The population of this city may be estimated at seventy-five thousand.*

The Administration of Valladolid lies between 18° 12′ and 21° 10′ N. latitude, and 102° and 105° W. longitude; being bounded on the south by the South Sea and part of Mexico; on the east and north-east by the latter administration; and on the north by that of Guanaxuato. Its greatest length from north-east to south-west is two hundred and thirty miles, and its greatest width east and west one hundred and ninety miles. The population may be estimated at three hundred and sixty thousand. Its capital of the same name is situated in about 20° N. latitude, 103° 25′ W. longitude. Population unknown.†

The administration of Mexico lies between 16° 30′ and 21° 30′ N. latitude, 99° and 105° W. longitude, and is bounded on the south by the South Sea, on the east by the governments of Puebla and Vera Cruz, on the north by that of St. Luis, and on the west by Valladolid and Guanaxuato. Its greatest length north and south may be three hundred and sixty miles, and its greatest width, which is on the western ocean, is two hundred miles. The population may be estimated at one million five hundred thousand souls. ‡ The capital (which is that of the whole kingdom) is Mexico, any description of which would be superfluous; I will therefore only say from every information I could obtain from persons who had resided in it for years, that it does not contain above two hundred thousand. Its being the residence of the Vice-roy, (whose court is more splendid than that of Madrid,) its central position as to the two ports of Acapulco and Vera Cruz, together with the rich and luxuriant vale which surrounds it, will give to Mexico, whenever the Spanish Americans burst the present bonds of slavery in which they are enthralled, and become a free, great, and happy people, all those advantages which great wealth, a

---

* Humboldt states the population of the administration for the year 1803, at six hundred and thirty thousand five hundred, and of the city nineteen thousand five hundred. Pol Ess. Vol. ii. pp. 227, 230. E.

† Administration, three hundred and seventy-six thousand four hundred; city, eighteen thousand. Pol. Ess. Vol. ii. pp. 208 and 224. E.

‡ According to Humboldt, one million five hundred and ten thousand eight hundred; of the capital, one hundred and eleven thousand and thirty-seven. Vol. ii. pp. 3 and 183. E.

THE INTERIOR OF NEW SPAIN.

large population, and a commanding situation, concentrate; and assuredly render it one of the greatest cities in the world. In point of population, it is now in the second rank, but in beauty, riches, magnificence, and splendour it aspires to the first.

The Administration of Oaxaca lies between 16° and 18° N. latitude, and 98° and 112° W. longitude, being bounded on the south by the South Sea, on the west by the government of Puebla, on the north by Mexico and Vera Cruz, and on the east by the Province of Guatemala. Its greatest length east and west is two hundred and thirty miles, and its width north and south one hundred and seventy-five miles. The population may be estimated at five hundred and twenty thousand souls.* The capital is Oaxaca, in 17° 30′ N. latitude, 96° 25″ W. longitude.

The administration of Vera Cruz lies between 17° and 22° N. latitude, 98° and 101° W. longitude, and is bounded on the north and east by the Gulph of Mexico, on the south by Oaxaca, on the west by Puebla and Mexico. Its greatest length north-west and south-east is four hundred and thirty miles, and its width east and west not more than sixty miles. The population may be estimated at two hundred and twenty thousand. The capital is Vera Cruz, in 19° 10′ N. latitude, 98° 30′ W. longitude, which is the sole port of entry for all the kingdom on the Atlantic Ocean, as that of Acapulco is on the western. Its population may be estimated at thirty thousand souls.† This city was sacked by the English on the 17th May, 1683, since which the works for its defence have been made so very strong as almost to bid defiance to any attack from the sea.

The Administration of Puebla lies between 16° and 20° N. latitude, and 100° and 102° W. longitude; and is bounded on the south by the South Sea, on the east by Oaxaca and Vera Cruz, and on the north and west by Mexico, extending nearly three hundred miles in its greatest length from north to south, and one hundred and twenty in its greatest width from east to west. The population may be estimated at eight hundred thousand souls. Its capital is the city of La Puebla, in 19° 12′ N.

---

* The administration in 1803, five hundred and thirty-four thousand eight hundred; the capital, in 1792, twenty-four thousand. Humb. Vol. ii. pp. 235 and 242. E.

† Administration in 1803, one hundred and fifty-six thousand; city, sixteen thousand. Humb. Vol. ii. pp. 250 and 267. E.

latitude, 100° 50' W. longitude, with an estimated population of eighty thousand souls.*

The Administration of Guanaxuato lies between 21° 30' and 22ᵘ 30' N. latitude, and 103° and 105° W. longitude; bounded on the south by Valladolid, on the east by Mexico, on the north by St. Luis Zacatecas, and on the west by Guadalaxara. Its greatest extent from north to south is seventy-five miles, and from east to west eighty-five. The population may be estimated at five hundred thousand souls.† Its capital city is Guanaxuato, in latitude 21° N., longitude 103ᵘ W.

The Administration of Zacatecas lies between 21° 20' and 24° 12' N. latitude, 103° and 105° 30' W. longitude; bounded on the north by the internal Province of Biscay, on the east by St. Luis, on the west by Guadalaxara, and on the south by Guanaxuato. Its greatest length is two hundred and ten miles north and south, and its greatest width a hundred and forty-five from east to west. Its population may be estimated at two hundred and fifty thousand two hundred and fifty souls.‡ The capital, Zacatecas, stands in 23ᵘ N. latitude and 104° W. longitude.

The Administration of St. Luis Potosi lies between 21° 20' and 28° 50' N. latitude, and 99° and 102° W. longitude, and includes Texas and St. Ander. It is bounded on the north by New Leon, on the east by the Province of St. Ander, on the south by Guanaxuato and Mexico, and on the west by Zacatecas. Its greatest length from east to west is a hundred and seventy miles. The population may be estimated at three hundred and eleven thousand five hundred souls. Its capital, St. Luis de Potosi, with a population of sixty thousand §, stands in 22° N. latitude, 103° W. longitude, and was founded in 1568.

The Province of Neuvo San Ander is bounded on the north by the Province of Texas, on the west by Neuvo Leon and Cogquilla, on the south by St. Luis, and on the east by the Atlantic Ocean. From north

---

* The administration, eight hundred and thirteen thousand three hundred; the capital, sixty-seven thousand eight hundred. Humb. Vol. ii. pp. 190 and 200. E.

† Administration, five hundred and seventeen thousand three hundred; capital forty-one thousand. Humb. Vol. ii. pp. 204 and 206. E.

‡ Administration, one hundred and fifty-three thousand and three hundred; capital, thirty-three thousand. Humb. Vol. ii. pp. 233, 234. E.

§ The administration, three hundred and thirty-four thousand nine hundred; capital, twelve thousand. Humb. Vol. ii. pp. 271 and 272. E.

to south it is about five hundred miles in length, but from east to west not more than one hundred and fifty. Its population may be estimated at thirty-eight thousand souls. The capital, New San Ander, is on the river of that name about forty miles from the sea, in 23° 45′ N. latitude, and 101° W. longitude.

The Kingdom of New Leon is bounded on the east by New San Ander, on the north by Cogquilla, on the west by Biscay, and on the south by St. Luis and Zacatecas. Its greatest length north and south is two hundred and fifty miles. Its population may be estimated at thirty thousand souls. Its capital, Montelrey, is situated on the head waters of Tiger river, which discharges itself into the Gulph of Mexico. The city of Montelrey contains about eleven thousand, and is the seat of the Bishop Don Dio Premiro, who visited the port of Natchitoches, when commanded by Captain Turner of the 2d United States regiment infantry. His Episcopal jurisdiction extends over New San Ander, New Leon, Cogquilla and Texas, and his salary is equal to one hundred thousand dollars per annum. Montelrey is situated in 26° N. latitude, and 102° W. longitude. There are many and rich mines near this city, from whence I am informed are taken one hundred mules' load of bullion in silver and gold monthly, which may be presumed to be not more than three-fifths of what is drawn from the mines, there being many persons who prefer never getting their metal coined, as it is then not so easily ascertained what they are worth, which is an important secret in all despotic governments.

The foregoing nine administrations, (or intendancies,) the Kingdom of Leon, and the Province of Nuevo San Ander, are included in the two audiences of Guadalaxara and Mexico, and form, I believe, the whole political government of the Vice-roy. But I am not positive whether his jurisdiction does not include the Audience of Guatemala, which lies to the south and includes the province proper of that name: that of Chiapa, Yucatan, Veragua, Costa Rica, and Honduras. An audience is the high court of appeals, in which the Vice-roy presides, and has two votes; it is intended as a check on his power and authority. The administrations are governed by intendants, who are officers of high rank, and always Europeans.

The longitude given is from the meridian of Paris. In the general view of New Spain, I shall take some notice of the manners, modes, force, &c., of the Vice-royalty; but as I do not pretend to be correctly informed respecting this quarter of the kingdom, and there being so many persons who have given statements on these heads, I shall confine my remarks principally to the internal provinces through which I passed, and on which I made my observations.

INTERNAL PROVINCES.

NEW MEXICO lies between 30° 30' and 440° N. latitude, and 104° and 108° W. longitude, and is the most northern province of the Kingdom of New Spain. It extends on the north-west into an undefined limit; it is bounded on the north and east by Louisiana, on the south by Biscay and Cogquilla, and on the west by Senora and California. Its length is unknown, its breadth may be one hundred miles, but the inhabited part is not more than four hundred miles in length, and fifty in breadth, lying along the River del Norte, from the 31" 30' to the 37° N. latitude. But in this space there is a desert of more than two hundred and fifty miles.

Air and Climate.—No person accustomed to reside in the temperate climate of the 36° and 37° N. latitude in the United States, can form any idea of the piercing cold experienced in that parallel in New Mexico. But the air is serene, not subject to damps or fogs, as it rains but once a year and some years not at all: it is a mountainous country, and the grand dividing ridges which separate the waters of the Rio del Norte from those of California, bordering it on the line of its western limits, and which are covered in some places with eternal snows, give a keenness to the air, which would never be calculated on in a temperate zone.

Timber and Plains.—The cotton-tree is the sole production of this province, except some scrubby pines and cedars at the foot of the mountains; the former borders the banks of the Rio del Norte, and its tributary streams. All the rest of the country presents to the eye a barren wild of poor land, scarcely to be improved by culture, and appears only capable of producing a scanty subsistence for the animals, which live on a few succulent plants and herbage.

THE INTERIOR OF NEW SPAIN.

Mines, Minerals, and Fossils.—There are no mines known in the province, except one of copper, situated in a mountain on the western side of the Rio del Norte in latitude 34° N. It is wrought, and produces twenty thousand mule loads of copper annually, furnishing that article for the manufactories of nearly all the internal provinces. It contains gold, but not quite in sufficient quantity to pay for its extraction, consequently it has not been pursued. There is near Santa Fé in some of the mountains a stratum of talc, which is so large and flexible as to admit of being subdivided into thin flakes, of which the greatest proportion of the houses in Santa Fé and all the villages to the north have their window-lights made.

Rivers.—The River del Norte takes its rise in the mountains, which give birth to the head waters of California, the Plate, Pierre, Jaune of the Missouri, and Arkansaw of the Mississippi, in 40° N. latitude, and 110° W. longitude (from Paris). Its course from its source to the Gulph of Mexico may be by its meanders estimated at two thousand miles; passing through the Provinces of New Mexico, part of Biscay, Cogquilla, and New San Ander, where it falls into the Gulph in 26° N. latitude. It cannot in any part of its course be termed a navigable stream, owing to sand bars in the flat country, and mountains in the upper part, with which its course is interrupted; but small boats might ascend as high as the Presidio de Rio Grande, in Cogquilla, and it might be navigable for canoes in various parts of its course. Even in the mountains above Santa Fé it afforded amply sufficient water for that species of navigation, and more than appeared to be flowing in its bed in the plains. This must be attributed to the numerous canals and the dry sandy soil, through which the river takes its course, and where much of the water that flows from the mountains is absorbed and lost. In the Province of New Mexico it is called the Rio del Norte, below it is termed the Rio Grande, but in no instance did I hear it called the Rio Bravo, as many of our ancient maps designated it. There are also in the limits of this province to the west, the Rivers San Rafael, San Xavier, River de los Dolores, also de los Anamas or Nabajos; all of which unite and form the Great Rio Colorado of California; the first two take their sources in the same mountains as the Rio del Norte, but on the western side.

The River Colorado by its meanders may be about one thousand miles in length, from its sources to its entrance into the head of the Gulph of California in the 33° N. latitude. It has been represented to me by men of information and research, to be navigable for three hundred miles above the gulph for square rigged vessels.

By this river and the Arkansaw, the best communication might be established between the two oceans in North America. There are represented to be various numerous and warlike nations of Indians on its banks. Through the whole of its course its shores are entirely destitute of timber, and I was informed that for three hundred miles there was not a tree ten inches in diameter.

The River Buenaventura empties into the Pacific Ocean to the North of California in 39° 30′ N. latitude, and takes its source in the Sierra Madre to the north of the Colorado and Del Norte. The Rio Gila heads opposite to the copper mines, and discharges itself into the Gulph of California, just below the Colorado in the 33° N. latitude. The Rio Puerco is a branch of the Rio del Norte, and comes from the north and joins that river about one hundred miles below the Presidio del Norte. None of the foregoing streams have the vestige of civilization on their shores, excepting the Rio del Norte.

Lakes.—I know of no lakes in the province except that of Tampanagos, the existence of which I rather look upon as fabulous. It is said to commence, according to Father Escalante, in the 40° N. latitude, and to have been explored to the 42° in a north-west direction, when it enlarged its dimensions, and the discoverer thought proper to return.

Animals.—North Mexico produces deer, elk, buffalo, cabrie, the grisley black bear, and wild horses, all of which are too well known to need description.

Population.—Its population is not far short of thirty thousand souls,* one-twentieth of which may be Spaniards from Europe (or Chapetones); four-twentieths Creoles; five-twentieths Mestis, and the other half civilized Indians.

Chief Town.—The capital is Santa Fé, situated on a small stream which empties into the Rio del Norte, on the eastern side, at the foot of

---

*Humboldt makes the population forty thousand two hundred, and that of the capital three thousand six hundred. Vol. ii. pp. 307 and 317. E.

THE INTERIOR OF NEW SPAIN. 305

the mountains which divide the waters of that river from the Arkansaw and Red rivers of the Mississippi, in 36° N. latitude and 109° W. longitude. It is of a long, rectangular form, extending about one mile from east to west on the banks of the creek. In the centre is the public square, one side of which forms the flank of the soldiers' square, which is closed, and in some degree defended by round towers in the angles which flank the curtains; another side of the square is formed by the palace of the Governor, his guard-houses, &c.; another is occupied by the priests and their suite, and the fourth by the chapitones, who reside in the city. The houses are generally only one story high, with flat roofs, and have a very mean appearance on the outside, but some of them are richly furnished, especially with plate. The secondary cities in the province are Albuquerque and Passo del Norte; the latter is the southern city of the province, as Taos is the most northern. But between the village of Sibilleta and the Passo, there is a wilderness of near two hundred miles.

Trade and Commerce.—New Mexico carries on a trade direct with Mexico and Biscay, also with Senora and Sinaloa. It sends out annually about thirty thousand sheep, tobacco, dressed deer and cabrie skins, some fur, buffalo robes, salt, and wrought copper vessels of a superior quality. It receives in return from Biscay and Mexico, dry goods, confectionary, arms, iron, steel, ammunition, and some choice European wines and liquors. From Senora and Sinaloa, gold, silver, and cheese. The following articles sell as stated in this province, which will shew the cheapness of provision, and the extreme dearness of goods: flour at two dollars per hundred, salt five dollars the mule load, sheep one dollar each, pork twenty-five dollars per hundred, beeves five dollars each, wine Del Passo fifteen dollars per barrel, horses eleven dollars each, mules thirty dollars each; superfine cloths twenty-five dollars per yard, fine ditto twenty dollars, linen four dollars, and all other dry goods in proportion. The journey with loaded mules from Santa Fé to Mexico and returning takes five months. They manufacture rough leather, segars, a vast variety and quantity of potter's ware, cotton, some coarse woolen cloths, and blankets of a superior quality. All these manufactures are carried on by the civilized Indians, as the Spaniards think it more honourable to be agriculturists than mechanics. The Indians likewise far exceed their conquerors in the fecundity and variety of genius in all mechanical operations.

Agriculture.—New Mexico has the exclusive right of cultivating tobacco. About two miles above the town of the Passo del Norte is a bridge over the river, where the road passes to the western side, at which place is a large canal that takes out an ample supply of water for the purpose of cultivation, which is carried on at this place in as great perfection as at any I visited in the province. There is a wall bordering the canal the whole way on both sides to protect it from the animals; and when it arrives at the village it is distributed in such a manner that each person has his fields watered in succession. At this place were as finely cultivated fields of wheat and other small grain as I ever saw. And also numerous vineyards, from which were produced the finest wine ever drank in the country, which was celebrated throughout all the provinces, and was the only wine used on the table of the commanding general.

They cultivate corn, wheat, rye, barley, rice, and all the common culinary plants of the same latitude in the United States. But they are at least a century behind us in the art of cultivation, for notwithstanding the numerous herds of cattle and horses, I have seen them frequently breaking up whole fields with the hoe. Their oxen draw by the horns after the French mode* But their carts are extremely awkward and clumsily made. During the whole of the time we were in New Spain I never saw one horse in a vehicle of any description, mules being made use of in carriages, as well as for the purpose of labour.

Antiquities.—On the River St. Francis, a large branch of the Gila which heads near the copper mines in New Mexico, and discharges itself into the Red river of California, are the remains of old walls and houses which are established to be the vestiges of the Mexicans on their route of emigration from the north-west to the plains of Mexico, where they finally established themselves. Those walls are of a black cement which increases in stability with age, and bids defiance to the war of time; the secret of its composition is now entirely lost. There are also found at this place many broken pieces of earthenware which still possesses the glazing as perfect as when first put on.

Aborigines.—The Kyaways wander on the sources of the Plate, and are supposed to be one thousand and nine men strong. They possess

---

* In this they only imitate the parent country. E.

THE INTERIOR OF NEW SPAIN.

immense herds of horses, and are at war with both the Pawnees and Ietans, as well as with the Sioux. They are armed with bows, arrows and lances, and follow the buffalo. This nation, the Ietans, and the Utahs speak the same language.

The Utahs wander on the sources of the Rio del Norte; they are supposed to be two thousand warriors strong, are armed in the same manner, and pursue the same game, as the Kyaways, but are a little more civilized, having more connection with the Spaniards, with whom however they are frequently at war. They were at this time at peace with them, but waging war with the Ietans.

A battle was fought between them and the Ietans, in September, 1806, near the village of Taos; there were about four hundred combatants in each army, but were separated by a Spanish Alcalde riding out to the field of battle. There were eight or ten killed on each side. The Utahs gave all the horses they had taken to the Spaniards. This shews, in a strong degree, the influence the Spaniards have over these Indians.

The Nanahaws are situated to the north-west of Santa Fé, and are frequently at war with the Spaniards. They are supposed to be two thousand warriors strong, and are armed in the same manner as the two preceding nations. This nation, as well as all others to the west of them, bordering on California, speak the language of the Apaches and Lee Panis, who are in a line with them to the Atlantic.

The Apaches are a nation of Indians, who extend from the Black Mountains in New Mexico to the borders of Cogquilla, keeping the frontiers of three provinces in a continual state of alarm and dread, and employing nearly two thousand dragoons to escort the caravans, protect the villages, and revenge the various attacks they are continually making on the subjects of His Catholic Majesty. They formerly extended from the entrance of the Rio Grande to the Gulph of California, and have waged a continual warfare with the exception of short truces, with the Spaniards, from the time they pushed their conquests back from Mexico into the internal provinces. It is extremely difficult to say what their numbers are at the present day, but they must be extremely reduced by their long and constant hostilities, together with the wandering and savage life they lead on the mountains, which is so injurious to an increase of population, and in which they are extremely pinched by famine.

At the commencement of their warfare, the Spaniards used to take their prisoners and make slaves of them, but finding that their unconquerable attachment to liberty made them surmount every difficulty and danger to return to their mountains, they adopted the practice of sending them to Cuba. This the Apaches no sooner learned than they refused to give or receive quarter, and in no instance have there been any taken since that period, except when surprised asleep, or knocked down and overpowered. Their arms are the bow and arrow, and the lance. The bow forms two semicircles, with a shoulder in the middle; the back of it is entirely covered with sinews, which are laid on in so nice a manner, by the use of some glutinous substance, as to be almost imperceptible; this gives great force to the elasticity of the weapon. Their arrow is more than the cloth yard of the English, being three feet and a half long, the upper part consisting of some light rush or cane, into which is inserted a shaft of about one foot, made of some hard seasoned light wood; the point is of iron, cane, or stone, and when the arrow enters the body, in attempting to extract it the shaft comes out of its socket and remains in the wound. With this weapon they shoot with such force as to go through the body of a man, at the distance of one hundred yards; and an officer told me, that in an engagement with them one of their arrows struck his shield and dismounted him in an instant. Their other weapon of offence is a lance of fifteen feet in length, which with both hands they charge over their heads, managing the horse principally with their knees. With this they are considered as an over-match for the Spanish dragoons single handed, but for want of the tactic can never stand the charge of a body that cuts in concert : they all have the shield. Some few are armed with guns and ammunition, taken from the Spaniards. These, as well as the archers, generally march to war on foot, but the lance men are always mounted.

Numerous are the anecdotes I heard related of their personal bravery, and the spirit of their partisan corps. Not long before I passed through, as a cornet with sixty-three dragoons was passing between New Mexico and Biscay, he was surrounded by about two hundred Apaches infantry, and instead of charging through them (as it was on the plain) he ordered his dragoons to dismount and fight with their carabines, by which means he and his whole party fell a sacrifice. Malgares related an instance when

THE INTERIOR OF NEW SPAIN.

he was marching with one hundred and forty men, and was attacked by a party of Apaches, both horse and foot, who continued the fight for four hours. Whenever the Spanish dragoons made a general charge the Apaches cavalry would retreat behind their infantry, who met the Spaniards with a shower of arrows, on which they immediately retreated, and even the gallant Malgares spoke of his cavalry breaking their infantry as a thing not to be thought of. How quickly would one full squadron of our troops have put them to flight and cut them to pieces? Malgares assured me that if the men had seconded the efforts and bravery of the Indian chieftain, they must have been defeated and cut to pieces; that in various instances he rallied his men and brought them up to the charge, and when they flew, retired indignantly in the rear. Seeing Malgares very actively engaged in forming and bringing up the men, he rode out a-head of his party and challenged him to single combat with his lance. This my friend refused as he said the chief was one of the stoutest men he knew, carried a remarkably heavy lance, and rode a very fine charger; but one of his corporals enraged to see them thus braved by the savage, begged permission to meet the "infidel." His officer refused his request, and ordered him to keep his ranks; but he reiterating his request, his superior in a passion told him to go.

The Indian chief had turned his horse to join his party, but seeing his enemy advancing, turned, and giving a shout, met him at full speed. The dragoon thought to parry the lance of his antagonist, which he in part effected, but not throwing it quite high enough, it entered his neck in front and came out at the nape, when he fell dead to the ground, and his victorious enemy gave a shout of victory, in which he was joined by all his followers. This enraged the Spaniards to such a degree that they made a general charge, in which the Indian cavalry again retreated not withstanding the entreaties of their gallant leader. In another instance a small smoke was discovered on the prairie, and three poor savages were surrounded by one hundred dragoons, and ordered to lay down their arms. They smiled at the officer's demand, and asked him if he could suppose that men who had arms in their hands would ever consent to become slaves? He being loth to kill them, held a conference for an hour, when finding that his threats had as little effect as his entreaties, he ordered his men to attack them at a distance, keeping out of the reach of their arrows, and firing at them with their carabines, which they did, the Indians never ceasing to resist as long as life remained.

In a truce which was once held, a captain was ordered to treat with some of the bands; he received their deputies with hauteur, and they could not come to terms; the truce was broken, the Indians retreated to their fastnesses in the mountains. In a day or two this same officer pursued them. They were in a place called the Door in the Mountains, where only two or three dragoons could enter at a time, and there were rocks and caves on the flanks. Between the Indians secreted themselves, until a number of the Spaniards had come in, when the Indians sounded a trumpet, and the attack began and continued on the side of the Apaches, until the captain fell, when the Indian chief caused the firing to cease, saying, that "the man who had so haughtily spurned the proffered peace was now dead." They made prisoner (for once) of a young officer who during the truce had treated them with great kindness, and sent him home safe and unhurt.

Some of the bands have made temporary truces with the Spaniards, and received from them twenty-five cents per diem each. These people hang round the fortifications of the country, drink, shoot, and dissipate their time; they are haughty and independent, and great jealousy exists between them and the Spaniards. An officer was under trial when I was in the country for anticipating an attack on his fortress, by attacking the chiefs of the supposed conspiracy, and putting them to death before they had time to mature and carry their plan into operation. The decision of his case I never learnt; but those savages who have been for some time around the forts and villages become by far the most dangerous enemies the Spaniards have when hostile, as they acquire the Spanish language, manners, and habits, and passing through the populated parts under the disguise of the civilized and friendly Indians, commit murders and robberies without being suspected. There is in the Province of Cogquilla a partisan by the name of Ralph, who, it is calculated, has killed more than three hundred persons. He comes into the town under the disguise of a peasant, buys provision, goes to the gambling tables and to mass, and before he leaves the village is sure to kill some person, or carry off a woman, which he has frequently done. Sometimes he joins travellers on the road, insinuates himself into their confidence, and takes his opportunity to assassinate them. He has only six followers, and from their knowledge of the country, their activity, and cunning, he keeps about three hundred dragoons continually employed. The government has offered one thousand dollars for his head.

The civilized Indians of the Province of New Mexico consist of what were formerly twenty-four different bands, the several names of which I was not able to learn. But the Keres were one of the most powerful; they form at present the population of St. Domingo, St. Philip's and Deis, and one or two other towns. They are men of large stature, round, full visage, fine teeth, and appear to be of a gentle, tractable disposition; they resemble the Osage more than any nation in my knowledge. Although they are not the vassals of individuals, yet they may properly be termed the slaves of the state; for they are compelled to do military duty, drive mules, carry loads, or in fact perform any other act of duty or bondage that the will of the commandant of the district, or any passing military tyrant, chooses to ordain. I was myself eye-witness of a scene which made my heart bleed for these poor wretches at the same time that it excited my indignation and contempt, that they should suffer themselves with arms in their hands to be beaten and knocked about, by beings no ways their superiors, unless a small tint of complexion could be supposed to give that superiority. Before we arrived at Santa Fé, one night we rested near one of the villages where resided the families of two of our horsemen. They took the liberty to pay them a visit in the night. Next morning the whole were called up, and because they refused to testify against their imprudent companions, several were knocked down from their horses by the Spanish dragoons with the butt end of their lances; yet with the blood streaking down their visage, and arms in their hands, they stood cool and tranquil! not a frown, not a word of discontent, or palliation escaped their lips. Yet, what must have been the boiling indignation of their souls, at the insults offered by the wretch, clothed with a little brief authority? But the day of retribution will come in thunder and in vengeance.

These savages are armed with bows and arrows, with lances or escopates. Although they are said to be converted to Christianity, they still retain many of their ancient superstitious feasts and ceremonies, one of which is so remarkable, that it must not be passed unnoticed. Once a year there is a great festival, prepared for three successive days, which they spend in eating, drinking, and dancing: near this scene of amusement is a dark cave, into which not a glimpse of light can penetrate, and in which are prepared places to repose on. To this place persons of both sexes and of all ages, (after puberty,) and of all descriptions, repair in the night, where there is an indiscriminate commerce of the votaries, as chance, fortune, and events may direct. These revels certainly have great affinity to some of the ancient mystic rites of Greece and Rome.

Government and Laws.—The government of New Mexico may be termed military in the pure sense of the word; for although they have their Alcaldes or inferior officers, their judgments are subject to a reversion by the military commandants of districts. The whole male population is subject to military duties, without pay, or emolument, and are obliged to find their own horses, arms, and provisions. The only thing furnished by their government is ammunition, and it is extraordinary with what subordination they act, when turned out on military service. A strong proof of this was exhibited in the expedition of Malgares to the Pawnees; his command consisting of one hundred dragoons of the regular service, and five hundred drafts from the province. He had continued down the Red river until their provisions began to be short; they then demanded of the Lieutenant where he was bound, and his intention. To this he haughtily replied, "wherever his horse carried him." A few mornings after he was presented with a petition (signed by two hundred of the militia) to return home. He halted immediately, and caused his dragoons to erect a gallows, then beat to arms, and the troops fell in: he separated the petitioners from the others, took the man who had presented him the petition, tied him up, gave him fifty lashes, and threatened to put to death on the gallows any man who should dare to murmur. This effectually silenced them, and quelled the rising spirit of sedition. But it was remarked, that it was the first instance of a Spaniard receiving corporal punishment ever known in the province.

Morals, Manners, &c.—There is nothing particularly characteristic in the inhabitants of this province that will not be embraced in my general observations on New Spain, except that the country being a frontier, and the people cut off as it were from the more populated parts of the kingdom, together with their continual wars with some one of the savage nations who surround them, render them the bravest, and most hardy subjects in New Spain; they are generally armed, and know the use of their weapons. Their want of gold and silver renders them laborious, in order that the productions of their industry may be the means of establishing the equilibrium between them and the other provinces, where those metals abound; and their isolated and remote situation causes them to exhibit in a superior degree, the heaven-like qualities of hospitality and kindness, in which they appear to endeavour to fulfil the injunctions of the Scripture, which enjoins us to feed the hungry, clothe the naked, and give comfort to the oppressed. I shall always take pleasure in expressing my gratitude for their noble reception of myself and poor lads.

Military Force.—There is but one troop of dragoons in all New Mexico, of the regular force, which is stationed at Santa Fé, and is one thousand strong. Of this the Governor is always the captain, styling himself captain of the royal troop of Santa Fé dragoons; but they are commanded by a first lieutenant, who is captain by brevet. The men capable of bearing arms may be estimated at five thousand, of those probably one thousand are completely armed, one thousand badly, and the rest not at all.

Religion.—The Catholic religion is well known, and with all others tolerated in the United States. It is practised here after the same manner as in the other provinces, and will be taken notice of generally; but it may not be impertinent to remark, that the clergy in this province are much more liberal than those nearer the Vice-royalty, where the terrors of the inquisition keep them in awe. In our presence they and the officers used to laugh openly at the terror and superstition in which the common people were held by them. Many of them were generous and friendly, and I certainly feel myself indebted to them for their polite and hospitable treatment.

History.—In the year 1594 two friars came out from Old Mexico to New Mexico, and were well received by the savages. They returned, and the ensuing year Juan de Onuate, a monk, went out and explored the country. On his return, one thousand troops and five hundred men, women, and children, came and settled on the Rio del Norte, at no very great distance from where Santa Fé now stands. They entered into an arrangement with the Indians, on the subject of their establishment; but a few years after they rose *en masse* and fell on the new settlers by surprise, killed most of the soldiers, and obliged them to retreat to the Passo del Norte, from which circumstance it acquired its name. Here they waited a reinforcement from Biscay, which they received, of seventy men and two field pieces; with these they commenced their march and finally arrived at Santa Fé, then the capital Indian village, which they immediately laid siege to. The Indians maintained themselves twenty-two days, when they surrendered and entered into a second negotiation. Since that time the inhabitants have been engaged in continual warfare with the various savage tribes, which surround them on all sides, who have been nearly ruining them on several occasions, and have obliged them to apply for reinforcements from Biscay and Senora.

A few years since the Ietans carried on a warm and vigorous war against them, but now are at peace, and considered as their firmest allies.

In the historical anecdotes of New Mexico, it may not be improper to record the name of James Pursley, the first American who ever penetrated the immense wilds of Louisiana, and shewed the Spaniards of New Mexico, that neither the savages who surround the deserts which divide them from the habitable world, nor the jealous tyranny of their rulers, was sufficient to prevent the enterprising spirit of the Americans from penetrating the arcanum of their rich establishments in the New World. Pursley was from near Baird's Town, Kentucky, which he had left in 1799. In 1802, with two companions, he left St. Louis and travelled west on the head of the Osage river, where they made a hunt; from thence they struck for the White river of the Arkansaw, and intended to descend it to Orleans, but while making preparations the Kanses stole their horses: having secured their peltries they pursued them into the village. The horses were there, but the Indians refused to give them up: Pursley saw his horse with an Indian on him going to the water at the edge of the town. He pursued him, and with his knife ripped open the horse's bowels. The Indian returned to the village, got his gun and came and snapped it at Pursley, who followed him into the village with his knife: the Indian took refuge in a lodge surrounded by women and children. This conduct struck the chiefs with astonishment, and admiration of the "mad Americans," as they termed them, and they returned the other horses to the hunters. Pursley and his companions now returned to the place

THE INTERIOR OF NEW SPAIN.

where they had buried their peltries, and determined to pursue the route by land to St. Louis; but some persons stole their horses a second time, when they were no great distance from the Osage river, on which they formed a rough canoe and descended that stream, nearly to its junction with the Missouri. Here they overset their canoe and lost their whole year's hunt, but saved their arms and ammunition, which are always the primary objects in a desert. On the Missouri they met Monsieur ——— in his barge, bound to the Mandanes. Pursley embarked with him for the voyage; his two companions preferred returning to their homes. On the arrival of the former at the point of destination, his employer despatched him on a hunting and trading tour, with some bands of the Paducas and Kyaways, with a small quantity of merchandize. In the ensuing spring they were driven by the Sioux from the plains into the mountains which give rise to the Plate, Arkansaw, &c., and it was their sign which we saw in such amazing abundance on the head waters of the Plate, their party consisting of nearly two thousand souls with ten thousand beasts. The Indians knowing they were approximate to New Mexico, determined to send Pursley with his companions and two of their body into Santa Fé, to know of the Spaniards if they would receive them amicably, and enter into a trade with them. This being acceded to by the Governor (Allencaster) the Indian deputies returned for their bands; but Pursley thought proper to remain with a civilized people, among whom a fortuitous event had thrown him, a circumstance which he assured me he had at one time entirely despaired of. He arrived at Santa Fé June, 1805, and had been following his trade (a carpenter) ever since, at which he made a great deal of money, except when working for the officers, who paid him little or nothing. He was a man of strong natural sense, and of undaunted intrepidity; and entertained me with numerous interesting anecdotes of his adventures with the Indians, and of the jealousy of the Spanish government. He was once nearly being hanged for making a few pounds of powder, which he innocently did, as he was accustomed to do in Kentucky, but which is a capital crime in these provinces. He still retained his gun, which he had with him during his whole tour, and spoke confidently that if he had two hours' start, not all the province could take him. He was forbidden to write, but was assured he should have a passport whenever demanded; he was obliged, however, to give security that he would not leave the country without the permission of the government. I brought letters out for him. He assured me that he had found gold on the head of the Plate, and had carried some of the virgin mineral in his shot pouch for months, but that being in doubt whether he should ever again behold the civilized world, and losing in his mind all the ideal value which mankind have stamped on that metal, he threw his sample away; that he had imprudently mentioned it to the Spaniards, who had frequently solicited him to go and shew a detachment of cavalry the place, but conceiving it to be in our territory he had refused, and was fearful that the circumstance might create a great obstacle to his leaving the country.

BISCAY lies between 24° and 33° N. latitude, and 105° and 111° W. longitude; is bounded on the north by New Mexico, on the west by Senora and Sinaloa, and on the east by New Leon and Cogquilla. It is six hundred miles in length, from north-west to south-east, and four hundred miles in width from east to west, taking it at its greatest extent.

Air and Climate.—The air is dry, and the heat very great at that time of the year which precedes the rainy season, which commences in June, and continues until September by light showers; during the other part of the year there is not the least rain or snow to moisten the earth. The atmosphere had therefore become so electrified, that when we halted at night, in taking off our blankets, the electric fluid would almost cover them with sparks; and in Chihuahua we prepared a bottle with gold leaf as a receiver, and collected sufficient fluid from a bear skin to give a considerable shock to a number of persons. This phenomenon was more conspicuous in the vicinity of Chihuahua than in any other part that we crossed.

Mines and Minerals.—This province abounds in gold and silver mines, which yield an immense quantity of those metals, but not so great a revenue to the King as those which are nearer the mint, and consequently present a greater facility to coinage. I am not acquainted with the proportion of the metals which the mineral yields in any instance, except in one of the silver mines at Chihuahua, which belonged to a friend of mine, who informed me that his mine yielded him thirteen and a half dollars per hundred weight. I went one day, accompanied by Robinson, through many of these furnaces, and noticed the method they pursued in analyzing

THE INTERIOR OF NEW SPAIN.

the mineral and extracting the metals. But as I had previously asked several Spanish officers to accompany me, who had always declined or deferred the thing to a future period, I conceived it probable it was too delicate a subject to make a minute inquiry into. I so far observed the process, however, as to learn, that the mineral was brought to the furnace from the mines in bags on mules, it was then ground or pounded into small lumps, not larger than the size of a nut, and precipitated into water (in a sieve which permitted the smaller particles to escape into a tub) through several progressive operations; from the small particles which remained at the bottom of the tub after it had been purified by the earthy particles, there was a proportoin of metal extracted by a nicer process, but the larger parts were put into a furnace, similar to our iron furnaces, and when it was in a state of fusion was let out into a bed of sand prepared for it, formed to make bars about the size of our common pig iron; average in value about two thousand five hundred dollars. The gold was drawn out into a mould similar to a bowl, and the pieces were stamped (as was each bar of silver) by the King's essayer of metals, with its value; being from eight to ten thousand dollars; they are then received into the King's treasury in payment, and in fact have a currency through the kingdom. There are vast speculations made on the coinage. As people who have not large capitals prefer selling their bullion in the internal provinces at a considerable discount, to being obliged to transport it to Mexico, in order to convert it into specie. The present C——— (I was informed) was engaged in that traffic, on which from the Province of Senora he sometimes made twenty-five per cent. But numbers of the proprietors who have no immediate use for their bullion, put it in their cellars, where it remains piled up to their posterity, of no service to themselves or to the community. There are at Chihuahua and its vicinity fifteen mines, thirteen of silver, one of gold, and one of copper, the furnaces for all of which are situated round the town in the suburbs, and present, except on Sundays, volumes of smoke arising in every direction; which are seen from a distance long before the spires of the city strike the view. It is incredible the quantity of cinders that surround the city, in piles ten or fifteen feet high. Next the creek they have formed a bank of them to check the encroachments of the stream, and it has presented an effectual barrier. I am told that a European employed some hands, and wrought at the cinders, and that they yielded one dollar twenty-five cents for each per day, but this not answering his expectations, he ceased his proceedings. At Mauperne there are one gold and seven silver mines.

At Durango there are many and rich mines, but I am unable to state the number. There are also gold mines in the Sierra Madre, near Alomas, and many others of which I have no knowledge. There is likewise in the province, about one hundred miles south of Chihuahua, a mountain or hill of loadstone. Walker, who had been on the ground and surveyed it, informed me, it appeared to be a solid stratum as regular as that of limestone, or any other of the species. He had brought home a square piece of near one and a half foot, and was preparing some to be sent to Spain, and likewise forming magnets to accompany it, in order that their comparative strength might be ascertained with magnets formed in Europe.

Rivers.—The Conchos is the largest in the province. It takes its source in the Sierra Madre, near Batopilis in 28° N. latitude, and discharges itself in the Rio del Norte in latitude 31°, after a course of about three hundred miles. It is the largest western branch of the Rio del Norte, and receives in its course the Rio Florida from the east, and St. Paubla from the west. Where we struck the Conchos, it appeared to be nearly as large as the Rio del Norte at the Passo. The Rio San Paubla is the largest western branch of the Conchos, and heads in 28° 50' N. latitude, and empties into the latter at Bakinao; its whole course is about one hundred and fifty miles, in summer nearly dry, and in the rainy season impassable. The Rio Florida takes its rise in latitude 26° 30' north, and after a course of about one hundred and fifty miles discharges itself into the Conchos. Guaxequillo is situated on its eastern bank about midway. The Rio Nasas is in part the line between Biscay and Cogquilla; it runs north and empties into the lake of Cayman; it is nearly dry in the summer season, but at some periods impassable.

Lakes.—Lake Cayman and Lake Parras are two small lakes situated at the foot of the mountains, and are full of fish.

Animals, Insects, &c.—There are some few bears, deer, and wild horses, but not in abundance. The scorpions of Durango exhibit the most remarkable instance of the physical effects of climate or air that I ever heard related. They come out of the walls and crevices in May

THE INTERIOR OF NEW SPAIN. 319

and continue about a fortnight in such numbers that the inhabitants never walk in their houses after dark without a light, and always shift or examine the bed clothes, and beat the curtains previous to going to rest; after which the curtains are secured under the bed. The precautions are similar to those we take with our moschetto curtains. The bite of these scorpions has been known to prove mortal in two hours. But the most extraordinary circumstance is, that by taking them ten leagues from Durango they become perfectly harmless, and lose all their venomous qualities. Query, does this arise from a change of air or of sustenance?

Population of Chief Towns.—The population of Biscay may be estimated at two hundred thousand;* of this three-twentieths may be Spaniards from Europe, five-twentieths Creoles, five-twentieths Mestis and Quatroons, and seven-twentieths Indians. Durango was founded in 1550. It is the principal city, and the seat of government for the Province of Biscay, and of the Bishop of Durango. Its population may be estimated at forty thousand souls.† It is situated in 25° N. latitude, and 107° W. longitude.

Pallalein, situated at the foot of the Sierra Madré, is supposed to contain twenty-five thousand souls.

Chihuahua, the place of residence of the Commandant General of the internal provinces, was founded in 1691, and is situated in 29° N. latitude, and 107° 30' W. longitude. Its population may be estimated at seven thousand;‡ it is of an oblong rectangular form, on the eastern side of a small stream, which discharges itself into the river Conchos. On its southern extremity is a small but elegant church. In the public square stands the church, the royal treasury, the town house, and the richest shops. At the western extremity another church, for the military; a superb hospital, belonging formerly to the Jesuits' possessions; the church of the Monks of St. Francis and St. Domingo; the military academy and Quartel del Tropa. On the northwest were two or three missions, very handsomely situated on a small stream, which comes in from the west. About one mile to the south of the town is a large aqueduct, which conveys the water round it, to the east, into the

---
* According to Humboldt, one hundred and fifty-nine thousand seven hundred. Pol. Ess. Vol. ii. p. 286. E.
† Twelve thousand, Humb. Ubi. Supra. p. 293. E.
‡ Eleven thousand six hundred. Ibid. p. 293. E.

main stream below the town, at the centre of which is seated a reservoir, from whence the water is conducted by pipes to the different parts of the city; and in the public square is to be a fountain, and *jet d'eau*, which will be both ornamental and useful. The principal church at Chihuahua was the most superb building we saw in New Spain. Its whole front being covered with statues of the apostles, and the different saints, set in nitches of the wall, and the windows, doors, &c., ornamented with sculpture. I never was within the doors, but was informed by Robinson, that the decorations were immensely rich. Some men whom we supposed entitled to credit, informed us that the church was built by a tax of twelve and a half cents laid on each ingot of gold, or silver, taken out of the mines in the vicinity in ———— years. Its cost, including the decorations, was one million five hundred thousand dollars, and when it was finished, there remained three hundred thousand dollars of the fund unappropriated. On the south side of Chihuahua is the public walk, formed by three rows of trees, whose branches nearly form a junction over the heads of the passengers below. At different distances there are seats for persons to repose themselves on; at each end of the walks there were circular seats on which (in the evening) the company collected, and amused themselves with the guitar, and songs in Spanish, Italian, and French, adapted to the voluptuous manners of the country. In this city, as well as in all others of any consideration, there are patroles of soldiers during the night, who stop every person at nine o'clock and examine them. My countersign was " Americans."

Trade, Commerce, and Manufactures.—Biscay trades with North Mexico, Senora, and the Vice-royalty; from the latter of which they bring on mules all their dry goods, European furniture, books, ammunition, &c. They furnish a great number of horses, mules, sheep, beeves, goats, &c., to the more populous parts of the kingdom, which have less spare ground for pasturage. Some persons make large fortunes by being the carriers from Mexico to Chihuahua, the freight being eight dollars per cent. and they generally put three hundred pounds on each mule. The merchants make their remittances twice a year in bullion. Goods sell at Chihuahua about two hundred per cent. above the prices of our Atlantic sea-port towns. Their horses average at six dollars, but some have been sold for one hundred, their trained mules at twenty dollars; but extraordinary matches for carriages have sold for four hundred dollars a pair. Rice sells for four dollars per hundred weight. They manufacture some few arms, blankets, stamp leather, embroidery, coarse cotton, and woollen cloths, and a species of carpetting. Their blankets average at two dollars, but some sell as high as twenty-five dollars.

Agriculture.—They cultivate wheat, corn, rice, oats, cotton, flax, indigo, and vines. What I have said relative to the cultivation of these articles in New Mexico will equally apply to this province; but it may be proper to observe here, that one of Nolan's men constructed the first cotton gin they ever had in the province, and that Walker had caused a few churns to be made for some private families, and taught them the use of them.

Timber, Plains, and Soil.—To the north of Chihuahua, about thirty miles to the right of the main road, there is some pine timber, and at a spring on this side of Carracal we saw one walnut tree, and on all the small streams there are shrubby cotton trees: with these few exceptions, the whole province is a naked, barren plain, which presents to the eye an arid unproductive soil; and more especially in the neighbourhood of mines, even the herbage appears to be poisoned by the qualities of the land.

Antiquities.—There are none in the province which came within my notice, except the Jesuit college and the church at Chihuahua, which were about one century old, and are used as hospitals. In these there was nothing peculiar except a certain solidity and strength, which appeared to surpass the other public buildings of the city.

Aborigines.—There are no uncivilized savages in this province, except the Apaches, of whom I have already spoken largely. The Christian Indians are so incorporated amongst the lower grades of Mestis that it is scarcely possible to draw the line of distinction, except at the ranchos of some nobleman or large land-holder, where they are in a state of vassalage. This class of people laid a conspiracy, which was so well concerted as to baffle the research of the Spaniards for a length of time, and to occasion them the loss of several hundreds of the inhabitants. The Indians used to go out from their villages in small parties; in a short time a part would return, with the report that they had been attacked by the Indians. The Spaniards would immediately send out a detachment in pursuit, when they were led into an ambuscade, and every soul cut off. They pursued this course so long that the whole province became alarmed at the rapid manner in which their enemies multiplied; but some circumstances leading to a suspicion, they made use of the superstition of these people for their ruin. Some officers disguised themselves like friars and went round amongst the Indians, pretending to be possessed of the spirit of prophecy. They preached up to them, that the day was approaching when a general deliverance from the Spanish tyranny was about to take place, and invited the Indians to join in promoting with them the work of God. The poor creatures came forward, and in their confessions stated the great hand that had already been put to the work. After they had ascertained the nature and extent of the conspiracy, and obtained a body of troops, they commenced the execution and put to death about four hundred of them. This struck terror and dismay through the Indian villages, and they dared not rise to support their freedom and independence.

Government and Laws.—In this province there is some shadow of civil law, but it is *merely a shadow*, as the following anecdotes may illustrate. An officer, on arriving at a village, demanded quarters for himself and troops. The supreme civil officer of the place sent him word that he must shew his pass-port. The military officer immediately sent a file of men, who brought the judge a prisoner before him, when he severely reprimanded the magistrate for his insolence, and obliged him to obey his orders instantly. This has been done by a subaltern, in a city of twenty thousand inhabitants. The only laws which can be said to be in force, are the military and ecclesiastical, between which there is a perfect understanding. The Governor is a brigadier-general, residing at Durango, and receives five thousand dollars in addition to his pay in the line. At the same time it is but proper to observe that there are ordinances to bear on each subject of civil discussion, but they are so corrupt, that the influence of family and fortune generally has *right* on its side. In each town is a public magazine for provision, where every farmer brings his grain and produce which he may have for sale, when he is sure to meet with a market, and should there be a scarcity the ensuing year, it is retailed out to the inhabitants at a reasonable rate: to this place all the citizens of the town repair to purchase.

Morals, Manners, &c.—There is nothing peculiar in the manners or morals of the people of this province, but a much greater degree of luxury among the rich, and misery among the poor, and corruption of morals more generally than in New Mexico. As to military spirit they have none; at a muster of a regiment of militia at Chihuahua, one of my men attended, and informed me that there were about twenty-five who had fire-arms and lances, fifty with bows and arrows and lances, and the remainder with lances, or bows and arrows only.

Military Force.—The regular military force of Biscay consists of one thousand one hundred dragoons, distributed as follows: On the frontiers of the deserts of New Mexico and Senora, at the forts of Elisiaira, Carracal, and St. Buenaventura, Presidio del Norte Janos, Tulinos, and St. Juan Baptist. Farther south are Chihuahua, Jeronime, Cayone, St. Paubla, Guaxequillo, and Conchos, with several other places, which are dependencies on these possessions. The complement of each of those posts is one hundred and fifty men, but may be averaged at one thousand one hundred in all; say one hundred at each post. The militia are not worthy particular notice.

Religion—Biscay is in the diocese of Durango, the Bishop's salary being estimated at one hundred thousand dollars per annum. The Catholic religion is here in its full force, but the inferior clergy are much dissatisfied. The people's superstition is so great that they are running after the Holy Father in the streets, and endeavouring to kiss the hem of his garment; and should the Bishop be passing the street all kneel, whether rich or poor.

History. I shall not presume to say anything on this subject, except that I believe this province has been populated about two hundred and seventy years.

SENORA lies between the 27° and 33° N. latitude 110° and 117° W. longitude from Paris; its greatest length from north to south being about four hundred and twenty, and its width from east to west three hundred and eighty miles. It is bounded on the north by New Mexico, on the west by California, on the south by Sinaloa and the Gulph, on the east by Biscay and New Mexico.

Air and Climate.—Dry, pure, and healthy generally; but near the Gulph the ground is marshy, and it is in some of the districts unhealthy.

Mines, Minerals and Fossils.—On these subjects I can only speak in general. It abounds in rich gold and silver mines, but more especially the former, in as much as the gold does not preserve its usual exchange with silver in that province. General Salcedo told me that in this province, the largest piece of pure gold had been found, ever yet discovered in New Spain, and it had been sent to the King to be put in his cabinet of curiosities.

Rivers.—Rio de la Ascencion is a short river which enters the Gulph of California, about the 31° N. latitude. Rio Yaqui heads on the borders of Biscay and Senora, and discharges itself in the Gulph of California at Guaymas, at 28° the N. latitude.

Timber, Plains, and Soil.—This province is like Biscay, destitute of timber, but has some rich soil near the sea.

Animals.—There are deer, cabrie, and bear: there are also remarkably large Guana lizards, which are said to weigh ten pounds, and are perfectly harmless; they are tamed by the inhabitants and trained to catch mice.

Population and Chief Towns.—The population of Senora may be estimated at two hundred thousand souls, of which three-twentieths probably are Spaniards, four-twentieths Creoles, six-twentieths Mestis, and seven-twentieths Indians. Arispe, the capital of Senora, and until twenty years past the seat of government of the internal provinces, is situated in 31° N. latitude, and 111° W. longitude, near the head of the river Yaqui. It is celebrated throughout the kingdom for the vast quantity of gold table utensils made use of in the houses, and for the urbanity and hospitality of the inhabitants. Its population is three thousand four hundred souls.*

Senora and Terrenate are the next cities in magnitude in the province, the latter to the north, the former to the south of the capital.

Trade and Commerce.—Senora trades with New Mexico and Biscay for the productions of those provinces, and with Old Mexico, both by land and sea, through the Gulph of California. It is celebrated for cheese, horses and sheep.

---

* The Province of Senora, one hundred and twenty-one thousand four hundred; the Arispe, seven thousand six hundred; Senora, six thousand four hundred. Humb. Vol. ii. pp. 296 and 305. E.

THE INTERIOR OF NEW SPAIN.

Agriculture.—They cultivate the same articles as in Biscay.

Aborigines—There are a number of savage nations bordering on Senora, which oblige the King to keep up a number of military posts on the northern and western frontiers. But the names of the tribes, as to any of their distinguished characters, I am unacquainted with; however it may not be improper to observe, that they are armed with bows, arrows, shield and lance, like their savage neighbours. The civilized Indians are in the same situation as in the other provinces.

Government and Laws.—Similar to those of Biscay; the Governor being a brigadier-general, receiving seven thousand dollars, in addition to his pay in the line.

Morals and Manners.—In every respect similar to those of Biscay, except that they are more celebrated for hospitality.

Military Force.—The regular military force of this province consists of nine hundred dragoons, and two hundred infantry, stationed as follows:—At Tubson, St. Cruz, Tubac, and Altac on the north, with one hundred dragoons each for a garrison. Fiuteras, Bacuachi, Bavispa, and Horcasitas, in the centre with three hundred dragoons and two hundred infantry; Buenavista on the south with one hundred dragoons as a garrison. The infantry mentioned above are a nation of Indians, called the Opejas, and are said to be the best soldiers in New Spain. I saw a detachment of them at Chihuahua, who appeared to be fine, stout, athletic men, and were the most subordinate and faithful troops I ever knew, acting like a band of brothers, and having the greatest attachment for their officers.

Religion.—Catholic, in the Diocese of Durango.

History.—I am unacquainted with its history, except that the seat of government of the internal provinces was formerly at Arispe, at which time the government of California was also under the Captain-Generalship of the internal provinces. But the removal of the seat of government to Chihuahua, and the disjunct situation of California, induced His Majesty to annex it to the Vice-Royalty. The increasing magnitude of the relations of New Spain with the United States, gave likewise an importance to the eastern interests, which induced the continuance of the seat of government at Chihuahua.

SINALOA lies between the 23° and 28° N. latitude, and 108° and 111° W. longitude, and is bordered on the north by Senora and Biscay, on the east by the latter, on the south by the Administration of Guadalaxara, and on the west by the Gulph of California. Its greatest length is three hundred miles north and south, and in width from east to west one hundred and fifty miles.

Air and Climate.—On the sea coast humid, but back dry and pure.

Mines, Minerals, and Fossils.—There are both gold and silver mines, but with their relative value or productions I am unacquainted.

Rivers.—Rio Fuerte takes its source in 27° N. latitude, and 110° W. longitude, and disembogues itself into the Gulph of California. It crosses the whole province, and is nearly one hundred and fifty miles long. Rio Culican is not more than fifty miles in length, and enters the Gulph of California in 25ᵁ N. latitude.

Timber, Plains, and Soil.—No timber; soil similar to Senora.

Animals.—Domestic only.

Population and Chief Towns.—Its population may be estimated at sixty thousand, not more than three-twentieths of whom are Spaniards, the remainder Creoles, Mestis, and Indians. Sinaloa is the capital, but its population, extent, &c., are to me unknown.

Agriculture.—The same as Senora.

Aborigines.—None who are not civilized.

Military Force.—One hundred dragoons for expresses, and the guard of the Governor.

Religion.—Catholic; in the diocese of the Bishop of Durango.

THE PROVINCE OF COGQUILLA lies between the 23° and 31° 30' N. latitude, and 101° and 105° W. longitude; its greatest length north and south may be five hundred miles, and in its greatest width east and west two hundred miles. It is bounded on the north by New Mexico and Texas, on the east by the latter, St. Ander and New Leon, on the south by the Administration of Zacatecas, and on the west by Biscay.

Air and Climate.—Pure and healthy, except about the middle of May, when the heat is intense, and sometimes a scorching wind is felt like the flame issuing from an oven or furnace, which frequently skins the face and affects the eyes. This phenomenon is felt more sensibly about the setting of the sun than at any other period of the twenty-four hours.

THE INTERIOR OF NEW SPAIN.

Mines, Minerals, and Fossils.—I know of no mines in this province except at Montelovez, and Sta. Rosa; the value of either of which I am unacquainted with; but those of Sta. Rosa are reputed to be as rich as any silver mines in the kingdom. Montelovez has none very considerable.

Rivers.—This province has no river of magnitude or consequence but the Rio Grande, which crosses its northern part in a south-east direction.

Lakes.—There is a small lake called the Agua Verde, situated on its western extremity, which gives rise to a small stream that discharges itself into the Rio del Norte.

Timber, Plains, and Soil.—From the River Nasas to the east the palmetto is found, which grows to the heighth of twenty and twenty-five feet, with a trunk of two or three feet diameter; its leaves are in the shape of a spear, and cover all the trunk when young, but fall off as the tree grows old; its wood is of a spongy nature, and from every information I could procure, is of the same species as that of the same name in the southern States. One hundred miles to the east of the Rio Grande, the oak timber commenced, being the first we had seen in the province, but it was very small and scrubby, and presented from this to the line of Texas (the River Mariana) a very perceptible gradation of the increase of vegetation of timber, in quality, luxuriance, and variety. The country now became very similar to the Indian territory.

Animals.—Deer, wild horses, and a few buffaloes and wild hogs.

Population and Chief Towns.—Montelovez is the capital of Cogquilla; it is situated on a small stream of water, and lies in 26° 33′ N. latitude, 103° 30′ W. longitude; it is about one mile in length, on a course north, 70° east by the main street; it has two public squares, seven churches, powder magazines, mills, King's hospital, and Quartel del Tropas. This is the principal military depot for the Provinces of Cogquilla and Texas. Its population may be estimated at three thousand five hundred souls. This city being the stated residence of His Excellency, Governor Cordero, has been ornamented by him with public walks, columns, and fountains, and made one of the handsomest cities in the internal provinces.

Sta. Rosa is about thirty-eight miles to the north-west of Montelovez, and is represented to be the most healthy situation in the provinces, and to have the best water and fruit. It is on some of the head waters of the River Millada. Its population is represented at four thousand souls.

Parras is situated on a small stream, and with its suburbs is supposed to contain seven thousand souls; and San Lorenzo, three miles to the north, five hundred souls. This place may be termed the vineyard of Cogquilla, the whole population pursuing no other occupation than the cultivation of the grape, and its name denotes the *branches of the vine*. At the Hacienda of San Lorenzo, where we halted, were fifteen large stills, and larger cellars, and a greater number of casks than I ever saw in any brewery in the United States. Its gardens were delightfully interspersed with figs, vines, apricots, and a variety of fruits, which are produced in the torrid zone. Fine summer houses, where were wine, refreshments, and couches to repose on, and where the singing of the birds was delightful. There were here likewise mills, and a fine water-fall.

The Presidio of Rio Grande is situated on that river, and is remarkable for nothing but three or four handsome missions, with which it is surrounded, a powder magazine, quarters for the troops, and a few iron field-pieces on miserable truck carriages. Population two thousand five hundred souls. The population of this province may be estimated at seventy thousand souls, not more than ten thousand of whom are Spaniards.

Trade, Commerce, and Manufactures.—This province receives all its merchandise from Mexico by land, and in return gives horses, mules, wines, gold, and silver. There is an annual fair held at Saltelo, in New Leon, at which an immense quantity of merchandise is disposed of, and where merchants of very large capitals reside.

Agriculture.—They cultivate the vine principally, with grain and corn sufficient for their own consumption, and to supply the greater part of Texas.

Aborigines.—The Apaches cover their north-west frontier. The Lee Panis are a nation who rove from the Rio Grande to some distance into the Province of Texas. Their former residence was on the Rio Grande, near the sea-shore. They are at present divided into three bands of three hundred, three hundred and fifty, and one hundred men each; are at war with the Ietans and Apaches, and at peace with the Spaniards. They have fair hair, and are generally handsome; and are armed with bows, arrows, and lances; they pursue the wild horses, of which they take numbers and sell them to the Spaniards.

THE INTERIOR OF NEW SPAIN.

Government and Laws.—Military and ecclesiastical power is all that is known or acknowledged in this province, but its administration was mild under their excellent governor Cordero. The Governor's civil salary is four thousand dollars per annum.

Morals and Manners.—It was evident to the least discerning eye, that as we diverged from those parts which produce such vast quantities of the precious metals, the inhabitants became more industrious, and there were fewer beggars; thus were the morals of the people of Cogquilla less corrupted than those of Biscay or New Leon, their neighbours.

Military Force.—There are four hundred dragoons maintained in this province, and stationed at Montelovez, Sta. Rosa, Presidio, Rio del Norte, San Fernandez.

Religion.—Catholic, but mild. It is in the Diocese of Durango.

History.—Cogquilla had not pushed its population as far as the Rio Grande in the year 1687, as at that time La Salle established himself at the entrance of that river, it being a wilderness; but Montelovez was established some time before this era; of its particular history I have no knowledge.

THE PROVINCE OF TEXAS lies between 27° 30′ and 35° N. latitude, 98° and 104° W. longitude; bordered on the north by Louisiana, on the east by the Territory of Orleans, on the west by Cogquilla and New Mexico, and on the south by New San Ander; its greatest length from north to south may be five hundred miles, and breadth from east to west three hundred and fifty.

Air and Climate.—It is one of the most delightful temperatures in the world, but being a country covered with timber, the new emigrants are generally sickly, which may very justly be attributed to the putrescent vegetable matter which they put into fermentation in clearing, and by remaining on the ground, inhaling all the air which arises from the effluvia, intermittents supervene and billious attacks, and in some instances malignant fevers. These remarks are proved by the observation of all the first settlers of our western frontiers, that those places which in the course of ten or fifteen years become perfectly healthy, are for the first two or three years quite the reverse, and generally cost them the loss of two or three members of their families. I presume that this dreadful effect might be remedied if the settlers would go with the working hands and fell the timber and destroy the vegetation in the spring, and in the fall when dry burn it, but not reside on the place for at least the first two years, in the course of which time the atmosphere would by these means not be affected by the morbid exhalations arising from the before-mentioned causes; and the place would be as healthy a residence as any other in the same climate.

Mines, Minerals, and Fossils.—The only mine known and worked is one of lead.

Rivers.—The River St. Antonio takes its source about one league to the north-east of the capital of the province, (St. Antonio,) and is navigable for canoes to its source, affording excellent fish, fine mill-seats, and water to every part of the town. It is joined by the River Mariana from the west, (which forms part of the line between Cogquilla and Texas,) and then discharges itself into the Rio Guadelupe, about fifty miles from the sea. At the town of St. Antonio it is about twenty yards wide, and in some places twelve feet in depth. The River Guadelupe takes its source about one hundred and fifty miles to the north-west of St. Antonio: where we crossed it, it was a beautiful stream of at least sixty yards in width, its waters are transparent and navigable for canoes. After receiving the waters of St. Antonio and St. Mark, it discharges itself into the south-west end of the Bay of St. Bernard. At the crossing of this river there is a range for the horses of St. Antonio, and a guard de cabello with an elegant site for a town.

The River St. Mark takes its source about one hundred miles north, twenty west of St. Antonio, and at the crossing of the road is thirty yards in width: a clear and navigable stream for canoes. By the road this river is only fourteen miles from the Guadelupe, into which it discharges itself.

The Red river takes its source in the Province of Cogquilla, in $33°$ N. latitude, $104°\ 30'$ W. longitude, but bending its course east, enters the Province of Texas; and after a winding course of about six hundred miles disembogues itself into the Bay of St. Bernard; in the $29°$ N. latitude. Where the road traverses, it was at least one hundred and fifty yards wide, and has a guard of dragoons stationed on its banks; its waters are of a reddish cast, from whence it probably derived its name: this stream is navigable for boats of three or four tons burthen.

The River Brassos takes its source in the Province of Cogquilla, in $34°$ N. latitude, and $105°$ W. longitude, enters the Province of Texas,

THE INTERIOR OF NEW SPAIN.

and discharges itself into the Gulph of Mexico in 28° 40' after a course of seven hundred miles; it is the largest river in the province, and where the road crosses is three hundred yards wide, and navigable for large keels. From the appearance on its banks it must rise and fall one hundred feet, its waters were red and turbid, its banks well timbered and a rich prolific soil. Here was kept the only boat I recollect to have seen in the provinces.

The River Trinity takes its source in 34° N. latitude, and 99° W. longitude, and discharges itself into Galveston's bay, in 29° 30' N. latitude. By its meanders it is about three hundred miles in length; where the road crosses it is about sixty yards in width, with high steep banks covered with timber, and a rich luxuriant soil.

The Rivers Natchez and Angelina are small streams of about twenty yards in width, and discharge themselves after forming a junction into the Trinity.

The River Toyac is a small stream which discharges itself into the Gulph of Mexico, in the same bay as the Sabine, in about 29° 50' N. latitude, and 97° W. longitude.

The Sabine river, the present limits between the Spanish dominions and the territories of the United States in that quarter, takes its source in about the 33° N. latitude, and enters the Gulph of Mexico in 29° 50'. It may be three hundred miles in length by its meanders, and at the road about fifty yards in width: here the Spaniards keep a guard and ferry-boat.

Lakes.—Some small ones near the head of the Guadelupe, and some branches of Red river.

Timber, Plains and Soil.—This province is well timbered for one hundred miles from the coast, but has some small prairies interspersed through its timbered land; taken generally it is one of the richest, most prolific, and the best watered countries in North America, for the residence of man, and the production of the necessaries of life.

Animals.—Buffalo, deer, elk, wild hogs, and wild horses; the latter of which are in such large numbers as to afford supplies for all the savages who border on the province, the Spaniards, and vast droves for the other provinces of the United States, which find their way out, notwithstanding the trade being contraband. They go in such large gangs that it is requisite to keep an advanced guard of horsemen, in order to frighten them away; for should they be suffered to come near your horses and mules which you drive with you, by their snorting, neighing, &c., they alarm them, and are freqently joined by them and taken off, notwithstanding all the exertions of the dragoons to prevent them. A gentleman told me he saw seven hundred beasts carried off at one time, not one of which was ever recovered. In the night they frequently carry off the droves of travellers' horses, and even come within a few miles of St. Antonio, and entice away the horses in the vicinity. The method pursued by the Spaniards in taking them is as follows: they take a few fleet horses and proceed into the country where the wild animals are numerous; they build a large inclosure, with a door which enters into a smaller inclosure: from the entrance of the large pen they project wings out into the prairie to a great distance, and then set up bushes, &c., to induce the horses when pursued to enter within these wings. After these preparations are made, they keep a lookout for a small drove; for if they unfortunately should start too large a one, they either burst open the pen or fill it up with the dead bodies, and the remainder run over them and escape; in which case the party is obliged to leave the place, as the stench arising from the putrid carcasses would be insupportable, and in addition to this, the pen would not receive others. But should they succeed in driving in a few, say two or three hundred, they select the handsomest and youngest, noose them, and take them into the small inclosure, then turn out the others. After which, by starving, preventing them from taking any repose, and continually keeping them in motion, they subdue them by degrees, and finally break them to submit to the saddle and bridle. For this business I presume there is no nation in the world superior to the Spaniards of Texas.

Population and Chief Towns.—St. Antonio, the capital of the province, lies in 29° 50′ N. latitude, 101° W. longitude; is situated on the head waters of the river of that name, and perhaps contains two thousand souls, most of whom reside in miserable mud-wall houses, covered with thatch grass roofs; the town is laid out on a very grand plan: to the east of it, on the other side of the river, is the station of the troops. About two, three, and four miles from St. Antonio are three missions, formerly flourishing and prosperous. These buildings for solidity, accommodation, and even majesty, were surpassed by few that I met with in New Spain. The resident priest treated us with the greatest hospitality, and was respected and beloved by all who knew him. He made a singular observation relative to the aborigines, who had formerly formed the population of these establishments under the charge of the monks. I asked him what had become of the natives? He replied, that it appeared to him that they could not exist under the shadow of the whites, as the nations who formed these missions had been nurtured and taken all the care of that was possible, and put on the same footing as the Spaniards; yet they had, notwithstanding, dwindled away, until the other two had become entirely depopulated; and the one where he resided had not more than sufficient to perform his household labour. From this he had formed an idea that God never intended them to form one people, but that they should always remain distinct and separate.

Nacogdoches is merely a station for troops, and contains nearly five hundred souls; it is situated on a small stream of the River Toyac.

The population of Texas may be estimated at seven thousand; these are principally Spanish creoles; some French, some Americans, and a few civilized Indians and half-breeds.

Trade and Commerce.—This province trades with Mexico, by Montelrey and Montelovez for merchandize, and with New Orleans by Natchitoches, but the latter, being contraband, is liable to great damage and risks: they give in return specie, horses, and mules.

Agriculture.—The American emigrants are introducing some little spirit of agriculture near to Nacogdoches and the Trinity; but the oppression and suspicions they labour under prevent their proceeding with that vigour which is necessary to give success to the establishment of a new country.

Aborigines.—The Tancards are a nation of Indians who rove on the banks of Red river, and are six hundred men strong; they follow the buffalo and wild horses, and carry on a trade with the Spaniards. They are armed with the bow, arrow, and lance; are errant and confined to no particular district. They are a tall, handsome people: in conversation they have a peculiar clucking, and express more by signs than any savages I ever visited; in fact, language appears to have made less progress than among any other.

They complain much of their situation and the treatment of the Spaniards; are extremely poor, and, except the Apaches, were the most independent Indians we observed in the Spanish territories: they possess large droves of horses. There are a number of other nations, now nearly extinct, some of which are mentioned by Dr. Sibley in a report he made to the government on these subjects. A few, and very few indeed, of these nations have been converted by the missions, and these are not in that state of vassalage which the Indians farther to the south are held in.

Government and Laws.—Perfectly military, except as to the ecclesiastical jurisdiction.

Morals and Manners.—Being on the frontiers, where buffalo and wild horses abound in great numbers, and not engaged in any war with savages who are powerful, they have adopted a mode of living by following those animals, which have been productive of a more errant disposition round the capital (St. Antonio) than in any other of the provinces But Cordero, by restricting (by edicts) the buffalo hunts to certain seasons, and obliging every man of family to cultivate so many acres of land, has, in some degree, checked the spirit of hunting, or wandering life, which had been hitherto so very prevalent; and has endeavoured to introduce, by his example and precepts, a general urbanity and suavity of manners, which rendered St. Antonio one of the most agreeable *séjours* that we met with in the provinces.

Military Force.—There were in Texas, at the time I came through, nine hundred and eighty-eight men, from the actual returns of the troops which I have seen, two hundred of whom were from St. Ander and New Leon, under the command of Governor Herrara. The disposition of those troops are as follows: three hundred and eighty-eight at St. Antonio; four hundred at the cantonment of ———, on the Trinity; one hundred at the Trinity, and one hundred at Nacogdoches. The militia (a rabble) are made the more respectable by a few American riflemen, who are incorporated among them; they are about three hundred in number, including bow and arrow men.

Religion.—Catholic, but much relaxed.

History.—To me unknown, except what might be extracted from various authors on that subject.

THE INTERIOR OF NEW SPAIN.

General Remarks on New Spain.—To become acquainted with all the civil and political institutions of a country, requires a perfect knowledge of the language, a free ingress to the archives, and residence of some years. Even then we can scarcely distinguish between the statute law and the common law, derived from custom, morals, and habits: under these circumstances, it cannot be expected that I should be able to say much on the subject, as I possess none of the above advantages; but I will offer a few observations.

To a stranger, it is impossible to define the limits of the military and ecclesiastical jurisdictions, in every affair which relates to the citizens, and, in fact, with the soldiery the force of superstition is such, that I am doubtful whether they would generally obey one of their officers in direct violation of the injunction of their religious profession. The audiences of Mexico and Guadalaxara were formed, no doubt, as a check on the immense power of the Vice-Roy. The number of members composing each, is to me unknown; but they are formed of the Vice-Roy as president with two votes, generals, and bishops. To their jurisdiction, the appeals from the judgment of the intendants, and all subordinate officers, may be made in civil cases; but the military and ecclesiastical decisions are distinct: yet for all this semblance of justice, should an individual dare to make the appeal, and not succeed in establishing the justice of his claim to redress, he is certainly ruined. And where justice is so little attended to when opposed to power and wealth, as in the Spanish provinces, the appeal is a desperate remedy. This tribunal, or legislative body, enacts all the laws for the general regulations of their divisions of the kingdom.

The Captain-Generalship of the internal provinces appeared to me to be much more despotic, for the laws or regulations were issued in the form of an order, merely, without any kind of a preamble whatsoever, except sometimes it was said, "by order of the King." And such was the style of the governors of provinces.

Morals, Manners, &c.—For hospitality, generosity, docility, and sobriety, the people of New Spain exceed any nation perhaps on the globe: but in national energy, or patriotism, enterprise of character, and independence of soul, they are perhaps the most deficient. Yet there are men who have displayed bravery to a surprizing degree, and the Europeans who are there, cherish with delight the idea of their gallant ancestry. Their women have black eyes and hair, fine teeth, and are generally brunettes. I met but one exception to this rule at Chihuahua, of a fair lady, and she by way of distinction was called the girl with light hair. They are all inclining a little to *en bon point*, but none (or few) are elegant figures. Their dresses are generally short jackets and petticoats, and high-heel shoes, without any head dress: over this they have a silk wrapper which they always wear, and when in the presence of men affect to bring it over their faces; but as we approached the Atlantic and our frontiers, we saw several ladies who wore the gowns of our country women, which they conceive to be more elegant than their ancient costume. The lower class of the men are generally dressed in broad-brimmed hats, short coats, large waistcoats and small clothes, always open at the knees, owing, I suppose, to the greater freedom it gives to the limbs on horseback, a kind of leather boot or wrapper bound round the leg, somewhat in the manner of our frontier men's leggins, and gartered on. The boot is of a soft pliable leather, but not coloured. In the eastern provinces the dragoons wear over this wrapper a sort of jack-boot made of seal leather, to which are fastened the spurs by a rivet, the gaffs of which are sometimes near an inch in length. But the spurs of the gentlemen and officers, although clumsy to our ideas, are frequently ornamented with raised silver work on the shoulders, and the strap embroidered with silver and gold thread. They are always ready to mount their horses, on which the inhabitants of the internal provinces spend nearly half the day. This description will apply generally for the dress of all the men of the provinces for the lower class, but in the towns, amongst the more fashionable ranks, they dress after the European or United States mode, with not more distinction than we see in our cities from one six months to another. Both men and women have remarkably fine hair, and pride themselves in the display of it.

Their amusements are music, singing, dancing, and gambling; the latter is strictly prohibited, but the prohibition is not much attended to. The dance of —— is performed by one man and two women, who beat time to the music, which is soft and voluptuous, but sometimes changes to a lively gay air, whilst the dancers occasionaly exhibit the most indelicate gestures. The whole of this dance impressed me with the idea of an isolated society of once civilized beings, but now degenerated into a medium

THE INTERIOR OF NEW SPAIN.

state, between the improved world and the children of nature. The fandango is danced in various figures and numbers. The minuet is still danced by the superior class only; the music made use of is the guitar, violin, and singers, who in the first described dance, accompany the music with their hands and voices, having always some words adapted to the music, which are generally of such a tendency as would in the United States occasion every lady to leave the room.

Their games are cards, billiards, horse-racing, and cock-fighting, the first and last of which are carried to the most extravagant lengths, the parties losing and winning immense sums. The present Commandant-General is very severe with his officers in these respects, frequently sending them to some frontier post, in confinement for months, for no other fault than having lost large sums at play.

At every town of consequence is a public walk, where the ladies and gentlemen meet and sing songs, which are always on the subject of love, or the social board. The females have fine voices and sing in French, Italian and Spanish, the whole company joining in the chorus. In their houses the ladies play on the guitar, and generally accompany it with their voices. They either sit down on the carpet cross-legged, or loll on a sofa. To sit upright in a chair appeared to put them to great inconvenience, and although the better class would sometimes do it on our first introduction, they soon demanded liberty to follow their old habits. In their eating and drinking they are remarkably temperate. Early in the morning you receive a dish of chocolate and a cake; at twelve you dine on several dishes of meat, fowls, and fish; after which you have a variety of confectionary, and indeed an elegant dessert: then drink a few glasses of wine, sing a few songs, and retire to take the siesta, or afternoon nap, which is done by rich and poor; and about two o'clock the windows and doors are all closed, the streets deserted, and the stillness of midnight reigns throughout. About four o'clock they rise, wash, and dress, and prepare for the dissipation of the night. About eleven o'clock some refreshments are offered, but few take any, except a little wine and water and a little candied sugar.

The Government have multiplied the difficulties for Europeans mixing with the Creoles or Mestis, to such a degree, that it is difficult for a marriage to take place. An officer wishing to marry a lady not from Europe, is obliged to acquire certificates of the purity of her descent for two hundred years back, and transmit them to the court, when the licence will be returned; but should she be the daughter of a person of the rank of captain or upwards, this nicety vanishes, as their rank purifies the blood of the descendants.

The general subjects of the conversation of the men are women, money, and horses, which appear to be the only objects in their estimation worthy of consideration. Having united the female sex with their money and their beasts, and treated them too much after the manner of the latter, they have eradicated from their breasts every sentiment of virtue, or of ambition, to pursue the acquirements which would make them amiable companions, instructive mothers, or respectable members of society. Their whole souls, with a few exceptions, like the Turkish ladies, are taken up in music, dress, and the little blandishments of voluptuous dissipation. Finding that the men only require these as objects of gratification to the sensual passions, they have lost every idea of the feast of reason and the flow of soul which arise from the intercourse of two refined and virtuous minds, whose inmost thoughts are open to the inspection and admiration of each other, and whose refinements of sentiment heighten the pleasures of every gratification.

The beggars of the City of Mexico alone are estimated at sixty thousand souls, what must be the number through the whole kingdom? And what reason can it be owing to, that, in a country superior to any in the world for riches in gold and silver, producing all the necessaries of life, and most of its luxuries, there should be such a vast proportion of the inhabitants in want of bread and clothing? It can only be accounted for by the tyranny of the government, and the luxuries of the rich: the government striving by all the local restrictions possible to be invented, without absolutely driving the people to desperation, to keep Spanish America dependent on Europe.

Trade, Commerce, Manufactures, and Revenue.—The trade and commerce of New Spain are carried on with Europe and the United States by the port of Vera Cruz solely, and with the East Indies and South America by Acapulco, and even then under such restrictions of productions, manufactures, and time, as to render it almost of no consequence as

THE INTERIOR OF NEW SPAIN.

to the general prosperity of the country. Were all the numerous bays and harbours of the Gulph of Mexico and California opened to the trade of the world, and a general licence given to the cultivation of all the productions which the country is capable of yielding, with freedom of exportation and importation, with proper duties on foreign goods, the country would immediately become rich and powerful, a proper stimulus would be held out to the poor to labour, when certain of finding a quick and ready sale for the productions of their plantations or manufactories. The country abounds in iron ore, yet all the iron and steel, and articles of manufactures are obliged to be brought from Europe, the manufacturing or working of iron being strictly prohibited. This occasions the necessary utensils of husbandry, arms, and tools, to be enormously high, and forms a great check to agriculture, improvements in manufactures, and military skill. The works of the Mexicans in gold, silver, and painting, shew them naturally to have a genius, which, with cultivation and improvement, might rival the greatest masters of either ancient or modern schools. Their dispositions and habits are peculiarly calculated for sedentary employments, and I have no doubt, if proper establishments were made, they would soon rival, if not surpass, the most extensive woollen, cotton or silk manufactures of Europe. Their climate is adapted for raising the finest cotton in the world, and their sheep possess all the fineness of wool for which they are so celebrated in Spain. Besides this they have immense quantities of raw materials, which they have on hand, wool selling for a mere song, and, in fact, they scarcely take the half from the fleece of the sheep for the coarse manufactories of the country, and for making beds.

I cannot presume to state the revenues of the country, but am credibly informed that the mint coins per annum at least fifty millions of dollars in silver, and fourteen millions of dollars in gold, the one-fifth of which amounts to twelve millions eight hundred thousand. The duties on foreign goods, and the amount paid by the purchasers of monopoly, may make four millions more, which would make the annual revenue sixteen millions eight hundred thousand. The civil list of the kingdom amounts to five hundred and eighty thousand. The military, seven millions one hundred and eighty-nine thousand two hundred, making, with the civil list, seven millions seven hundred and sixty thousand two hundred, which deducted from sixteen millions eight hundred thousand, leaves a clear revenue for the King from his

Mexican dominions of nine millions thirty thousand eight hundred. The clergy are not included in this estimate, as they receive their revenues through their own proper channel, and although the best paid officers in the government cost the King nothing in a direct way, yet the dreadful manner in which they oppress and impoverish his subjects would render it better policy to abolish their impositions and pay them a direct salary out of the public treasury.

The European troops are some of the choicest regiments from Spain, consequently we may put them on the supposition that they are well disciplined and officered by men of honour and science. The regular troops of the kingdom, who are in the Vice-Royalty, acting from the stimulus of ambition and envy, are supposed to be equal to their brethren from Europe. The militia with the regular officers are likewise good troops, but are not held in such high estimation as the other corps. These three corps, forming a body of twenty-three thousand two hundred and eighty-eight men, may be called the regular force of the kingdom, as the militia of one hundred and thirty-nine thousand five hundred, would in my estimation be of no more consequence against the regular troops of any civilized power, than the ancient aborigines of the country were against the army of Cortes. The particular observations which follow, must be considered as applying to the troops of the internal provinces, unless specified to the contrary. The appearance of the Spanish troops is certainly (at a distance) à la militaire. Their lances are fixed to the side of the saddle under the left thigh, and slant about five feet above the horse; on the right the carabine is slung in a case to the front of the saddle (or pummel) crossways, the breech to the right hand, and on each side of the saddle behind the rider is a pistol; below the breech of the carabine is slung the shield, which is made of sole leather trebled, sewed together with thongs, with a band on the inside, to slip the left arm through; those of the privates are round, and about two feet in diameter. The officers and non-commissioned officers have them of an oval form, bending on both sides, in order to permit the arrow to glance, and they have in general the arms of Spain with Don Carlos the fourth, gilt on the outside, with various other devices, which add much to the elegance of their appearance on horseback, but are only calculated to be of service against savages, who have no fire-arms. The dragoons of the Vice-Royalty do not make use

THE INTERIOR OF NEW SPAIN.

RETURN OF MILITARY FORCE IN NEW SPAIN.

Provinces and Places.	Disciplined and Regular European Troops.			Regular Troops of the Country.			Militia, with Regular Field Officers, and under Pay.			Probable Armed Citizens.	
	Cavalry.	Artillery.	Infantry.	Cavalry.	Artillery.	Infantry.	Cavalry.	Artillery.	Infantry.	Fire-arms.	Bows, Arrows, and Lances.
Xalapa Ina. Vera Cruz..	....	200	2,000	2000	....	....	3,000	....	1,000	....	....
Vera Cruz and Sea-ports.	....	800	2,000	....	....	....	600	....	2,000	....	....
Mexico	1,000	....	....	....	....	1,000	3,400	1,000	....	....	....
Different Prov. and V.-Royalty	....	....	....	....	....	....	....	....	....	15,000	80,000
New Mexico	....	....	....	100	....	....	....	....	....	1,000	4,000
Biscay	....	....	....	1,100	....	....	....	....	....	5,000	8,000
Senora	....	....	....	900	....	200	....	....	....	5,000	8,000
Sinaloa	....	....	....	100	....	....	....	....	....	3,000	6,000
Cogquilla	....	....	....	400	....	....	....	....	....	1,000	2,000
Texas	....	....	....	488	....	....	....	....	....	500	1,000
Total	1,000	1,000	4,000	5,088	....	1,200	7,000	1,000	3,000	30,500	109,000

```
                CAVALRY.  ARTILLERY.  INFANTRY.
European........  1,000     1,000       4,000      Cavalry.....13,088
Regular Troops mixed.. 5,088  ....      1,200      Artillery... 2,000
Trained Militia...  7,000    1,000      3,000      Infantry.... 8,200

       Total...13,088      2,000        8,200    Total..23,288 Disciplined Effective Force.
                                                  30,500 Undisciplined Militia.
                                                 109,000 Bow, Arrow, and Lance-men.

                                                 162,788 Total Force.
```

of the lance or shield, but are armed, equipped, and clothed after the modern manner, as are also the dragoons of the eastern provinces. When they recently expected to be opposed by the American troops, they were deprived of their lance and shield, and received the straight cutlass, in their stead.

Their dress is a short blue coat, with a red cape and cuff without facings, leather or blue cotton velvet small clothes and waistcoat; the small clothes always open at the knees: the wrapping boot with the jack boot, and permanent spurs over it; a broad-brimmed high-crowned wool hat with a ribbon round it of various colours, generally received as a present from some female, which they wear as a badge of favour of the fair sex, and a mark of their gallantry.

Their horses are small and slender limbed, but very agile, and are capable of enduring great fatigue. The equipments of the horses are, to our ideas, awkward, but I believe them superior to the English, and they have the advantage over us, as to the skill of the rider as well as the quality of the horse, as their bridles have a strong curb which gives them so great a mechanical force that I believe it almost practicable with it to break the jaw of the horse. The saddle is made after the Persian model, with a high projecting pummel, or, as anciently termed, bow, and is likewise raised behind; this is merely the tree. It is then covered by two or three coats of carved leather, and embroidered workmanship, some with gold and silver in a very superb manner. The stirrups are of wood closed in front, carved generally in the figure of a lion's head or some other beast; they are very heavy, and to us present a very clumsy appearance. The horseman seated on his horse has a small bag tied behind him, his blankets either under him or lying with his cloak between his body and the bow, which makes him at his ease. Thus mounted it is impossible for the most vicious animals to dismount them. They will catch another horse, when both are running nearly at full speed, with a noose and hair rope, with which they will soon choak down the beast they are pursuing. In short, they are probably the most expert horsemen in the world.

At each port is a store, called the King's, where it was the original intention of the government that the soldiers should be supplied with provisions, clothing, arms, &c., at a cheap rate; but it being a post generally given to some young officer to make his fortune, they are subject to great impositions. When a dragoon joins the service he receives from the King five horses and two mules, and this number he is always obliged to keep good from his own pocket; but when he is discharged, the horses and mules receive the discharge mark, and become his private property. They engage for five or ten years, at the option of the soldier. But in the bounty there is a very material difference. It is extremely easy to keep up the corps, as a private dragoon considers himself upon an equality with most of the citizens, and infinitely superior to the lower class; and it is not unfrequent to see men of considerable fortune marrying the daughters of sergeants and corporals.

The pay of the troops of New Spain varies with the locality, but may be averaged in the internal provinces as follows:

A colonel, four thousand five hundred dollars per annum; lieutenant-colonel, four thousand; major, three thousand; captain, two thousand four hundred; first lieutenant, one thousand five hundred; second lieutenant, one thousand; ensign, eight hundred; sergeant, three hundred and fifty; corporal, three hundred; private, two hundred and eighty-eight. With this pay they find their own clothes, provisions, arms, accoutrements, &c., after the first equipments.

Corporal punishment is contrary to the Spanish ordinances; they punish by imprisonment, putting in the stocks, and death; but as a remarkable instance of the discipline and regularity of conduct of the provincial troops, I may mention, that although marching with them, and doing duty as it were for nearly four months, I never saw a man receive a blow; or put under confinement for one hour. How impossible would it be to regulate the turbulent dispositions of the Americans with such treatment? In making the foregoing remark, I do not include officers, for I saw more rigourous treatment exercised towards some of them than ever was practised in our army.

The discipline of their troops is very different from ours: as to tactics, or military manœuvres, they are not held in much estimation; for during the whole of the time I was in the country, I never saw a corps of troops exercising as dragoons, but frequently marching by platoons, sections, &c., in garrison, where they serve as infantry, with their carabines. In these manœuvres they were also very deficient. On a march, a detachment of cavalry generally encamp in a circle. They relieve their guards at night, and as soon as they halt the new guard is formed on foot, with their carabines, and then march before the Commandant's tent, where the commanding officer of the guard cries the invocation of the Holy Virgin three times. The commanding officer replies, it is well. They then retire and mount their horses, and are told off, some to act as guard of the horses, as cavalry; others as guard of the camp, as infantry. The old guards are then paraded and relieved, and the new sentinels take post. The sentinels are singing half their time, and it is no uncommon thing for them to quit their post to come to the fire, go for water, &c. In fact, after the officer is in bed, frequently the whole guard comes in; yet I never knew any man punished for these breaches of military duty.

Their mode of attack is by squadrons on the different flanks of their enemies, but without regularity or concert, shouting, hallooing, and firing their carabines, after which, if they think themselves equal to the enemy, they charge with a pistol and then the lance. But from my observations on their discipline, I have no hesitation in declaring that I would not be afraid to march over a plain with five hundred infantry, and a proportionate allowance of horse artillery of the United States army, in the presence of five thousand of these dragoons. Yet, I do not presume to say, that an army with that inferiority of numbers would do to oppose them, for they would cut off your supplies, and harass your march and camp night and day, to such a degree as to oblige you in the end to surrender to them without ever having come to action; but if the event depended on one engagement, it would terminate with glory to the American arms. The conclusion must not however be drawn, that I infer from this they are deficient in physical firmness more than other nations, for we see the savages, five hundred of whom would on a plain fly before fifty bayonets, on other occasions brave danger and death in its most horrid shapes, with an undaunted fortitude never surpassed by the most disciplined and hardy veterans. But it arises solely from the want of discipline and confidence in each other, as is always the case with undisciplined corps; unless stimulated by the god-like sentiment of love of country, which these poor fellows know nothing of.

The travelling food of the dragoons in New Mexico, consists of a very excellent species of wheat biscuit, and shaved meat well dried, with a vast quantity of red pepper, of which they make bouilli and then pour it on their broken biscuit, when it becomes soft and excellent eating. Farther south they use great quantities of parched corn meal and sugar, as practised by our hunters, each dragoon having a small bag. They thus live, when on command, on an allowance which our troops would conceive little better than starving, never except at night attempting to eat any thing like a meal, but biting a piece of biscuit, or drinking some parched meal and sugar, with water during the day.

From the physical as well as moral properties of the inhabitants of New Spain, I do believe they are capable of being made the best troops in the world, possessing sobriety, enterprise, great physical force, docility, and a conception equally quick and penetrating.

The modes of promotion in the internal provinces are singular, but probably productive of good effects. Should a vacancy of first lieutenant offer in a company, the captain commanding nominates, with the senior second lieutenant (who by seniority would fill the vacancy) two other lieutenants to the General, giving his comments on the three. The General selects two, for nomination to the court, from whom is selected the fortunate candidate, whose commission is made out and forwarded. As the letters of nomination are always kept secret, it is impossible for the young officers to say who is to blame, should they be disappointed, and the fortunate is in a direct way to thank the King only for the ultimate decision. The method is the same with the superior grades to the colonel.

The King of Spain's ordinances for the government of his army are generally founded on justice and a high sense of honour: I could not procure a set from any of the officers to take to my quarters, consequently my observations on them were extremely cursory. They provide that no old soldier shall ever be discharged the service unless for infamous crimes. When a man has served with reputation for fifteen years and continues, his pay is augmented, twenty years he receives another augmentation; twenty-seven years he receives the brevet rank and pay of an ensign, and thirty-two those of a lieutenant, &c. These circumstances are a great stimulus, although not one in a thousand arrive at the third period, when they are permitted to retire from the service with full pay and emoluments. All sons of captains, or of grades superior, are entitled to enter the King's school as cadets, at the age of twelve years. The property of an officer or soldier, who is killed on the field of battle, or dies of his wounds, is not liable to be taken for debt, and is secured, as well as the King's pension, to the relatives of the deceased.

Court martials for the trial of a commissioned officer must be formed of general officers; but this clause subjects the officers of the provinces to a great species of tyranny, for the Commanding-General has taken upon himself to punish for all offences not capital, consequently according to his own judgment and prejudices, and from which there is only an appeal to the King. Difficult indeed, must it be for the complaints of a subaltern to reach the ears of His Majesty through the numerous crowds of sycophants who surround him, one half of whom are probably in league with the oppressor. This practice likewise deprives an officer of the most sacred of all rights, the being tried by his peers, for should he be sent to Mexico or Europe for trial, it is possible he may not be able to take half the testimony which is necessary to his complete justification.

There is another principle defined by the ordinances which has often been the cause of disputes in the service of the United States, viz.: The commandant of a post in the Spanish service, if barely a captain, receives no orders from a general, should one arrive at his post, unless that general should be superior in authority to the person who posted him; for, says the ordinance, he is responsible to the King alone for his post. This principle, according to my ideas, is very injurious to the interest of any country that adopts it. We will say for example that a post of great importance, containing immense military stores, is likely to fall into the hands of the enemy; a superior officer to the commandant receives the information, and repairs to the post, and orders him immediately to evacuate it. The commandant feeling himself only responsible to the authority who placed him in that position, refuses to obey, and the magazines and place are lost! The principle is likewise subversive of the very foundation of military subordination and discipline, whereby an inferior should in *all cases* obey a superior, who alone should be responsible for the effect arising from the execution of his orders. It will readily be believed that in thus advocating implicit obedience to the orders of a superior, I do not suppose the highest improbabilities, or impossibilities, such as a command from him to turn your arms against the constituted authority of your country, or to be an engine of his tyranny, or the pander

THE INTERIOR OF NEW SPAIN.

of his vices; these are cases wherein a man's reason alone must direct him, and are not and cannot be subject to any human rule whatever.

Religion.—Its forms are topics with which I am very imperfectly acquainted, but, having made some enquiries and observations on the subject, I will freely communicate them, fearful, at the same time, that I may lay myself open to the severe criticism of persons who have in any degree applied themselves to the study of theology or the ritual of the Catholic Church.

The Kingdom of New Spain is divided into four archbishopricks, viz.: Mexico, Guadalaxara, Durango, and St. Luis Potosi; under these again are the subbishopricks, deacons, curates, &c., each of whom is subject and accountable to his immediate chiefs for the districts committed to his charge, and the whole are again subject to the ordinances of the high court of inquisition, held at the capital of Mexico; whence are fulminated the edicts of censure against the heresies and impious doctrines of the modern philosophy, both as to politics and religion. I am credibly informed that the influence of that tribunal is greater in His Catholic Majesty's Mexican dominions than in any Catholic country in Europe, or perhaps in the world. A few years since they condemned a man to the flames for asserting and maintaining some doctrine which they deemed heretical; and also a Jew who was imprudent enough to take the image of Christ from the cross and put it under the sill of his door, saying privately, he would make the dogs walk over their God. This court likewise examines and condemns all books of a modern sentiment, either as to religion or politics, and excommunicates any one in whose hands they may be found. I recollect to have seen one of its decrees published in the Mexican *Gazette*, condemning a number of books as heretical and contrary to the sacred principles of the Holy Catholic Church, and the peace and durability of the government of His Catholic Majesty. Amongst these were mentioned Helvetius on Man, J. J. Rousseau's Works, Voltaire's, Mirabeau's, and a number of others of that description, and even at so great a distance as Chihuahua an officer dared not take Pope's Essay on Man to his quarters, but used to come to mine to read it.

The salaries of the archbishops are superior to those of any officers in the kingdom, that of the Bishop of Mexico being estimated at one hundred and fifty thousand dollars per annum, while the Vice-Roy has but eighty thousand, and fifty thousand allowed for his table, falling short of the Bishop twenty thousand dollars. These incomes are raised entirely from the people, who pay no tax to the King, but give one-tenth of their yearly income to the clergy, besides the fees of confessions, bulls, burials, baptisms, marriages, and a thousand other impositions, which the corruption of priestcraft has introduced, and have been kept up by the superstition and ignorance of the people. Notwithstanding all this, the inferior clergy, who do all the slavery of the office, are liberal and well informed men. I scarcely saw one who was not in favour of a change of government. They being generally Creoles by birth, and always kept in subordinate grades, without the least shadow of a probability of rising to the superior dignities of the Church, their minds have been soured to such a degree that I am confident in asserting they will lead the van whenever the standard of independence is raised in the country.

Politics.—It has often been a subject of discussion with politicians, in what manner a mother country should treat her distant and powerful colonies, in order to retain them the longest in their subjection. For the history of all nations and all ages has proved, that no community of people separated from another by an immense ocean, feeling their power, strength, and independence, will remain long subject to the parent state purely from the ties of consanguinity and similarity of habits, manners, and religion. Society itself having arisen from the mutual wants, fears, and imbecility of the infancy of human institutions, a large body of that society will remain no longer subject to another branch, at the immense distance of a thousand leagues, than until they feel their maturity and capability of providing for their own wants, and their own defence. We may, therefore, draw a conclusion that no political course of conduct whatever will eventually prevent their separation. But there is a line of conduct which certainly must retard it in a great measure, and prudence would dictate to the mother country the policy of giving way without a struggle to an event beyond her power to prevent. The two great examples of English and Spanish America are before our eyes. England gave us free liberty to pursue the dictates of our own judgment with respect to trade, education, and manners, by which means we increased in power, learning, and wealth, with a rapidity unexampled in the annals of the world; and, on the first attempt to infringe the rights which we had enjoyed, asserted

THE INTERIOR OF NEW SPAIN.   349

that claim which nature and the locality of our situation gave us a right to demand, and power to defend. Had Great Britain yielded to the storm with grace and dignity, she would have secured our gratitude, ancient prejudices, and affections in her favour ; but by a long and arduous conflict, the murder of thousands of our citizens, the destruction of the country, the profanation of our altars, and the violation of every right, divine and human, she implanted into the breasts of the Americans an antipathy, approaching nearly to horror, a desire of revenge almost hereditary, and destroyed the bonds of brotherhood that might have subsisted between the two countries, and it will take ages of just conduct from her to the United States to rectify the evil. Spain pursued a different line of conduct towards her Mexican dominions, which were settled by Europeans sixty years previous to any part of the United States, and might be termed a conquered kingdom, rather than the settlement of a savage country. This country she has therefore bound up in all the ligatures of restrictions, monoplies, prohibitions, seclusions, and superstition ; and she has so carefully secluded all light from bursting in on their ignorance, that they have vegetated like the acorn in the forest; until the towering branches have broken through the darkness of the wild which surrounded them and let in the light of heaven. The approximation of the United States, with the gigantic strides of French ambition, have begun to rouse up their dormant qualities, and to call into motion the powers of their minds, on the subject of their political situation. Instances of their disposition for independence were exhibited in their feeble attempts at a revolution on the 15th of January, 1624, under the Vice-Royalty of Don Diego Carrello Galves; the insurrection on the 8th of June, 1692; and more recently in 1797 under the Count de Galves, when they proclaimed him King of Mexico, in the streets of the capital, and one hundred and thirty thousand souls were heard proclaiming, "Long live Galves King of Mexico." It was then only for him to have *willed it*, and the Kingdom of Mexico was lost to Charles IV. forever. But preferring his loyalty to his ambition, he rode out to the mob, attended by his guards, with his sword in hand, crying out, "Long live His Catholic Majesty Charles the Fourth," and threatening to put to instant death with his own hand, any persons who refused immediately to retire to their houses. This dispersed the people. In another quarter of the kingdom an immense number had collected and proclaimed him king; he sent ten thousand men against them, dispersed them, and had four beheaded. These firm measures saved the country at that period. Galves received the greatest honours from the court of Spain, but was poisoned in a short time after, fulfilling the maxim, "That it is dangerous to serve jealous tyrants," for they always conceive that the same power who stilled the ocean's rage, can at will raise the storm into all the majesty of overwhelming fury. Thus by taking his life, the court of Spain was relieved from the dread of his influence over the Mexicans. England would naturally have been the power they would have looked up to in order to form an alliance to secure their independence; but the insatiable avarice and hauteur exhibited by that nation in her late descent at La Plata, with the disgrace of her arms, has turned their views to other quarters. They have therefore directed their eyes towards the United States, as brethren of the same soil in their vicinity; who have within their power ample resources of arms, ammunition, and even men, to assist in securing their independence; and who in that event would secure to themselves the almost exclusive trade of the richest country in the world for centuries, and to be her carriers as long as the two nations exist. For Mexico, like China, will never become a nation of mariners, but must receive the ships of all the world into her ports, and give her bullion in exchange for the productions of their different countries. What would not be the advantages the United States would reap from this event? Our numerous vessels would fill every port, and from our vicinity enable us to carry off at least nine-tenths of her commerce. Even on the coast of the Pacific no European nation could vie with us: there would also be a brisk inland trade carried on with the southern provinces via Red river, and having a free entrance into all their ports, we should become their factors, agents, guardians, and, in short, their tutelar genius, as the country fears but hates France and all Frenchmen and measures. It therefore remains for the government of the United States to decide, whether, if Buonaparte should seize on the crown of Spain, they will hold out a helping hand, to emancipate another portion of the western hemisphere from the bonds of European tyranny and oppression, or by a different policy suffer six hundred thousand people to become in the hands of French intrigue, enterprise, and tactics, a scourge to our south-western boundaries, which would oblige us to keep up a large and respectable

THE INTERIOR OF NEW SPAIN.

military force, and continually render us liable to a war, on the weakest and most vulnerable part of our frontiers.

Twenty thousand auxiliaries from the United States under good officers, joined to the independence of the country, are at any time sufficient to create and effect the revolution. Those troops can be raised and officered in the United States, but must be paid and supported at the expence of Mexico. It would be requisite, that, not only the General commanding, but every officer, down to the youngest ensign, should be impressed with the necessity of supporting a strict discipline, to prevent marauding, which should in some instances be punished with death, in order to evince to the citizens that you came as their friends and protectors, not as their plunderers and tyrants; also the most sacred regard should be had not to injure the institutions of their religion, thereby shewing them we had a proper respect to all things in any way connected with the worship of the Deity, while at the same time we permitted every man to adore Him agreeably to the dictates of his own judgment.

Z. M. PIKE,
Captain, First United States Regiment of Infantry.

Washington,
12th *April,* 1808.

APPENDIX.

(No. I.)

To General Wilkinson.

St. Charles, 17th July, 1806.

DEAR SIR,
WE arrived here last evening all well, except some of the soldiers from fatigue, as in the present state of the water we were obliged to row altogether.

We were disappointed in not obtaining any information from St. Louis, or baggage for the Pawnees. I do not know how it will be digested by them.

* * * * * * * *

We likewise were disappointed in not receiving a line from you, as we had expected, in the hopes of which I shall yet detain until twelve o'clock, and then take my departure. Our Osage conduct themselves pretty well, and are very obedient to orders; at first they had an idea a little too free relative to other people's property, but at present stand corrected.

I understood from you that they were equipped by Mr. Tillier, with everything necessary for their voyage to their towns, consequently, although they have been applying to me for a variety of articles, none of which they have been gratified with, but powder and ball, which are necessary for their own defence.

The General will pardon this scrawl, and should he send an express after us, will please to let Mrs. Pike know of the opportunity.

I am, dear Sir,
With high respect,
Your obedient servant,
(Signed)   Z. M. PIKE.

(No. II.)

To General Wilkinson.

St. Charles, 19th July, 1806.—In the morning.

DEAR GENERAL,
ENCLOSED you have one of the articles, subscribed by Mr. Henry, mentioned in my note of yesterday. I hope the General may approve of the contents.

APPENDIX.

Lieutenant Wilkinson and Dr. Robinson marched (with one soldier) this morning, and the boats have proceeded under the conduct of Bellenger; I shall overtake them in an hour or two.

Numerous reports have been made to the Indians, calculated to impress them with an idea that there is a small army of their enemies waiting to receive us at the entrance of the Grand Osage. But I have partly succeeded in scouting the idea from their minds.

No news of Chouteau nor the Pawnees' trunks.

I am, dear General,
Your obedient servant,
(Signed)   Z. M. PIKE.

(No. III.)

To General Wilkinson.

Village de Charette, evening of the 22d July, 1806.

DEAR SIR,

FINDING no prospect of meeting with a private conveyance for our letters, in time sufficient to find you previous to your setting sail, which would be entirely too late to secure my deserter, and give you the other information they contain, I have hired the bearer to ride express to Belle Fontaine, for which I have promised him eight dollars; which, taking into view his ferriages, &c., cannot be deemed high, and I hope the General will please to order the military agent to discharge the same.

The weather has at length become settled, and we set sail to-morrow with our boats newly, and much better, arranged.

I am, General, with sincere esteem,
And high respect,
Your obedient servant,
(Signed)   Z. M. PIKE.

To General Wilkinson.

Village de Charette, 22d July, 1806.

DEAR GENERAL,

I HAVE the honour to acknowledge the receipt of your two obliging favours of the 18th and 19th instant, the particular contents of each shall be punctually attended to.

I assure you, Sir, that I am extremely pleased with the idea that Messrs. ——— and ——— will meet with their merited reward, and I on my part, am determined to shew them that it is not their sinister movements that can derange the objects of our voyage; the greatest embarrassment they have yet occasioned me has been by the detention of the Pawnees' baggage, who have been much mortified on the occasion. But I question much if under similar impressions and circumstances, many white men would have borne their loss with more philosophy than our young savages.

APPENDIX. 355

I conceive that I cannot dispose of one of my guns better than to give it to Frank, whose *fusee* was left at Chouteau's; also, each of them a soldier's coat; this is all the remuneration I will pretend to make them, and I hope it may bring them to a good humour.

You will probably be surprised at the slow progress we have made, but are already informed of the cause of our detention at St. Charles. We have since been detained two days, on account of the rain; and although we were able to prevent the water from entering immediately on the top of the boat where it was covered, yet the quantity which she made at both ends occasioned so much dampness under the loading as to injure both my own corn and that of the Indians, with other small articles, which they had at various times taken from under the loading, and not returned to their proper places; but they appear satisfied that we have paid all possible attention to prevent injury, as much, and indeed more, to their baggage than our own.

In consequence of the above, (and with a design to write you,) I halted here to-day, which I hope we shall usefully employ in drying our baggage, cleaning our arms, and putting ourselves in a posture of defence. Lieutenant Wilkinson has experienced no inconvenience from his march by land with the Indians, and the event has proved the necessity of some officer accompanying them, as he informs me he found it necessary to purchase some beeves for their consumption on the route, for which he drew on the superintendent of Indian affairs, and he will write to you more particularly on the subject. They were absent from the boat four days, and had he not been with them, they would have supplied themselves by marauding, to the great offence of our good citizens.

I am informed that a party of forty Sacs were at Boon's Lick, above the Osage river, a few days since, but I by no means conceive on the route to intercept us, as the people pretend at this place.

Three days since one of my men complained of indisposition, and went on shore to march; he has never joined the party, and from various reasons, I conceive has deserted. I have therefore enclosed an advertisement, which if the General will please to cause to be posted at St. Louis, Kaskaskias, and Lusk's Ferry on the Ohio, I conceive he will be caught.

I have written to Captain Daniel Bissell on the occasion, but hope the General will enforce my request to that gentleman, as to his being brought to trial. I was much mortified at the event, not only on account of the loss of the man, but that my peculiar situation prevented me from pursuing him, and making him an example.

With respect to the Ietans, the General may rest assured I shall use every precaution previous to trusting them, but as to the mode of conduct to be pursued towards the Spaniards, I feel more at a loss, as my instructions lead me into the country of the Ietans, part of which is no doubt claimed by Spain, although the boundaries between Louisiana and New Mexico have never yet been defined. In consequence of which, should I encounter a party from the villiages near Santa Fé, I have thought it would be good policy to give them to understand, that we were about to join our troops near Natchitoches, but had been uncertain about the head waters of the rivers over which we passed; but, that *now*, if the Commandant approved of it, we would pay him a visit of politeness, either by deputation, or the whole party, but if he refused, signify our intention of pursuing our direct route to the post below. At all events I flatter myself I may secure an unmolested retreat to Natchitoches. But if the Spanish jealousy, and the instigation of domestic traitors, should induce them to make us prisoners of war, (in time of peace,) I trust to the magnanimity of our country for our liberation, and a due reward to their opposers, for the insult and indignity offered their national honour. However, unless they give us ample assurances of just and honourable treatment, according to the custom of nations in like cases, I would resist, if even the inequality was as great as at the affair of Bender, or the Straits of Thermopylæ.

Will you pardon the foregoing as the enthusiasm of a youthful mind, yet, not altogether unimpressed by the dictates of prudence.

I hope the General will be persuaded, that with his son, I shall act as I would to a brother, endeavouring in all cases to promote his honour and prosperity.

I am, dear General,
Your sincere friend,
And obedient humble servant,
(Signed)   Z. M. PIKE.

N. B. In consequence of indisposition, &c., Lieutenant Wilkinson will steer one boat and I the other.

(No. IV.)

To General James Wilkinson.

Five leagues below the River Osage, 26th *July*, 1806.

DEAR GENERAL,

I HALT a moment, in order to say we have arrived thus far all safe, although our savages complain much of fatigue, &c.

The bearer had been sent by Mr. Sangonet to examine the Osage river, and reports that they could not get their canoes up the river more than sixty miles; if so, we have a bad prospect before us; but go we will, if God permits.

I am, dear General,
Your obedient servant,
(Signed)   Z. M. PIKE.

We have been detained several days by the Indians.

(No. V.)

To General James Wilkinson.

Park on the Osage river, 14th *Aug.*, 1806.

DEAR SIR,

BY Baptiste la Tulip I send this letter, who informs me he bears letters to Chouteau, informing him that a party of the Little Osages have marched to war against

APPENDIX. 357

the Kanses, and a party of the Grand Osages left the village expressly to make war on the white people on the Arkansaw. This latter step the White Hair did every thing in his power to prevent, but could not. If true, what are we to think of our *bons amis* the Osage?

But to ——— must we ascribe the stroke against the Kanses, who I am informed sent a message to the Osage nation to *rase* the Kanses village entirely. On this subject I intended to have been more particular, and substantiate it by proofs; but present circumstances seem to give credibility to it. On my arrival at the village more particular enquiry shall be made on the subject.

Yesterday morning Lieutenant Wilkinson, the Doctor, interpreter, and one soldier, marched with the Indians, as they were very apprehensive of an attack. The people in the canoe heard them crying, and saw them on their march.

Nothing extraordinary has yet taken place on our route, except our being favoured with a vast quantity of rain, which I hope will enable us to ascend to the village.

What face will the Indians receive us with? and to whom are we to ascribe their hostile disposition, unless the traitors of St. Louis?

Lieutenant Wilkinson is in very good health, and will lament his having missed this opportunity of assuring his parents of his love and affection.

I am, dear General,
Your obedient servant,
(Signed)   Z. M. PIKE.

(No. VI.)

To Lieutenant Pike.

Cantonment, Missouri, August 6, 1806.

SIR,

IN consequence of the receipt of the inclosed letters, I have thought proper to send you an express, to enable you to announce to the Osage the designs of their enemies, that they may take seasonable measures to circumvent them. You will not fail, in addition to the within talk, to enhance our paternal regard for this nation, by every proper expression; but are to keep clear of any conflict in which they may be involved, though you are to avoid the appearance of abandoning them. If it should be the Potowatomies' intention to carry their threat into execution, it is probable they will not attempt to make the blow before the falling of the leaves, and in the meantime the Osages should establish a chain of light scouts along the coast of the Missouri, to ascertain with certainty the approach of their enemy.

It is reduced to a certainty that ——— and a society of which he is the ostensible leader, have determined on a project to open some commercial intercourse with Santa Fé, and as this may lead to a connection injurious to the United States, and will, I understand, be attempted without the sanction of law or the permission of the executive, you must do what, consistently, you can to defeat the plan. No good can be derived to the United States from such a project, because the prosecution of it will

APPENDIX.

depend entirely on the Spaniards, and they will not permit it, unless to serve their political as well as their personal interests. I am informed that the ensuing autumn and winter will be employed in reconnoitring and opening a connection with the Ietans, Pawnees, &c.; that this fall, or the next winter, a grand magazine is to be established at the Osage towns, where these operations will commence; that ——— is to be the active agent, having formed a connection with the Ietans. This will carry forward their merchandize within three or four days' travel of the Spanish settlements, where they will deposit it, under a guard of three hundred Ietans. ——— will then go forward with four or five attendants, taking with him some jewelry and fine goods. With these he will visit the Governor, to whom he will make presents, and implore his pity by a fine tale of sufferings which have been endured by the change of government: that they are left here, with goods to be sure, but not a dollar's worth of bullion, and therefore they have adventured to see him, for the purpose of praying his leave for the introduction of their property into the province. If he assents, then the whole of the goods will be carried forward; if he refuses, then ——— will invite some of his countrymen to accompany him to his deposit, and having there exposed to them his merchandize, he will endeavour to open a forced or clandestine trade; for he observes the Spaniards will not dare to attack his camp. Here you have the plan, and you must take all prudent and lawful means to blow it up.

In regard to your approximation to the Spanish settlements, should your route lead you near them, or should you fall in with any of their parties, your conduct must be marked by such circumspection and discretion, as may prevent alarm or conflict, as you will be held responsible for consequences. On this subject I refer you to my orders. We have nothing new respecting the pending negotiations in Europe, but from Colonel Cushing I understand the Spaniards below are behaving now with great courtesy.

By the return of the bearer you may open your correspondence with the secretary of war; but I would caution you against anticipating a step before you, for fear of deception and disappointment. To me you may, and must, write fully and freely, not only giving a minute detail of every thing past worthy of note, but also of your prospects and the conduct of the Indians. If you discover that any tricks have been played from St. Louis, you will give them to me with names, and must not fail to give particulars to the secretary of war, with names, to warn him against improper confidence and deception. Enclose your despatch for me to Colonel Hunt, and it will follow me by a party which I leave for the purpose. It is interesting to you to reach Natchitoches in season to be at the seat of government pending the session of Congress; yet you must not sacrifice any essential object to this point. Should fortune favour you on your present excursion, your importance to our country will, I think, make your future life comfortable.

To shew you how to correct your watch by the quadrant, after it has been carefully adjusted, preparatory to your observing on the eclipses of the satellites of Jupiter, I send you a very simple plan, which you will readily understand: a bason of water, in some place protected from the motion of the air, will give you a fairer artificial horizon than Mercury. I think a tent, with a suitable aperture in the side of it, would do very well. I have generally unroofed a cabin. Miranda has botched his business. He has lost his two schooners captured, and himself in the Leander returned to Jamaica. The French have a squadron of four frigates at Porto Rico, and of five sail of the line with Jerome Bonaparte at Martinique. I consider them lost.

Your children have been indisposed; but Mrs. Pike writes you. She appears well. My regards to your associates, and may God protect you.

(Signed)   J. WILKINSON.

(No. VII.)

To General Wilkinson.

Camp Independence, near the Osage Towns, August 28, 1806.

DEAR GENERAL,

YOU will, no doubt, be much surprised to perceive by the date of this letter that we are still here: but we have been unavoidably detained by a variety of circumstances.

I had the happiness to receive your express the day of my arrival, the bearer having arrived the night before, and have attended particularly to its contents.

On the 19 inst. I delivered your *parole* to the Cheveu Blanc, and on the 21st held a grand council of both towns, and made the necessary communications and demands for horses, on the subject of making peace with the Kanses, accompanying me to the Pawnees, down the Arkansaw, and if there were any *brave* enough to accompany me the whole voyage.

They requested one day to hold council in the villages previous to giving an answer. Three days passed before I received any; their determination was as follows:—From the Grand Osage village, or the Cheveu Blanc, we are accompanied by his son, and *Jean Le Fou*, the second chief of the village, with some young men not known, and he furnishes us four horses.

The Little Osage send the brother of the chief (whom I really find to be the third chief of the village) and some young men unknown, and furnish *six* horses!! This is their present promise, but four of the ten are yet deficient. With these I am merely capable of transporting our merchandize and ammunition. I shall purchase two more, for which I find we shall be obliged to pay extravagant prices.

I sincerely believe that the two chiefs, White Hair and The Wind, have exerted all their influence; but it must be but little when they could only procure ten horses out of seven or eight hundred.

I have taken an exact survey of the river to this place, noting particular streams, &c., a protracted copy of which Lieutenant Wilkinson forwards by this opportunity. Since our arrival here I have ascertained the variation of the compass to be 6° 30' E., the latitude, by means of several observations, 37° 26' 17" N., and by an observation of three different nights, obtained two immersions of Jupiter's satellites, which will enable us to ascertain every geographical object in view.

APPENDIX.

On the same night I arrived near the village, there was a Mr. Baptiste Du Chouquet, alias Larme, with two men, arrived in a small canoe, and went immediately to the lodge of the White Hair, whose conduct, with that of our resident interpreter, appears (in my estimation) to have changed since I sent Lieutenant Wilkinson to demand to see Baptiste's passport, if he had one: if not, to bring him to camp, which was done. I detained him two days, until I had made an enquiry of White Hair, who said he had merely mentioned to him that Labardie was coming with a quantity of goods. Finding I could substantiate nothing more criminal against him than his having entered the Indian boundaries without a passport, and not being able to send him back a prisoner, I detained him a sufficient time to alarm him, and then took his deposition (a copy of which is enclosed to the attorney-general), and wrote Dr. Brown on the occasion, and requested him to enter a prosecution against these men.

Barroney informs me that he has not the least doubt but ——— was at the bottom of this embassy, although in the name of ———, as after the arrival of Baptiste, the Indians frequently spoke of ———, and declared, if he had come, he could have obtained horses plenty.

Our interpreter, also, (Maugraine,) I do believe to be a perfect creature of ———; he has almost positively refused to accompany me, (although I read your order on the subject,) alleging he was only engaged to interpret at this place, notwithstanding he went last year to the Arkansaw for Mr. Chouteau without difficulty. I have not yet determined on the line of conduct to be pursued with him, but believe, on his giving a positive refusal, I shall use military law. What the result will be is uncertain; but to be thus braved by a scoundrel will be lessening the dignity of our government. He is married into a powerful family, and appears, next to the White Hair, to have the most influence in the Grand village. The General will please to observe that much of the foregoing rests on conjecture, and therefore will give it its due weight. But to him I not only write as my General, but as a paternal friend, who would not make use of my open communications, when not capable of being substantiated by proofs.

We have heard nothing of the Potowatomies; but should they come in a few days, they will meet with a warm reception, as all are ready to receive them.

Since my arrival here many Spanish medals have been shown me, and some commissions. All I have done on the subject is merely to advise their delivery below, when they would be acknowledged by our government. Many have applied for permission to go to Saint Louis, none of which I have granted, except to the son of Sans Oreille, who goes down to make enquiry for his sister.

I have advanced our express some things on account, and forward his receipts; also, some trifles to Barroney, whom I have found to be one of the finest young men I ever knew in his situation, and appears to have entirely renounced all his Saint Louis connections, and is as firm an American as if born one: he of course is entirely discarded by the people of Saint Louis, but I hope he will not suffer for his fidelity.

On the chart forwarded by Lieutenant Wilkinson is noted the census which I caused to be taken of the village of the Little Osage; that of the Grand Osage I shall likewise obtain—they are from actual enumeration. Lieutenant Wilkinson will (if nothing extraordinary prevents) descend the Arkansaw, accompanied by Ballenger and two men, as the former is now perfectly acquainted with the mode of taking courses and protracting his route, and the latter appears as if he had not the proper capacity for it, although a good dispositioned and brave man.

           I am, dear sir,
             Your obedient servant,
         (Signed)   Z. M. PIKE.

To General Wilkinson.

                   29th August, 1806.
  DEAR SIR,

I WILL continue my communications, by relating that The Wind has come in and informed me that the other two horses which he promised have been withdrawn by their owners. He appeared really distressed, and I conceive I do him justice in believing that he is extremely mortified at the deceptions which have been passed on him.

It is with extreme pain I keep myself *cool* amongst the difficulties which these people appear to have a disposition to throw in my way; but I have declared to them that I shall go on, even if I collect our tents and other baggage (which we shall be obliged to leave together) and burn them on the spot.

I have sold the batteau which I brought up (and which was extremely rotten) for one hundred dollars, in merchandize, the price of this place, which I conceive was preferable to leaving her to destruction, as I am afraid I do the barge (for which I demanded one hundred and fifty dollars), although I leave her under charge of The Wind and shall report her to Colonel Hunt.

I shall despatch the express to-morrow, as he complains much of the detention, &c., and as I hope nothing worthy of note will occur at this place previous to our departure, I hope the General will believe me to be, and should this be my last report to have been, his sincerely attached friend and

              Obedient servant,
         (Signed)   Z. M. PIKE.

To General J. Wilkinson.

               Osage Towns, 30*th August*, 1806.
  DEAR SIR,

I HAVE brought Mr. Noal, alias Maugraine, to reason, and he either goes himself or hires, at his expence, a young man who is here who speaks the Pawnees language, and in many other respects is preferable to himself; but he will be the bearer of the express to Saint Louis.

The Cheveu Blanc requested me to inform you that there is a murderer (an Osage) in his village, who killed a Frenchman on the Arkansaw; but owing to the great dissensions and schisms of the Arkansaw faction, he is fearful to deliver him up, without some of his friends having agreed to it, and his authority being strengthened by a formal demand from you, when he assures me he shall be brought down a prisoner. Indeed the Cheveu Blanc appears to be very delicately situated, as the village on the Arkansaw serves as a place of refuge for all the young, daring, and discontented; and added to which, they are much more regularly supplied with ammunition, and, should not our government take some steps to prevent it, they will ruin the Grand village, as they are at liberty to make war without restraint, especially on the nations who are to the west, and have plenty of horses. The Chief says he was promised, at Washington, that these people should be brought back to join him; but, at present, many of his village are emigrating there.

Owing to the difficulty of obtaining horses, Mr. Henry returns from this place. In-descending the Mississippi I will request him to pay his respects to you.

I last evening took the census of the Grand village, and found it to be

Men 502
Boys......................341
Women and Girls..........852

Total............1,695

Lodges................214

The express waits, which I hope the General will accept as an excuse for this scrawl, having witten him fully on the 28th and 29th inst.

I am, dear General,
Your ever sincere friend and obedient servant,
(Signed)   Z. M. PIKE, Lt.

(No. VIII.)

To the Hon. Henry Dearborn, Secretary War Department.

Pawnee Republic, 1st Oct., 1806.

SIR,

WE arrived here on the 25th ult. after a tedious march of three hundred and seventy-five miles, the distance (as I conceive) being very much augmented by the Osages, who accompanied us, leading us too far to the south, owing to their great fear of the Kanses. We suffered considerably with thirst, but our guns furnished us amply with buffalo meat.

We delivered in safety, to the Chief, the two young Pawnees who had lately visited Washington, and caused to be explained to the nation, the parole which they bore from the President of the United States.

On our arrival, we found the Spanish and American flags both expanded in the village, and were much surprised to learn, that it was not more than three or four weeks, since a party of Spanish troops (whose number were estimated by the Indians of this town at three hundred) had returned to Santa Fé; and further learnt that a large body of troops had left New Mexico, and on their march had met with the villagers of the Pawnee Mahaws, who were on one of their semi-annual excursions; that they encamped together, and entered into a treaty; but after this, the Pawnees raised their camp in the night, and stole a large portion of the Spaniards' horses. This circumstance induced them to halt on the Arkansaw with the main body of the troops, and to send forward the party who appeared at this village; who proposed to this Chief to join a party of his warriors to their troops, march to and entirely destroy the village of the Pawnee Mahaws; this proposition he had prudence enough to reject, although at war with that nation. The Spanish officer informed him that his superior, who remained at the Arkansaw, had marched from Santa Fé, with an intention of entering into a treaty with the following nations of Indians, viz.: The Kanses, the Pawnee Republic, the Grand Pawnees, Pawnee Loups, Otoes, and Mahaws; and had with him a grand medal, commissions, and four mules for each; but by the stroke of the Pawnee Mahaws, the plan was disconcerted, except only as to this nation. The commissions are dated Santa Fé, 15th June, 1806, and signed Governor General, &c., &c., of New Mexico, and run in the usual style of Spanish commissions to savages, as far as I was capable of judging of their contents.

The Chief further informed me, that the officer who commanded the said party, was too young to hold councils, &c.; that he had *only* come to open the road, but that in the spring his superior would be here, and teach the Indians what was good for them; and that they would build a town near them. In short, it appears to me to have been an expedition expressly for the purpose of striking a dread into those different nations of the Spanish power, and to bring about a general combination in their favour. Under these impressions, I have taken the earliest opportunity of reporting the infringement of our territory, in order that our government may not remain in the dark, as to the views of her neighbour. I effected a meeting at this place, between a few Kanses and Osages, who smoked the pipe of peace and buried the hatchet, agreeably to the wishes of their great father; in consequence of which a Kans has marched for the Osage nation, and some of the latter propose to accompany the former to their village; whether this good understanding will be permanent, I will not take on me to determine; but, at least, a temporary good effect has succeeded. From the Osage towns, I have taken the courses and distances, by the route we came, marking each river or rivulet we crossed, pointing out the dividing ridges, &c. The waters which we crossed were the head of the Osage, White, and Verdigrise rivers, (branches of the Arkansaw,) and the waters of the Kanses river. The latitude of this place, I presume, will be in about 30° 30' N., and I hope to obtain every other astronomical observation, which will be requisite to fix its geographical situation beyond dispute. I expect to march from here in a few days, but the future prospects of the voyage are entirely uncertain, as the savages strive to throw every impediment in our way, agreeably to the orders received from the Spanairds. Being seated on the ground, and writing on the back of a book, I hope will plead my excuse for this scrawl.

I am, sir, with high respect,
Your obedient servant,
(Signed) Z. M. PIKE.

APPENDIX.

To General J. Wilkinson.

Pawnee Republic, 2d Oct., 1806.

DEAR GENERAL,

INCLOSED you have a copy of my letter from this place, to the secretary of war, in order that should you think any communication on the contents necessary, you may have a perfect command of the information given the war department, and will be the more capable of illustrating the subject.

You will perceive by the said communication, that we were led considerably out of our course by our guides, and in my opinion not less than one hundred miles; this was entirely owing to the pusillanimity of the Osages, who were more afraid of the Kanses than I could possibly have imagined.

You will likewise perceive the council which took place between those nations (under our auspices) and its effects, but which I candidly confess, I have very little hopes will be productive of a permanent peace, as none of the principal men of either nation were present; but as both are anxious for a cessation of hostilities, perhaps it may have the desired effect.

Two of the Kanses chiefs have said they will pursue the voyage with me agreeably to my orders; I do not yet know whether they will descend the Arkansaw with Lieutenant Wilkinson, or continue on to Red river with me, but they have their own selection.

The General will no doubt be struck with some surprise to perceive that so large a party of Spanish troops have been so lately in our territory; no doubt at first you would conclude that it must have been militia; but when informed that their infantry was armed with muskets and bayonets, and had drums; that the men wore long mustaches and whiskers, which almost covered the whole of their faces; their cavalry armed with swords and pistols, and that regular guards and patroles were kept by horse and foot, you may probably change your opinion.

The route by which they came, and returned, was by no means the direct one to Santa Fé, and why they should have struck so low down as the Grand Saline, unless they had an idea of striking at the village of the Grand Pest, or conceived the Saline in their territory, I cannot imagine.

On our arrival here, we were received with great pomp and ceremony, by about three hundred men on horseback, and with great apparent friendship by the Chief. The Osage (one chief and four warriors) were presented with eight horses, the Kanses who arrived two days after, were also presented with horses. The day after, we assembled the four principal chiefs to dine, after which, I presented the Principal with a double barrelled gun, gorget, and other articles, (this man wore the grand Spanish medal,) and to the second the small medal you furnished me, with other articles; and to each of the others a gorget in their turn. Those presents I conceived would have a good effect, both as to attaching them to our government, and in our immediate intercourse.

At the council, which was held a day or two afterwards, I presented them with merchandize, (which at this place should be valued at two hundred and fifty dollars,)

APPENDIX.

and after explaining their relative situation as to the Spanish and American governments, I asked on my part, if they would assist us with a few horses, an Ietan prisoner who spoke Pawnee, to serve as an interpeter, an exchange of colours, and finally, for some of their chiefs to accompany us, to be sent to Washington. The exchange of the colours was the only request granted at the time; and for particular reasons (which Lieutenant Wilkinson related) I thought proper to return them to the Chief; and after spending two or three anxious days, we were given to understand, that our requests could not be complied with in the other points, and were again strongly urged by the head Chief to return the way we came, and not prosecute our voyage any further. This brought on an explanation as to our views towards the Spanish government, in which the Chief declared, that it was the intention of the Spanish troops to have proceeded further towards the Mississippi, but that he objected to it, and they listened to him and returned; he therefore hoped we would be equally reasonable. But finding I still determined on proceeding, he told me in plain terms (if the interpreter erred not) that it was the will of the Spaniards we should not proceed; which not answering, he painted innumerable difficulties which he said lay in the way; but finding all his arguments had no effect, he said, "It was a pity," and was silent.

This day I sent out several of my party to purchase horses, but know not how we shall succeed, as the Kanses have intimated an' idea, that the Chief will prohibit his people from trading with us.

The Pawnees and the Ietans are at war; the latter killed six of the former in August last, consequently the effecting any communication with the Ietans by means of this nation is impossible.

If God permits, we shall march from here in a few days, and at the Arkansaw I shall remain until I build two small canoes for Lieutenant Wilkinson (whose party will consist of Ballenger and two or three men, with three Osage). Those canoes will be easily managed, and in case of accident to one, the other will still be sufficient to transport their baggage.

I am informed, that in a few days he will meet French hunters, and probably arrive at the village of the Grand Pest in a fortnight; and as all the Osage nation are apprized of his descent, I conceive he will meet with no insurmountable difficulties.* The Ietans are at open war with the Spaniards, so that could we once obtain an introduction, I conceive we should meet with a favourable reception. Yet how it is to be brought about, I am much at a loss to determine, but knowing that, at this crisis of affairs, an intimate connection with that nation might be extremely serviceable to my country, I shall proceed to find them; in hopes to discover some means through the French, Osage, and Pawnee languages, of making ourselves understood.

Any number of men (who may reasonably be calculated on) would find no difficulty in marching the route we came with baggage waggons, field artillery, and all the usual appendages of a small army; and if all the route to Santa Fé should be of

---

* This was erroneous, but it was my impression at the time.

APPENDIX.

the same description, in case of war, I would pledge my life (and what is infinitely dearer, my honour) for the successful march of a reasonable body of troops, into the Province of New Mexico.

I find the savages of this country less brave, but possessing much more duplicity, and by far a greater propensity to lying and stealing, than those I had to pass through in my last voyage.

I am extremely doubtful if any chief of these nations can be induced to prosecute the voyage with us, as their dread of the Ietans, and the objections of the Pawnees, seem to outweigh every argument and inducement to the contrary.

October 3d—The Pawnee Chief has induced the Kanses to return to their villages, by giving them a gun and promising horses, with many frightful pictures drawn if they proceeded.

The Osages lent me five horses, which their people who accompanied us were to have led back, but receiving fresh ones from the Pawnees, they would not be troubled with them. In fact, it was a fortunate circumstance, as four of the horses I obtained of the Osage have such bad backs they cannot proceed, and we shall be obliged to leave them; and not purchasing here with facility, I should have been obliged to have sacrificed some of our baggage. I therefore sent them a certificate for each horse, on the Indian agent below, which I hope the General will order him to discharge.

I know the General's goodness will excuse this scrawl, as he is well acquainted with the situation it must be written in, and at the same time, believe me to be his sincere friend and

           Most obedient humble servant,
  (Signed)   Z. M. PIKE.

(No. IX.)

To General J. Wilkinson.

Arkansaw, 24th Oct., 1806. Latitude 37° 44′ 9″ N.

DEAR GENERAL,

OUR party arrived here on the 15th inst., myself and Dr. Robinson on the 19th, we having been out to seek the trace of the Spanish troops, missed the party, and were not able to join them until the fourth day.

The river being very regular, Lieutenant Wilkinson had calculated to proceed on the day following, on the most direct route for the Red river, but shortly after my joining considerable rain fell and raised the river, and we have been ever since preparing wooden and skin canoes for that gentleman and party to descend in.

The river is between three and four hundred yards in width; generally flat low banks, not more than two or three feet high, and the bed a sand-bank from one side to the other. *

The want of water will present the greatest obstacle to the progress of the party who descend the Arkansaw, as they have no cause to fear a scarcity of provision,

APPENDIX.

having some bushels of corn on hand, and at their option to take as much dried meat as they think proper, hundreds of pounds of which are lying on scaffolds at our camp; and they are likewise accompanied by the choice of our hunters.

Under these circumstances, and those stated in my letter from the Pawnees, I can assert with confidence, there are no obstacles I should hesitate to encounter, although those inseparable from a voyage of several hundred leagues through a wilderness inhabited only by savages, may appear of the greatest magnitude to minds unaccustomed to such enterprizes.

Lieutenant Wilkinson and party appear in good spirits, and shew a disposition which must vanquish every difficulty.

We were eight days travelling from the Pawnee village to the Arkansaw, (our general course S. 10° W.,) several of which we lay by nearly half, owing to various circumstances; my course made it one hundred and fifty miles, but could now march it in one hundred and twenty. Lieutenant Wilkinson has copied and carries with him a very elegant protracted sketch of the route, noting the streams, hills, &c., that we crossed; their courses, bearings, &c., and should I live to arrive, I will pledge myself to shew their connections, and general direction with considerable accuracy, as I have myself spared no pains in reconnoitring or obtaining information from the savages in our route.

From this point, we shall ascend the river until we strike the mountains, or find the Ietans; and from thence bear more to the S. until we find the head of the Red river, where we shall be detained some time, after which nothing shall cause a halt until my arrival at Natchitoches.

I speak in all these cases in the positive mood, as, so far as lies in the compass of human exertions, we command the power; but I pretend not to surmount impossibilities, and I well know the General would pardon my anticipating a little to him.

The General will probably be surprised to find that the expenses of the expedition will more than double the contemplated sum of our first calculations, but I conceived the Spaniards were making such great exertions to debauch the minds of our savages, that economy might be very improperly applied. And I likewise have found the purchase of horses to be attended with much greater expense than was expected at St. Louis. For these reasons, and when I advert to the expenses of my two voyages, (which I humbly conceive might be compared with the one performed by Captains Lewis and Clark,) and the appropriations made for theirs, I feel a consciousness, that it is impossible for the most rigid to censure my accounts.

I cannot yet say if I shall sacrifice my horses at Red river, but every exertion shall be made to save them for the public; some if in good condition would be fine ones, and average between fifty and sixty dollars. Should the fortune of war at length honour me with a company, I hope the General will recollect his promise to me, and have the men now under my command attached to it; and on my arrival I shall take the liberty of soliciting his influence, that they may obtain the same, or similar rewards, to those conferred on the men who accompanied Captain Lewis, as I will

APPENDIX.

make bold to say, that they have in two voyages, incurred as great dangers, and gone through as many hardships.

I am, dear General,
Your ever attached friend and obedient servant,
Z. M. PIKE.

N. B. Dr. Robinson presents his respectful compliments, and is sanguine in the success of our expedition.

(No. X.)

The following report was written by Lieutenant Wilkinson at a time when it was expected I had been cut off by the savages. In consequence of which it alludes to transactions relative to the expedition previously to our separation, which I have since corrected, but the adventures of his party after our separation are given in his own words.

Z. M. PIKE.

To His Excellency General Wilkinson,
Commander in Chief of the United States' Army.

New Orleans, April 6th, 1807.

SIR,

AGREEABLY to your order dated in June, 1806, I took my departure from Belle Fontaine, under the command of Lieutenant Pike, early in July. The Missouri being well up, we found the navigation as favourable as could have been expected. On the 28th of the same month we reached the mouth of the Osage river, which we found a pellucid, tranquil stream, with the exception of a few trifling ripples, and a fall of about six feet in two-thirds of a mile, called the Old Man's rapid. The river abounds with various kinds of good fish, especially the soft shell turtle, which we took in great numbers. The banks of the river are generally formed by craggy cliffs, and not unfrequently, you perceive stupendous rocks projecting over the water, out of which issue excellent springs. The most remarkable natural curiosity which I observed, is a pond of water, about three hundred toises in circumference, six miles above the Yungar, on a rising piece of ground considerably above the level of the river, which keeps one continued height, is perfectly pure and transparent, and has no outlet, by which to discharge itself.

On the 12th of August, the Osages appeared dissatisfied with the tedious movement of our barges, and expressed a wish to cross the prairie to their villages, in case an escort was allowed them. I immediately volunteered my services, and we parted with the boats at the mouth of Grande river, the spot where our ransomed prisoners were taken the preceding winter by the Potowatomies.

We reached the village of the Little Osages, after a fatiguing and laborious march of six days across an arid prairie.

APPENDIX. 369

When within a mile of the town, the Chief Tuttasuggy, or The Wind, desired a regular procession might be observed, and accordingly he placed me between himself and his first warrior, and the ransomed captives followed by files. Half a mile from the village we were met by one hundred and fifty horsemen, painted and decorated in a very fanciful manner. These were considered as a guard of honour, and on our approach opened to the right and left, leaving us a sufficient space to pass through.

A few hundred yards in advance on the right I perceived sixty or more horsemen, painted with a blue chalk, which when the Chief observed, he commanded a halt, and sent forward his younger brother Nezuma, or the Rain that Walks, with a flag and silk handkerchief, as a prize for the swiftest horseman. At a given signal they started off at full speed, the two foremost taking the flag and handkerchief, and the rest contenting themselves with having shewn their agility and skill.

As I entered the village, I was saluted by a discharge from four swivels, (which the Indians had taken from an old fort erected by the Spaniards on the river,) and passed through a crowd of nearly a thousand persons, part of whom I learnt were of the 'Grand village. I was immediately, but with ceremony, ushered into the lodge of the Soldier of the Oak, who, after having paid me some very handsome compliments, courteously invited me to eat of green corn, buffalo meat, and water melons about the size of a twenty-four pound shot, which, though small, were highly flavoured.

After Lieutenant Pike's arrival with the boats we formed our camp on the bank of the river equi-distant from the villages of the Grand and Little Osages, and he selected a situation for making his observations, which he did not complete until the 28th of the month. The 29th and 30th were devoted to packing as conveniently and carefully as possible the mathematical instruments and a small quantity of provisions. And on the 1st of September, we commenced our march for the Pawnee Republic, and entered on that vast and extensive prairie, which lies between the Missouri and the Rio del Norte.

We coursed the Osage river to its source, and almost immediately after crossed some of the small branches of Grande river, which enters the Arkansaw about seven hundred miles from the Mississippi. After passing the Grande river, which we found to be sixty or eighty yards wide, we marched a whole day before we reached the waters of the Kanses, and were agreeably suprised to find ourselves on the bank of a bold running stream. Between this and the village of the Pawnees, we crossed two strongly impregnated salines, which passed over a sandy country, almost destitute of herbage' and after a painful march under an oppressive sun, over an irregular and broken surface, we arrived at the town of the Republican Pawnees on the 25th of September. We were met the day before by a number of warriors, whom curiosity had led thus far to see us, among whom was the third consequential character of the Republican party; for you must know that the village is composed of the followers of a dissatisfied warrior who first made this establishment, and the adherents of a regular chief of the Grand Pawnees, who migrated thither some few years since with his family, and usurped the power of the Republican warrior. To such a pitch does this party spirit prevail, that you easily perceive the hostility which exists between the adherents of the two chiefs. Early on the morning of the 25th we were joined by a few more savages of distinction, headed by the brother of Characterick, or the White Wolf, Chief of the nation, who was to act as master of the ceremonies to our formal entry. Preparatory to our march, we had our men equipped as neatly as circumstances would admit. About mid-day we reached the summit of a lofty chain of ridges, where we were requested to halt and wait the arrival of the Chief, who was half a mile from us, with three hundred horsemen, who were generally naked, (except having buffalo robes and breech cloths,) and painted with white, yellow, blue, and black clay. At the word of the Chief the warriors divided, and pushing on at full speed, flanked us on the right and left, yelling in a most diabolical manner. The Chief advanced in front, accompanied by Iskatappe or the Rich man, the second great personage of the village, and his sons, who were clothed in scarlet cloth. They approached slowly, and when within a hundred yards, the three latter halted, and Characterick advanced in great state, and when within a few paces of us stretched out his hand and cried "bon jour;" thus ended the first ceremony. We moved on a mile further, and having gained the summit of a considerable hill we discovered the village directly at its base. We were here again halted, and the few Osages who accompanied us were ordered in front and seated in rank entire. The Chief squatted on his hams in front of them, and filled a calumet, which several different Indians took from him and handed to the Osages to smoke. This was called *Horse Smoke*, as each person who took the pipe from the Chief intended presenting the Osages a horse. Mr. Pike and Dr. Robinson afterwards accompanied the Chief to his lodge, and I moved on with the detachment, and formed our camp on the opposite bank of the Republican fork of the Kanses river, on a commanding hill, which had been selected as the most favourable situation for making observations, though very inconvenient on account of wood and water, which we had to transport nearly a quarter of a mile.

At a council held some few days after our arrival, Lieutenant Pike explained to them the difference of their situation to what it had been a few years past. That now they must look up to the President of the United States as their great father, and that he had been sent by him, to assure them of his good wishes, &c., &c. That he perceived a Spanish flag flying at the council lodge door, and was anxious to exchange one of their great father's for it, and that it was our intention to proceed on further to the westward, to examine this our newly acquired country. To this, a singular and extraordinary response was given; in fact, an objection started in direct opposition to our proceeding farther to the west; however they gave up the Spanish flag, and we had the pleasure to see the American standard hoisted in its stead.

At the same council, Characterick observed, that a large body of Spaniards had lately been at his village, and that they promised to return and build a town adjoining his. The Spanish Chief, he said, mentioned that he was not empowered to counsel with him; that he came merely to break the road for his master, who would visit him in the spring with a large army, and that he further told him the Americans were a little people, but were enterprizing, and one of those days would stretch themselves even to his town, and that they took the lands of Indians and would drive off their game. And how very true, said Characterick, has the Spanish Chieftain spoken? We demanded to purchase a few horses, which was prohibited us, and the friendly communication which had existed between the town and our camp was stopped. The conduct of our neighbours assumed a mysterious change; our guards were several times alarmed, and finally appearances became so menacing as to make it necessary for us to be on our guard day and night.

It was obvious that the body of Spaniards who preceded us but a few weeks in their mission to this village, were the regular cavalry and infantry of the Province of Santa Fé, as they had formed their camps in regular order; and we were informed they kept regular guards, and that the beats of their drums were uniform morning and evening. The Spanish leader further delivered to Characterick, a grand medal, two mules, and a commission bearing the signature of the Governor, civil and military, of Santa Fé. He also had similar marks of distinction for the Grand Pawnees, the Pawnee Mahaws, Mahaws proper, Ottoes, and Kanses.

On the 6th of October we made some few purchases of miserable horses at the most exorbitant prices, and on the 7th, unmoved by the threats of the Chief relative to our proceeding farther to the west, we marched in a close and compact body until we passed their village, and took the large Spanish beaten trace for the Arkansaw river. We passed the following day, an encampment of the Spaniards, where we counted sixty-nine fires. On the 9th, as usual, made an easy march, and about noon when we halted to refresh ourselves, were overtaken by three hundred Pawnees, on their way to the salines of the Kanses to hunt buffalo. Their every act shewed a strong disposition to quarrel, and in fact they seemed to court hostility, but finding us without fear, and prepared to a man, they offered no outrage, and having grazed our horses an hour we parted from this turbulant band. Slung our packs and proceeded on to Solomon's fork of the Kanses, and pitched our tents on an old encampment of the Spaniards, whose trace we were following, as we found the next morning many tent pins, made of wood different from any in that country. At mid-day, Lieutenant Pike, Dr. Robinson, and the interpreter Baroney, pushed on to search for water, and I remained with the troops. I pushed on as briskly as our poor half famished horses would permit, and at night-fall could discover nothing of Mr. Pike, and had not a tree in view. This induced me to quicken my pace, and as darkness had rendered my compass useless, I coursed by the Polar star, but the horizon becoming overcast, I halted on a naked stony prairie, without water or grass for our horses. On the following morning I directed my course more to the southward, and about ten o'clock came to the creek and encampment of Lieutenant Pike. Late in the evening of the same day, after passing over a mountainous tract of country, we reached the Grand saline, which we found so strongly impregnated, as to render corn unpalatable when boiled in it. On the 12th, after a distressing day's march, we reached the second or small saline, and on the following day encamped on the most western branch of the Kanses river.

APPENDIX.

We were detained on the morning of the 13th by a small rain, but as time was pressing, we marched about noon, crossed the dividing ridge of the Kanses and Arkansaw rivers, and halted on a small branch of the latter.

For several days past we had been so bewildered by buffalo paths, that we had lost the Spanish trace, and this being an object of moment, we resolved to make search for it. Accordingly, on the following day at noon, Mr. Pike and Dr. Robinson struck off from the party a due west course, and I marched the detachment for a copse of wood, which we could barely discern in the south-west, and reached it about midnight.

At day-break I was awoke by my old and faithful Osage, who informed me that we were on the banks of the Arkansaw river. I immediately arose and discovered my tent to have been pitched on the margin of a watercourse, nearly four hundred yards wide, with banks not three feet high, and a stream of water running through it, about twenty feet in width, and not more than six or eight inches deep.

I remained here four days in great anxiety and suspense, as neither Mr. Pike nor Dr. Robinson made their appearance, nor could be found, although I had all my hunters in search of them; but I was agreeably surprised on the fifth day early in the morning, by their arrival. It appeared our apprehensions were mutual, as they expected I had been cut off, and I believed they had been murdered.

On the 17th it commenced raining and continued for several days, during which time the river rose so much as to fill its bed from bank to bank. Lieutenant Pike having determined that I should descend the Arkansaw, we cut down a small green cotton wood, and with much labour split out a canoe, which being insufficient, we formed a second of buffalo and elk skins. .

After the rain had ceased, the weather became extremely cold, and on the 27th in the evening, a severe snow storm commenced, and continued nearly all night. In the morning the river was almost choaked with drifting ice, but the sun bursting out at noon, the ice disappeared. I took leave of Mr. Pike, who marched up the river, at the moment I embarked on board my newly constructed canoe; but unfortunately we had not proceeded more than one hundred yards when my boats grounded, and the men were obliged to drag them through sand and ice five miles to a copse of wood on the south-western bank. I here hauled up my canoe, formed a kind of cabin of it, and wrapped myself up in my buffalo robe, disheartened and dissatisfied with the commencement of my voyage. The night was severely cold, and in the morning the river was so full of ice, as to prevent all possibility of proceeding. The day continued stormy, with snow from the north-west.

On the 30th the river was frozen up, and towards evening the water had run off, and left the bed of the river covered with ice. This circumstance determined me to leave my canoes, and course the river by land. Accordingly, on the 31st of October, after having thrown away all my cloathing and provision, except half a dozen tin cups of hard corn for each man; I slung my rifle on my shoulder, and with my buffalo robe at my back, and circumferenter in my hand, I recommenced my march with a light and cheerful heart. My only apprehension was the meeting with

APPENDIX.

detached bands of the Pawnees, who I am confident would have brought myself and my five men to action, and the consequence was very obvious.

On the 1st, 2d and 3d of November, I marched over high and barren hills of sand, and at the close of each day, passed strongly impregnated salines, and perceived the shores or the river to be completely frosted with nitre. The face of the country as I descended looked more desolate than above; the eye being scarcely able to discern a tree, and if one was discovered, it proved to be a solitary cotton-wood, stinted in growth by the sterility of the soil. The evening of the 3d instant, I encamped on the bank of the river, without a tree or even a shrub in view. On the 4th we experienced heavy rain, but hunger and cold pressed me forward. After marching ten miles, I reached a small tree, where I remained in a continued rain for two days. At the expiration of this time, having exhausted my fuel, I had again to push off in a severe storm, and formed my camp at the mouth of a bold running stream, whose northern bank was skirted by a chain of lofty ridges.

On the 8th, in the morning, it having cleared up, I began my march early, and it appeared as if we had just gotten into the region of game, for the herds of buffalo, elk, goat, and deer, surpassed credibility. I do solemnly assert, that if I saw one I saw more than nine thousand buffaloes during the day's march.

On the 10th in the evening, after a severe day's march, I encamped on the bank of a large creek, and discovered for the first time on the river, a species of wood differing from the cotton tree. I assure you the sight was more agreeable than a person would imagine; it was like meeting with an old acquaintance, from whom you had been separated a length of time. I even began to think myself approximating civilized settlements, although I was just entering on the hunting ground of the Osages. The buffalo and goats disappeared on the 12th, or rather we had passed their range, and entered that of the deer only. Our marches now lay through rich narrow bottoms from one hundred and fifty to two hundred yards wide.

On the 15th, discovering timber sufficiently large to form canoes, I felled a couple of trees, and commenced splitting out. I would have proceeded farther by land, but as my men were almost worn out with fatigue, and the game grew scarce, I conceived it most advisable to rest for a short time, and kill my winter store of meat. This I effected by the 24th, and on the same day completed the canoes.

On the 25th I again attempted the navigation of the river, but was as unfortunate as at first, for my boat grounded after floating a few hundred yards, and the men were consequently compelled to ply with their shoulders instead of their paddles.

The following day I passed the Negracka (Ninnescak), at whose mouth commence the craggy cliffs which line a great part of the shores of the Arkansaw.

On the 28th the provision canoe overset, and I lost nearly all my stock of meat. This accident was rendered the more distressing by an almost total loss of my ammunition, which, unfortunately, was in the same canoe.

On the 30th I fell in with a band of Grand Osages, who were in pursuit of buffalo cows; the Chief of the party insisted on my remaining with him a day, and sent out his young men to hunt for me.

APPENDIX.

In the afternoon two Indians of the Little Osage nation joined us, with a horse and mule, and brought me a message from Tattasuggy, or The Wind, who, it appeared, was lying very ill, about twenty miles across the prairie, and wished to see me. As he was a particular favourite of·mine, I left my canoes in charge of the men, and passed with a guide to the Chief's temporary village. I found him extremely unwell, with what I conceived to be a dropsy, for his abdomen was very much swollen. He seemed gratified at the sight of me, and observed that he was poor and pitiful, for the reason that he was a friend to the Americans. He said that Chouteau, after he had arrived at their villages last fall, had treated him like a child, and had taken to Washington his younger brother Nezuma, or the Rain that Walks, and intended making him chief of the nation; that Chouteau told him he was a bad man, was an American, but that the Spaniards were going to war with America, and that in a short time they would claim all this country again; that he prevented the traders allowing a credit, whereby his family were much distressed. This I clearly perceived, for they were even destitute of a whole blanket.

This Nezuma, whom Chouteau took on to Washington last fall with his wife, I am better acquainted with than perhaps Mr. Chouteau himself. In the first place I marched with him from St. Louis to his town, and he started with us to visit the Pawnees, but the mean and pitiful wretch got alarmed, and sneaked off without even advising us of his departure. He has no more command in the village than a child, is no warrior, and has not even the power to controul the will of a single man of his nation. Whether this youth is entitled to a grand medal, you may judge from the foregoing statement. Indeed, Sir, our grand medals have become so common, that they do not carry with them the respect which they should. I recollect one of the deputation who was at the seat of government the year before the last, came out with a large medal and an intermediate sized one. On our arrival at the villages, I calculated on his acting a conspicuous part of the play, but, to my utter astonishment, he was not permitted to sit among the chiefs, or even the warriors at the council.

You well know, Sir, how particular the Spaniards, and the British especially, have been in their distribution of medals, and if I mistake not, an Iowa Chief, who had been to the seat of government, and there received a small medal, returned it in preference to giving up a large British medal, as he valued it more because it was a certain distinguishing mark of a Chief.

You gave to Mr. Pike an intermediate sized medal for one of the Pawnee chiefs, which he presented Iskatappe, who having remarked the medals pendant from the necks of the two Pawnee young men had been at Washington, demanded of what utility it would be to him? The only Spanish medals in the Pawnee nation are those worn by Characterick, or the White Wolf, and his son.

The following sarcastic remark was made by the son of the Belle Oiseau, a chief of the first standing among the Grand Osages whilst living, and who, unfortunately, was killed by the Sacs, on his way to Washington, with the first deputation. The son of White Hair, with Shenga Wassa, or Beautiful Bird, was to accompany us to the Pawnee village, but the former proved recreant, and, at the crossing of Grand

APPENDIX.

river, said he would return home. "Shame on you," said the latter, "what a pity it is so great and honourable a medal should be disgraced by so mean a heart."

You will pardon this digression, but I would wish to convince you, from what I have seen of Indians, how very requisite it is to use the utmost caution in the distribution of our presents and marks of distinction.

Before I set out to visit Tattasuggy, the ice had commenced drifting in large sheets, and on my return I found it running from shore to shore; I however pushed off, and drifted with it.

The night of the 2d of December was intensely cold, but hunger obliged me to proceed, and we fortunately reached the mouth of the Neskalonska river, without accident or injury, excepting that one of my men got frosted. This day we passed two salines, which enter on the south-west side.

The severity of the weather increased, and the river froze over on the morning of the 3d. This circumstance placed me in a situation truly distressing, as my men were almost naked; the tatters which covered them were comfortless, and my ammunition was nearly exhausted.

The men solicited me to hut, but I was resolved by perseverance and exertion to overcome, if in my power, the obstacles opposed to my progress.

' The Neskalonska is about one hundred and twenty yards wide, shoal, and narrow at its mouth, but deepens and spreads after you turn the first point. On this stream the Grand and Little Osages form their temporary fall hunting camps, and take their peltries. When the severity of winter sets in, the Grand Osages retire to Grosse Isle on the Verdigris or Wasetihoge, and the Little Osages to one of its small branches, called Possitonga, where they remain during the hard weather, and from thence return to their towns on the Neska, or Osage river.

On the 6th the ice began to drift, and I immediately pushed off with it, but as my evil stars would have it, my boats again grounded, and being in the middle of the river, my only alternative was to get out and drag them along for several miles, when we halted to warm our benumbed feet and hands. The next day several large cakes of ice had blocked up the river, and we had to cut our way through them with axes. The boats as usual grounded, and the men bare legged and bare footed, were obliged to leap into the water. This happened so frequently that two more of my men got badly frosted.

On the 8th one of my canoes was driven on a bank of ice, during a snow storm, and did not overtake me until the evening of the 9th, and then in so shattered a condition, that she could hardly be kept above water, and the poor fellows who were in her were almost frozen.

On the 10th, about noon, I passed Grand saline, or the Newsewketonga, which is of a reddish colour, though its water is very clear. About two days' march up this river you find the prairie grass on the south-west side incrusted with salt, and on the north-east bank fresh water springs, and lakes abounding with fish. This salt the Arkansaw Osages obtain by scraping it off the prairie with a turkey's wing into a wooden trencher. The river does not derive its name from its saline properties, but the quantities of salt that may always be found on its banks, and is at all seasons of the year portable.

On the 20th, in the afternoon, we passed another saline with water equally as red as the former, and more strongly impregnated with salt.

After encountering every hardship, to which a voyage is subject in small canoes at so inclement a season of the year, I arrived on the 23d instant, in a storm of hail and snow, at the wintering camp of Cashesegra, or Big Track, chief of the Osages who reside on Verdigris river. On the following day I gave him your talk, and received his reply, which it is unnecessary to recount fully, as it was merely a description of his poverty and miserable situation. He however said, that he had been informed the United States intended erecting factories on the Osage river, and that he was anxious to have one near to his own village, and for the purpose, he was willing to give the United States the tract of country lying between the Verdigris and Grand rivers. A factory, with a garrison of troops stationed there, would answer the double purpose of keeping in order those Indians who are the most desperate and profligate part of the whole nation, and more fully impressing them with an idea of our consequence, and gaining more firmly their friendship. It also would tend to preserve harmony among the Choctaws, Creeks, Cherokees, and Osages of the three different villages, who are in a constant state of warfare; and further, it would prevent the Osages making excursions into the country of the poor and peaceably disposed Choctaws, and might have some effect in confining the Spaniards to their own territorial limits.

On the 27th I passed the mouths of the Verdigris and Grand rivers, the former being about one hundred, and the latter one hundred and thirty yards wide; these streams enter within a quarter of a mile of each other. Below the mouth of Grand river commenced the rapids, which continue for several hundred miles down the Arkansaw.

About fifty-eight or sixty miles up the Verdigris is situate the Osage village. This band, some four or five years since, were led by the Chief Cashesegra, to the waters of the Arkansaw, at the request of Pierre Chouteau, for the purpose of securing their trade; the exclusive trade of the Osage river having at that time been purchased from the Spanish governor, by Manuel Liza, of St. Louis. But though Cashesegra be the nominal leader, Clermont, or the Builder of Towns, is the greatest warrior and most influential man, and is more firmly attached to the interests of the Americans, than any other chief of the nation. He is the lawful sovereign of the Grand Osage, but his hereditary right was usurped by Pahuska, or White Hair, while Clermont was yet an infant. White Hair, is in fact, a chief of Chouteau's creating, as well as Cashesegra, and neither has the power, nor disposition to restrain their young men from the perpetration of an improper act, fearing lest they should render themselves unpopular.

On the 29th I passed a fall of near seven feet perpendicular, and at evening was visited by a scout from an Osage war party, and received from them a man by the name of M'Farlane, who had been trapping up the Pottoe. We passed about

APPENDIX. 377

noon this day the mouths of the River des Illinois, which enters on the north-east side, and the Canadian river which puts in from the south-west. The latter river is the main branch of the Arkansaw, and is equally as large as the other.

On the 31st I passed the mouth of Pottoe, a deep though narrow stream, which puts in on the south-west, and also the River au Milieu that enters from the north-east.

On the evening of the 6th January, I reached the plantation of a Mr. Labourne, and was more inhospitably treated than by the savages themselves.

On the 8th passed the two upper Arkansaw or Quapaw villages, and on the 9th, after passing the lower Quapaw town, and a settlement of Choctaws, arrived at the post of Arkansaw.

The surface of the country between the Osage towns and the Pawnee village is generally broken and naked, the soil, sterile, and abounding with flint and lime stones. As you approach the waters of the Kanses it becomes hilly and sandy. The same may be said of the country between the Pawnee village and the Arkansaw, but after passing the ridge which separates the waters of the Kanses and Arkansaw, the surface becomes more regular and less stony.

Below the Verdigris, the shores of the Arkansaw are generally lined with cane, and consequently consist of rich bottoms. I was informed by the Indians that the country to the north-west of the Osage village, abounds with valuable lead mines, but I could make no discovery of any body of mineral.

The survey from the Arkansaw post to the Mississippi, I fear is not correct, as I was so ill when I descended that part of the river, as to be confined to my blanket.

I have the honour to subscribe myself
Your faithful and obliged
Humble and obedient servant,
JAMES B. WILKINSON,
1st Lieut. 2d United States regt. of Infantry.

(No. XI.)

LETTER TO GOVERNOR ALLENCASTER.

Santa Fé, 3d March, 1807.

SIR,

ON the arrival of your troops at my encampment last month, under the command of Lieutenant Don Ignacio Saltelo and Mr. Bartholomew, they informed me, that Your Excellency had directed them to assure me that I should be escorted through your dominions to the source of Red river, as our being on the frontiers of your province gave cause to suspicion. I conceived it more proper to comply with the request, and repair to Santa Fé, in order to explain to Your Excellency any circumstance which might appear extraordinary, but on my arrival here, am informed by

Your Excellency, that it is necessary that myself and troops pass by Chihuahua, in the Province of Biscay, more than two hundred leagues out of my route. I have demanded of Your Excellency to know if we are to be considered as prisoners of war? You inform me you do not consider us in that light. Not to embarrass Your Excellency with many demands, I only request to receive it from under your hands, in what manner I am to consider myself, and the orders for my passing into the country; also whether the expence of the voyage is to be considered as defrayed by the government of Spain or the United States? Excuse my language, as I am not much accustomed to writing in French, but Your Excellency having no person who understands English, obliges me to attempt that language.

I am, Sir, &c.
(Signed)   Z. M. PIKE.

TRANSLATION.

THE 1st Lieutenant of the Anglo-American troops, named Z. Montgomery Pike with the party of soldiers under his command, having been met with by the troops under my orders at four day's journey from the seat of government, in this province, which is under my charge; he was required personally to appear, which he voluntarily did, complying with the orders of the senior Commanding General of these internal provinces. I bade the said Lieutenant proceed on his march with his party, equipped with horses, provisions, and equipage, under charge of an officer and sixty men of our troops, with orders to introduce him to the said Commanding General, in the town of Chihuahua. I permitted the said party to carry their arms and ammunition; actuated by proper considerations, and to comply with the petition of the said Anglo American. I certify the foregoing contents to be accurate.

(Signed)   JOACHIM REAL ALLENCASTER.

Santa Fé, 3d March, 1807.

(No. XII.)

To Governor Allencaster.

St. Fernandez, March 7th, 1807.

SIR,

ON my arrival at this village, and meeting with Dr. Robinson, he informed me, that he acknowledged to Lieutenant Malgares to belong to my party. As this acknowledgment, in fact, only interested himself, I am constrained to explain to Your Excellency, my reasons for having denied his connection with me. He marched from St. Louis with my detachment as a volunteer, after having with much pains and solicitation obtained permission from the General for that purpose. On our arrival on the Rio del Norte (then supposed to be the Red river) he left the party in order to come to Santa Fé, with a view of obtaining information as to trade, and collect some debts due to persons in the Illinois. On my being informed of his embarrassments, I conceived it would be adding to them to acknowledge his having accompanied a military

APPENDIX. 379

party on to the frontiers of the province—and conceived myself bound in honour and friendship to conceal it; but scorning any longer the disguise he had assumed, he has left me at liberty to make this acknowledgement to Your Excellency, which I hope will sufficiently exculpate me in the opinion of every man of honour and of the world, for having denied a fact, when I conceived the safety of a friend in a foreign country to be concerned in the event. The above statement will be corroborated by Lieutenant Wilkinson, and he will be reclaimed by the United States as a citizen, agreeably to our treaties with Spain, regulating the intercourse, commerce, &c., between the two nations. I felt disposed to enter into an expostulation with Your Excellency, as to the deception practised on me by the officers who came out with your invitation to enter the province, but will refrain, and only request that my sergeant and party may be ordered to follow with all possible despatch, as he has all my astronomical instruments and cloathing, except what I now wear. I have found Lieutenant Malgares to be what you stated him, a gentleman and a soldier, and I sincerely wish the fortune of war may one day enable me to shew the gentlemen of the Spanish army, with whom I have had the honour of forming an acquaintance, with what gratitude I appreciate their friendship and politeness, and none more highly than Your Excellency's.

With sincere, &c.
(Signed)   Z. M. PIKE.

(No. XIII.)

To His Excellency General Salcedo.

Chihuahua, 6th April, 1807.

SIR,

HAVING been for near the space of a year absent from my country, and the probability of its being yet two or three months before I arrive in the territory of the United States, the necessity of passing through some hundred leagues of foreign territory, with the distressed situation of my troops, induce me to apply to Your Excellency for a necessary supply of money. Any arrangement which may be conceived proper for the repayment, I will cheerfully adopt, either to pay it to the Spanish consul at New Orleans, or the ambassador of His Catholic Majesty at Washington.

The sum which I conceive will answer the present purposes of myself and troops, is one thousand dollars, for which I will give you such vouchers as Your Excellency may conceive proper.

I have the honour to assure Your Excellency
of my high respect, and to be .
Your obedient servant,
(Signed)   Z. M. PIKE.

TRANSLATION.

For the 1st Lieut. Montg. Pike.

According to the solicitation you have made in your letter of yesterday, that from the royal treasury of this place there should be delivered you one thousand dollars.

(which you say are necessary for the accommodation of the troops of the United States of America, which you have under your charge) or whatever other sum you choose to demand; and the government of the United States shall refund the said sum to the Senor Marquis de Casa Yrujo; I have directed the formula for you to sign of four corresponding and quadruplicate receipts.

God preserve you many years,
(Signed)   NIMESIO SALCEDO.

(No. XIV.)

To His Excellency Brig.-Gen. Don Nimesio Salcedo, Commandant General of the Interior Provinces of the Kingdom of New Spain.

Chihuahua, 14th April, 1807.

SIR,

ON my marching from Sante Fé, Governor Allencaster informed me that my papers would be considered as a sacred deposit until my arrival at this place, when Your Excellency would examine and take them into consideration. When they were examined and taken possession of, I explained without disguise the nature and contents of each, conceiving that those only which had any relation to the object of my expedition could be interesting, and that merely a copy of the chart, and translations of the official papers would be taken. You must be conscious, Sir, that it was in my power to have secreted or destroyed every trace of my voyage and plans, previous to my arrival at Chihuahua, but resting satisfied that no rupture had taken place between His Catholic Majesty and the States I have the honour to serve, which would be a justification for the seizure of my papers, I preferred leaving them in *statu quo*, to using duplicity, which in some degree always implicates the character of a military man. Admitting the country which I explored to be contested between the two governments, each would naturally wish to obtain information as to its geographical situation, in order that they might form correct ideas as to what would be their mutual interest, founded on justice and the honour and dignity of the nation, in forming the line of demarcation. This was the view of the United States government in the expedition which I had the honour to command, and the loss of the geographical sketches taken, might be the occasion of a suspension of the final line of limits, and consequently the delay of an amicable adjustment of the now existing differences between the two governments. Your Excellency may not have any intention to detain my papers, which I had only begun to suppose from your returning part by Lieutenant Walker; in which case you will please to excuse this intrusion: but I will add, that if you have it in view, should you be pleased to examine them with particularity, you will find that there are letters from General Wilkinson as well as his son to me, also from the latter to his father and mother, and others, which are by no means of a political nature, or at least not as respects to the relations existing between the government of Spain and the United States, and therefore

APPENDIX.

can by no means be interesting to Your Excellency. The book which contains my charts also contains part of the sketches of a voyage to the source of the Mississippi, which, I presume cannot be interesting to the Spanish government. But to conclude, I have only to request of Your Excellency to know if it is your intention to seize on my papers, now in your possession? if so, that you may cause me to be furnished with, or suffer me to take, a copy of them, and that I may receive a certificate from under your hand of the number, nature, &c., of the said papers, and the reason for their seizure, in order that my government may be enabled to make the proper application to the Spanish court for an explanation. My reason for applying to Your Excellency so early on this subject, is, that on the arrival of my men who are still in the rear, I might be prepared to march in a short period of time, for under the present aspect of affairs I feel conscious that I am as anxious to arrive on the territories of the United States, as Your Excellency must be for me to quit the dominions of His Catholic Majesty. In all events, I hope you will believe me to be with the highest sentiments of personal respect,

Your most obedient servant,
(Signed)   Z. M. PIKE.

(No. XV.)

To his Excellency General Wilkinson.

Chihuahua, 20th April, 1807.

MY DEAR GENERAL,

NEVER did I sit down to address you with a heart so oppressed with anxiety and mortification; but knowing the uncertainty which must exist as to the fate of myself and party, I conceive it proper to attempt a communication, although I think it extremely uncertain, owing to the difficulty of the route, and to various circumstances which are not to be communicated in a letter, whether it may ever come to hand, or at least, previous to my arrival at the territories of the United States. I was detained in the mountains of Mexico until the month of January, and in February found myself, with eight of my party only, on the head branches of the Rio del Norte, which I then conceived to be the sources of the Red river, our information making the latter extend the whole distance between the former and the Arkansaw, although its sources are some hundred miles below either of the others.

Here I was encountered by two officers and one hundred men, who bore orders from the Governor of New Mexico to cause me and my party to march to the capital of that province; but his request was in the most polite style, and in fact, the commanding officer assured me there was not the least constraint, but that His Excellency desired a conference, and that I then should be conducted by the most direct route, to the navigable part of the Red river, from whence I could immediately descend to Natchitoches. Although dubious of the faith of the invitation, and being in a situation where I could have defended myself as long as my provision lasted, or until I might probably have escaped in the night; yet knowing the pacific intentions of our government, and the particular instructions of my General as to my conduct in case of a rencontre with a body of Spanish troops, I conceived it most proper to comply with the demand and repair to Santa Fé; and, as the rest of my party who remained in the mountains were many of them invalids, and not in a situation to be able to return, I conceived it most proper to leave orders for them to follow, accompanied by an escort of Spanish troops left for that purpose.

On my arrival at Santa Fé, His Excellency Governor Allencaster informed me it was necessary that I should immediately march to Chihuahua, in the Province of Biscay, in order to present myself to his Excellency the Commandant General N. Salcedo, for further orders. This being, so different from what I had been taught to expect, I demanded of Governor Allencaster, in a written communication, to know if I was to consider myself and party as prisoners of war? He replied in the negative. We marched on the following day, and arrived at this place on the 2d instant, from whence I am informed by the General, I shall march on the arrival of the remainder of my party for Natchitoches.

I must here acknowledge myself and party under infinite obligations to the friendship and politeness of all the Spanish officers, and in a particular manner to the Commandant General of these Provinces.

Should the politics of our country make it necessary to augment the army previous to my arrival, I hope the General will approve of my aspiring to a considerable promotion in the new corps. Should the line of demarkation be amicably adjusted between the United States and Spain, I hope to obtain the appointment of one of the commissioners, as I make bold to assert that with respect to the arrangements necessary, and a knowledge of the country through which the line must pass, I am better instructed than any other officer of my age in our service; and, if joined to a colleague of profound astronomical knowledge, we could surmount every difficulty. I likewise beg leave to suggest to Your Excellency that I conceive the information I hold of considerable consequence in the determination of the line of limits, and that (it not already determined) I can throw considerable light on the subject.

I hope Your Excellency will be pleased to forward orders for me to Natchitoches informing me if I am to descend to Orleans or proceed to the federal city? and if the latter, permitting me to pass by Louisiana, in order to visit and arrange the affairs of my family, to whom I beg the favour of my General to communicate the certainty of the existence of myself and Dr. Robinson, who begs to be sincerely remembered to you.

The General will pardon the requests I have made of him, knowing the confidence of my heart in the paternal and soldierly esteem which he has manifested for him, who has the honour to be,

    With every sentiment of esteem,
     Respect, and high consideration,
      Dear General,
       Your obedient humble servant,
        (Signed) Z. M. PIKE.

APPENDIX. 383

(No. XVI.)

TRANSLATION.

To Montgomery Pike, First Lieutenant of Infantry.

OF the papers connected with the expedition, which, by orders of the United States government, you have made from the St. Louis of the Illinois, into the settlements of New Mexico, and which you yourself separated from the others which you brought here, and put into my hand the day of your arrival, there have been found an inventory, and certificate respecting each of them accompanying it, and deposited in the office the 17th current for the purpose therein expressed. The judgment on which remains for the decision of the King my Lord; and shall be reported in the secret archives of this Captain-Generalship. Considering that you have indicated in your summons official to this government the greatest desire to arrive at the territories of the States, I have resolved that you prepare to continue your voyage in two or three days, in consequence of which the necessary arrangements shall be made, such as you, with the people of your expedition, have experienced until your arrival at this place.

God preserve you many years,

(Signed) NIMESIO SALCEDO.

Chihuahua, 23d April, 1807.

TRANSLATION.

INVENTORY of the Papers of the Lieutenant of Infantry of the United States of America, Montgomery Pike, detained by the superior government and Commandant-General of the interior provinces of New Spain; as belonging to a voyage which he executed from St. Louis of the Illinois, to the territories of New Mexico, to visit the Indian nations, and reconnoitre the country, appearing to have been his expedition undertaken at the charge of the government of the said United States and by orders of General Wilkinson: *

No. 1. Letter from General Wilkinson to Pike, dated 24th of June, 1806.
2. Another from the same to Pike, 18th July, 1806.
3. Another from the same to another officer, 19th July, 1806.
4. . Another from the same to Pike, dated 6th August, 1806.
5. Letter from Lieutenant Wilkinson to his father, 27th October, 1806.
6. Another from ditto to ditto, 28th October, 1806.
7. Letter from Pike to General Wilkinson, 22d February, 1806.
8. Ditto from Lieutenant Wilkinson to Lieutenant Pike, 26th October, 1806.
9. Proclamation of General Wilkinson, prohibiting any citizen of the United States trading with the Indian nations, without permission from the government, dated 10th July, 1805.
10. A letter from Charles Jonet, agent for the Indians, to General Wilkinson dated 10th July, 1806.

---

* See my account of the seizure of the papers, April 2d, 1807.

APPENDIX.

11. Notes of Lieutenant Pike on the voyage from New Mexico to Chihuahua, of four pages.
12. A rough manuscript of the Missouri and Osage rivers.
13. Letter from Sergeant Ballenger to General Wilkinson, unsealed.
14. Letter from Lieutenant Wilkinson to Pike, without date.
15. A certificate in the French language of a certain Baptiste Larme, found in the Osage nation, and specifying his motives for being there.
16. A bundle of papers in the French language, which contained notes on the harangues and manifestoes, which Lieutenant Pike had delivered to the Indian nations.
17. A passport of Lieutenant Pike to the Indian Winafricure, a captain of the little Osage.
18. A small draft or map of the country, which is situated between the Mississippi and Santa Fé, with a description of that town and a notice of having met with three thousand Camanches.
19. A book in octavo, a manuscript which contains the diary of Lieutenant Pike, from January, 1807, to the 2d March in the same year, when he arrived at Santa Fé, in seventy-five pages.
20. A book in quarto, manuscript, in pasteboard, with copies of letters to the Secretary of War and General Wilkinson, and various observations, astronomical, &c., relative to the commission of the Lieutenant, in sixty-seven pages.
21. A manuscript book in folio, containing different plans of countries, &c., with a diary with rhumbs, distances, and worked observations, and meteorological tables, which arose from a revisal of the voyage, by the said Lieutenant Pike, in forty pages.

Don Francisco Valasco, first officer of the secretaries of the Captain-Generalship of the internal provinces of New Spain, and Juan Pedro Walker, Officer of the company of horse of the royal presidio of Janos, Certify that the Lieutenant of American infantry, Montgomery Pike, when presented to the Commandant-General of the beforementioned provinces, Don Nimesio Salcedo, produced a small trunk, which he brought with him.* And that in the presence of the undersigned, he opened it himself and took out different books and papers. When having separated with his own hands, all that appeared to be or that he said were private, or had no connection with the voyage; he delivered the remainder to the demand of the Commandant-General, which were solely those comprehended in the foregoing inventory which we have made, and for the verification of which we have annexed our signature.

          (Signed)   FRANCISCO VALASCO.
Chihuahua, 8th April, 1807.   JUAN PEDRO WALKER.

---

* The falsity, want of candour, and meanness exhibited in this certificate is manifest, and was an imbecile attempt to shew that all my actions were voluntary and that in the delivery of my papers, there was no degree of constraint.

APPENDIX.

(No. XVII.)

To His Excellency General Nimesio Salcedo.

Chihuahua, April 14th, 1807.

SIR,

I HOPE Your Excellency will not attribute it to presumption, or a disposition to intrude, when I address you on a subject foreign from my official duties, and on which I can only speak as an individual: but I should feel myself wanting in humanity, and that attention which every man owes to his fellow creatures in distress, were I to remain silent; and more especially when those are my compatriots, and some of them formerly my companions—now in a strange country, languishing out their days far from relations and friends, with hardly a dawn of hope remaining of ever again being blessed with the view of their native homes. It is scarcely necessary to add that I allude to the unfortunate companions of Nolan, who having entered the territories of His Chatholic Majesty in a clandestine manner, equally in violation of the treaties between the two governments, the laws of the United States, and those of Spain, could not be reclaimed or noticed by their country. Yet, from every information I have received on the subject, the men of the party were innocent, believing that Nolan had passports from the Spanish governor to carry on the traffic of horses. I pretend not to justify the many irregularities of their conduct since in the Spanish dominions, but hope that it may be viewed with an eye of clemency, as they are most of them very illiterate, having received scarcely any education. David Pharo was formerly a subaltern in a company of infantry of the United States, commanded by my father, the time I served as a volunteer, but left service, (as I have been informed,) owing to some irregularities of conduct. His having been once my companion entitles him at present to my particular attention; yet I will here mention to Your Excellency, a circumstance which may appear, if known, in an unfavourable light, viz.: About 15 days past I was informed Pharo was in town, and that he desired to see me. I was extremely mortified at receiving the information, as I conceive he must have left his post in a clandestine manner, yet I could not find in my heart to refuse the interview which I gave, but determined at the same time to inform you of the circumstance, conceiving that you could not look on it as a matter of much criminality.

But to conclude, I have to beg of Your Excellency, if in your power and consistent with the line of conduct you conceive proper to pursue, to inform me if anything can be done towards restoring those poor fellows to their liberty, friends, and country, and in a particular manner I intercede for Pharo. If it is out of the power of the General to grant them leave to return to the United States, I beg to know if there is any objection to my taking out letters to their fathers, wives, &c.? I should not have addressed this letter to the General, had I not conceived the fate of those men to be at his disposal, as he had suffered one of them to join the service of His Catholic Majesty; neither do I request the honour of any other than a verbal reply, as I write in the character of an individual, and not as an officer of the United States.

I am, sir, with high consideration,
Your humble obedient servant,
(Signed)   Z. M. PIKE.

APPENDIX.

(No. XVIII.)

To His Excellency, Governor Salcedo.

Natchitoches, 20th August, 1807.

SIR,

PREVIOUS to my departure from Chihuahua, we had entered so fully into the subject of the seizure of my papers, that I should never have made another appeal, until I made one through our government to the ambassador of His Catholic Majesty, had I not received orders to that effect, it not being known at the time these restrictions were given that the propriety of the seizure had been contested between Your Excellency and myself. But as you have now had time fully to reconsider the business, it may not appear in the same light that it did when I had the honour to address you before. Your Excellency may be induced to conceive that the measure of seizing my notes, plans, meteorological and astronomical observations, &c., for part of the Mississippi, Missouri, Osage, Kanses, and Arkansaw rivers, waters acknowledged by the Spanish government to be within the known territories of the United States, may not be justifiable. Whatever may be your opinion on these subjects, I am at an entire loss to conceive how and upon what principles you could involve in that seizure, letters from individuals to individuals, the contents of which could in no wise be interesting to the Spanish government. I have therefore once more to appeal to Your Excellency, with a hope, that the time you have had for deliberation may induce you to conceive it proper, and but an act of justice, to deliver up the papers seized at Chihuahua, and hope Your Excellency will have the goodness to address them to me in a packet, to the care of the commanding officer of this place. If the continuation of an amicable understanding between the two nations is an object of estimation in the mind of Your Excellency, the final demarcation of limits must be considered as the first good step to be taken towards its accomplishment; and to enable my government to form a correct idea on that subject, it was requisite they should be well acquainted with the geographical situation of the heads of the Arkansaw and Red rivers, the former part of which I had accomplished, and could with all ease have carried the remaining part of that object into execution, (after discovering my mistake of the Rio del Norte for the Red river,) had I been permitted by the Governor of North Mexico; instead of which I was hurried through the country to Chihuahua, without having time given for the absent part of my party and baggage to join me, by which means I was obliged to appear in a garb and manner incompatible with the rank I have the honour to hold; and which in some degree offered an indignity to the country whose commission I bear. And to add to my mortification, I was then deprived of the information I had obtained at the risk of our lives and the suffering of unknown miseries. The information contained in my notes was not only of a geographical nature, but also such as would enable the executive of the United States to take some steps to ameliorate the barbarous state of the various savage tribes whom I visited, and I may be permitted to add, would have added in some small degree to the acquirements of science, which are for the general benefit of mankind. When I left Chihuahua, I was informed my sergeant and party were detained near that place, in order

APPENDIX.

that they might not be permitted to join me, that by a separate examination they might be intimidated to make a declaration to justify the conduct observed towards us. This I am conscious must have failed, but I am at an entire loss to conceive why they should have been detained until this time, when Your Excellency assured me they should follow me immediately. Their detention has been of considerable private injury to myself, and an insult to my government. When I marched from Chihuahua, Your Excellency officially informed me that everything was prepared for my transport to our lines; but I was much surprised to have to pay for the hire of horses, &c. demanded of me, at the first place where we changed our escort. As I neither conceived it just that I should pay for the involuntary tour I had taken through your territories, neither was I prepared to do it. But, as your officers were responsible, and gave their receipts for the transports, and from the orders received by Captain Viana at Nacogdoches, I was obliged to hire beasts to take me to Natchitoches, although an escort of your troops were furnished.

I here with the greatest pleasure embrace the opportunity of acknowledging the polite treatment I received from your officers in general on my route; but in a particular manner to Colonels Cordero and Herrara, to Captains Barelo and Viana, with Lieutenant Malgares; to all of whom it would be my greatest pleasure to have it in my power to return the compliment. Will Your Excellency do me the honour to present my high respects to your lady, and my compliments to Mr. Truxillo and Father Rocus.

I am, sir, with the most
Profound consideration,
Your obedient servant,
(Signed) Z. M. PIKE, Capt.

(No. XIX.)

To Captain Pike, U. S. Army.

New Orleans, May 20th, 1807.

DEAR SIR,

AFTER having counted you among the dead, I was most agreeably surprised to find, by a letter from General Salcedo, received a few days since,* that you were in

*THE FOLLOWING IS THE LETTER HERE REFERED TO.

From General Salcedo to General Wilkinson,
Dated Chihuhua, 8th April, 1807.

EXCELLENT SIR,

ON the 16th of February last, John Robinson appeared before the Governor of NEW MEXICO, saying that he was a Frenchman, inhabitant of St. Louis, which place he had left on the 15th June last year, with the view of going to the country of the Pawnees, to make recoveries, that having received information that his debtors had directed their steps to the said province, he had concluded to follow them in company with fifteen other persons, who went for the purpose of hunting on the rivers Arkansaw, and Colorado (Red river); that in the neighbouring mountains the two last of his company had left him, his possession and that he proposed sending you, with your party, to our frontier post. I lament that you should lose your papers, but shall rely much on your memory, and although it was unfortunate that you should have headed Red river, and missed the object of your enterprize, yet I promise myself that the route over which you have passed will afford some interesting scenes, as well to the statesman as the philosopher. You will hear of the scenes in which I have been engaged, and may be informed that the traitors whose infamous designs against the constitution and government of our country I have detected, exposed, and destroyed, are vainly attempting to explain their own conduct by inculpating me; and among other devices they have asserted that yours and Lieutenant Wilkinson's enterprize was a premeditated co-operation with Burr. Being on the wing for Richmond, in Virginia, to confront the arch traitor and his host of advocates, I have not leisure to commune with you as amply as I could desire; let it then suffice to you for me to say, that of

for which reason he saw himself under the necessity of proceeding to the Ietan Indians, to whom he explained his situation, and who accordingly agreed to conduct him.

On the 25th of the same month of February, at the distance of four days' journey from the town of Santa Fé, and nine leagues west of its settlements, at the place called the Ojo Caliente (Hot Springs) near the confluence of Rio Grande del Norte (Great North river), and that known under the name of Rio de los Conejos (of Rabbits), a detachment of the garrison of the said Province of New Mexico, met Montgomery Pike, 1st Lieutenant of the infantry of the United States, with eight men of the said infantry who, on being given to understand that he must be conducted to the said town, consented to accompany them.

It was then settled that two of his men should remain on the spot, with half of His Catholic Majesty's detachment, to wait for six others who had not yet arrived, and he proceeded to the Governor's, to whom he declared, that his being in that neighbourhood was owing solely to his having been lost, and having mistaken the Rio del Norte for the Colorado. But this officer, in compliance with the orders of his superior officer, forwarded the said 1st Lieutenant, with the six men of the American army, and the above-mentioned John Robinson, to this capital. They arrived here on the 2d inst., and the said officer, on being presented to me, laid before me in the same manner as he had done to the Governor of Santa Fé, the papers relative to his mission, the correspondence he had carried on with Your Excellency since it commenced, with his journals and note-books. Your Excellency is not ignorant of the repeated representations made by the King's Minister in the United States, the Marquis of Casa Calvo, whilst he was in Louisiana, summoning the American government not to carry into effect any projects of extending its expeditions into territories unquestionably belonging to His Majesty. You must, therefore, without any further observations or remarks on my part, be satisfied that these documents contain evident, unequivocal proofs, that an offence of magnitude has been committed against His Majesty; and that every individual of this party ought to have been considered as prisoners on the very spot. Notwithstanding such substantial and well-grounded motives that would have warranted such a measure, wishing to give the widest latitude to the subsisting system of harmony and good understanding, and above all, firmly persuaded that Your Excellency will take such steps as your judgment may suggest, as best calculated to prevent any bad consequences on the occasion, I have concluded to keep in this general government all the papers presented by Lieutenant Pike, and to give him and his men full liberty to return to Your Excellency, after having treated them with attention, and offered them every assistance they stood in need of.

I am without reserve and beyond expression, your most obedient, humble, respectful, and faithful servant, and pray that God may preserve Your Excellency many years.

(Signed)   SALCEDO.

APPENDIX.

the information you have acquired, and the observations you have made, you must be cautious, extremely cautious, how you breathe a word, because the publicity may excite a spirit of adventure adverse to the interests or our government, or injurious to the maturation of those plans, which may be hereafter found necessary and justifiable by the government.

I leave Colonel Cushing in command of the district, with plenary powers, and have informed him that you have leave to repair to St. Louis, by the most direct route, the moment you have communicated to me in duplicate the results of your travels, voluntary and involuntary, in relation to clime, country, population, arts, agriculture, routes, distances and military defence. The President will be impatient to have whatever you have acquired, and to the detailed account a sketch must be added, and the original and duplicate addressed to me at the city of Washington, with the least possible delay. You may make up your report at Natchitoches, and proceed from thence to the Washita, and from thence to the Askansaw, or you may descend to Fort Adams, and proceed thence to St. Louis, by the most convenient route. Colonel Cushing, whom I leave in command of the district, has my orders in your favour, and will give you every indulgence; but as an expedition is now in motion up the Arkansaw, to explore it to its source and further north-west, it is highly important you should, either in person or by two or three confidential men, send forward to the Arkansaw every information which you may deem essential to the success of the enterprize. A Mr. Freeman, under the chief direction of Mr. Dunbar, of Natchez, has the controul of this operation. The escort, which consists of thirty-five select non-commissioned officers and privates, is commanded by Lieutenant Wilkinson seconded by Lieutenant T. A. Smith. This detachment, with two boats suitably equipped, will reach Natchez in eight or ten days from the present, and will proceed with all possible despatch. You will address your communications to Lieutenant Wilkinson, who, after many hardships and difficulties, reached this place about the 1st of March. He has finished a pretty good traverse of the river, and his journal is interesting. I think the present party will winter near the Arkansaw Osages, about six hundred miles by the river from the Mississippi. The President mentioned you and your explorations to the source of the Great river, in his address to congress, in handsome terms, and I am convinced he has a proper sense of your merits, and will do you ample justice. I offer you leave to go immediately to your family, because I apprehend it will be most desirable; yet, if you possess in your information aught which you may desire to communicate in person, you are at liberty to proceed, by the shortest route, to the seat of government, near which you will find me, if alive, three or four months hence.

I pray you to attend particularly to the injunctions of this hasty letter, and to believe me, whilst I am your general,

                Your friend,

(Signed)   JAMES WILKINSON.

APPENDIX.

(No. XX.)

To General Wilkinson.

Natchitoches, 5th July, 1807.

DEAR GENERAL,

ONCE more I address you from the land of freedom, and under the banners of our country. Your esteemed favour of the 20th May now lies before me, in which I recognize the sentiments of my General and friend, and will endeavour, as far as my limited abilities permit, to do justice to the spirit of your instructions.

I must premise to Your Excellency that my letter of the 20th April, dated at Chihuahua, went through a perusal by General Salcedo, previous to his forwarding it.

That letter stated the mode of my being brought into Santa Fé, and I will now state to Your Excellency the proceeding on the subject of my papers. I will omit the hauteur of the reception given me by Governor Allencaster, for a more particular communication, which changed afterwards to extreme politeness.

Being under no restrictions previous to arriving at Santa Fé, I had secreted all my papers which I conceived necessary to preserve, leaving my book of charts, my orders, and such others as might lead the Governor to know me in my proper character and to prevent his suspicions being excited to a stricter enquiry.

On examining my commission, orders, &c., he told me to remove my trunk to my own quarters, and that on the morrow he would converse with me on the subject. I had caused the men to secrete my papers about their bodies, conceiving this to be safer than leaving them in the baggage; but in the evening, finding the ladies of Santa Fé were treating them to wine, &c., I was apprehensive their intemperance might discover the secret, and took them from all but one (who had my journal in full) who could not be found, and put them in my trunk, conceiving the inspection was over; but next morning an officer, with two men, waited on me and informed me he had come for me to visit the Governor, and had brought these two men to take up my trunk. I immediately perceived I was out-generalled. On my arrival at the Governor's house, His Excellency demanded if I had the key. My reply was in the affirmative; when he observed "it is well;" my trunk should be a sacred deposit in the charge of the officer, who would escort me to Chihuahua; for which place, after dinner, I marched, under the escort of Lieutenant Don Faciendo Malgares, and sixty-five men. The character of this officer I beg leave to introduce to the attention of your Excellency, as an European possessing all the high sense of honour which formerly so evidently distinguished his nation, as the commandant of the six hundred troops who made the expedition to the Pawnees, as an officer of distinguished merit, who in his mode of living fully justified the pomp and style of his actions, who outshines many of their governors of provinces, and whom in my future reports I shall have frequent occasion to quote. He observed to me, "The Governor informs me, sir, your trunk is under restrictions, but your word of honour as a soldier that no papers shall be taken out, and you have free ingress, as usual." I gave it, and I presume it is scarcely necessary to add it was religiously adhered to.

APPENDIX. 391

On our arrival at Chihuahua, the general demanded my trunk, and on its being opened and the papers laid on the table, he took them in hand one by one, and demanded the purport of each, which truth obliged me to declare; and had I been disposed to have equivocated, Ensign Walker, of His Catholic Majesty's service, who stood present and assisted in the examination, could immediately have detected the fraud; also His Excellency understands sufficient of the English language to discover the general purport of any paper.

After going through them in this manner, and separating them into two piles, he observed to me, "you will leave those papers for my inspection, and in the mean while, in concert with ensign Walker, (who will give the Spanish translation,) you will give me a detailed account of your route, views, destination, &c., and during that time I will examine the papers now before me." To this I agreed, flattering myself that it was his intention to return me my papers, by his demanding a sketch; also, so great was my confidence in the all-protecting name of my country, I conceived it was a greater step than the General would venture to take, to seize on the papers. But when I had finished the proposed sketch and presented it, and found a still further delay, I addressed the General on the subject, when, after a few days, some were returned, but I was officially informed, that " the remaining papers were seized, but would be kept in the secret cabinet of that Captain-Generalship, until the pleasure of His Catholic Majesty was known,"—at the same time I had presented to me a certificate specifying the number and contents of those detained, and stating that they were assorted by own hand, and voluntarily. This assertion was so contrary to truth, honour, and the line of conduct a general should have pursued with a young gentleman, that I took the liberty of telling one of the officers who signed the certificate that it was incorrect. But as Sergeant Meek was still in the rear, with nearly all my baggage, I took care to give him orders that none of the said baggage should be opened, except by force, which will evince that, although I preferred acting like a gentleman to obliging General Salcedo to resort to rough treatment, it was not a voluntary surrender of my papers. But the General will please to recollect that my journals were saved at Santa Fè, which were continued and are entire to this post; a fortunate circumstance of the Doctor's having copied my courses and distances through all the route (except an excursion we made to the source of the River La Plate) to the Spanish territories, preserved them. These will enable me to exhibit a correct chart of the route, although not so minutely as the one seized on, which was laid down daily by the eye and angular observations. Thus my only essential papers lost were my astronomical observations, meteorological tables, and a book containing remarks on minerals, plants, &c., with the manners, population, customs, &c., of the savages; but the results of the former were in part communicated, and probably my journal may supply part of the others, and our memories will make the loss of the latter of but little consequence. While in the Spanish territories I was forbidden the use of pen and paper, notwithstanding which I kept a journal, made meteorological observations, took courses and distances, from the time I entered their country until my arrival at this place, all of

APPENDIX.

which I brought safe off in the men's guns (where I finally secreted my papers) without detection.

From our unremitting attention day and night, the immense territory they led us through, and the long time we were in their country, I have been able to collect (I make bold to assert) a correct account of their military force, regular and irregular; also, important and interesting information on geographical situations, political sentiments, and dispositions of the people of every class, the manners, arts, resources, riches, revenues, value and productions of their mines, situation, &c., &c., with the annual revenues paid Bonaparte; and had we possessed as great a knowledge of the Spanish language when we entered the territories as when we left them, our information would have been nearly as complete as I could have wished it, if sent expressly for the purpose of acquiring it, by the open authority of His Majesty. But the French language was greatly beneficial, in which my communications were sometimes made. By the Sergeant, who is still in the rear, and was never suffered to join me, as General Salcedo conceived he should probably procure some information from him, which he could not if immediately under my orders, I expect many other communications of importance from many individuals, who promised to forward them by him. But I presume the General has found himself in an error, as I perceive by a letter from him to Governor Cordero, the Sergeant killed one of his men, in consequence of some improper conduct, and the General accuses him of great intractability, as he is pleased to term it. From the foregoing statement Your Excellency will observe that I yet possess immense matter, the result of one year's travel, in a country deserted and unpopulated, which has been long the subject of curiosity to the philosopher, the anxious desire of the miser, and the waking thoughts and sleeping dreams of the man of ambition and aspiring soul, and in our present critical situation, I do conceive immensely important, and which opens a scene for the generosity and aggrandizement of our country, with a wide and splendid field for harvests of honour for individuals. But my papers are in a mutilated state, from the absolute necessity I was under to write on small pieces in the Spanish country; also, from being injured in the gun barrels, some of which I fired three times off to take out the papers. These circumstances would make it necessary, in the first place, to take a rough copy as they stand; then it will be necessary to assort the matter, as military, political, moral, trade, clime, soil, &c., all now form an undigested mass: then, sir, the combining each, the plotting, &c., would take up a time of considerable extent for one man; and to make duplicates after they were in order could not be done in three months. The General may recollect it was nearly that period before my reports were completed last year, although assisted by Mr. Nau and the Sergeant-Major, and sometimes by Lieutenants Wilkinson and Graham. Also, with respect to the Spanish country, I must know the extent of the objects in view, in order to embrace those points in my reports; and, further, my dear sir, my health is by no means the most perfect, my eyes being so extremely weak that it is almost impossible for me to continue for one hour with the pen in my hand, and by that time I have a considerable pain in my breast. From

APPENDIX. 393

these circumstances my General will perceive the almost impracticability of my complying with the contents of his letter as to duplicate reports from this place; but I shall immediately commence the business of arranging and digesting my papers, and will proceed with the labour with every perseverance my situation will permit of until the arrival of my sergeant and the residue of the party (should they not retard more than twenty days) when I shall proceed immediately to St. Louis, and from thence through Kentucky, Virginia, &c., to the federal city, making no unnecessary delay, and all the whole of the route prosecuting my business at every leisure moment. When at Washington I flatter myself with your assistance and advice. As I propose taking courses, distances, &c., from thence to St. Louis, it will be making the tour of the greatest part of Louisiana, crossing the main rivers at different points, when I am certain, with the survey of the Missouri by Captains Lewis and Clark, my own of the Mississippi, Lieutenant Wilkinson's of the Lower Arkansaw (which river I surveyed to its source) and Mr. Dunbar's of Red river, may be formed the completest survey of Louisiana ever yet taken.

The instruments I had with me I wish the General to inform me in what light they stood, as most of them were ruined in the mountains by the falling of the horses from precipices, &c., and I left an order at Chihuahua for the sergeant to sell them at a certain price, as the addition of a land carriage of five hundred leagues would not add to their benefit. Baroney, if alive, is with my sergeant, and has proved a noble fellow in his line, and I beg liberty to recommend him to some appointment near the Kanses, should any offer. I must further add the following anecdote of my men, in whose breasts lay the whole secret of my papers, and whom frequently, when in the Spanish territories, I was obliged to punish for outrages committed in a state of intoxication, yet never did one offer, or show a disposition to discover it. It is certain they knew instant death would follow; but still their fidelity to their trust is remarkable. I have charged them as to communications, and shall dispose of them in such a manner as not to put it in their power to give things much publicity. Dr. Robinson has accompanied me the whole route, is still with me, and from whom I take a pleasure in acknowledging I have received important services, as my companion in dangers and hardships, and counsellor in difficulties, and to whose chemical, botanical, and mineralogical knowledge, the expedition was greatly indebted: in short, sir, he is a young gentleman of talents, honour, and perseverance, possessing, in my humble opinion, a military turn of mind, and would, I believe, in case of an augmentation of the army, enter, if he could obtain a rank above a subaltern. I hope the General will be pleased to have my copies forwarded by Lieutenant Wilkinson, so that I can command the use of them at Washington; also, all my letters written him during the expedition, as they contain information I wish to refer to, and the copies were seized. Dr. Sibley has informed me the expedition up the Arkansaw is suspended, which supersedes the necessity of my sending the express ordered.

I congratulate the General on the safe arrival of Lieutenant Wilkinson, and am sorry to hear of the difficulties he encountered. I have been obliged to draw money

APPENDIX.

of the Spanish government, which I have to pay to their ambassador at Washington. I supported those of my men who were with me all the time in the Spanish country, being separated from my baggage, and never permitted to have it join me, and having been presented to the Commandant-General in a blanket cappot: I was under the necessity of going into very considerable expense to support what I not only considered my own honour, but the dignity of our army. This, where a captain's pay is two thousand four hundred dollars per annum, was a ruinous thing to my finances; but I hope it may be taken into due consideration.

After making myself pretty perfect in the French language, I have obtained such a knowledge of the Spanish as to make me confident in asserting, that in three or four years I will with ease make myself master of the latter, Italian, and Portugueze, sufficiently to read all, and speak and write the Spanish. The Doctor has even exceeded me in that point. I mention this to the General, as I know the interest he takes in the improvement of his military protégé.

We had heard in the Spanish dominions of the convulsions of the western country, originating in Mr. Burr's plans, and that you were implicated; sometimes that you were arrested, sometimes superseded, &c. Those reports (although I never gave credit to them) occasioned me great unhappiness, as I conceived that the shafts of calumny were aiming at your fame and honour, in a foreign country, where they had hitherto stood high, and were revered and respected by every class. At St. Antonio Colonel Cordero informed me of the truth of the statement, which took a load from my breast and made me comparatively happy, and I hope ere long the villainy will be unmasked and malignity and slander hide their heads. The before-mentioned gentleman sent you by me a box of Spanish chocolate, which I shall forward to Colonel Cushing. Governor Herrara said the maliciousness of the world was such as to forbid his writing, but begged to be sincerely remembered to you. A letter addressed to me, Cincinnati, Ohio, may possibly reach me on my route, when I hope to receive the approbation of my conduct. Many letters written to me, addressed to this place, have been secreted or destroyed: probably the General can give me a hint on the subject.

These ideas have made a deep impression on my mind, and did not an all-ruling passion sway me irresistibly to the profession of arms and the paths of military glory, I would long since have resigned my sword for the rural cot, where peace, health, and content would at least be our inmates, should not our brows be crowned with laurel.

I must now conclude, as this letter has far exceeded the bounds proposed when commenced; but the effusions of my heart are such on its contents, that I could not limit them to a more contracted space. Excuse my scrawl, as I am entirely out of patience, but believe me to be,

    Dear General,
     With high respect and esteem,
      Your obedient servant,
   (Signed)   Z. M. PIKE, Captain.

THE END.

www.ingramcontent.com/pod-product-compliance
Lightning Source LLC
Chambersburg PA
CBHW022119290426
44112CB00008B/740